Youth Suicide and Bullying

Youth Suicide and Bullying

Challenges and Strategies for Prevention and Intervention

EDITED BY

PETER GOLDBLUM

DOROTHY L. ESPELAGE

JOYCE CHU

BRUCE BONGAR

Oxford University Press is a department of the University of Oxford.
It furthers the University's objective of excellence in research, scholarship,
and education by publishing worldwide.

Oxford New York
Auckland Cape Town Dar es Salaam Hong Kong Karachi
Kuala Lumpur Madrid Melbourne Mexico City Nairobi
New Delhi Shanghai Taipei Toronto

With offices in
Argentina Austria Brazil Chile Czech Republic France Greece
Guatemala Hungary Italy Japan Poland Portugal Singapore
South Korea Switzerland Thailand Turkey Ukraine Vietnam

Published in the United States of America by
Oxford University Press
198 Madison Avenue, New York, NY 10016

Library of Congress Cataloging-in-Publication Data

Youth suicide and bullying : challenges and strategies for prevention and
intervention / edited by Peter Goldblum, Dorothy L. Espelage, Joyce Chu, Bruce Bongar.
pages cm
Includes bibliographical references and index.
ISBN 978-0-19-995070-6
1. Bullying. 2. Bullying in schools. 3. Youth—Suicidal behavior. 4. Suicide—
Prevention. I. Goldblum, Peter.
BF637.B85Y68 2015
362.28'70835—dc23
2014017940

9 8 7 6 5 4 3
Printed in the United States of America
on acid-free paper

This book is dedicated to all of the children who live in fear of being bullied and to all of those who have stepped in to help them survive.

CONTENTS

ACKNOWLEDGMENT

This book would not have been possible without the dedicated editorial assistance from Samantha Pflum and Lisa De La Rue. Throughout the process—from inception to completion—they worked tirelessly to help conceive, organize, communicate with authors, carefully review chapters, and participate in writing several chapters. Always with good spirit and quick turnaround, they helped make the editorial process go through without a hitch.

The editors are indebted to our chapter authors who held to the mission of providing state-of-the-science materials that helped bridge the multiple disciplines represented in the book in a way useful for a range of readers.

And finally, each editor would also like to express gratitude to our partners, Michael, Ray, Kenney, and Karen, who have graciously waited and supported us as we spent way too much time on professional projects.

ABOUT THE EDITORS

Peter Goldblum, Ph.D., MPH, is a professor of psychology at Palo Alto University, where he is co-director of the Multicultural Suicide Research Center and the Center for LGBTQ Evidence-based Applied Research (CLEAR). An early pioneer in the development of public health approaches for the lesbian, gay, bisexual, and transgender (LGBT) community, he helped initiate an integrative community approach to AIDS prevention and mental health services through the San Francisco Department of Public Health, sometimes referred to as the "San Francisco Model." His research and clinical practice related to suicide and bullying among LGBT people began in 1984 with his dissertation research, and he continues it through today, publishing articles and book chapters on the topic. Other books written by Dr. Goldblum include: *Strategies for Survival: A Gay Men's Health Manual for the Age of AIDS* (1987, St. Martin's Press) and *Working with AIDS Bereavement* (1998, University of California, San Francisco [UCSF] AIDS Health Project). He received the American Psychological Association [APA] Division 44 Distinguished Contributions to Education and Training Award in 2013.

Dorothy L. Espelage, Ph.D., is the Edward William Gutgsell and Jane Marr Gutgsell Endowed Professor at the University of Illinois, Urbana–Champaign. She has engaged in research on bullying, homophobic name-calling, and teenage sexual and dating violence for the last 20 years. She is the author of over 120 peer-reviewed articles and 25 chapters. Dr. Espelage has conducted several randomized clinical trials on bully prevention programs and has studied the overlap between various forms of youth violence.

Joyce Chu, Ph.D., is an associate professor of clinical psychology at Palo Alto University (PAU) in California. She co-leads the Multicultural Suicide Research Center and the Ethnic Minority Mental Health Research Group at PAU, where her work is focused on depression and suicide in ethnic minority adult and geriatric populations. She has an interest in advancing the assessment and prevention of suicide for cultural minorities, and has published a cultural theory and model of suicide with her collaborators Peter Goldblum and Bruce Bongar. As part of this work, she and her colleagues have developed a tool to assist clinicians in accounting for cultural influences on suicide risk. Dr. Chu's work is community-collaborative and aims to understand barriers to service-use and to develop culturally congruent outreach and service options for underserved communities, particularly the Asian

Americans. She also directs the PAU Diversity and Community Mental Health Program, whose goal is to train future psychologists to work in the community mental health settings, and co-directs the Center for Excellence in Diversity at PAU.

Dr. Chu earned her bachelor's and master's degrees in psychology at Stanford University, her doctorate in clinical psychology from the University of Michigan, and did a postdoctoral fellowship at the University of California, San Francisco. In 2012, she was awarded the Samuel M. Turner Early Career Award for Distinguished Contributions to Diversity in Clinical Psychology from the American Psychological Association Society of Clinical Psychology. In 2013, she was chosen for the Asian American Psychological Association Early Career Award for Distinguished Contribution to Research.

Bruce Bongar, Ph.D., ABPP, graduated from the University of Wisconsin (with distinction) with a degree in psychology in 1972, and received his doctorate from the University of Southern California in 1977. Dr. Bongar is the Calvin Professor of Psychology at the Pacific Graduate School of Psychology at Palo Alto University in Palo Alto, California, and former Consulting Professor in the Department of Psychiatry and the Behavioral Sciences at Stanford University School of Medicine. Early in his career, Dr. Bongar developed strong interests in identifying the risk factors associated with suicidal behavior and other clinical emergencies, and he has remained a very prolific contributor to the scholarly literature and research in this area. He is past president of the Section on Clinical Emergencies and Crises of Division 12 (Clinical Psychology) of the American Psychological Association (APA). The American Association of Suicidology recognized Dr. Bongar for his work by the early-career-achievement Edwin S. Shneidman Award (1993) for outstanding contributions to research in suicidology, and the Louis I. Dublin Award (2004) for significant lifetime career contributions to research in suicidology. In 2008, Professor Bongar was presented with the Florence Halpern award from the Division of Clinical Psychology of the APA for his distinguished contributions to the profession of clinical psychology. In 2010, he also was awarded the Career Achievement Award from the Section on Clinical Emergencies and Crises of the Division of Clinical Psychology of APA for his work on suicide and life-threatening behaviors. Professor Bongar's current scholarly and research projects include the investigation and prevention of suicide in active-duty military and veteran populations, bullying and suicide, and multicultural approaches to the assessment, management and treatment of the suicidal patient.

CONTRIBUTORS

Sheri Bauman, Ph.D.
University of Arizona
College of Education
Department of Disability and Psychoeducational Studies
Tucson, AZ

Leonard C. Beckum, Ph.D.
Palo Alto University
Stanford University
Palo Alto, CA

Alan L. Berman, Ph.D.
The American Association of Suicidology
Washington, DC

Whitney Bliss, B.A.
Palo Alto University
Department of Clinical Psychology
Palo Alto, CA

Bruce Bongar, Ph.D., ABPP
Palo Alto University
Stanford University School of Medicine
Department of Psychiatry and Behavioral Sciences
Palo Alto, CA

Catherine P. Bradshaw, Ph.D.
Johns Hopkins Center for the Prevention of Youth Violence
Johns Hopkins Bloomberg School of Public Health
Baltimore, MD

Joyce Chu, Ph.D.
Palo Alto University
Diversity and Community Mental Health Program
Center for Excellence in Diversity
Palo Alto, CA

Dewey Cornell, Ph.D.
University of Virginia
Curry School of Education
Charlottesville, VA

Christopher D. Corona, M.A.
The Catholic University of America
Department of Psychology
Washington, DC

Lisa De La Rue, M.A.
University of Illinois at Urbana–Champaign
Department of Educational Psychology
Champaign, IL

Jeffrey Duong, B.A.
Johns Hopkins Center for the Prevention of Youth Violence
Johns Hopkins Bloomberg School of Public Health
Baltimore, MD

Dorothy L. Espelage, Ph.D.
University of Illinois at
Urbana-Champaign
Department of Educational Psychology
Child Development Division
Champaign, IL

Amy Fairchild, Ph.D., MPH
Columbia University
Mailman School of Public Health
Department of Sociomedical Sciences
New York, NY

Rebecca Floyd, M.A., M.S.
Palo Alto University
Department of Clinical Psychology
Palo Alto, CA

David M. Frost, Ph.D.
Columbia University
Mailman School of Public Health
New York, NY

Polly Y. Gipson, Ph.D.
University of Michigan
Department of Psychiatry
Ann Arbor, MI

Peter Goldblum, Ph.D., MPH
Palo Alto University
Center for LGBTQ Evidence-Based
Applied Research (CLEAR)
Department of Clinical Psychology
Palo Alto, CA

Mark L. Hatzenbuehler, Ph.D.
Columbia University
Mailman School of Public Health
Department of Sociomedical Sciences
New York, NY

Michael L. Hendricks, Ph.D., ABPP
Washington Psychological Center
Washington, DC

Jennifer Hirsch, Ph.D., ABPP
Columbia University
Mailman School of Public Health
Department of Sociomedical Sciences
New York, NY

Melissa K. Holt, Ph.D.
Boston University School of Education
Department of Counseling Psychology
Boston, MA

Arthur M. Horne, Ph.D.
The University of Georgia
The William A. & Barbara R. Owens
Institute for Behavioral Research
Athens, GA

Cynthia Hudley, Ph.D.
University of California-Santa Barbara
Gervitz Graduate School of Education
Santa Barbara, CA

Iulia I. Ivan, Ph.D.
Palo Alto University
Department of Clinical Psychology
Palo Alto, CA

David A. Jobes, Ph.D.
The Catholic University of America
Department of Psychology
Washington, DC

Cheryl A. King, Ph.D.
University of Michigan
Mary A. Rackham Institute
Ann Arbor, MI

Anat Brunstein Klomek, Ph.D.
Interdisciplinary Center (IDC)
Schneider Children's Medical Center of
Israel
School of Psychology
Herzliya, Israel

Joseph Kosciw, Ph.D.
Gay Lesbian Straight Education
Network (GLSEN)
Washington, DC

Susan P. Limber, Ph.D.
Clemson University
Institute on Family and Neighborhood
Life
Clemson, SC

Handrea Anita Logis, M.S.
University of Illinois at
Urbana-Champaign
Champaign, IL

Sabina K. Low, Ph.D.
Arizona State University
T. Denny Sanford School of Social and Family Dynamics
Tempe, AZ

Johnson Ma, M.A.
Palo Alto University
Department of Clinical Psychology
Palo Alto, CA

Roxana Marachi, Ph.D.
San José State University
Connie L. Lurie College of Education
San José, CA

Ilan H. Meyer, Ph.D.
University of California–Los Angeles, School of Law
The Williams Institute
Los Angeles, CA

Kimberly J. Mitchell, Ph.D.
University of New Hampshire
Crimes Against Children Research Center
Durham, NH

Laura Mufson, Ph.D.
Columbia University Medical Center
Department of Psychiatry
New York, NY

Constance Nathanson, Ph.D.
Columbia University
Mailman School of Public Health
Department of Sociomedical Sciences
New York, NY

Sheila Nezhad, M.A.
University of California–Los Angeles
The Williams Institute
Los Angeles, CA

Amanda B. Nickerson, Ph.D.
University of Buffalo Graduate School of Education
Alberti Center for Bullying Abuse Prevention
Buffalo, NY

Dan Olweus, Ph.D.
University of Bergen
Research Center for Health Promotion (HEMIL)
Bergen, Norway

Kiel Opperman, M.A.
University of Michigan
Department of Psychiatry
Ann Arbor, MI

Pamela Orpinas, Ph.D.
The University of Georgia
The William A. & Barbara R. Owens Institute for Behavioral Research
Athens, GA

Richard Parker, Ph.D.
Columbia University
Mailman School of Public Health
Department of Sociomedical Science
New York, NY

Samantha Pflum, M.S.
Palo Alto University
Department of Clinical Psychology
Palo Alto, CA

V. Paul Poteat, Ph.D.
Boston College
Lynch School of Education
Boston, MA

Jane Riese, MSW, LSW
Clemson University
Institute on Family and Neighborhood Life
Clemson, SC

Ian Rivers, Ph.D.
Brunel University London
School of Sport and Education
Uxbridge, England

Philip C. Rodkin, Ph.D.
University of Illinois at Urbana–Champaign
Department of Educational Psychology
Champaign, IL

Laura Sciacca, M.A.
Palo Alto University
Department of Clinical Psychology
Palo Alto, CA

Andrew Edmund Slaby, M.D., Ph.D., M.P.H.
New York University and New York Medical College
NYU Langone Medical Center
New York, NY

Marlene J. Snyder, Ph.D.
Clemson University
Institute on Family and Neighborhood Life
Clemson, SC

Laura A. Szalacha, Ed.D.
The Ohio State University
College of Nursing
Columbus, OH

Rylan J. Testa, Ph.D.
Palo Alto University
Department of Clinical Psychology
Palo Alto, CA

Teceta Thomas Tormala, Ph.D.
Palo Alto University
Department of Clinical Psychology
Palo Alto, CA

Toni Orrange Torchia, B.A.
University of Buffalo Graduate School of Education
Alberti Center for Bullying Abuse Prevention
Buffalo, NY

Kim Westheimer, Ph.D.
Human Rights Campaign
Department of Public Education and Outreach
Washington, DC

Michele L. Ybarra, MPH, Ph.D.
Center for Innovative Public Health Research
Internet Solutions for Kids
San Clemente, CA

PART ONE

Overview: State of the Science and Current Challenges

1

Facing the Challenges of Preventing Youth Suicide and Bullying

PETER GOLDBLUM, DOROTHY L. ESPELAGE, JOYCE CHU, BRUCE BONGAR, SAMANTHA PFLUM, AND LISA DE LA RUE ■

On September 22, 2010, Tyler Clementi, an 18-year-old university freshman, jumped to his death from the George Washington Bridge in New York City following an incidence of cyberbullying that publicly exposed him kissing another man. This incident and the following media explosion (over 300 print stories that year) stimulated a national discussion on the role of bullying and harassment in youth suicide. It also highlighted the prevalence of peer victimization of lesbian, gay, bisexual, transgender, and questioning (LGBTQ) youth. The response to this incident, and several other highly publicized suicide deaths that appeared to be related to bullying, has come both from official sources, including President Obama, and from community efforts to protect vulnerable youth.

This book identifies and addresses the challenges of youth bullying and suicide in a balanced and scientific manner. Through the inclusion of nationally recognized authorities within the fields of both bullying and suicide, this book serves as a one-stop source for state-of-the-science information and perspectives that can inform further research and the promotion of scientifically based interventions that are systematic and cost-effective. We believe that, along with general recommendations to prevent these phenomena, policies and approaches must come from a working collaboration between concerned citizens and professionals who consider their own unique community-contextual factors to help communities take control of their own public health. We see the audience for our work as including those who either work with youth as school staff, practitioners, youth advocates, researchers, or parents, or who are at the forefront of developing or informing policies to prevent these behaviors. Finally, we hope that the approach that we take integrating an educational and public health view of the problem will promote new directions in training students in education, health sciences, and public health.

The association between bullying and suicide is not simple. While research supports a connection between bullying involvement and suicidality (Kim & Leventhal, 2008), it is important to view this relationship within the broader socio-ecological context, and recognize that bullying is just one potential risk factor in a constellation of other risk and protective factors (Chapter 3; this volume).

Bullying has been, and continues to be, viewed as an educational challenge. Given the documented adverse educational outcomes for youth involved in bullying, explanations and program development have been the purview of educational science and educators (American Educational Research Association, 2013). More recently, bullying is also being framed as a public health issue because of the concurrent associations among bullying, school violence, and suicide behaviors (Masiello & Shroeder, 2014). Inherently, public health issues have an impact on the settings where youth spend their time, including both formal educational (e.g., schools) and informal educational settings (e.g., youth centers, extracurricular activities). Thus, in this book we draw upon both educational and public health science to address the challenges associated with youth bullying and suicide. We feel that an integration of these fields offers an enhanced perspective from which to study, to understand, and to address the challenges associated with these phenomena.

Although researchers have called attention to bullying in schools and youth communities for two decades in the United States and over four decades internationally, it has only been in the last few years that bullying was recognized as a serious American public health concern. Unfortunately, the awareness came at a time when educational systems had come under greater scrutiny regarding academic accountability, often overly focused on academic test scores, with a concomitant de-emphasis on the social or emotional well-being of youth, teachers, or staff. Thus, the anti-bullying movements and campaigns were launched within educational environments of extreme chaos. Developmental psychologist Urie Bronfenbrenner (2001) noted "increased cynicism and disillusionment among American adolescents and youth" (p. 186), and suggested that students were continuing to show declines in their level of social competence and character. In tandem, rates of youth suicide were continuing to cause concern. This awareness also came at a time when access to mental health services for families was increasingly difficult. No two systems within the United States are in more chaos than those addressing education and mental health. Deep fissures exist among our citizens as to how to proceed in each of these domains. Cultural values and socio-political divisions have hampered efforts to build and implement efficient and efficacious systems of care to protect the health and safety of our children. Not giving in to the pervasive cynicism, we are encouraged by recent efforts by multiple U.S. federal agencies (e.g., Departments of Education and Justice, Centers for Disease Control) to address bully and suicide prevention (http://www.stopbullying.gov/blog/categories/Federal-Partners-Bullying-Prevention) by partnering with nonprofit organizations (e.g., the Gay, Lesbian, Straight Education Network [GLSEN]). These partners are committed to a long-term working relationship to prevent bullying, its associated mental health challenges, and the potential link to the life-threatening problem of suicide behaviors. In this book, we will showcase projects that strive to use both science and community participation to provide effective suicide and bullying prevention programs (see Part V: Educational Approaches, in this book).

SOCIAL-ECOLOGICAL VIEW

Consistent with Bronfenbrenner's (1979) social-ecological framework, much of research presented in this book rests on the conception that all social problems are located within multiple systems that are affected by and in turn affect each other. Many scholars have started to extend Bronfenbrenner's (1986) model of child development to encompass social-ecological factors associated with bullying involvement. In the area of school bullying and peer victimization, the social-ecological model focuses on understanding how individual characteristics of children interact with their environmental contexts or systems to promote or prevent victimization and perpetration (Espelage, 2012; Hong & Espelage, 2012). As advances in developmental science emerged, Bronfenbrenner and colleagues offered a reformulation of the social-ecological model, including the introduction of chaos theory into this model (Bronfenbrenner & Evans, 2000), suggesting that chaos in the various structures can exacerbate risk factors.

The structures or locations with which children have direct contact are referred to as their *microsystem*, including peers, family, community, and schools. The interaction between components of the microsystem is referred to as the *mesosystem*. An example of a mesosystem is the interrelations between the family and school, such as parental involvement in their child's school. The *exosystem* is the social context with which the child does not have direct contact, but that affects him or her indirectly through the microsystem. Examples would be teacher or staff perceptions of the school environment, and opportunities for professional development around bullying, school violence, or school climate. The *macrosystem* level is commonly regarded as a cultural "blueprint," which may determine the social structures and activities in the various levels (Bronfenbrenner, 1997). This level includes organizational, social, cultural, and political contexts, which influence the interactions within other system levels (Bronfenbrenner, 1997). The final level of the social-ecological framework, the *chronosystem* level, includes consistency or change (e.g., historical or life events) of the individual and the environment over the life course (e.g., changes in family structure).

It is our belief that bullying involvement and the risk for suicidal behavior can be significantly reduced if we consider prevention and intervention efforts that take into account the complex direct and indirect (interaction) effects of a youth's environment. Thus, observations and theories pertaining to etiology and treatment must fit together into a comprehensive approach to address these problems. Based on cross-cultural and community mental health perspectives, strategies that target specific behaviors and attitudes need to be evaluated within a broader context.

SCIENTIFIC CHALLENGE

Defining the Problem

As we apply the social-ecological framework to the intersection of bullying and suicide, it quickly becomes evident that to fully realize the impact of the multiple structures on these behaviors requires complex, multilevel, and multi-informant studies. First and foremost, there have to be consistent definitions and assessments of both bullying and suicide behaviors. Once there is agreement on these primary definitions, further defining the interaction between these two is required. Having consensus as to definitions is necessary before adequate surveillance and data collection are possible. The definitional challenge inherent in both "bullying" and "suicide" has plagued their independent study for some time. As we begin to combine their study into a larger public health problem, additional challenges arise. For example, what do we call the phenomenon? Some have suggested "bully-related suicide" (even more provocative, "bullicide"), a term that implies a necessarily causal link; others are more comfortable with simple associative terms such as "bullying and suicide behavior." We have selected the second, broader term in order to avoid an *a priori* assumption that the two target behaviors are necessarily causally linked.

A rigorous debate has emerged about how best to define bullying and how to distinguish it from other forms of aggression and/or peer victimization (American Educational Research Association, 2013; Rodkin, Espelage, & Hanish, in press). One of the first, predominant definitions of bullying, which continues to be used in the literature and in the legal arena, is as follows: "A student is being bullied or victimized when he or she is exposed, repeatedly and over time, to negative actions on the part of one or more students" (Olweus, 2010, p. 11). More recent definitions of bullying emphasize observable or non-observable aggressive behaviors, the repetitive nature of these behaviors, and the imbalance of power between the individual or group perpetrator and the victim (Gladden, Vivolo-Kantor, Hamburger, & Lumpkin, 2014; Ybarra, Espelage, & Mitchell, 2014). An imbalance of power exists when the perpetrator or group of perpetrators has more physical, social, or intellectual power than the victim. In a recent examination of a nationally representative study, early and late adolescents who perceived their perpetrator as having more power reported greater adverse outcomes (e.g., depression, suicidal ideation) than did victims who did not perceive a power differential (Ybarra, Espelage, & Mitchell, 2014).

In 2010, the Department of Education and the Centers for Disease Control and Prevention collaborated to develop a uniform *research* definition. This group defined *bullying* as follows:

> Bullying is any unwanted aggressive behavior(s) by another youth or group of youths who are not siblings or current dating partners that involves an observed or perceived power imbalance and is repeated multiple times or is highly likely to be repeated. Bullying may inflict harm or distress on the targeted youth including physical, psychological, social, or educational harm. (Gladden et al., 2014, p. 7)

These behaviors include verbal and physical aggression that ranges in severity from making threats, spreading rumors, and social exclusion, to physical attacks causing injury. As defined, bullying can occur face-to-face or through technology (e.g., cell phones, computers). Finally, some bullying behaviors may overlap with aggression that meets the legal definition of *harassment*, but not all incidents of harassment constitute bullying. Given that bullying co-occurs with other forms of aggression and school violence (Espelage, Basile, & Hamburger, 2012; Rodkin, Espelage, & Hanish, in press), educators and scholars should not limit themselves to collecting data only on bullying, but should include data on all forms of aggression and victimization. Educators and scholars should also comply with clear and accepted definitional distinctions of "bullying," "aggression," and "harassment."

A similar debate has ensued regarding the definition of *suicidality*. The comparison between studies related to suicide behavior has been hampered by inconsistent terminology. "Suicidality" often refers simultaneously to suicidal ideation and suicidal behavior. "Suicidal ideation" refers to thinking about, considering, or planning for suicide (Crosby, Ortega, & Melanson, 2011), while "suicidal behavior" refers to self-directed actions that are conducted with the intention to kill oneself. The behavioral component of this definition can also encompass acts of preparation for a suicide attempt, such as gathering a method of suicide (e.g., purchasing a gun, collecting sleeping pills), or preparing for one's death by suicide (e.g., giving away possessions, writing a suicide note) (Crosby et al., 2011).

The term *parasuicide* is also used to denote a non-lethal but self-inflicted and injurious act (Bongar, 1991). This term has been frequently utilized to describe self-harming behaviors that occur without the intention to die, including the cutting, burning, and bruising of one's own body. In more recent suicidality literature, the term *non-suicidal self-injury* (NSSI) has been used in place of *parasuicide* (Nock, Joiner, Gordon, Lloyd-Richardson, & Prinstein, 2006). Both NSSI and parasuicide differ from suicide attempts, which refer to direct efforts to end one's own life (Nock et al., 2006).

A "suicide attempt" is any act of self-inflicted bodily damage done with self-destructive intent (Bongar, 1991). Suicidality is evaluated on a continuum of lethality based on the potential for self-inflicted death. All cases of potentially dangerous self-inflicted injury should be regarded as suicide attempts, regardless of the victim's explanation for the acts. "Dangerousness," in this sense, refers to the attempter's belief that his or her actions could feasibly endanger his or her life (Bongar, 1991). "Completed suicide," which may occur after multiple suicide attempts over time, is defined as the "act of taking one's own life" (Bongar, 1991, p. 6). Obviously, suicide and bullying studies will benefit from common use of language and consensus regarding what data are collected, by whom, and in what form.

Size of the Problem

The majority of extant research indicates that involvement in bullying in any capacity is associated with higher rates of suicidal ideation and behaviors, with cross-sectional studies finding increased odds ratios of 1.4–10.0 (Kim & Leventhal, 2008). Most of the research on the links between bully/peer victimization and suicidal behaviors has been conducted outside of the United States, but a 2009 paper examined the association between peer victimization and suicidal ideation and attempts across three nationally representative samples of U.S. adolescents (Kaminski & Fang, 2009). Youth victimized by their peers were 2.4 times more likely to report suicidal ideation and 3.3 times more likely to report a suicide attempt than youth who reported not being bullied.

Although there is fairly consistent evidence that there is an increased suicide risk for those involved in bullying, evidence suggests that risk might vary for youth who are bully perpetrators, victims, bully-victims (those who both bully and are victims), or bystanders. For instance, some studies have shown that the association between suicidal ideation and bullying is stronger for targets of bullying than for perpetrators (e.g., Rigby & Slee, 1999). However, another study found that after controlling for depression, the association between bullying and suicidal ideation was strongest for bully perpetrators (Kaltiala-Heino, Rimpela, Marttunen, Rimpela, & Rantanen, 1999). Another study of middle school youth reported that the bully–suicide association was minimized when depression and delinquency were considered for all youth (Espelage & Holt, 2013). Whereas multiple studies have found that bully-victims report more suicidal ideation and behaviors than do uninvolved youth, victims, or perpetrators (e.g., Klomek et al., 2007), there are other studies that do not support this pattern. For instance, Herba and colleagues (2008) found that there were no differences in levels of suicidal ideation between bully-victims and uninvolved youth. These studies point to the complexity of assessing suicide risk based on the level of involvement youth have in the bully-victim-bystander dynamic.

Similarly, mixed findings exist with regard to whether the association between bullying and suicidal ideation varies by sex. Klomek and colleagues (2009) found that bullying victimization at age eight was associated with later suicide attempts and completed suicides after controlling for depression and conduct problems, but this was the case only for girls. The authors speculate that this sex difference might have emerged given that girls are more likely to experience relational victimization, whereas boys are more likely to experience physical victimization, and relational victimization might have a longer-lasting impact. On the other hand, other studies have found that boys might be at greater risk. For instance, male bullies showed higher than average levels of suicidal ideation in one study of a community population (Rigby & Slee, 1999), and in a sample of Italian youth seeking psychological help, suicidal ideation was predicted by being bullied at school only for boys (Laukkanen et al., 2005). According to Poteat and Rivers (in this volume Chapter 10), research comparing sexual and gender minority and heterosexual youth has consistently shown that sexual minority youth report higher levels of suicidality (Eisenberg & Resnick, 2006; Remafedi, French, Story, Resnick, & Blum, 1998; Robinson & Espelage, 2011; Russell & Toomey, 2012). However, peer victimization does not appear to explain all of the mental health disparities between lesbian, gay, bisexual (LGB) and heterosexual youth (Robinson & Espelage, 2012).

CULTURAL CHALLENGE

A core belief and value underlying this book is that cultural differences must be taken into consideration when addressing the causes and remedies of suicide and bullying. How to include culture in the broad study of psychological phenomena is still widely debated. Generally, the editors of the book work from a multicultural perspective. According to Hall (2014), "multicultural psychology views human behavior as influenced by an individual's culture and the cultures surrounding and acting on the individual" (p. 3). There has been debate among scholars over whether all groups qualify as "cultural." Some scholars believe that the term *culture* should be reserved for the groups that transmit their values, traditions, and norms across generations. This would exclude groups who developed their group identity later in life, such as sexual and gender minorities and those who are disabled. Other scholars argue that any group that "share[s] some themes, issues, or experiences (language, trauma, social class, race, sexual orientation, hobbies) constitute[s] culture" (Dunn & Hammer, 2014, p. 44). Rather than argue over who qualifies for the name of "culture," the editors of this book believe that a fine-grained examination of group identities (including multiple identities), norms, expectations, and stresses should be carried out in order to calculate the effect that culture has on the issue under study. Given that cultural factors—including ethnic, sexual, and gender identities—have been identified as playing a significant role in both suicide and bullying risk, we have taken a broad view of "multiculturalism" to include a wide range of individuals who identify with social groups consistently over time. In Part III: Cultural Perspectives we provide five chapters that discuss the connection between culture and youth suicide and bullying.

BROADER EDUCATIONAL CHALLENGES

As noted by Kathleen Sebelius (former U.S. Secretary of Health and Human Services) and researchers who have studied bullying, prevention efforts to date have had limited success in producing sustainable reductions in rates of bullying and peer victimization (Chapter 18; this volume). Much of this research has attempted to identify programs that could be scaled for implementation in all schools and communities. This one-size-fits-all approach is not consistent with the tenets underlying a social-ecological view of social development. More specifically, the social-ecological model argues for interventions that are tailored to where the problem is situated and should target unique risk and protective factors in each school, community, or other ecology. Furthermore, all schools and communities vary in their readiness to develop or implement prevention programs. For example, some communities have unlimited resources, while others have few to no resources. Therefore, efforts must be made to identify cost-conscious approaches so that all youth, including those in economically disadvantaged communities, can learn to manage conflicts and address bullying before mental health issues arise. To optimize our prevention and intervention efforts, research and programs that are developed need to be iterative in nature, wherein data and knowledge gained from one study could be used to adapt and modify programs to fit the unique ecology of each community. This iterative approach should also consider developmental and cultural characteristics that can enhance the saliency and potency of programs. A nice example of this is Espelage et al. (Chapter 18; this volume) in which data from focus groups with teachers and students who completed three years of a social-emotional learning program were used by program developers in producing variations of the curriculum.

Additional focus from a public health perspective on the intersection of youth suicide and bullying could have a positive impact on the field. One clear advantage of adopting a public health framework is the focus on developing empirical, data-driven programs rather than feel-good or favored approaches (e.g., empower bystanders, youth media campaigns in schools). However, there are also potential disadvantages to relying completely on framing youth suicide and bullying as a "public health" issue. Public health interventions require a strict delineation and definition of target health-oriented behaviors. This singular focus may limit the emphasis of educationally relevant goals, including character education, academic performance, civility, creativity, and ethics. Thus, from an education perspective, character education is a worthy goal in its own right, not only as a mediator for increasing health promotion. In this book, we argue for an understanding of the problem of youth suicide and bullying from both an educational and a public health framework.

Major values-based divisions exist in the United States, creating a broader political challenge. Communities have become increasingly polarized around issues related to education and the role of schools in instilling values. Most parents want their children to be respectful to others, but parents also differ in their beliefs whether this is the school's responsibility to impart. Differences in cultural perspectives impact what parents encourage schools to teach their children and what they oppose. In a pluralistic society, there is a challenge to integrate anything into schools that does not directly affect academics, test scores, college readiness, and vocational training. Educational systems are embedded within communities that are deeply divided in their tolerance for non-academic material being delivered in schools. This is problematic for the prevention of and intervention in youth suicide and bullying, given that schools are often where youth are victimized and subsequently placed at risk for depression, suicidality, and other psychological sequelae.

Indeed, there is tremendous pressure on schools and school boards to address youth suicide and bullying, yet they are expected to do this in a time of limited resources and greater accountability for academic performance. At the same time, bully prevention has become hyper-commercialized, such that non-scientific approaches are being marketed to schools, which in the end has widened the science-to-practice gap. Regardless, schools need guidance to either design prevention efforts that fit their culture and climate or they need assistance in adopting and tailoring prevention programs that fit their climate.

PUBLIC HEALTH CHALLENGE

Public Health Definitions

In 1988 the Institute of Medicine (IOM) defined public health as "what we, as a society, do collectively to assure the condition in which people can be healthy" (Masiello & Schroeder, 2014, p. 5). This sense of collaboration and community participation to assure the health of its people is basic to all communities and is the responsibility of all citizens, both professionals and laypersons. By framing the phenomena of youth suicide and bullying from a public health perspective, validated and standardized approaches to planning, problem-solving, and prevention are made available. Furthermore, well-established institutions and funding sources such as the Centers for Disease Control (CDC) and the National Institutes of Health (NIH) are now available to provide national-level technical and financial assistance. As the field moves forward in this direction, however, we must be mindful of potential limitations in conceptualizing the problem entirely from this framework. The charge of public health is to reduce or eradicate specific risks in order to have measureable impact on specific medical or social problems. This framework may prove overly stringent and reductionist for addressing some of the broader sociocultural issues inherent in the bullying and suicide challenge among youth. We therefore recommend a hybrid approach that borrows from public health, yet is mindful of larger academic and character-building objectives that are essential to a public-education approach. As always, wisdom is required to determine which problems and concerns are best addressed by the highly focused public health model, and when educational processes are better suited. This selection largely will be determined by the program outcome (e.g., reduction in bullying behavior among third-grade girls vs. a greater appreciation of the role of civility within our society).

THE HISTORY OF PUBLIC HEALTH

Early efforts at disease control focused on sanitation (water, air, sewage) in the mid-1800s, evolving into the personal hygiene movement, with its focus on health education of vulnerable groups such as mothers, infants, and schoolchildren in early 1900s (Adams, Amos, & Munro, 2002). In the mid-1970s, new definitions of "health" were advanced; "health" began to be seen as being more than the absence of disease, including "a state of complete physical, mental, and social well-being" (Salazar, Crosby, & DiClemente, 2013, p. 4). This broader definition of health was incorporated into strategies focused on reducing specific unhealthy behaviors while increasing healthy behaviors, thus ushering in the era of "health promotion." In 2012, the White House Conference entitled "Federal Partners in Bullying Prevention Summit" launched a national initiative to reduce bullying as a factor in youth suicide and framed the interaction as a public health problem. At that conference, Secretary Sebelius noted:

> . . . our nation faced a number of tragic incidents involving children and teenagers who, having been bullied, felt like they had nowhere to turn and took their own lives. It seized the nation's attention. And for many, it was a wakeup call. Bullying is not just a harmless rite of passage, or an inevitable part of growing up. It threatens the health and well-being of our young people. It's destructive to our communities and devastating to our future. (http://www.stopbullying.gov/)

PUBLIC HEALTH FRAME OF YOUTH BULLYING AND SUICIDE

Throughout its history, the public health model has emphasized prevention rather than cure. Conceptualized as an "upstream approach" (Salazar et al., 2013), prevention focuses on the reduction of factors that impact the initiation of a specified disease or injury. Rather than focusing on treating and eliminating disease on the individual level, public health approaches are "synonymous with large population events or programs" (Masiello & Schroeder, 2014, p. 6). The CDC mission statement notes that prevention efforts intend "to promote health and quality of life by preventing and controlling disease, injury, and disability" (Salazar ct al., 2013, p. 11). Prevention approaches are often divided into three levels: primary, secondary, and tertiary. Primary approaches are applied universally across the population. Large-scale anti-bullying advertisements and national anti-bullying laws and policies fall into this category. These approaches are cost-effective and may significantly reduce the extent of damage before it happens. Secondary prevention is more targeted at individuals and groups at risk and aims to "minimize consequences through early detection" (Salazar et al., 2013, p. 11). The approach can be more tailored to the needs and cultural sensitivities of individuals who may require additional efforts to engage in health promotion. Programs designed to reduce bullying and increase positive bystander responses fall into this category. Tertiary prevention efforts are designed to mitigate the consequences of disease or an injury after the fact (Salazar et al., 2013, p. 16). Individual and family counseling for bully perpetrators and victims falls into this category of prevention activities.

CRITIQUE OF THE PUBLIC HEALTH APPROACH

A criticism that has been leveled at some programs addressing public health problems is that they are atheoretical. Without a clear view of the determinants (causes) of bullying and suicide and how these determinants interact, programs to alter health behaviors are just shots in the dark. Furthermore, interventions that are not grounded in well-researched theories of change are often applied inconsistently and may lead to negative or inconsistent results. On the other hand, not all innovative, grassroots programs start from an atheoretical perspective, and they may be effective due to sensitivity to cultural or socio-political nuances regarding the population. If these programs are to be successfully transported to other communities, careful reverse-engineering may be necessary to determine the active program components and to provide clear instruction for replication and dissemination.

Most public health problems are complex. Scientific work may be fragmented and may be conducted by scientists who do not communicate with each other, do not publish in the same professional journals, and do not attend the same professional conferences. This "silo" phenomenon has hindered progress in understanding the complexities of bullying and suicide. Therefore, one of the goals of this book is to help improve communication among all stakeholders. Not only do youth suicide and bullying need unified explanatory models, evidence-based approaches must be synthesized to address multifactorial determinants. Recent advances in scientific explanations of psychosocial elements of suicide and the cultural determinants of suicide and bullying are reported in this volume to ground the discussion of evidence-based practice in these areas (see Chapters 13, 14, and 15; this volume).

Current public-health intervention science places great emphasis on the development of programs that have been demonstrated to work, otherwise known as *evidence-based practice*. Evidence-based public health calls for "a solid knowledge base on disease frequency and distribution, on the determinants and consequences of disease, and on the safety, efficacy, and effectiveness of interventions and their costs" (Eriksson, 2000, p. 1). While there is little debate that the systematic nature of the scientific method is preferable to more hit-or-miss methods, dispute still exists concerning what is required for a method to qualify as "evidence-based." For example, in both medicine and the behavioral sciences, the role of randomized controlled trial (RCT) methodology is being questioned for socially oriented programs. Less debated is the benefit of reliable and valid pre- and post-intervention assessments that focus on target behaviors to determine successful outcomes.

A corollary of strictly evidence-based practice is that implementation of best-practice protocols should be held to high standards of fidelity. By "fidelity," we mean that protocols should be strictly adhered to in order to determine whether the outcomes (or lack thereof) derive from the proper or improper use of the protocol. Maintenance of quality control is clearly necessary to consistently and effectively apply interventions. On the other hand, overly rigid application of interventions that do not match client or community needs may render sound approaches ineffective due to participant resistance. Within the psychotherapy literature, there is currently an active debate regarding what is meant by "fidelity" and whether cultural adaptation of treatments is a worthy goal. Guillermo Bernal and his colleagues (2009) describe the dilemma in this way:

> Promoting a systematic approach to treatment is a double-edged sword: on one hand, greater structure for researchers and practitioners are [*sic*] attractive features for those who espouse a scientist-practitioner model to psychology practice or training. On the other hand, such systematization can potentially increase the risk of adopting a one-size-fit [*sic*] all approach to interventions and intervention research that is contradictory in practice to what the movement intended to promote in spirit (i.e., competent practice). (p. 361)

These authors recommend cultural adaptation procedures (Bernal et al., 2009) that alter evidence-based treatments to better fit schools' and communities' personal and cultural characteristics. Cultural adaptations may include augmenting recruitment activities, language, intervention procedures, or cultural matching of provider and participant. Other authors (McHugh, Murray, & Barlow, 2009) also question whether strict fidelity may present a barrier for dissemination of programs due to the lack of certain organizational structures and prohibitive costs. These authors argue that, rather than rigid compliance with treatment manuals, principle-based programs that target specific behavioral goals with more flexible therapeutic procedures may be more adaptable to actual service sites (McHugh et al., 2009). An additional benefit to these guidance-orientated procedures is that it allows community-based practitioners room for innovation. Staying within the scientific method, these programs would need to routinely incorporate evaluation tools with demonstrated reliability and validity to assess changes in the target behavior from baseline through completion, and even at follow-up intervals.

PUBLIC HEALTH APPLICATION: COMMUNITY PLANNING AND DECISION-MAKING

Public health problems require participation from a broad spectrum of those affected within a community. Using the social ecological model provides a framework to identify stakeholders in the problem on multiple levels. These stakeholders may reside locally or be many miles apart, and it can be difficult to know who is in charge. Large national and international problems like youth bullying and suicide may have many agencies working on the same problem, completely unaware of each other. Even within local communities, there may be a lack of coordination and planning, thus duplicating services and wasting scarce resources. Public health philosophy encourages cross-disciplinary collaboration, joint decision-making and planning, and a public–private partnership. In fact, having active leadership and involvement (buy-in) from concerned citizens is usually predictive of a strong response. At the same time, activities to assess community needs, develop priorities, establish work plans, and institute a strong multilevel evaluation before and after the intervention are considered good scientific practice.

Several groups have outlined a public health approach to youth violence and bullying. The following guidelines are adapted from Public Heath Approaches to Bullying Prevention (Masiello & Schroeder, 2014), based on documents created for the CDC and the World Health Organization (WHO) approaches to violence prevention: As communities plan integrated strategies to reduce the number and impact of youth bullying and suicide, an overarching planning process may take the following into consideration.

1. Define the problem clearly. Educate yourself as to existing definitions of desired outcomes, demographics, and potential mediating factors. Whenever possible, use existing quantitative data available for local, school, or state health. In addition, make every effort to define the "who" "what," "when," "why," and "how" associated with the issue at hand. Qualitative data (interviews and focus groups) may give insights into local issues and mechanisms that drive local situations and unique community resources. Familiarize yourself with current scientific literature on bullying and suicide (see Part II in this book: Defining the Problem: Prevalence, Predictors, and Protectors).
2. Determine the risk and protective factors involved within your population (geographic, ethnic, sexual and gender minorities, age groups). In other words, what are the direct and associated correlates of the issue you are wishing to correct or improve? A careful review of cultural literature will help reduce bias among planners and program designers, as well as increase the cultural competence of providers and participants (see Part III: Cultural Perspectives). Understanding the causes of suicidality and bullying is essential in determining the type of community approach you select (Part IV: Explanatory Models).
3. Carefully select and implement an intervention program that best fits your specific community profile of risks and protective factors, has a documented scientific track record of effectiveness in reduction of these risks and increasing protective factors, and determine how to apply the application with the highest level of fidelity to determine whether the program should be replicated as is, or altered to improve its effectiveness. Part V provides several examples of bullying and suicide interventions in detail, written by the program developers, to assist you in selecting the approach that is best for your situation. Part VI provides insights into levels of approaches that are consistent with the social-ecological

perspective, ranging from school-based interventions to national legal and policy initiatives.

4. Evaluate what you are doing throughout the initiative, including the planning process and the buy-in from consumers. A valid and reliable outcome-evaluation tool must focus on the specific observable and measurable changes that determine the success of the program. Clearly defining objectives beforehand and collecting relevant data throughout allows program data to be easily and accurately reported, and provides relevant information for facilitating decisions related to program alterations and or continuation. Furthermore, this same information is typically required by funders and serves as the basis for ongoing funding.
5. Disseminate information (e.g., reports, professional articles, presentations at conferences) to all stakeholders. Publicly report the evaluation findings and engage in an informed decision (based on evaluation data) about whether to continue or alter the program, and how to proceed. Timely and accurate reports to funders will increase the chances for continuation of worthy programs. Feedback to program developers will be invaluable to the continued refinement and development of their programs.

In conclusion, in order to move forward in addressing the challenges of youth bullying and suicide, we recommend an integrative approach that addresses the scientific, cultural, educational, and public health aspects of the problem. In the chapters that follow, you will find expert and scientifically grounded perspectives on each of these areas. In the final section, we provide a synthesis of the recommendations made in these chapters to facilitate our readers' ability to put these recommendations into action.

REFERENCES

Adams, L., Amos, M., & Munro, J. (2002), *Promoting Health: Policies and Practice.* London: Sage Publications.

American Educational Research Association (2013). *Prevention of Bullying in Schools, Colleges, and Universities: Research Report and Recommendations.* Washington, DC: American Educational Research Association.

Bernal G., Jimenez-Chafey, M. I., & Rodriquez, M. M. D. (2009). Cultural adaptation of treatments: A resource for considering culture in evidence-based practice. *Professional Psychology: Research and Practice, 40*(4), 361–368. doi: 10.1037/a0016401

Bongar, B. M. (1991). The knowledge base. In B. M. Bongar (Ed.), *The Suicidal Patient: Clinical and Legal Standards of Care* (pp. 1–32). Washington, DC: American Psychological Association.

Bronfenbrenner, U. (1997). Ecological models of human development. In *Readings on the Development of Children, 1993*, 37–43.

Bronfenbrenner, U. (1979). *The Ecology of Human Development.* Boston, MA: Harvard University Press.

Bronfenbrenner, U. (1986). Ecology of the family as a context for human development: Research perspectives. *Developmental Psychology, 22*(6), 723–742. doi: 10.1037/0012-1649.22.6.723

Bronfenbrenner, U. (2001). Growing chaos in the lives of children, youth, and families. In *Making Human Beings Human: Bioecological Perspectives on Human Development* (p. 186). Thousand Oaks, CA: Sage.

Bronfenbrenner, U., & Evans, G. W. (2000). Developmental science in the 21st century: Emerging questions, theoretical models, research designs and empirical findings. *Social Development, 9*(1), 115–125. doi: 10.1111/1467-9507.00114

Crosby, A. E., Ortega, L., & Melanson, C. (2011). *Self-Directed Violence Surveillance: Uniform Definitions and Recommended Data Elements*. Atlanta, GA: Centers for Disease Control and Prevention, National Center for Injury Prevention and Control.

Dunn, S. D., & Hammer, E. D. (2014). On teaching multicultural psychology. In F. T. L. Leong, L. Comas-Diaz, G. C. Nagayama-Hall, V. C. McLoyd, & J. E. Trimble (Eds.), *APA Handbook of Multicultural Psychology* (Vol. *1*) (pp. 43–58). Washington, DC: American Psychological Association.

Eisenberg, M. E., & Resnick, M. D. (2006). Suicidality among gay, lesbian and bisexual youth: The role of protective factors. *Journal of Adolescent Health, 39*, 662–668. doi:10.1016/j.jadohealth.2006.04.024

Eriksson, C. (2000). Learning and knowledge-production for public health: A review of approaches to evidence-based public health. *Scandinavian Journal of Public Health, 28*, 298–308. doi: 10.1080/1403490050500555

Espelage, D. L. (2012). Bullying prevention: A research dialogue with Dorothy Espelage. *Prevention Researcher, 19*(3), 17–19.

Espelage, D. L., & Holt, M. K. (2013). Suicidal ideation and school bullying experiences after controlling for depression and delinquency. *Journal of Adolescent Health, 53*, S27–S31. doi: 1016/j.jadohealth.2012.09.017

Espelage, D. L., Basile, K. C., & Hamburger, M. E. (2012). Bullying experiences and co-occurring sexual violence perpetration among middle school students: Shared and unique risk factors. *Journal of Adolescent Health, 50*, 60–665. doi:10.1016/j.jadohealth.2011.07.015

Gladden, R. M., Vivolo-Kantor, A. M., Hamburger, M. E., & Lumpkin, C. D. (2014). *Bullying Surveillance Among Youths: Uniform Definitions for Public Health and Recommended Data Elements, Version 1.0.* Atlanta, GA; National Center for Injury Prevention and Control, Centers for Disease Control and Prevention, and U.S. Department of Education.

Hall, C. C. I. (2014). The evolution of the revolution: The successful establishment of multicultural psychology. In F. T. L. Leong, L. Comas-Diaz, G. C. Nagayama-Hall, V. C. McLoyd, & J. E. Trimble (Eds.), *APA Handbook of Multicultural Psychology* (Vol. *1*) (pp. 3–18). Washington, DC: American Psychological Association.

Hall, G. C. N. (2014). *Multicultural Psychology* (2nd ed.). New York: Pearson.

Herba, C. M., Ferdinand, R. F., Stijnen, T., Veenstra, R., Oldehinkel, A. J., Ormel, J., & Verhulst, F. C. (2008). Victimisation and suicide ideation in the TRAILS study: specific vulnerabilities of victims. *Journal of Child Psychology and Psychiatry, 49*(8), 867–876.

Hong, J. S., & Espelage, D. L. (2012). A review of research on bullying and peer victimization in school: An ecological systems analysis. *Aggression and Violent Behavior, 17*, 311–312. doi: 10.1016/j.avb.2012.03.003

Kaltiala-Heino, R., Rimpelä, M., Marttunen, M., Rimpelä, A., & Rantanen, P. (1999). Bullying, depression, and suicidal ideation in Finnish adolescents: School survey. *British Medical Journal, 319*, 348–351. doi: 10.1136/bmj.319.7206.348

Kaminski, J. W., & Fang, X. (2009). Victimization by peers and adolescent suicide in three US samples. *Journal of Pediatrics, 155*(5), 683–688. doi:10.1016/j.jpeds.2009.04.061

Kim, Y. S., & Leventhal, B. (2008). Bullying and suicide. A review. *International Journal of Adolescent Medicine and Health, 20*(2), 133–154. doi: 10.1515/IJAMH.2008.20.2.133

Klomek, A. B., Marrocco, F., Kleinman, M., Schonfeld, I. S., & Gould, M. S. (2007). Bullying, depression, and suicidality in adolescents. *Journal of the American Academy of Child & Adolescent Psychiatry, 46*(1), 40–49. doi: 10.1097/01.chi.0000242237.84925.18

Klomek, A. B., Sourander, A., Niemelä, S., Kumpulainen, K., Piha, J., Tamminen, T., . . . & Gould, M. S. (2009). Childhood bullying behaviors as a risk for suicide attempts and completed suicides: A population-based birth cohort study. *Journal of the American Academy of Child & Adolescent Psychiatry, 48*(3), 254–261.

Laukkanen, E., Honkalampi, K., Hintikka, J., Hintikka, U., & Lehtonen, J. (2005). Suicidal ideation among help-seeking adolescents: Association with a negative self-image. *Archives of Suicide Research, 9*, 45–55. doi: 10,1080/13811110590512930

Masiello, M. G., & Shroeder, D. S. (2014). *A Public Health Approach to Bullying Prevention*. Washington, DC: American Public Health Association.

McHugh, R. K., Murray, H. W., & Barlow, D. H. (2009). Balancing fidelity and adaptation in the dissemination of empirically supported treatments: The promise of transdiagnostic interventions. *Behavior Research and Therapy, 47*, 946–953. doi: 10.1016/j.brat.2009.07.005

Nock, M. K., Joiner, T. E., Gordon, K. H., Lloyd-Richardson, E., & Prinstein, M. J. (2006). Non-suicidal self-injury among adolescents: Diagnostic correlates and relation to suicide attempts. *Psychiatry Research, 144*, 65–72. doi: 10.1016/j.psychres.2006.05.010

Olweus, D. (2010). Foundations for understanding bullying. In S. R. Jimerson, S. M. Swearer, & D. L. Espelage (Eds.), *The Handbook of Bullying in Schools: An International Perspective* (pp. 9–33). New York: Routledge.

Rigby, K., & Slee, P. T. (1999). Suicidal ideation among adolescent school children, involvement in bully/victim problems and perceived low social support. *Suicide and Life-Threatening Behavior, 29*, 119–130.

Remafedi, G., French, S., Story, M., Resnick, M. D., & Blum, R. (1998). The relationship between suicide risk and sexual orientation: Results of a population-based study. *American Journal of Public Health, 88*, 57–60. doi: 10.2105/AJPH.88.1.57

Robinson, J. P., & Espelage, D. L. (2011). Inequities in educational and psychological outcomes between LGBTQ and straight students in middle and high school. *Educational Researcher, 40*, 315–330. doi: 10.3102/0013189X11422112

Robinson, J. P., & Espelage, D. L. (2012). Bullying explains only part of LGBTQ-heterosexual risk disparities: Implications for policy and practice. *Educational Researcher, 41*(8), 309–319. doi: 10.3102/0013189X12457023

Rodkin, P. C., Espelage, D. L., & Hanish, L. D. (in press). A relational perspective on the social ecology of bullying. *American Psychologist*.

Russell, S. T., & Toomey, R. B. (2012). Men's sexual orientation and suicide: Evidence for U.S. adolescent-specific risk. *Social Science and Medicine, 74*, 523–529. doi: 10.1016/j.socscimed.2010.07.038

Salazar, L. F., Crosby, R. A. & DiClemente, R. J. (2013). Health behavior in the context of the "new" public health. In R. J. DiClemente, R. Salazar, & R. A. Crosby (Eds.), *Health Behavior Theory for Public Health*. Burlington, MA: Jones and Bartlett.

Ybarra, M., Espelage, D. L., & Mitchell, K. J. (2014). Differentiating youth who are bullied from other victims of peer-aggression: the importance of differential power and repetition. *Journal of Adolescent Health*. Online first, 1–8.

2

Comment Chapter

Bullying and Suicide Prevention: Taking a Balanced Approach That Is Scientifically Informed

JEFFREY DUONG AND CATHERINE P. BRADSHAW

As with most public health issues, highly publicized events or tragedies are often what it takes to capture the attention of the general public and policy makers. A number of incredibly troubling teen deaths by suicide have drawn the nation's attention to the issues of bullying and suicide. While the increased awareness of these two public health concerns is well deserved, the media publicity has inadvertently led many to assume a causal link between bullying and suicide (Arseneault, Bowes, & Shakoor, 2010). Although bullying and suicide share some common risk and protective factors, studies have shown that the association between these two forms of violence is often complex and indirect (Suicide Prevention Resource Center [SPRC], 2011). In fact, most youth who are bullied do not become suicidal. Other risk factors such as mental illness (Karch, Logan, McDaniel, Floyd, & Vagi, 2013; Klomek et al., 2008, 2013) and a lack of social support (Pisani et al., 2013) may contribute to suicidal behaviors. In this commentary, we aim to provide a balanced approach in reviewing the literature on the potential link between bullying and suicide, and identify research areas requiring attention. We also provide recommendations for addressing bullying and suicide from a public health perspective.

WHAT THE SCIENCE TELLS US ABOUT THE LINK BETWEEN BULLYING AND SUICIDE

Epidemiological research reveals that suicide and bullying are significant public health problems affecting youth in the United States. Suicide is the fourth leading cause of death for children between the ages of 5 and 14, and the second leading cause of death for those between the ages of 15 and 24 (Hoyert & Xu, 2012). Meanwhile, bullying is one of the most common forms of victimization experienced by young people in the United States. Approximately 20% to 28% of middle school and high school students indicate on self-report surveys that they have been bullied within the past year (Robers, Kemp, & Truman, 2013).

The growing concern over bullying led the Obama Administration to launch a partnership between several federal agencies to raise awareness about bullying, promote ongoing efforts to prevent and reduce bullying, identify effective bullying interventions and strategies, and facilitate partnerships between bullying prevention stakeholders and organizations (Bryn, 2011). Despite these national efforts over the past few years, there has been limited evidence that the prevalence of bullying has changed significantly (Bradshaw, Pas, & Zablotsky, 2014; Robers et al., 2013).

Children and youth who are involved in bullying are at increased risk for numerous negative outcomes. Victims of bullying frequently report physical health problems, lower school engagement, and reduced academic performance (Cornell, Gregory, Huang, & Fun, 2013). Youth who are victimized often experience feelings of depression and anxiety that may persist through adulthood (Copeland, Wolke, Angold, & Costello, 2013). In light of these findings regarding the mental health correlates and potential consequences of bullying, it is not surprising that some youth involved in bullying are at increased risk for suicide (Copeland et al., 2013). Data from the National Violent Death Reporting System (NVDRS) also suggest that school problems, depressed mood, substance abuse problems, and other life crises that are prevalent among victims of bullying are also common among youth suicide decedents (Karch et al., 2013).

Although the prevalence of suicidal behaviors is greater among youth involved in bullying compared to those who are uninvolved (Copeland et al., 2013), the scientific literature has not yet established a causal relationship between bullying and suicide. Furthermore, most victims of bullying do not become suicidal (SPRC, 2011). Rather, there may be vulnerable groups of youth who are victimized and at greater risk for suicide, such as sexual minorities (Poteat, Mereish, DiGiovanni, & Koenig, 2011; Poteat, O'Dwyer, & Mereish, 2012; Robinson & Espelage, 2011). Youth with disabilities may also be at risk for increased victimization (Rose, Espelage, Aragon, & Elliott, 2011; Sullivan & Bradshaw, 2012). As the scientific literature has shed light on the complex association between bullying and suicide, a more balanced approach is clearly necessary for addressing these issues.

A PUBLIC HEALTH APPROACH TO PREVENTING BULLYING AND SUICIDE

Adopting a public health perspective is imperative to effectively reduce bullying and suicide. This entails using scientifically informed approaches to raise awareness about bullying and suicide, as well as disseminating accurate information based on what is known from empirical research. Furthermore, prevention efforts should include universal strategies to enhance protective factors for all youth, selective interventions to modify early antecedents of bullying and suicide for youth at risk, and indicated efforts for youth already engaged in these behaviors (Mrazek & Haggerty, 1994; O'Connell et al., 2009). Considering the importance of balanced and integrative approaches to prevent bullying and suicide, here we present specific action-oriented recommendations guided by a public health framework to address these concerns.

Temper the "Causal" Message in Media Coverage of Bullying-Related Suicides

We need to be cautious not to overstate the association between bullying and suicide in media reports (SPRC, 2011). Most of the research on the association between bullying and suicide has been cross-sectional, which cannot determine temporality. Furthermore, although recent longitudinal studies provide more compelling evidence on the link between bullying and suicide (e.g., Copeland et al., 2013; Klomek et al., 2008, 2013), they are insufficient to establish causality. We also generally see that the association between bullying involvement (typically as a bully/victim) and suicidal thoughts or behaviors can be accounted for by mental health problems (Copeland et al., 2013; Klomek et al., 2008, 2009). More longitudinal studies are needed to clarify the temporal link between bullying and suicide before causal inferences can be made (Klomek et al., 2008; Klomek et al., 2013).

Integrate Bullying and Suicide Prevention Efforts

The scientific research has shown that youth bullying and suicide share a common set of risk and protective factors, such as emotion regulation problems, impulsivity, social support, and connectedness (O'Brennan, Bradshaw, & Sawyer, 2009; Zenere & Lazarus, 2009). Tiered prevention approaches may be useful strategies for integrating bullying and suicide prevention efforts and targeting the many risk and protective factors for these concerns (Waasdorp, Bradshaw, & Leaf, 2012). Universal programs such as Positive Behavioral Interventions and Supports (PBIS; Horner, Sugai, & Anderson, 2010), Second Step (Espelage, Low, Polanin, & Brown, 2013), and the Good Behavior Game (GBG; Wilcox et al., 2008) target early risk and protective factors for bullying and suicide, which make youth less likely to exhibit these negative outcomes (Ialongo et al., 1999; Wilcox et al., 2008). Due to their school-wide approach that targets multiple risk factors, universal interventions may offer a synergistic strategy to prevent bullying and suicide (Domitrovich et al., 2010).

Selective intervention strategies, such as Coping Power (Lochman et al., 2012), are particularly effective at identifying students at risk for other behavioral problems later in life. Meanwhile, indicative intervention strategies, such as the Incredible Years Program (Webster-Stratton & Herman, 2008), target youth showing early signs of social and emotional problems. Because selective and indicative interventions play an important role in identifying youth at risk for violent behavior, or those already involved, they may potentially be a platform for disseminating gatekeeper training to adults. These interventions would enable adults to identify and refer youth at risk for suicide to mental health service programs.

Promote Positive and Supportive School Climates

Promoting positive and supportive school climates is an important strategy for effective bullying and suicide prevention (Birkett, Espelage, & Koenig, 2009).

Bolstering a positive and supportive school climate involves creating a school culture that fosters respect, caring, and inclusiveness. Students must be also able to make healthy connections with adults in school (Blum, 2005; O'Brennan, Waasdorp, & Bradshaw, 2014). Research has identified a number of strategies that are critical to promoting a favorable school climate and student connectedness. These include providing opportunities for students, teachers, and administrators to work collaboratively and establish clear rules, as well as school policies, regarding behavioral expectations and consequences for when they are violated (Bradshaw et al., 2008; Olweus et al., 2007).

Teachers should receive training on classroom management and intervention strategies (Duong & Bradshaw, 2013). Adults should also intervene consistently with problematic behavior (Olweus et al., 2007). Furthermore, it is crucial for adults to be able to model appropriate behaviors and reinforce the positive behaviors of students. In areas where bullying frequently occurs (e.g., hallways, cafeteria, playground), increased adult supervision is necessary. Finally, it is important to develop effective support systems for students such that they can feel safe to seek help from adults if their peers have threatened them or if they feel unsafe in their school environment (Whitted & Dupper, 2005). Many of the evidence-based programs cited earlier (e.g., PBIS or GBG) include some of these critical features, and thus could be integrated to address risk and protective factors for bullying and suicide (Bradshaw et al., 2008).

Provide Training on Identifying and Responding to Risk Factors for Suicide

Effective prevention efforts should incorporate screening programs and gatekeeper training in schools (Wyman et al., 2008). School staff should be trained to identify students who appear to be struggling. Specifically, learning to identify risk factors for bullying and suicide is necessary (Espelage & Swearer, 2003). Equally important is for schools to develop policies and protocols for how staff should respond to students who are at risk for bullying and suicide. Strategies should be evidence-based as well. For example, research highlights the importance of timely referrals to appropriate mental health services for students at risk for bullying or suicide (Greene, 2003). Thus, ensuring access to mental health services and supports is pivotal in addressing these concerns. School-based mental health professionals also perform a variety of key functions in prevention efforts (Weist, Lever, Bradshaw, & Owens, 2013). Therefore, school districts need to ensure the availability of school-based mental health professionals (e.g., school psychologists, school counselors, and social workers), as these individuals can provide frontline mental health support for students at risk for suicide.

Start Prevention Early

Youth typically begin to engage in bullying behaviors prior to when suicidal behaviors tend to emerge (Klomek et al., 2009). Accordingly, it is crucial to prevent bullying in early childhood. Through early prevention, educators and mental health practitioners can identify students at risk for later behavior problems, including both suicidal behavior and conduct problems. Programs can then target children in a developmental stage before suicide problems (often) emerge. For youth already involved in bullying, it is imperative to assess their risk for suicide (Rigby & Slee, 1999).

Utilize Comprehensive Strategies That Involve Families, Schools, and Communities

Studies have consistently shown that risk factors spanning multiple ecological levels are associated with bullying and suicide. Bullying and suicide research efforts often emphasize using an ecological perspective to study these issues. Research supports adopting a comprehensive approach that involves families, schools, and communities to reduce violence (Mann et al., 2005). For example, parents are important stakeholders in preventing bullying and suicide. They play an important role in talking with their children about bullying and suicide and can advance school-based prevention efforts. Their participation is also necessary for resolving bullying situations that involve their children (Waasdorp, Bradshaw, & Duong, 2011). Meanwhile, prevention programs that involve the community may lead to special opportunities for intervention and outreach (Lindstrom-Johnson et al., 2011). Social marketing campaigns, for instance, can be used to reach large groups (Knox et al., 2003). Furthermore, communications can be tailored to specific groups that may play a role in prevention and early intervention (e.g., police officers or medical professionals) (Srabstein et al., 2008).

CONCLUSION

Bullying and suicide are complex phenomena that have gained considerable attention from policymakers, families, educators, and the general public over the past few years. This level of public attention provides the rare opportunity for action through developing policy, increasing prevention programming, and altering social norms. It is increasingly vital that we adopt a public health approach to address these two concerns. A critical component of this approach is the application of solid epidemiological research. Thus, it is important not to overstate a potentially causal association between bullying and suicide, either in the public's eye or in the research. Rather, a balanced approach is necessary when communicating research findings, particularly regarding such a sensitive and evocative issue such as youth suicide. Moreover, studies suggest that bullying and suicide share some common risk and protective factors. Accordingly, integrating prevention strategies could be a potentially efficient method for addressing both concerns. As some subgroups of youth may be particularly vulnerable to both bullying and suicide (e.g., youth with mental health concerns), a public health approach incorporating universal, selective, and indicated prevention efforts is critical to addressing these two serious health risks. Bolstering protective factors while simultaneously addressing risk factors is important to support vulnerable youth effectively. Although the school environment is a central ecological context for addressing these concerns, family, peer, and broader community contexts are also key considerations in effective prevention efforts. Indeed, addressing the link between bullying and suicide using a scientifically informed and balanced approach will be crucial to achieving the vision of safety and health for all youth.

REFERENCES

Arseneault, L., Bowes, L., & Shakoor, S. (2010). Bullying victimization in youths and mental health problems: "Much ado about nothing." *Psychological Medicine*, *40*(5), 717–729. Available at http://dx.doi.org/10.1017/S0033291709991383.

Birkett, M., Espelage, D. L., & Koenig, B. (2009). LGB and questioning students in schools: The moderating effects of homophobic bullying and school climate on negative outcomes. *Journal of Youth and Adolescence*, *38*(7), 989–1000. Available at http://dx.doi.org/10.1007/ 10.1007/s10964-008-9389-1.

Blum, R. W. (2005). A case for school connectedness. *Educational Leadership*, *62*(7), 16–20.

Bradshaw, C. P., Koth, C. W., Bevans, K. B., Ialongo, N., & Leaf, P. J. (2008). The impact of school-wide positive behavioral interventions and supports (PBIS) on the organizational health of elementary schools. *School Psychology Quarterly*, *23*(4), 462–473. Available at http://dx.doi.org/10.1037/a0012883.

Bradshaw, C. P., Pas, E. T., & Zablotsky, B. (2014). Examining eight-year trends in bullying and related attitudes and behaviors: A population-based study of youth grades 4–12. Manuscript submitted for publication.

Bryn, S. (2011). Stop bullying now! A federal campaign for bullying prevention and intervention. *Journal of School Violence*, *10*(2), 213–219. Available at http://dx.doi.org/ 10.1080/15388220.2011.557313.

Copeland, W. E., Wolke, D., Angold, A., & Costello, J. (2013). Adult psychiatric outcomes of bullying and being bullied by peer in childhood and adolescence. *JAMA Psychiatry*, *70*(4), 419–426. Available at http://dx.doi.org/10.1001/jamapsychiatry.2013.504.

Cornell, D., Gregory, A., Huang, F., & Fan, X. (2013). Perceived prevalence of teasing and bullying predicts high school dropout rates. *Journal of Educational Psychology*, *105*(1), 138–149. Available at http://dx.doi.org/10.1037/a0030416.

Domitrovich, C. E., Bradshaw, C. P., Greenberg, M. T., Embry, D., Poduska, J. M., & Ialongo, N. S. (2010). Integrated models of school-based prevention: Logic and theory. *Psychology in the Schools*, *47*(1), 71–88. Available at http://dx.doi.org/10.1002/pits.20452.

Duong, J., & Bradshaw, C. P. (2013). Using the extended parallel process model to examine teachers' likelihood of intervening in bullying. *Journal of School Health*, *83*(6), 422–429. Available at http://dx.doi.org/10.1111/josh.12046.

Espelage, D. L., Low, S., Polanin, J. R., & Brown, E. C. (2013). The impact of a middle school program to reduce aggression, victimization, and sexual violence. *Journal of Adolescent Health*, *53*(2), 180–186. Available at http://dx.doi.org/10.1016/j.jadohealth.2013.02.021.

Espelage, D. L., & Swearer, S. M. (2003). Research on school bullying and victimization: What have we learned and where do we go from here? *School Psychology Review*, *32*(3), 365–383.

Greene, M. B. (2003). Counseling and climate change as treatment modalities for bullying in school. *International Journal for the Advancement of Counselling, 25*(4), 293–302. Available at http://10.1023/B:ADCO.0000005528.59128.32.

Horner, R. H., Sugai, G., & Anderson, C. M. (2010). Examining the evidence base for school-wide positive behavior support. *Focus on Exceptional Children, 42*(8), 1–14.

Hoyert, D. L., & Xu, J. (2012). Deaths: Preliminary data for 2011. *National Vital Statistics Reports, 61*(6). Retrieved May 12, 2014, from http://www.cdc.gov/nchs/data/nvsr/nvsr61/nvsr61_06.pdf.

Ialongo, N. S., Werthamer, L., Kellam, S. G., Brown, C. H., Wang, S., & Lin, Y. (1999). Proximal impact of two first-grade preventive interventions on the early risk behaviors for later substance abuse, depression, and antisocial behavior. *American Journal of Community Psychology, 27*(5), 599–641. Available at http://dx.doi.org/10.1023/A:1022137920532.

Karch, D. L., Logan, J., McDaniel, D. D., Floyd, C. F., & Vagi, K. J. (2013). Precipitating circumstances of suicide among youth aged 10–17 years by sex: Data from the national violent death reporting system, 16 states, 2005–2008. *Journal of Adolescent Health, 53*(1), S51–S53. Available at http://dx.doi.org/10.1016/j.jadohealth.2012.06.028.

Klomek, A. B., Kleinman, M., Altschuler, E., Marrocco, F., Amakawa, L., & Gould, M. S. (2013). Suicidal adolescents' experiences with bullying perpetration and victimization during high school as risk factors for later depression and suicidality. *Journal of Adolescent Health, 53*(1), S37–S42. Available at http://dx.doi.org/10.1016/j.jadohealth.2012.12.008.

Klomek, A. B., Sourander, A., Kumpulainen, K., Piha, J., Tamminen, T., Moilanen, I., . . . Gould, M. S. (2008). Childhood bullying as a risk for later depression and suicidal ideation among Finnish males. *Journal of Affective Disorders, 109*(1), 47–55. Available at http://dx.doi.org/10.1016/j.jad.2007.12.226.

Klomek, A. B., Sourander, A., Niemelä, S., Kumpulainen, K., Piha, J., Tamminen, T., . . . Gould, M. S. (2009). Childhood bullying behaviors as a risk for suicide attempts and completed suicides: a population-based birth cohort study. *Journal of the American Academy of Child & Adolescent Psychiatry, 48*(3), 254–261. Available at http://dx.doi.org/10.1097/CHI.0b013e318196b91f.

Knox, K. L., Litts, D. A., Talcott, G. W., Feig, J. C., & Caine, E. D. (2003). Risk of suicide and related adverse outcomes after exposure to a suicide prevention programme in the US Air Force: cohort study. *British Medical Journal, 327*(7428), 1376. Available at http://dx.doi.org/10.1136/bmj.327.7428.1376.

Lindstrom-Johnson, S. R., Finigan, N. M., Bradshaw, C. P., Haynie, D. L., & Cheng, T. L. (2011). Examining the link between neighborhood context and parental messages to their adolescent children about violence. *Journal of Adolescent Health, 49*(1), 58–63. Available at http://dx.doi.org/10.1016/j.jadohealth.2010.10.014.

Lochman, J. E., Boxmeyer, C. L., Powell, N. P., Qu, L., Wells, K., & Windle, M. (2012). Coping power dissemination study: Intervention and special education effects on academic outcomes. *Behavioral Disorders, 37*(3), 192–205.

Mann, J. J., Apter, A., Bertolote, J., Beautrais, A., Currier, D., Haas, A., . . . & Hendin, H. (2005). Suicide prevention strategies. *JAMA: Journal of the American Medical Association, 294*(16), 2064–2074. Available at http://dx.doi.org/10.1001/jama.294.16.2064.

Mrazek, P. J., & Haggerty, R. J. (1994). *Reducing Risks for Mental Disorders: Frontiers for Preventive Intervention Research*. Washington, DC: Institute of Medicine, National Academy Press.

O'Brennan, L. M., Bradshaw, C. P., & Sawyer, A. L. (2009). Examining developmental differences in the social-emotional problems among frequent bullies, victims, and bully/victims. *Psychology in the Schools, 46*(2), 100–115. Available at http://dx.doi.org/ 10.1002/pits.20357.

O'Brennan, L. M., Waasdorp, T. E., & Bradshaw, C. P. (2014). Strengthening bullying prevention through school staff connectedness. *Journal of Educational Psychology.* Advance online publication. Available at http://10.1037/a0035957

O'Connell, M. E., Boat, T., & Warner, K. E. (Eds.). (2009). *Preventing Mental, Emotional, and Behavioral Disorders Among Young People: Progress and Possibilities.* Washington, DC: National Academies Press.

Olweus, D., Limber, S. P., Flerx, V. C., Mullin, N., Riese, J., & Snyder, M. (2007). *Olweus Bullying Prevention Program: Schoolwide Guide.* Center City, MN: Hazelden.

Pisani, A. R., Wyman, P. A., Petrova, M., Schmeelk-Cone, K., Goldston, D. B., Xia, Y., & Gould, M. S. (2013). Emotion regulation difficulties, youth–adult relationships, and suicide attempts among high school students in underserved communities. *Journal of Youth and Adolescence, 42*(6), 807–820. Available at http://dx.doi.org/10.1007/s10964-012-9884-2.

Poteat, V. P., Mereish, E. H., DiGiovanni, C. D., & Koenig, B. W. (2011). The effects of general and homophobic victimization on adolescents' psychosocial and educational concerns: The importance of intersecting identities and parent support. *Journal of Counseling Psychology, 58*(4), 597–609. Available at http://dx.doi.org/10.1037/a0025095.

Poteat, V. P., O'Dwyer, L. M., & Mereish, E. H. (2012). Changes in how students use and are called homophobic epithets over time: Patterns predicted by gender, bullying, and victimization status. *Journal of Educational Psychology, 104*, 393–406. Available at http://dx.doi.org/ 10.1037/a0026437.

Rigby, K., & Slee, P. (1999). Suicidal ideation among adolescent school children, involvement in bully–victim problems, and perceived social support. *Suicide and Life-Threatening Behavior, 29*(2), 119–130. Available at http://dx.doi.org/10.1111/j.1943-278X.1999.tb01050.x.

Robers, S., Kemp, J., & Truman, J. (2013). *Indicators of School Crime and Safety: 2012.* (NCES 2013-036/NCJ 241446). Washington, DC: National Center for Education Statistics, U.S. Department of Education, and Bureau of Justice Statistics, Office of Justice Programs, U.S. Department of Justice.

Robinson, J. P., & Espelage, D. L. (2011). Inequities in educational and psychological outcomes between LGBTQ and straight students in middle and high school. *Educational Researcher, 40*, 315–330. Available at http://dx.doi.org/10.3102/0013189X11422112.

Rose, C. A., Espelage, D. L., Aragon, S. R., & Elliott, J. (2011). Bullying and victimization among students in special education and general education curricula. *Exceptionality Education International, 21*(2), 2–14.

Srabstein, J., Joshi, P., Due, P., Wright, J., Leventhal, B., Merrick, J., . . . Riibner, K. (2008). Prevention of public health risks linked to bullying: a need for a whole community approach. *International Journal of Adolescent Medicine and Health, 20*(2), 185–200. Available at http://dx.doi.org/10.1515/IJAMH.2008.20.2.185.

Suicide Prevention Resource Center. (SPRC; 2011). *Issue Brief: Suicide and Bullying.* Newton, MA: Suicide Prevention Resource Center.

Sullivan, T. N., & Bradshaw, C. P. (2012). Introduction to the special issue of *Behavioral Disorders*: Serving the needs of youth with disabilities through school-based violence prevention efforts. *Behavioral Disorders, 37*(3), 129–132.

Waasdorp, T. E., Bradshaw, C. P., & Duong, J. (2011). The link between parents' perceptions of the school and their responses to school bullying: variation by child characteristics and the forms of victimization. *Journal of Educational Psychology, 103*(2), 324–335. Available at http://dx.doi.org/10.1037/a0022748.

Waasdorp, T. E., Bradshaw, C. P., & Leaf, P. J. (2012). The impact of schoolwide positive behavioral interventions and supports on bullying and peer rejection: A randomized controlled effectiveness trial. *Archives of Pediatrics & Adolescent Medicine, 166*(2), 149–156. Available at http://dx.doi.org/10.1001/archpediatrics.2011.755.

Webster-Stratton, C., and Herman, K. C. (2008). The impact of parent behavior-management training on child depressive symptoms. *Journal of Counseling Psychology, 55*(4),473–484. Available at http://dx.doi.org/10.1037/a0013664.

Weist, M. D., Lever, N. A., Bradshaw, C. P., & Owens, J. (2013). Further developing school mental health: Reflecting on the past to inform the future. In Weist, M. D., Lever, N. A., Bradshaw, C. P., & Owens, J. (Eds.). *Handbook of School Mental Health: Advancing Practice and Research* (2nd ed.) (pp. 1–14). New York: Springer.

Whitted, K. S., & Dupper, D. R. (2005). Best practices for preventing or reducing bullying in schools. *Children & Schools, 27*(3), 167–175. Available at http://dx.doi.org/10.1093/cs/27.3.167.

Wilcox, H. C., Kellam, S. G., Brown, C. H., Poduska, J. M., Ialongo, N. S., Wang, W., & Anthony, J. C. (2008). The impact of two universal randomized first- and second-grade classroom interventions on young adult suicide ideation and attempts. *Drug and Alcohol Dependence, 95*, S60–S73. Available at http://dx.doi.org/10.1016/j.drugalcdep.2008.01.005.

Wyman, P. A., Brown, C. H., Inman, J., Cross, W., Schmeelk-Cone, K., Guo, J., & Pena, J. B. (2008). Randomized trial of a gatekeeper program for suicide prevention: 1-year impact on secondary school staff. *Journal of Consulting and Clinical Psychology, 76*(1), 104–115. Available at http://dx.doi.org/10.1037/0022-006X.76.1.104.

Zenere, F. J., & Lazarus, P. J. (2009). The sustained reduction of youth suicidal behavior in an urban, multicultural school district. *School Psychology Review, 38*(2), 189–199.

PART TWO

Defining the Problem: Prevalence, Predictors, and Protectors

3

Suicidal Risk as a Function of Bullying and Other Victimization Exposures

MELISSA K. HOLT

In the past decade, both bullying and suicide among youth have emerged as significant public health concerns, with prevalence rates highlighting the significant number of youth affected by each of these issues. Studies have found that approximately 20%–30% of youth are involved in bullying in some capacity, with rates varying depending on the type of bullying under consideration (e.g., rates of verbal bullying are higher than rates of physical bullying) (Dinkes, Kemp, & Baum, 2009; Spriggs, Iannotti, Nansel, & Haynie, 2007; Wang, Iannotti, & Nansel, 2009). Cyber bullying prevalence estimates have been less consistent, with rates ranging from approximately 10%–35% for victimization and 5%–20% for perpetration (Kowalski & Limber, 2007; Wang et al., 2009; Williams & Guerra, 2007). While suicidality is less common, prevalence rates are nonetheless concerning. For instance, recent national estimates indicate that among ninth- through twelfth-grade students, 15.8% have seriously considered suicide in the past year, 12.8% have made a suicide plan, and 7.8% have attempted suicide (Centers for Disease Control and Prevention, 2012). Furthermore, among 10–24-year-olds, suicide is the second leading cause of death (Centers for Disease Control and Prevention, 2010).

Efforts to understand and prevent both bullying and suicide among youth have been situated in a social-ecological framework (Benbenishty & Astor, 2005; Bronfenbrenner, 1977; Office of the Surgeon General & National Action Alliance for Suicide Prevention, 2012; Swearer & Espelage, 2011). This framework emphasizes that youth behaviors are shaped by individual characteristics and a range of nested contextual systems, with microsystems consisting of structures directly affecting youth (e.g., schools, peer groups, families) and mesosystems reflecting the interrelations among the microsystems. For bullying, risk and protective factors at each level of the social-ecology have been identified for bullies, victims, and bully-victims (Cook, Williams, Guerra, Kim, & Sadek, 2010). Similarly, factors that either increase or reduce the risk for youth suicide have been delineated (Suicide Prevention Resource Center & Rodgers, 2011). While there are some shared risk (e.g., sexual minority status) and protective (e.g., social support systems) factors for suicide and bullying, there are others that are unique or operate differently for each domain. For example, males are generally at greater risk for bullying involvement and completed suicide, whereas females are at greater risk for suicidal ideation and attempts (Centers for Disease Control and Prevention, 2012; Kann et al., 2011; Lubell & Vetter, 2006; Office of the Surgeon General & National Action Alliance for Suicide Prevention, 2012; Rothon, Head, Klineberg, & Stansfeld, 2011).

In recent years, bullying has been increasingly examined as a potential risk factor for suicidal ideation, attempts, and completed suicide (Kim & Leventhal, 2008). While research supports an association between bullying involvement and suicidality (Kim & Leventhal, 2008), it is important to view this relationship within the broader social-ecological context, and recognize that bullying is just one potential risk factor in a constellation of other risk and protective factors. Furthermore, given the overlap between bullying and other victimization exposures (Holt, Finkelhor, & Kantor, 2007) and the link between other victimization exposures and suicide (Fergusson, Boden, & Horwood, 2008), this chapter argues for the need to assess violence exposures more broadly to best understand suicide risk among youth.

BULLYING AND SUICIDE

According to a recent systematic review, bullying involvement in any capacity (i.e., as a bully, victim, or bully-victim) is associated with higher rates of suicidal ideation and behaviors, with odds ratios ranging from 1.4–10.0 (Kim & Leventhal, 2008). In line with the social-ecological framework, efforts have been made to further specify the conditions under which this association is strengthened or diminished. Some research has suggested that bullying involvement might be a more salient independent risk factor for suicidality among girls (Klomek et al., 2009), whereas other studies have found a stronger relationship for boys (Laukkanen, Honkalampi, Hintikka, Hintikka, & Lehtonen, 2005). Findings with respect to how types of bullying involvement are differentially related to suicidal ideation and attempts are similarly mixed. For instance, some studies have found a stronger association for victims (e.g., Rigby and Slee, 1999), whereas other studies have found perpetrators to be at greater risk (e.g., Kaltiala-Heino et al., 1999). Bully-victims have typically been identified as the group at greatest risk for short- and long-term psychological distress (Kaltiala-Heino, Rimpelä, Rantanen, & Rimpelä, 2000); and some, but not all, studies have found bully-victims to be at increased risk for suicidality as compared to uninvolved youth, bullies, and victims (Herba et al., 2008; Klomek, Marrocco, Kleinman, Schonfeld, & Gould, 2007). Finally, researchers have started to explore whether different forms of bullying show similar or divergent patterns of association with suicidality. For instance, one study of high school students found that physical and cyber bullying contributed relatively equally to predicting suicidal behavior (Litwiller & Brausch, 2013). In an investigation of Canadian adolescents, cyber-bullying perpetration and victimization were found to make unique contributions to suicidal ideation, beyond what was accounted for by physical, verbal, and relational bullying (Bonanno & Hymel, 2013).

As research moves beyond delineating the bivariate relation between bullying involvement and suicidality, a more nuanced understanding of this association has emerged. For instance, after accounting for the role of depression and delinquency, differences in suicidal ideation between uninvolved youth and victims and uninvolved youth and bully-victims became minimal (Espelage & Holt, 2013). Conversely, after accounting for depression and sociodemographic characteristics in a study of adults, those who were victims of childhood bullying victimization were twice as likely to report suicidal ideation as were their uninvolved peers (Allison, Roeger, & Reinfeld-Kirkman, 2009). Similarly, whereas at the bivariate level physical, verbal, and cyber bullying were associated with suicidal ideation for male and female adolescents, once other factors were considered (e.g., neighborhood disorder and parental investment), individual types of bullying victimization no longer remained significant predictors (Turner, Exum, Brame, & Holt, 2013). Additional research has identified mediating factors such as substance use and violent behavior as key factors explaining possible pathways between bullying involvement and suicide (Litwiller & Brausch, 2013).

Studies considering how other factors, in conjunction with bullying involvement, contribute to suicidality have found divergent patterns for girls and boys. In a prospective study of Finnish children, bullying perpetration and victimization were associated with suicide attempts and completed suicide for boys by the age of 25. However, after accounting for conduct problems and depression symptoms, there was no longer a significant association (Klomek et al., 2009). Conversely, in this same study, bullying victimization at age eight remained a significant predictor of suicide attempts and completed suicides in early adulthood for girls in multivariate analyses that controlled for conduct and depression symptoms. Another study found that "meaning in life"— the belief that one's life has a purpose—mediated between bullying victimization and suicidal ideation for female adolescents, but for male adolescents, "meaning in life" played a moderating role between bullying victimization and suicidal ideation (Henry et al., 2013). Therefore, it appears that different factors might be salient for girls and boys.

Longitudinal studies have also contributed to an enhanced understanding of which youth involved in bullying might be at greatest risk for suicidal ideation or attempts. For instance, one study found that, in contrast to high school students reporting suicidal ideation only at baseline, individuals who reported both bullying perpetration and suicidal ideation at baseline reported more suicidal ideation at a two-year follow-up (Klomek et al., 2013). Similarly, a study of hospitalized suicidal adolescents found that, at baseline, youth who reported bullying perpetration also reported heightened levels of suicidal ideation (King, Horwitz, Berona, & Jiang, 2013). In this same study, while many youth engaged in bullying perpetration at baseline ceased such behaviors over the next 12 months, those at the 12-month follow-up who identified as perpetrating bullying behaviors (regardless of their involvement at baseline) also reported more suicidal ideation. Finally, emerging evidence suggests that the mental health implications of bullying might continue into adulthood. Specifically among males, bully-victim status in childhood was associated with suicidality in early adulthood (Copeland, Wolke, Angold, & Costello, 2013).

OTHER VIOLENCE EXPOSURES AND SUICIDE

While victimization and perpetration perhaps most commonly occur within the bullying context among youth, violence exposures also occur in other realms, and these additional victimization forms are important to consider as contributors to psychological functioning. In a nationally representative sample of children from birth to 17, approximately 10% had experienced some form of childhood maltreatment, and approximately 25% had witnessed or been indirectly exposed to violence (Finkelhor, Turner, Ormrod, & Hamby, 2009). Among high school students, 9.4% reported dating-violence victimization, and 8% reported forced sexual intercourse (Centers for Disease Control and Prevention, 2012). Furthermore, approximately half of adolescents reported experiencing sexual harassment during the course of a school year (Hill & Kearl, 2011). Singular forms of victimization have been correspondingly linked to a range of deleterious outcomes, including depression, suicidal ideation, and anxiety (Baldry & Winkel, 2003; Holt & Espelage, 2005). Moreover, for the subset of youth who incur multiple forms of victimization, there is a particularly heightened level of psychological distress (Finkelhor, Ormrod, & Turner, 2007).

Studies have linked bullying involvement—as a bully, victim, or bully-victim—to other victimization forms, including child maltreatment, dating violence, sexual harassment, and exposure to domestic violence (Espelage, Basile, & Hamburger, 2012; Holt et al., 2007; Miller et al., 2013). Little research, however, has addressed the extent to which bullying, in conjunction with other victimization exposures, uniquely or cumulatively influences mental health. In one study of elementary students, without considering other victimization exposures, all types of bullying involvement (i.e., as a bully, victim, or bully-victim) predicted internalizing problems, but once additional victimizations were accounted for, only victim and bully-victim statuses remained significant predictors (Holt et al., 2007). In another investigation focused specifically on suicide, Borowsky and colleagues (2013) found that, among bullies and victims involved in non-physical forms of bullying, physical and sexual abuse were two of the risk factors related to suicidal ideation or attempts (Borowsky, Taliaferro, & McMorris, 2013). This nascent research area suggests that, without considering how bullying and other victimization forms individually and cumulatively relate to suicidality indicators, there will be a restricted ability to identify the most at-risk youth, and similarly, to design the most effective prevention programs in either domain.

Conclusion and Suggestions

There is an increasing body of research supporting the association between bullying involvement and suicidality. Furthermore, studies are moving toward identifying nuances of this association, reflecting a broader social-ecological orientation that recognizes the importance of considering a range of individual and contextual variables affecting youth behaviors and functioning. This chapter highlights the importance of attending to bullying involvement and other victimization exposures conjointly. Through considering a broad range of victimization exposures, school counseling staff and other mental health professionals will be better equipped to assess the risk for mental health problems, including suicide.

Based on the issues highlighted in this chapter, specific recommendations for professionals who work with youth include the following.

Medical and Mental Health Providers

- Medical providers, most notably pediatricians, should screen for a range of victimization exposures, including bullying, during well-child visits.

Parents and Teachers

- Professionals working in schools or other youth-serving organizations should assess victimization exposures in the home and community as well as in other peer contexts (e.g., dating relationships) when working with youth involved in bullying. By understanding victimization exposures more comprehensively, suicide risk can be better determined.
- Parents and teachers should be alert to a range of factors increasing risk for youth suicide, including not only bullying involvement, but also factors such as depression and substance use.

Policy Makers

- Policy makers should recognize the complex nature of bullying involvement as it relates to other victimization exposures and suicidality, and use these findings to guide the development of new policies and the modification of existing ones.

Researchers

- Future research should continue to explore factors at each level of the social-ecological context that might modify the association between bullying involvement and suicide risk, and to clarify whether particular forms of bullying or types of involvement heighten risk. Understanding how the youth more peripherally involved in bullying might be affected is also important (Rivers & Noret, 2013). Also, given discrepant findings across studies, research could consider study characteristics that might explain differences in results. For instance, preliminary research suggests that the way in which bullying is measured affects the apparent strength of the relationship between bullying involvement and suicidal ideation and attempts (Holt et al., 2013). As new research findings emerge that are grounded in the social-ecological framework, both bullying and suicide-prevention efforts will be enhanced significantly. In turn, efforts will more effectively address two major current public health concerns for the youth population: bullying and suicide.

REFERENCES

Allison, S., Roeger, L., & Reinfeld-Kirkman, N. (2009). Does school bullying affect adult health? Population survey of health-related quality of life and past victimization. *Australian and New Zealand Journal of Psychiatry, 43*(12), 1163–1170. doi: 10.3109/00048670903270399

Baldry, A. C., & Winkel, F. W. (2003). Direct and vicarious victimization at school and at home as risk factors for suicidal cognition among Italian adolescents. *Journal of Adolescence, 26*(6), 703–716. Available at http://dx.doi.org/10.1016/j.adolescence.2003.07.002.

Benbenishty, R., & Astor, R. A. (2005). *School Violence in Context: Culture, Neighborhood, Family, School, and Gender.* New York: Oxford University Press.

Bonanno, R. A., & Hymel, S. (2013). Cyber bullying and internalizing difficulties: Above and beyond the impact of traditional forms of bullying. *Journal of Youth and Adolescence, 42*(5), 685–697. doi: 10.1007/s10964-013-9937-1

Borowsky, I. W., Taliaferro, L. A., & McMorris, B. J. (2013). Suicidal thinking and behavior among youth involved in verbal and social bullying: Risk and protective factors. *Journal of Adolescent Health, 53,* S4–S12. Available at http://dx.doi.org/10.1016/j.jadohealth.2012.10.280.

Bronfenbrenner, U. (1977). Toward an experimental ecology of human development. *American Psychologist, 32,* 513–531. Available at http://dx.doi.org/10.1037/0003-066X.32.7.513.

Centers for Disease Control and Prevention. (2012). Youth risk behavior surveillance—United States, 2011. *Morbidity & Mortality Weekly Report Surveillance Summaries 2012* (Vol. 61, pp. SS–4). Atlanta, GA.

Centers for Disease Control and Prevention, National Center for Injury Prevention and Control, Web-based Injury Statistics Query and Reporting System (2010). Retrieved July 5, 2013, from http://www.cdc.gov/injury/wisqars/index.html.

Cook, C. R., Williams, K. R., Guerra, N. G., Kim, T. E., & Sadek, S. (2010). Predictors of bullying and victimization in childhood and adolescence: A meta-analytic investigation. *School Psychology Quarterly, 25*(2), 65–83. doi: 10.1037/a002014910.1037/a0020149.supp (Supplemental)

Copeland, W. E., Wolke, D., Angold, A., & Costello, E. (2013). Adult psychiatric outcomes of bullying and being bullied by peers in childhood and adolescence. *JAMA Psychiatry, 70*(4), 419–426. doi: 10.1001/jamapsychiatry.2013.504

Dinkes, R., Kemp, J., & Baum, K. (2009). Indicators of School Crime and Safety: 2009. NCES 2010-012/NCJ 228478: National Center for Education Statistics. Retrieved July 3, 2013, from: http://nces.ed.gov/.

Espelage, D. L., Basile, K. C., & Hamburger, M. E. (2012). Bullying experiences and co-occurring sexual violence perpetration among middle school students: Shared and unique risk factors. *Journal of Adolescent Health, 50,* 60–65.

Espelage, D. L., & Holt, M. K. (2013). Suicidal ideation and school bullying experiences after controlling for depression and delinquency. *Journal of Adolescent Health, 53,* S27–S31. doi: 1016/j.jadohealth.2012.09.017

Fergusson, D. M., Boden, J. M., & Horwood, L. J. (2008). Exposure to childhood sexual and physical abuse and adjustment in early adulthood. *Child Abuse and Neglect, 32*(6), 607–619. Available at http://dx.doi.org/10.1016/j.chiabu.2006.12.018.

Finkelhor, D., Ormrod, R. K., & Turner, H. A. (2007). Polyvictimization and trauma in a national longitudinal cohort. *Development and Psychopathology, 19*(1), 149–166. doi: 10.1017/S0954579407070083

Finkelhor, D., Turner, H., Ormrod, R., & Hamby, S. L. (2009). Violence, abuse, and crime exposure in a national sample of children and youth. *Pediatrics, 124*(5), 1411–1423. doi: 10.1542/peds.2009-0467

Henry, K. L., Lovegrove, P. J., Steger, M. F., Chen, P. Y., Cigularov, K. P., & Tomazic, R. G. (2013). The potential role of meaning in life in the relationship between bullying victimization and suicidal ideation. *Journal of Youth and Adolescence, 43*, 221–232. doi: 10.1007/s10964-013-9960-2

Herba, C. M., Ferdinand, R. F., Stijnen, T., Veenstra, R., Oldehinkel, A. J., Ormel, J., & Verhulst, F. C. (2008). Victimization and suicide ideation in the trails study: Specific vulnerabilities of victims. *Journal of Child Psychology and Psychiatry, 49*(8), 867–876. doi: 10.1111/j.1469-7610.2008.01900.x

Hill, C., & Kearl, H. (2011). *Crossing the Line: Sexual Harassment at School*. Washington, DC: American Association of University Women.

Holt, M. K., & Espelage, D. L. (2005). Social support as a moderator between dating violence victimization and depression/anxiety among African American and Caucasian adolescents. *School Psychology Review, 34*(3), 309–328.

Holt, M. K., Finkelhor, D., & Kantor, G. K. (2007). Hidden forms of victimization in elementary students involved in bullying. *School Psychology Review, 36*(3), 345–360.

Holt, M., Vivolo-Kantor, A., DeGue, S., Holland, K., Matjasko, J., Wolfe, M., Reid, J. (2013, May 29). Bullying and its relation to suicidal ideation and behaviors: A meta-analysis. In Vivolo, A. (chair), *Addressing Youth Bullying by Applying Steps in the Public Health Model*. Paper presented at the Society for Prevention Research Annual Conference, San Francisco, CA.

Kaltiala-Heino, R., Rimpelä, M., Marttunen, M., & Rimpelä, A., & Rantanen, P. (1999). Bullying, depression, and suicidal ideation in Finnish adolescents: School survey. *British Medical Journal, 319*, 348–351. doi: 10.1136/bmj.319.7206.348

Kaltiala-Heino, R., Rimpelä, M., Rantanen, P., & Rimpelä, A. (2000). Bullying at school—an indicator of adolescents at risk for mental disorders. *Journal of Adolescence, 23*(6), 661–674. doi: 10.1006/jado.2000.0351

Kann, L., Olsen, E. O., McManus, T., Kinchen, S., Chyen, D., & Harris, W. A. (2011). Sexual identity, sex of sexual contacts, and health-risk behaviors among students in grades 9–12—Youth risk behavior, surveillance, selected sites, United States, 2001–2009. *MMWR Surveillance Summaries, 60*, 1–133.

Kim, Y. S., & Leventhal, B. (2008). Bullying and suicide. A review. *International Journal of Adolescent Medicine and Health, 20*(2), 133–154. doi: 10.1515/IJAMH.2008.20.2.133

King, C. A., Horwitz, A., Berona, J., & Jiang, Q. (2013). Acutely suicidal adolescents who engage in bullying behavior: 1-year trajectories. *Journal of Adolescent Health, 53*, S43–S50. Available at http://dx.doi.org/10.1016/j.jadohealth.2012.09.016.

Klomek, A. B., Kleinman, M., Altschuler, E., Marrocco, F., Amakawa, L., & Gould, M. A. (2013). Suicidal adolescents' experiences with bullying perpetration and victimization during high school as risk factors for later depression and suicidality. *Journal of Adolescent Health, 53*, S37–S42. doi: 1016/j.jadohealth.2012.12.008

Klomek, A. B., Marrocco, F., Kleinman, M., Schonfeld, I. S., & Gould, M. S. (2007). Bullying, depression, and suicidality in adolescents. *Journal of the American Academy of Child & Adolescent Psychiatry, 46*(1), 40–49. doi: 10.1097/01.chi.0000242237.84925.18

Klomek, A. B., Sourander, A., Niemelä, S., Kumpulainen, K., Piha, J., Tamminen, T., . . . Gould, M. S. (2009). Childhood bullying behaviors as a risk for suicide attempts and completed suicides: A population-based birth cohort study. *Journal of the American Academy of Child & Adolescent Psychiatry, 48*(3), 254–261. doi: 10.1097/CHI.0b013e318196b91f

Kowalski, R. M., & Limber, S. P. (2007). Electronic bullying among middle school students. *Journal of Adolescent Health, 41*(6), S22-S30. doi: 10.1016/j.jadohealth.2007.08.017

Laukkanen, E., Honkalampi, K., Hintikka, J., Hintikka, U., & Lehtonen, J. (2005). Suicidal ideation among help-seeking adolescents: Association with a negative self-image. *Archives of Suicide Research, 9*, 45–55. doi: 10,1080/13811110590512930

Litwiller, B. J., & Brausch, A. M. (2013). Cyber bullying and physical bullying in adolescent suicide: The role of violent behavior and substance use. *Journal of Youth and Adolescence, 42*, 675–684. doi: 10/s10964-013-9925-5

Lubell, K. M., & Vetter, J. B. (2006). Suicide and youth violence prevention: The promise of an integrated approach. *Aggression and Violent Behavior, 11*(2), 167–175. doi: 10.1016/j.avb.2005.07.006

Miller, S., Williams, J., Cutbush, S., Gibbs, D., Clinton-Sherrod, M., & Jones, S. (2013). Dating violence, bullying, and sexual harassment: Longitudinal profiles and transitions over time. *Journal of Youth and Adolescence, 42*(4), 607–618. doi: 10.1007/s10964-013-9914-8

Office of the Surgeon General, & National Action Alliance for Suicide Prevention. (2012). *2012 National Strategy for Suicide Prevention: Goals and Objectives for Action*. Washington, DC: Health and Human Services.

Rigby, K. and Slee, P.T. (1999). Suicidal ideation among adolescent school children, involvement in bully/victim problems and perceived low social support. *Suicide and Life-Threatening Behavior, 29*,119–130.

Rivers, I., & Noret, N. (2013). Potential suicide ideation and its association with observing bullying at school. *Journal of Adolescent Health, 53*, S32–S36. doi: 10.1016/j.jadohealth.2012.10.279

Rothon, C., Head, J., Klineberg, E., & Stansfeld, S. (2011). Can social support protect bullied adolescents from adverse outcomes? A prospective study on the effects of bullying on the educational achievement and mental health of adolescents at secondary schools in East London. *Journal of Adolescence, 34*(3), 579–588. doi: 10.1016/j.adolescence.2010.02.007

Spriggs, A. L., Iannotti, R. J., Nansel, T. R., & Haynie, D. L. (2007). Adolescent bullying involvement and perceived family, peer and school relations: Commonalities and differences across race/ethnicity. *Journal of Adolescent Health, 41*(3), 283–293. doi: 10.1016/j.jadohealth.2007.04.009

Suicide Prevention Resource Center, & Rodgers, P. (2011). *Understanding Risk and Protective Factors for Suicide: A Primer for Preventing Suicide*. Newton, MA: Education Development Center, Inc.

Swearer, S. M., & Espelage, D. L. (2011). A social-ecological framework of bullying among youth. In D. L. Espelage & S. M. Swearer (Eds.), *Bullying in North American Schools* (pp. 1–12). New York: Routledge.

Turner, M. G., Exum, M. L., Brame, R., & Holt, T. J. (2013). Bullying victimization and adolescent mental health: General and typological effects across sex. *Journal of Criminal Justice, 42*, 53–59. doi: 10.1016/j.jcrimjus.2012.12.005

Wang, J., Iannotti, R. J., & Nansel, T. R. (2009). School bullying among adolescents in the United States: Physical, verbal, relational, and cyber. *Journal of Adolescent Health, 45*(4), 368–375. doi: 10.1016/j.jadohealth.2009.03.021

Williams, K. R., & Guerra, N. G. (2007). Prevalence and predictors of Internet bullying. *Journal of Adolescent Health, 41*(6), S14–S21. doi: 10.1016/j.jadohealth.2007.08.018

4

Bullying and Mental Health

AMANDA B. NICKERSON AND TONI ORRANGE TORCHIA ■

Bullying, once regarded as a rite of passage, is now recognized as a serious mental health and public health issue. Bullying is a form of aggressive behavior that includes an intention to cause physical or psychological harm, a power imbalance that makes it difficult for the target to defend himself or herself, and repeated occurrence (Nansel et al., 2001; Olweus, 1993). Bullying can be physical (e.g., hitting, kicking), verbal (e.g., name calling), indirect (e.g., exclusion, rumor spreading), or electronic, also known as cyber-bullying (Crick, Casas, & Ku, 1999). Mental health is "a state of well-being in which every individual realizes his or her own potential, can cope with the normal stresses of life, can work productively and fruitfully, and is able to make a contribution to her or his community" (World Health Organization, 2011). In this chapter, the impact of bullying on various aspects of mental health, including emotional functioning, relationships, academic performance, and other outcomes, is reviewed for perpetrators, targets, bully-victims, and bystanders.

PERPETRATORS

Bullying others is associated with a range of concurrent and long-term externalizing problems. Students who bully others are more likely than their peers to engage in other high-risk behaviors, such as weapon-carrying (Dukes, Stein, & Zane, 2010) and substance abuse (Carlyle & Steinman, 2007; Kaltiala-Heino, Rimpelä, Rantanen, & Rimpelä, 2000; Kim, Catalano, Haggerty, & Abbott, 2011). Bullying behavior may be a precursor to escalating problems in later life. In a seminal study, Olweus (1991) found that 60% of students identified as bullies in middle school had at least one lifetime criminal conviction, with 35% to 40% of bullies having three or more criminal convictions in later life. More recent studies have found that former bullies are more likely to engage in violent crime (Farrington & Ttofi, 2011; Lösel & Bender, 2011), and to have more criminal convictions and traffic violations than their peers (Renda, Vassallo, & Edwards, 2011; Sourander et al., 2011). Individuals identified as bullying someone else at least once in their youth by self- or parent-report are also at increased risk for a diagnosis of antisocial personality disorder in young adulthood (Copeland, Wolke, Angold, & Costello, 2013). Bullies are more likely than their peers to sexually harass others later in life (Espelage, Basile, & Hamburger, 2012). They are also more aggressive in general, especially toward their spouses (Kim et al., 2011). Individuals who bullied others are more likely than their peers to use alcohol, marijuana, and other drugs in young adulthood (Farrington & Ttofi, 2011; Kim et al., 2011).

Bullying others is related not only to externalizing problems, but also to academic and physical problems. Students who bully others have been found to have poorer school adjustment and less school success (e.g., difficulty completing homework, problems getting along with others) than both targets and typical peers (Brown & Taylor, 2008; Nansel, Haynie, & Simons-Morton, 2003). In addition, these students are more likely to feel sad and unsafe in school than their peers who are not involved in bullying (Glew, Fan, Katon, Rivara, & Kernic, 2005). Perpetration also has physical implications, with females who bully others reporting higher rates of anorexia (Kaltiala-Heino et al., 2000). Bullies are also at higher risk for psychosomatic problems than non-involved peers, although these rates are lower than those for victims and bully-victims (Gini & Pozzoli, 2009).

There is a growing body of literature indicating that bullying others is also associated with depression, suicidal ideation, and suicide attempts (Klomek, Marrocco, Kleinman, Schonfeld, & Gould, 2007; Nickerson & Slater, 2009). Suicidal ideation is present in 43% of physical bullies, and suicidal behavior is present for 35% of this group, compared to less than 12% for uninvolved peers (Espelage & Holt, 2013). Additional research has found that males who frequently bullied others at age 8 were at increased risk for suicidality at age 25 compared to their non-involved peers (Klomek et al., 2009).

It is important to note that bullying accounts for only a small amount of the variance in suicidality (Hinduja & Patchin, 2010; Kowalski & Limber, 2013), indicating the need to distinguish specific risk and protective factors associated with this complex issue. Self-injurious behavior and increased negative emotionality have been indicated as risk factors across groups; however, a history of physical or sexual abuse, bringing weapons to school, mental health problems, running away from home, and self-identifying as being overweight are also risk factors for suicide among perpetrators (Borowsky, Taliaferro, & McMorris, 2013). Feelings of connectedness to parents and having caring friends were found to be protective factors for all youth involved in bullying; for perpetrators, connectedness to other caring adults such as relatives or community members was an additional protective factor (Borowsky et al., 2013).

TARGETS

Targets of bullying experience higher levels of emotional distress and mental health issues than their peers, including sadness, loneliness, and withdrawal (Kochenderfer & Ladd, 1996; Storch & Masia-Warner, 2004; van Oort, Greaves-Lord, Ormel, Verhulst, & Huizink, 2011). They also display other internalizing symptoms including anxiety and depression (Hugh-Jones & Smith, 1999; Kochenderfer & Ladd, 1996), with a comprehensive meta-analysis postulating a reciprocal relationship between peer victimization and internalizing behaviors (Reijntjes, Kamphuis,

Prinzie, & Telch, 2010). Targets of bullying may have a poor sense of self, perceiving themselves as failures and outcasts (Hugh-Jones & Smith, 1999). Peer victimization, although not limited to bullying per se, has been associated with characterological self-blame (i.e., attributions about victimization being due to internal, stable, and uncontrollable factors), loneliness, and low self-worth (Graham & Juvonen, 1998).

In addition to the victimization that targets experience, they often have other social difficulties with their peers. They are likely to have a low social status, marked by rejection and lack of acceptance by their peers (Ivarsson, Broberg, Arvidsson, & Gillberg, 2005; Salmivalli, Lagerspetz, Björkqvist, Österman, & Kaukiainen, 1996). Lack of reciprocated friendships and corresponding loneliness can also lead to more peer victimization (Boulton, Trueman, Chau, Whitehead, & Amatya, 1999). Furthermore, the targets of bullying tend to develop social connections with other victims, which can exacerbate their social problems and minimize the likelihood of peers' intervening to assist them when they are bullied (Salmivalli, Huttunen, & Lagerspetz, 1997). Targets of bullying are also at higher risk for other forms of victimization, such as physical and emotional maltreatment by parents, and sexual assaults (Duncan, 1999). Students who are victimized repeatedly and in different ways (e.g., sexual abuse, bullying, sexual harassment) have poorer psychosocial outcomes than other victims and peers (Holt & Espelage, 2003).

Victimization is also associated with poor school outcomes, including lack of connectedness and feeling unsafe in school (Glew et al., 2005). Targets often engage in withdrawal and escape behaviors such as avoiding or skipping school, which can have an adverse impact on their academic and social development (Batsche & Knoff, 1994; Kochenderfer & Ladd, 1996). Individuals who are victimized by their peers may be less successful academically (Brown & Taylor, 2008; Glew et al., 2005), particularly when they have other risk factors, such as aggressive behavior or low support from teachers and parents (Beran & Lupart, 2009).

Peer victimization is also associated with physical symptoms, such as abdominal pain and frequent visits to medical professionals (Greco, Freeman, & Dufton, 2010). A meta-analysis of 11 studies with over 150,000 children between the ages of 7 and 16 revealed that victims and bully-victims were at higher risk for psychosomatic problems than their uninvolved peers (Gini & Pozzoli, 2009). A possible causal mechanism is blunted cortisol levels, as adolescents who were bullied have been shown to have lower levels of cortisol than their non-victimized peers, a pattern typically associated with prolonged stress that is present in individuals with post-traumatic stress disorder (Knack, Jensen-Campbell, & Baum, 2011). Peer victimization can also result in a poorer body image and lower self-esteem (Lunde, Frisén, & Hwang, 2006), as well as the development of eating disorders in young women (Bond, Carlin, Thomas, Rubin, & Patton, 2001).

The negative impact of victimization can be long-lasting, and depressive symptoms have been found to persist even decades after the bullying occurred (Carlyle & Steinman, 2007; Ttofi, Farrington, Lösel, & Loeber, 2011). Additionally, the impact of childhood victimization has been associated with an increased risk for stress symptomology (Newman, Holden, & Delville, 2004), and anxiety disorders in adulthood (Copeland et al., 2013; Sourander et al., 2007). Janson and Hazler (2004) found that when asked to recall a time they were victimized, targets experienced physical arousal (i.e., elevated heart rate and skin conductance) similar to traumatic reactions experienced by those who had been in combat or sexually assaulted. Previous victimization also influences job success. Victims have been found to earn less money as adults than their non-victimized peers (Brown & Taylor, 2008); they also have higher rates of job changes and termination (Sansone, Leung, & Wiederman, 2013).

Targets of bullying have a greater likelihood of experiencing suicidal ideation and making suicide attempts than their peers (Klomek et al., 2007; Meltzer, Vostanis, Ford, Bebbington & Dennis, 2011; Nickerson & Slater, 2009; Ttofi et al., 2011). According to Karch, Logan, McDaniel, Floyd and Vagi (2013), one in eight individuals who had experienced school-related problems prior to their suicide had reported being bullied. Adults who recalled being bullied as children were more likely to report suicidal behaviors than non-involved individuals, even after controlling for depressive symptoms (Meltzer et al., 2011). Additional research by Klomek and colleagues (2009), found that girls, but not boys, who were frequently victimized at age 8 were more likely to attempt suicide by age 25 than those who were not frequently victimized. This relationship persisted even when conduct and depressive symptoms were considered.

Despite the significant relationship between victimization and suicidality, researchers have noted that experiencing bullying accounts for less than 7% of the variance in suicidality (Hinduja & Patchin, 2010; Kowalski & Limber, 2013). It is important to note that the risk for suicidal ideation and behavior increases substantially with repeated victimization (Klomek et al., 2007; Schneider, O'Donnell, Stueve, & Coulter, 2012). Recent work by Borowsky and colleagues (2013) has found that a history of physical and sexual abuse, mental health issues, running away from home, self-injurious behavior, and increased negative emotionality were significant risk factors for suicidality among targets. Protective factors included feeling connected to parents, other adults, and peers, in addition to having a positive attitude about school (Borowsky et al., 2013).

Numerous factors have been found to influence and mediate the negative impact of victimization, including the perception of the victimization experience and isolation. Students who perceive themselves to be victims of bullying have poorer psychosocial adjustment than students who do not believe they have been victimized (Juvonen, Nishina, & Graham, 2000). In their work examining both self-blaming attributions and the impact of ethnic majority status on context in peer victimization, Graham, Bellmore, Nishina, and Juvonen (2009) found that characterological self-blame mediated the relationship between peer victimization and maladjustment for Latinos and African-Americans in schools where they were the majority ethnic group. The researchers conceptualize this as an indicator of a social misfit, where outcomes are more negative for individuals whose behavior deviates from social norms within a particular context. Interestingly, students who were harassed themselves but did not witness other students being harassed experienced elevated feelings of humiliation and anger compared to students who had been both a victim and a witness in the same day (Nishina & Juvonen, 2005). This suggests that seeing others experience similar victimization may mediate the relationship between victimization and psychological effects, probably due to reducing feelings of isolation. Indeed, victimized students who also feel isolated in school report elevated levels of stress (Newman et al., 2004). Furthermore, students who are defended by a peer have better psychosocial adjustment and social standing (Sainio, Veenstra, Huitsing, & Salmivalli, 2010). Parental support for females, and teacher, classmate, and school support for males moderate the relationship between victimization and internalizing distress (Davidson & Demaray, 2007).

BULLY-VICTIMS

Recent research has revealed a distinct subgroup of youth, "bully-victims," who report both bullying others and being victimized (Haynie et al., 2001). These youth exhibit more problem behaviors (e.g., drinking, smoking, rule violations, theft, property damage), depressive symptoms, and lower social competence than peers who are either bullied or who bully others (Haynie et al., 2001; Veenstra et al., 2005). Long-term gender differences have been found among bully-victims, with increased rates of depressive disorders and panic disorder for males and females and increased risk of agoraphobia for females as young adults (Copeland et al., 2013).

Bully-victims have also been found to have greater difficulties associated with school. Bully-victims have poor academic achievement, lack a sense of connectedness, and are less likely to feel safe and involved in school than their peers (Cunningham, 2007; Glew et al., 2005; O'Brennan, Bradshaw, & Sawyer, 2009). Risk factors for low school bonding include past bullying, being female, having friends who bully, acceptance of bullying, and perceptions that teachers had low behavioral expectations (Cunningham, 2007).

The associations between bully-victim status and physical well-being have also been documented. A meta-analysis by Gini and Pozzoli (2009) identified bully-victims as more likely to develop psychosomatic problems than non-involved peers. In addition, increased rates of bulimia have been found among male bully-victims; both male and female bully-victims have increased rates of anorexia (Kaltiala-Heino, Rimpelä, Rantanen, & Rimpelä, 2000).

Although a significant issue among all bullying groups, bully-victims have been found to have the highest rates of suicidality, with rates as high as 60% for ideation and 44% for suicidal behaviors (Espelage & Holt, 2013). Researchers have found conflicting results related to gender and suicidality within the bully-victim group. Increased rates of suicidality have been reported among young adult males who were bully-victims in childhood and adolescence (Copeland et al., 2013; Klomek et al., 2009), whereas other findings indicate higher rates among females (Espelage & Holt, 2013). Significant risk factors for suicidality among bully-victims include self-injurious behavior and negative emotionality, but connectedness to parents and having caring friends were found to be protective factors (Borowsky et al., 2013).

BYSTANDERS

Bullying has been conceptualized as a "group process" (Salmivalli et al., 1996), with peer bystanders witnessing more than 80% of bullying episodes but intervening less than 20% of the time (Atlas & Pepler, 1998; Hawkins, Pepler, & Craig, 2001). Although less is known about the impact of bullying on bystanders, Rivers (2011) makes a cogent argument that bystanders take different roles in bullying situations, and may suffer mental health consequences similar to children who witness domestic violence and other types of abuse. Indeed, children who witness bullying and do not intervene report this to be an emotionally isolating experience (Hutchinson, 2012). Empirical studies have also found that bystanders report increased anxiety, depression, hostility, and paranoia (Nishina & Juvonen, 2005; Rivers, Poteat, Noret, & Ashurst, 2009). When college students were asked to recall observing bullying incidents, they reported elevated levels of trauma symptomology similar to that of survivors of natural disasters and mass-shooting witnesses (Janson & Hazler, 2004).

SUMMARY AND CONCLUSIONS

A review of the literature indicates that bullying has concomitant and long-term effects on perpetrators, targets, and even bystanders. These effects include internalized and externalized symptoms, interpersonal relationship difficulties, physical problems, substance abuse, and impaired functioning in school, work, and community contexts. Clearly, this is a salient public health and mental health issue. Research has begun to reveal factors that place individuals involved in bullying at greater risk for negative outcomes, such as multiple victimization experiences, characterological self-blame, being bullied and bullying others, and lack of support. Connectedness and social support appear to be key protective factors, underscoring the important role of parents and teachers, medical and mental health providers, and policy makers.

Suggestions for Providers, Parents, Teachers, and Policy Makers

Medical and Mental Health Providers

- Ask about peer relationships and bullying as part of routine visits.
- Educate parents about the prevalence of bullying, its impact, and signs to look for.
- Stay attuned to the relationship between bullying and stress, anxiety, depression, conduct problems, body-image distortions, and physical symptoms to assess and intervene accordingly.
- Use evidence-based interventions matched to symptoms associated with the effects of bullying.
- Conduct suicide and threat assessments to determine the level of risk and intervention needs.

Parents and Teachers

- Be attuned to signs that could suggest a child is suffering from involvement in bullying (e.g., physical signs of bruises, torn clothing; behavioral indicators of withdrawal, avoidance).
- Keep lines of communication open about peer relationships.
- Model, explicitly teach, and reinforce social-emotional skills (e.g., resolving conflict, feeling empathy, accepting others).
- Refer to a mental health professional if concerned about signs of depression, anxiety, or aggression.

- Advocate comprehensive approaches in schools, such as Positive Behavior Support, social-emotional learning, and creating norms of accepting and willingness to intervene to help others.

Policy Makers

- Conceptualize bullying within the larger framework of mental health and public health concerns.
- Promote policies that (1) use data at the local level, (2) promote training, education, and coordinated preventive efforts, and (3) use evidence-based interventions instead of reliance on zero tolerance and punitive approaches.

REFERENCES

Atlas, R. S., & Pepler, D. J. (1998). Observations of bullying in the classroom. *Journal of Educational Research*, *92*, 86–99. doi: 10.1080/00220679809597580

Batsche, G. M., & Knoff, H. M. (1994). Bullies and their victims: Understanding a pervasive problem in the schools. *School Psychology Review*, *23*, 165–177.

Beran, T., & Lupart, J. (2009). The relationship between school achievement and peer harassment in Canadian adolescents: The importance of mediating factors. *School Psychology International*, *30*, 75–91. doi: 10.1177/0143034308101851

Bond, L., Carlin, J. B., Thomas, L., Rubin, K., & Patton, G. (2001). Does bullying cause emotional problems? A prospective study of young teenagers. *British Medical Journal*, *323*, 480–483. doi: 10.1136/bmj.323.7311.480

Boulton, M. J., Trueman, M., Chau, C., Whitehead, C., & Amatya, K. (1999). Concurrent and longitudinal links between friendship and peer victimization: Implications for befriending interventions. *Journal of Adolescence*, *22*, 461–466. doi: 10.1006/jado.1999.0240

Borowsky, I. W., Taliaferro, L. A., & McMorris, B. J. (2013). Suicidal thinking and behavior among youth involved in verbal and social bullying: Risk and protective factors. *Journal of Adolescent Health*, *53*, S4–S12. doi: 10.1016/j.jadohealth.2012.10.280

Brown, S., & Taylor, K. (2008). Bullying, education and earnings: Evidence from the National Child Development Study. *Economics of Education Review*, *27*, 387–401. doi: 10.1016/j.econedurev.2007.03.003

Carlyle, K. E., & Steinman, K. J. (2007). Demographic differences in the prevalence, co-occurrence, and correlates of adolescent bullying at school. *Journal of School Health*, *9*, 623–629. doi: 10.1111/j.1746-1561.2007.00242.x

Copeland, W. E., Wolke, D., Angold, A., & Costello, J. (2013). Adult psychiatric outcomes of bullying and being bullied by peers in childhood and adolescence. *JAMA Psychiatry*, *70*, 422–426. doi: 10.1001/jamapsychiatry.2013.504

Crick, N. R., Casas, J. F., & Ku, H. (1999). Relational and physical forms of peer victimization in preschool. *Developmental Psychology*, *35*, 376–385. doi: 10.1037/0012-1649.35.2.376

Cunningham, N. J. (2007). Level of bonding to school and perception of the school environment by bullies, victims, and bully victims. *The Journal of Early Adolescence*, *27*, 457–478. doi:10.1177/0272431607302940

Davidson, L. M., & Demaray, M. (2007). Social support as a moderator between victimization and internalizing-externalizing distress from bullying. *School Psychology Review, 36*, 383–405.

Dukes, R. L., Stein, J. A., & Zane, J. I. (2010). Gender differences in the relative impact of physical and relational bullying on adolescent injury and weapon carrying. *Journal of School Psychology, 48*, 511–532. doi: 10.1016/j.jsp.2010.08.001.

Duncan, R. D. (1999). Maltreatment by parents and peers: The relationship between child abuse, bully victimization, and psychological distress. *Child Maltreatment, 4*, 45–55. doi: 10.1177/1077559599004001005

Espelage, D. L., Basile, K. C., & Hamburger, M. E. (2012). Bullying perpetration and subsequent sexual violence perpetration among middle school students. *Journal of Adolescent Health, 50*, 60–65. doi: 10.1016/j.jadohealth.2011.07.015

Espelage, D. L., & Holt, M. K. (2013). Suicidal ideation and school bullying experiences after controlling for depression and delinquency. *Journal of Adolescent Health, 53*, S27–S31. doi: 10.1016/j.jadohealth.2012.09.017

Farrington, D. P., & Ttofi, M. M. (2011). Bullying as a predictor of offending, violence and later life outcomes. *Criminal Behaviour and Mental Health, 21*, 90–98. doi: 10.1002/cbm.801

Gini, G., & Pozzoli, T. (2009). Association between bullying and psychosomatic problems: A meta-analysis. *Pediatrics, 123*, 1059–1065. doi: 10.1542/peds.2008-1215

Glew, G. M., Fan, M., Katon, W. J., Rivara, F. P., & Kernic, M. A. (2005). Bullying, psychosocial adjustment, and academic performance in elementary school. *Archives of Pediatric and Adolescent Medicine, 159*, 1026–1031. doi: 10.1001/archpedi.159.11.1026

Graham, S., Bellmore, A., Nishina, A., & Juvonen, J. (2009). "It must be me": Ethnic diversity and attributions for peer victimization in middle school. *Journal of Youth and Adolescence, 38*, 487–499. doi: 10.1007/s10964-008-9386-4

Graham, S., & Juvonen, J. (1998). Self-blame and peer victimization in middle school: An attributional analysis. *Developmental Psychology, 34*, 587–599. doi: 10.1037/0012-1649.34.3.587

Greco, L. A., Freeman, K. E., & Dufton, L. (2010). Overt and relational victimization among children with frequent abdominal pain: Links to social skills, academic functioning, and health service use. *Journal of Pediatric Psychology, 32*, 319–329. doi: 10.1093/jpepsy/jsl016

Hawkins, L. D., Pepler, D. J., & Craig, W. M. (2001). Naturalistic observations of peer interventions in bullying. *Social Development, 10*, 512–527. doi: 10.1111/1467-9507.00178

Haynie, D. L., Nansel, T., Eitel, P., Davis-Crump, A., Saylor, K., Yu, K., & Simons-Morton, B. (2001). Bullies, victims, and bully/victims: Distinct groups of at-risk youth. *Journal of Early Adolescence, 21*, 29–49. doi: 10.1177/0272431601021001002

Hinduja, S., & Patchin, J. W. (2010). Bullying, cyberbullying, and suicide. *Archives of Suicide Research, 14*, 206–221. doi: 10.1080/13811118.2010.494133

Holt, M. K., & Espelage, D. L. (2003). A cluster analytic investigation of victimization among high school students: Are profiles differentially associated with psychological symptoms and school belonging? *Journal of Applied School Psychology, 19*, 81–98. doi: 10.1300/J008v19n02_06

Hugh-Jones, S., & Smith, P. K. (1999). Self-reports of short- and long-term effects of bullying on children who stammer. *British Journal of Educational Psychology, 69*, 141–158. doi: 10.1348/000709999157626

Hutchinson, M. (2012). Exploring the impact of bullying on young bystanders. *Educational Psychology in Practice, 28*, 425–442. doi:10.1080/02667363.2012.727785

Ivarsson, T., Broberg, A. G., Arvidsson, T., & Gillberg, C. (2005). Bullying in adolescence: Psychiatric problems in victims and bullies as measured by the Youth Self-Report (YSR) and the Depression Self-Rating Scale (DSRS). *Norwegian Journal of Psychiatry, 59*, 365–375. doi:10.1080/08039480500227816

Janson, G. R., & Hazler, R. J. (2004). Trauma reactions of bystanders and victims to repetitive abuse experiences. *Violence and Victims, 19*, 239–255. doi: 10.1891/vivi.19.2.239.64102

Juvonen, J., Nishina, A., & Graham, S. (2000). Peer harassment, psychological adjustment, and school functioning in early adolescence. *Journal of Educational Psychology, 2*, 349–359. doi: 10.1037/0022-0663.92.2.349

Kaltiala-Heino, R., Rimpelä, P. R., Rantanen, P., & Rimpelä, A. (2000). Bullying at school: An indicator of adolescents at-risk for mental disorders. *Journal of Adolescence, 23*, 661–674. doi: 10.1006/jado.2000.0351

Karch, D. L., Logan, J., McDaniel, D. D., Floyd, C. F., & Vagi, K. J. (2013). Precipitating circumstances of suicide among youth aged 10–17 years by sex: Data from the National Violent Death Reporting System, 16 States, 2005–2008. *Journal of Adolescent Health, 53*, S51–S53. doi: 10.1016/j.jadohealth.2012.06.028

Kim, M. J., Catalano, R. F., Haggerty, K. P., & Abbott, R. D. (2011). Bullying at elementary school and problem behavior in young adulthood: A study of bullying, violence, and substance use from age 11 to age 21. *Criminal Behaviour and Mental Health, 21*, 136–144. doi: 10.1002/cbm.804

Klomek, A. B., Marrocco, F., Kleinman, M., Schonfeld, I. S., & Gould, M. S. (2007). Bullying, depression, and suicidality in adolescents. *Journal of the American Academy of Child and Adolescent Psychiatry, 46*, 40–49. doi: 10.1097/01.chi.0000242237.84925.18

Klomek, A. B., Sourander, A., Niemelä, S., Kumpulainen, K., Piha, J., Tamminen, T., . . . Gould, M. S. (2009). Childhood bullying behaviors as a risk for suicide attempts and completed suicides: A population-based birth cohort study. *Journal of the American Academy of Child & Adolescent Psychiatry, 48*, 254–261. doi: 10.1097/CHI.0b013e318196b91f

Knack, J. M., Jensen-Campbell, L. A., & Baum, A. (2011). Worse than sticks and stones? Bullying is associated with altered HPA axis functioning and poorer health. *Brain and Cognition, 77*, 183–190. doi: 10.1016/j.bandc.2011.06.011

Kochenderfer, B. J., & Ladd, G. W. (1996). Peer victimization: Cause or consequence of school maladjustment? *Child Development, 67*, 1305–1317. doi: 10.1111/j.1467-8624.1996.tb01797.x

Kowalski, R. M., & Limber, S. P. (2013). Psychological, physical, and academic correlates of cyberbullying and traditional bullying. *Journal of Adolescent Health, 53*, S13–S20. doi: 10.1016/j.jadohealth.2012.09.018

Lösel, F., & Bender, D. (2011). Emotional and antisocial outcomes of bullying and victimization at school: A follow-up from childhood to adolescence. *Journal of Aggression, Conflict, and Peace Research, 3*, 89–96. doi: 10.1108/17596591111132909

Lunde, C., Frisén, A., & Hwang, C. P. (2006). Is peer victimization related to body esteem in 10-year-old girls and boys? *Body Image, 3*, 25–33. doi: 10.1016/j.bodyim.2005.12.001

Meltzer, H. H., Vostanis, P. P., Ford, T. T., Bebbington, P. P., & Dennis, M. S. (2011). Victims of bullying in childhood and suicide attempts in adulthood. *European Psychiatry, 26*, 498–503. doi:10.1016/j.eurpsy.2010.11.006

Nansel, T., Haynie, D. L., & Simons-Morton, B. G. (2003). The association of bullying and victimization with middle school adjustment. *Journal of Applied School Psychology, 19*, 45–61. doi: 10.1300/J008v19n02_04

Nansel, T. R., Overpeck, M, Pilla, R. S., Ruan, W. J., Simons-Morton, B., & Scheidt, P. (2001). Bullying behaviors among US youth: Prevalence and association with psychosocial adjustment. *Journal of the American Medical Association, 285*, 2094–2100. doi:10.1001/jama.285.16.2094

Newman, M. L., Holden, G. W., & Delville, Y. (2004). Isolation and the stress of being bullied. *Journal of Adolescence, 28*, 343–357. doi: 10.1016/j.adolescence.2004.08.002

Nickerson, A. B., & Slater, E. D. (2009). School and community violence and victimization as predictors of suicidal behavior for adolescents. *School Psychology Review, 38*, 218–232.

Nishina, A., & Juvonen, J. (2005). Daily reports of witnessing and experiencing peer harassment in middle school. *Child Development, 76*, 435–450. doi:10.1111/j.1467-8624.2005.00855.x

O'Brennan, L. M., Bradshaw, C. P., & Sawyer, A. L. (2009). Examining developmental differences in the social-emotional problems among frequent bullies, victims, and bully/victims. *Psychology in the Schools, 46*, 100–115. doi: 10.1002/pits.20357

Olweus, D. (1991). Bully/victim problems among school children: Basic facts and effects of a school based intervention program. In I. Rubin & D. Pepler (Eds.), *The Development and Treatment of Childhood Aggression* (pp. 411–447). Hillsdale, NJ: Erlbaum.

Olweus, D. (1993). *Bullying at School: What We Know and What We Can Do.* New York: Blackwell Publishing.

Reijntjes, A., Kamphuis, J. H., Prinzie, P., & Telch, M. J. (2010). Peer victimization and internalizing problems in children: A meta-analysis of longitudinal studies. *Child Abuse & Neglect, 34*, 244–252. doi: 10.1016/j.chiabu.2009.07.009

Renda, J., Vassallo, S., & Edwards, B. (2011). Bullying in early adolescence and its association with anti-social behaviour, criminality and violence 6 and 10 years later. *Criminal Behaviour and Mental Health, 21*, 117–127. doi: 10.1002/cbm.805

Rivers, I. (2011). Morbidity among bystanders of bullying behaviors at school: Concepts, concerns, and clinical/research issues. *International Journal of Adolescent Medicine and Health, 24*, 11–16. doi: 10.1515/ijamh.2012.003

Rivers, I., Poteat, V. P., Noret, N., & Ashurst, N. (2009). Observing bullying at school: The mental health implications of witness status. *School Psychology Quarterly, 24*, 211–22. doi: 10.1037/a0018164

Sainio, M., Veenstra, R., Huitsing, G., & Salmivalli, C. (2010). Victims and their defenders: A dyadic approach. *International Journal of Behavioural Development, 35*, 144–151. doi: 10.1177/0165025410378068

Salmivalli, C., Huttunen, A., & Lagerspetz, K. (1997). Peer networks and bullying in schools. *Scandinavian Journal of Psychology, 38*, 305–312. doi: 10.1111/1467-9450.00040

Salmivalli, C., Lagerspetz, K., Björkqvist, K., Österman, K., & Kaukiainen, A. (1996). Bullying as a group process: Participant roles and their relations to social status within the group. *Aggressive Behavior, 22*, 1–15. doi: 10.1002/(SICI)1098-2337

Sansone, R. A., Leung, J. S., & Wiederman, M. W. (2013). Self-reported bullying in childhood: Relationships with employment in adulthood. *International Journal of Psychiatry in Clinical Practice, 17*, 64–68. doi: 10.3109/13651501.2012.709867

Schneider, S. K., O'Donnell, L., Stueve, A., & Coulter, R. W. S. (2012). Cyberbullying, school bullying and psychological distress: A regional census of high school students. *American Journal of Public Health, 102*, 171–179. doi: 10.2105/AJPH.2011.300308

Sourander, A., Jensen, P., Ronning, J. A., Niemela, S., Helenius, H., Sillanmaki, L.,...Almqvist, F. (2007) What is the early adulthood outcome of boys who bully or are bullied in childhood? The Finnish "From a Boy to a Man" study. *Pediatrics, 120,* 397–404. doi: 10.1542/peds.2006-2704

Sourander, A., Klomek, A. B., Kumpulainen, K., Puustjärvi, A., Elonheimo, H., Ristkari, T.,...& Ronning, J. A. (2011). Bullying at age eight and criminality in adulthood: Findings from the Finnish nationwide 1981 birth cohort study. *Social Psychiatry Psychology and Epidemiology, 46,* 1211–1219. doi: 10.1007/s00127-010-0292-1

Storch, E. A., & Masia-Warner, C. (2004). The relationship of peer victimization to social anxiety loneliness in adolescent females. *Journal of Adolescence, 27,* 351–62. doi: 10.1016/j.adolescence.2004.03.003

Ttofi, M. M., Farrington, D. P., Lösel, F., & Loeber, R. (2011). Do the victims of school bullies tend to become depressed later in life? A systematic review and meta-analysis of longitudinal studies. *Journal of Aggression Conflict and Peace Research, 3,* 63–73. doi: 10.1108/17596591111132873

van Oort, F. V. A., Greaves-Lord, K., Ormel, J., Verhulst, F. C., & Huizink, A. C. (2011). Risk indicators of anxiety throughout adolescence: The Trails Study. *Depression and Anxiety, 28,* 485–494. doi: 10.1002/da.20818

Veenstra, R., Lindenberg, S., Oldehinkel, A. J., De Winter, A. F., Verhulst, F. C., & Ormel, J. (2005). Bullying and victimization in elementary schools: A comparison of bullies, victims, bully/victims, and uninvolved preadolescents. *Developmental Psychology, 41,* 672–682. doi: 10.1037/0012-1649.41.4.672

World Health Organization (2011). Mental health: A state of well-being. Retrieved April 5, 2013, from http://www.who.int/features/factfiles/mental_health/en/index.html.

5

Suicidal Ideation and Bullying

An Ecological Examination of Community Impact

PAMELA ORPINAS AND ARTHUR M. HORNE

Bullying and other forms of peer aggression can have a devastating effect on children and adolescents. Children who are the targets of bullying are more likely than students who are not bullied to have worse academic grades and suffer from anxiety, depression, and psychosomatic symptoms (Fekkes, Pijpers, & Verloove-Vanhorick, 2004; Gini & Pozzoli, 2013; Orpinas & Horne, 2006). Some may think of committing suicide, and a few do indeed attempt to take their lives. Adolescents who think of or plan to commit suicide are in dire need for help. They may not see a solution to their problems, and they may be desperate enough to believe that suicide is the only way out of their situation.

Suicidal ideation—thoughts and plans to commit suicide—is complex, and frequently is not an isolated event in the life of adolescents. Beyond bullying, teens who report thinking about suicide frequently report other behavioral and emotional problems, such as exhibiting impulsive or aggressive behaviors, being aggressive with a dating partner, and using alcohol and drugs (Ackard, Eisenberg, & Neumark-Sztainer, 2007; Nahapetyan, Orpinas, Holland, & Song, 2013). The fact that problem behaviors tend to co-vary, creating a problem behavior syndrome, has been explained by problem behavior theory (Jessor et al., 2003) and by empirical research. Although the focus of the present study is the association between suicidal ideation and aggression, expanding the analysis to other problem behaviors will help researchers and educators develop a comprehensive view of the problem and thus implement more effective programs.

To develop community interventions to prevent suicidal ideation and adolescent aggression, it is fundamental to understand the ecological contributors of risk factors (those associated with an increased likelihood of the health-compromising behaviors) and protective factors (those associated with a reduced likelihood of the health-compromising behaviors) to adolescent development and well-being. Bronfenbrenner's (1979) ecological model is useful for understanding the multiple contributors that are critical in comprehending how problems develop. For example, risk and protective factors from different levels of the ecological model can help explain healthy adolescent development (Figure 5.1; adapted from Orpinas & Horne, 2006). As Figure 5.1 illustrates, the primary influences on the child are the family, the school, and the community. Each area of connection can provide both risk and protective factors related to healthy emotional and behavioral development, and the levels of influence greatly affect both aggression and suicidal ideation.

The model highlights the importance of maintaining positive relationships with significant people. From an ecological perspective, having positive relationships with adults who are important to the adolescent—such as parents and teachers—as well as with peers, may mitigate the potential risk factors for suicidal ideation and aggression. Not surprisingly, research has shown consistently that having supportive parents, maintaining good parent–child communication, and showing warmth in family relationships reduces the risk for suicidal ideation and suicide behaviors, as well as the risk of being involved in peer aggression (O'Donnell, O'Donnell, Wardlaw, & Stueve, 2004). Conversely, negative family

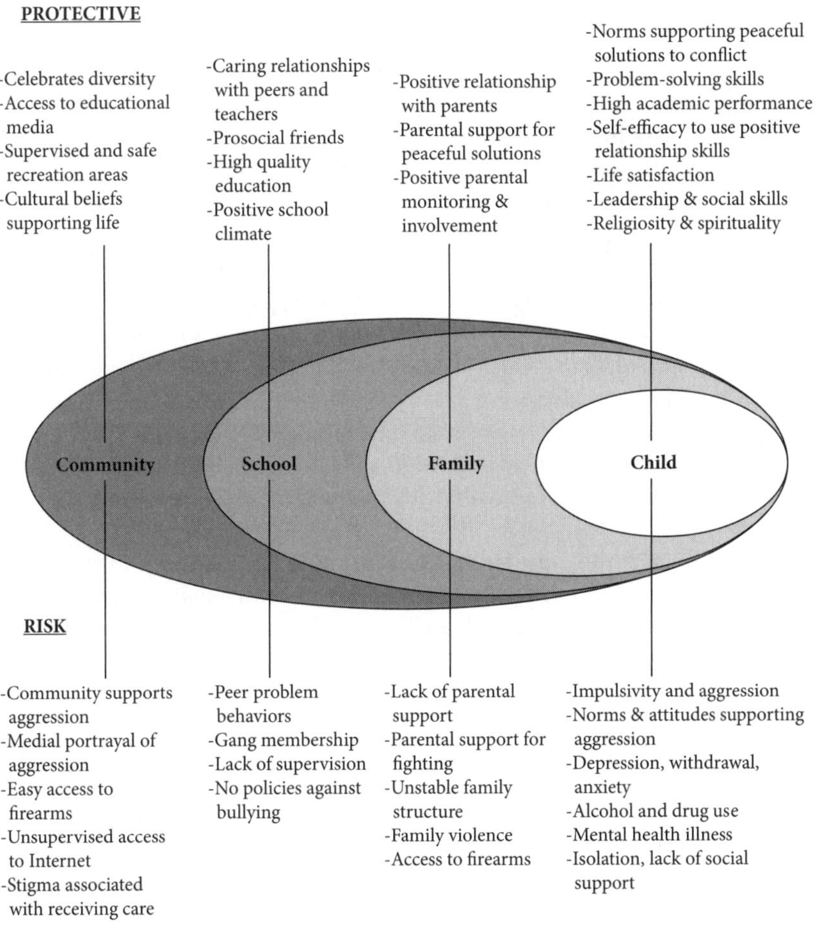

Figure 5.1 Protective and risk factors for bullying and suicidal ideation at multiple levels of the ecological model.

relationships increase those risks. Similarly, feeling connected and supported by teachers also may reduce suicidality, as well as the initiation or escalation of other health-risk behaviors (De Luca, Wyman, & Warren, 2012; McNeely & Falci, 2004). Connection with peers is different from connection with teachers, as some peers may support academic and other conventional behaviors, while others may promote drug use, aggression, and delinquency. What is clear, however, is that having more social networking opportunities and overall positive relationships with other students will reduce social isolation and the likelihood of suicidal ideation (Rutter & Behrendt, 2004).

Overall, adolescents who do not feel supported by friends and caring adults are more likely to report suicidal ideation and violence (Rutter & Soucar, 2002). The present study takes this conclusion a step further by examining the cumulative effect of lacking support from peers, teachers, and parents or caregivers on suicidal ideation and on peer aggression (Rutter, Maughan, Mortimore, Ouston, & Smith, 1979; Trentacosta et al., 2008).

PRESENT STUDY

The goal of this study was to expand understanding of the impact of social interactions on adolescents' suicidal ideation and aggressive behaviors. The study had two objectives. The first objective was to describe factors associated with suicidal ideation among tenth-graders. Using the ecological model, we examined behavioral factors (peer aggression and victimization, dating aggression and victimization, drug use, and delinquency) and perceptions of positive relationships with peers, teachers, and parents or caregivers. We hypothesized that tenth-graders who reported suicidal ideation would be more likely to report peer and dating aggression and victimization, as well as drug use and delinquency. We also hypothesized that students who report suicidal ideation would report worse relationships with peers, teachers, and caregivers.

The second objective was to examine the cumulative effect of not having positive relationships on both suicidal ideation and peer aggression and victimization. We examined three levels of relationships: with peers, teachers, and parents or caregivers.

Based on the present study, current research, and our experience working with schools, the last section of this chapter provides recommendations for healthcare providers, parents, teachers, mental health workers, and policy makers for promoting healthy child development.

METHODS

Sample

Data for this study were taken from tenth-graders participating in the *Healthy Teens Longitudinal Study*. We invited a randomly selected sample of adolescents attending schools in northeast Georgia to participate in this study. The nine participating schools varied in demographic composition, proportion of students receiving free or reduced-price lunch, and urban or rural location; but, as a whole, these schools represent the region. This cohort of students completed annual surveys from the sixth to the twelfth grade. Of the students who agreed to participate (n = 745) in sixth grade, 624 re-consented to continue in the study in high school. Questions about suicide were only asked in high school. Of these students, 31 did not answer the questions about suicide in tenth grade. Thus, the final sample consisted of 593 students (48% girls, 52% boys; 48% White, 36% Black, 11% Latino).

Procedures

Data were collected online using school computers. Trained research assistants supervised the data-collection process and answered questions. Students received a small monetary incentive for completing the survey. All procedures, including parents' written permission, were approved by the university's institutional review board.

Measures

Suicidal Ideation

Two questions from the *Youth Risk Behavior Survey* measured serious thoughts and plans to attempt suicide (Centers for Disease Control and Prevention, 2012). Response categories were (0) *no* and (1) *yes*. Participant who responded affirmatively to having had thoughts and/or plans were classified as having suicidal ideation.

Problem Behaviors

Subscales from the *Problem Behavior Frequency Scales* (Farrell, Kung, White, & Valois, 2000) measured peer aggression perpetration and victimization, drug use, and delinquency. *Peer aggression perpetration* (18 items, α = .91) measures physical aggression (7 items), non-physical aggression (5 items), and relational peer aggression (6 items). The correlation among the three types of aggressive behaviors was high (physical and non-physical = .74, physical and relational = .63, non-physical and relational = .67). *Peer aggression victimization* (12 items, α = .87) measured overt (6 items) and relational victimization (6 items). The correlation between overt and relational victimization was.48. *Drug use* (6 items, α = .89) examined frequency of using alcohol, tobacco, and marijuana. *Delinquency* (8 items, α = .84) included questions about truancy, cheating, stealing, graffiti, and damaging school property. Response categories ranged between (1) *never* and (6) *20 or more times*. Scales were computed by averaging the scores across items. Thus, all scales ranged between 1 and 6, with higher scores indicating more of the construct.

Dating Violence

Students who indicated that they had dated during the 3 months prior to the survey answered questions about dating violence. *Dating violence perpetration* (13 items, α = .93) and *dating violence victimization* (13 items, α = .91) measured the frequency of specific aggressive behaviors (e.g., pushing, slamming against the wall, punching, scratching) against or from a dating partner (Foshee, 1996). The instructions were: "Thinking about the last 3 months, how often has a boyfriend/girlfriend (someone that you dated, gone out with, gone steady with) done the following things to you? Only include it when the person did it to you first. In other words, don't count it if they did it to you in self-defense." Response categories ranged from (0) *never* and (3) *10 or more times*. Both scales were computed by averaging all items. Thus, both scales ranged between 0 and 3, with higher values indicating more aggression.

Positive Relationships

Two subscales from the *Student Classroom Climate* measured *student–student relationships* (7 items, α = .77) and *teacher–student relationships* (4 items, α = .79) (Miller-Johnson, Sullivan, Simon, & Multisite Violence Prevention Project, 2004). Examples of items of the student–student relationship scale are: "Students are kind and supportive of one another" and "Students make friends easily." Examples of items of the teacher–student relationship scale are: "Teachers treat students with respect" and "Teachers praise students more often than they criticize them." Response categories ranged from (1) *strongly disagree* and (4) *strongly agree*. Both scales were computed by averaging all items. Thus, both scales ranged between 1 and 4 with higher values indicating more positive relationships.

Parental Involvement

Parental involvement (12 items, α = .92) evaluates the caregiver's involvement in daily activities and routines (e.g., "How often did you have a friendly talk with your parent?" and "How often did you and your parent do things together at home?"), as well as knowledge of the child's whereabouts (e.g., "How often did you talk with your parent about what you had actually done during the day?") (Gorman-Smith, Tolan, Zelli, & Huesmann, 1996). The scale was computed by averaging all items. The scale ranged between 1 and 5, with higher scores indicating more parental involvement.

RESULTS

Overall, 11.5% (*n* = 68) of participating tenth-graders reported suicidal ideation (14.1% of girls and 9.1% of boys). Mean scores of students who reported suicidal thoughts were significantly higher than mean scores of students who did not report suicidal thoughts, in all measures of problem behaviors: peer aggression (perpetration and victimization), dating violence (perpetration and victimization), drug use, and delinquency (Table 5.1).

Mean scores of students who reported suicidal thoughts were significantly lower than scores of students who did not report suicidal thoughts in all measures of positive relationships: peers, teachers, and parents (Table 5.1). Student–student and teacher–student relationships were strongly correlated (.57), but the correlation of these two variables with parental involvement was low (.16 and .25, respectively).

Table 5.1. Comparison of Means of Predictor Variables by Report of Suicidal Ideation—Tenth-Graders

Correlates	No suicidal ideation Mean (SD)	Suicidal ideation Mean (SD)	F	P Value
PROBLEM BEHAVIORS				
Peer aggression perpetration	1.48 (0.59)	2.05 (0.87)	48.72	< .0001
Peer aggression victimization	1.31 (0.47)	1.75 (0.72)	44.23	< .0001
Dating violence perpetration[a]	0.15 (0.30)	0.38 (0.56)	21.61	< .0001
Dating violence victimization[a]	0.18 (0.36)	0.41 (0.49)	16.11	< .0001
Drug use	1.35 (0.81)	1.89 (1.07)	24.95	< .0001
Delinquency	1.23 (0.49)	1.61 (0.70)	33.00	< .0001
POSITIVE RELATIONSHIPS				
Positive student–student relationship	2.70 (0.45)	2.45 (0.45)	17.56	< .0001
Positive student–teacher relationship	2.82 (0.56)	2.57 (0.58)	11.68	.001
Positive parental involvement	3.82 (1.06)	3.27 (1.11)	15.88	< .0001

[a] Calculated over students who reported dating.

To examine the cumulative effect of lacking positive relationships, we created a risk-factor index with the three relationship variables. Based on previous research, we dichotomized these variables by using a 30th percentile cutoff score (Forehand, Biggar, & Kotchick, 1998). Students in the worst 30th percentile were coded as 1 (risk), others were coded as 0 (no risk). The cutoff scores were 2.43 for student–student relationship, 2.50 for teacher–student relationship, and 3.33 for parental involvement. To create the relationship risk index, scores of the three variables were added. Thus the relationship risk index ranged between 0 (no risk) and 3 (risk on all three variables).

The proportion of students reporting suicidal ideation significantly increased, by approximately 10% for every level of risk (Table 5.2), $\chi 2$ (3) = 49.93, $p < .0001$. Similarly, mean scores of perpetration of aggression against peers significantly increased for each level of risk (Table 5.2), F (3, 549) = 24.95, $p < .0001$. Using Bonferroni correction to compare pairs, all groups' scores were significantly different, except mean scores of students with two or three risks. Mean scores for peer victimization also increased by level of risk, except for students in the highest risk category. Mean scores of students in the no-risk group were significantly lower than all other groups; mean scores of students in the 1-risk group were significantly

Table 5.2. Suicidal Ideation and Overall Aggression by Relationship Risk Index—Tenth-Graders

Relationship risk index	Sample size	Proportion reporting suicidal ideation[a]	Overall aggression perpetration mean (SD)	Overall aggression victimization mean (SD)
0 (no risk)	217	2.8%	1.31 (0.39)	1.19 (0.29)
1	177	10.2%	1.57 (0.67)	1.40 (0.59)
2	112	23.2%	1.83 (0.79)	1.57 (0.68)
3 (highest risk)	47	31.9%	1.97 (0.88)	1.54 (0.57)

[a] Proportion reporting suicidal ideation within each risk group.

higher than the no-risk group and significantly lower than the 2-risk group; students in the highest-risk group were only significantly different from the no-risk group, F (3, 549) = 16.63, $p < .0001$.

DISCUSSION

Peer aggression and victimization are critical problems in the lives of many students who contemplate suicide. As important as bullying is, though, it is also clear that suicidal ideation may be linked to other health-compromising behaviors, not just peer aggression.

This study demonstrated that suicidal ideation is not an isolated event in the lives of adolescents. It was associated with many other risk behaviors: peer aggression and victimization, alcohol and drug use, dating violence, and delinquency. Problem behavior theory posits that problem behaviors tend to coexist, and research has consistently supported this tenet (Jessor et al., 2003; Vazsonyi et al., 2008).

The ability and opportunity to establish positive social relationships with peers, teachers, and family is important to prevent suicidal ideation and reduce problems of peer violence. In the present study, the cumulative effect of the lack of positive relationships was most important. No single factor stood out as critical for explaining suicidal ideation. As the 10% increase in suicidal ideation for each increase in risk indicated, the cumulative effect was critical. Other studies have also highlighted the importance of cumulative risk for suicide prevention (Roberts, Roberts, & Xing, 2010). Even for students who may have a negative environment at home, having caring adults and peers at school or in the community is important to reduce their risk. This study highlights the importance of connection with multiple community groups. Thus, interventions addressing these problems should be comprehensive and ecological.

This study has some limitations. The sample is limited to one part of the United States. However, it is important to note that the sample was randomly selected from six school districts. Comparing means may mask the diversity of the population. For example, some students may be depressed and suicidal but not involved in other problem behaviors. Further research is needed to investigate how subgroups of individuals behave and what are the distinct factors that predict their behavior. The study is based on self-reported data, which may result in over- or under-reporting.

WHAT COMMUNITIES CAN DO: RECOMMENDATIONS FOR ACTION

We propose recommendations for actions, based on the outcomes of the present study and the cumulative work we and others have done examining most effective ways of addressing problems of aggression, bullying, social relationships, and suicide (Conyne & Horne, 2013; Espelage & Horne, 2008; Kenny, Horne, Orpinas, & Reese, 2009; Kiselica, Englar-Carlson, & Horne, 2008; Orpinas & Horne, 2006). Ideally, families, educators, and community personnel will work collaboratively to create a climate of respect in which students feel safe, welcome, and supported.

Suggestions for Medical Providers

The primary role of physicians, nurses, and other healthcare workers is the treatment of illnesses. However, they also have an important role in promoting healthier and safer lifestyles. Here are some steps to take.

- Attend trainings to handle appropriately adolescents' disclosure of emotional and behavioral problems. Many healthcare providers feel uncomfortable talking about suicide with their patients.
- Discuss with parents their access to guns. The first risk factor for adolescent suicide is access to guns at home. If healthcare providers suspect that the adolescent has suicidal thoughts, they should ask the parents to immediately remove any guns from their home.
- Educate the community. Reach out to community organizations to offer presentations, discussions, and information sessions to youth, parents, and caregivers. It is not enough to count on office visits to identify problems; medical providers should be engaged in community outreach efforts.

Suggestions for Mental Health Providers

The most common role for mental health providers is helping individuals with behavioral and emotional problems. However, in addition to helping students in distress, mental health workers should help parents and their children connect with community organizations.

- Work with all community agencies that engage adolescents. Many cities have a community connections system that coordinates the services of agencies that help meet the emotional, behavioral, educational, and economic needs of students. We work with "Whatever It Takes" (http://www.witathens.org/), a program established in our community. Program leaders identify high-risk neighborhoods and then recruit and train community members to work block by block to help families identify essential resources. They also work

with the local police, schools, and religious groups to reach out to high-risk families. Although it is hard to pinpoint which of these efforts has had the strongest impact, teen pregnancy, gangs, and high-school dropout rates have decreased and academic performance has improved in the most challenging neighborhoods.
- Provide training in the community, specifically focusing on strategies to increase family communication, reduce aggression and violence, enhance social support, and reduce risk factors for teen suicide.
- Work with police and judicial offices to encourage prevention. Early intervention and prevention are cost-effective ways of addressing problems.

Suggestions for Parents

No parent wants to think that their child may be contemplating suicide. Yet there is a real possibility that at some point the adolescent may consider it. While there are no surefire prevention efforts, parents can take several steps for prevention.

- Maintain open conversations and a nurturing relationship. A positive family relationship is a major protective factor against suicidal thoughts and against aggressive behaviors. Families that have a nurturing relationship, support each other, and use a problem-solving approach will engage one another in healthy dialogues, even if the topics are stressful or intimidating. Families should remember that family support and communication is not a "born characteristic" but one that can be developed, nurtured, and enhanced.
- Take time to listen. Although people have busy lives, a critical component of healthy families is taking time to be together, listen, talk, play, and have fun. Family members should set aside time daily or regularly to connect and share life events, hopes and dreams, as well as discuss and solve problems.
- Look for clues that there may be problems. Symptoms of emotional problems are: sleeping too little or excessively, becoming unkempt in clothing and personal hygiene, and having mood changes (seeming despondent, remorseful, anxious, or hyper-attentive). Symptoms can also include having outbursts of anger or aggression or, conversely, being withdrawn and isolated. Mood changes can reflect normal adolescent developmental phases, but they may represent important problems that need to be addressed. Changes in behavior can be discussed and explored in an open and supportive family relationship.
- Discuss health-related issues, including suicide, in the family. Families should recognize their values and beliefs that counter possible suicidal thoughts, and identify resources, such as religious, educational, medical, and community services.
- Examine family values related to aggression and substance abuse. Families will encourage the continuation of conflict when they support revenge instead of positive solutions, model aggression rather

than problem-solving, support coercion in place of mediation and cooperation, and approve self-medication through substance abuse. The problem-solving behaviors that the family models will become part of the child's repertoire of responses.
- Monitor children's time, whereabouts, and peers. Parents' understanding of where their children are, what they are doing, and whom they spend time with are key to supervision.
- Remove guns from home, if you suspect that your child is depressed. Having a gun at home is the most dangerous risk factor for adolescent suicide.

Suggestions for Educators

Teachers spend a considerable amount of time with young people. As a result, teachers may be aware of changes in behavior and mood not observed by others, including family members. Adolescents often identify their teachers as very important in their lives, and as among the most significant adults for providing guidance and advice.

- Develop an open and inviting classroom. The classroom climate is established by teachers; they set the environment for how students engage with one another and with the teacher. To be warm, inquisitive, engaged, and supportive is critical. All students deserve a classroom that epitomizes a culture of respect and dignity for all people.
- Recognize changes in mood or behavior. Teachers are often aware of changes in student demeanor, dress, and affect. As they observe whole classes and school populations, it is easy for them to recognize what is different or out of context.
- Set a climate of respect for all students in which there is no tolerance for bullying, aggression, or other forms of harassment. Teachers should attend immediately to put-downs, peer rejection, and name-calling, and spend some time in classes discussing the importance of connectedness and respect.
- Work with programs designed to address adolescents' concerns. We created the Safe and Welcoming Schools and Community program to work with schools to develop a better understanding of how to establish a warm and welcoming environment, one in which all members of the educational community can feel welcomed and valued. Many agencies can provide help to improve the quality of the school environment, both physical and social.
- Know that all children can learn. Students who perceive that their teachers do not believe that they will learn will respond by fulfilling the expectation, rebelling, or acting out.
- Recognize that not all time in education has to be on subject matter. Teachers should also focus on helping students develop problem solving, conflict resolution, and planning skills. The academic component is essential, but developing pro-social skills is also critical, for those skills will remain with students throughout their lives.

- Work with administrators to establish school policies against bullying and aggression. In addition, effective schools monitor all parts of the school and provide adult supervision that communicates that the school is a place of support and learning.

Suggestions for Policy Makers

Policy makers, including legislators and appointed officials, are often so focused on resolving the "conflict *du jour*" that they have difficulty engaging in long-term planning, yet that is what is needed to prevent aggression, bullying, and suicide.

- Turn to researchers who study aggression, violence, bullying, and suicide prevention. They have regional and national data on prevalence of the problems, the knowledge of risk and protective factors related to the community, the statistics about when and where the conflicts occur, and the information about evidence-based interventions. Researchers can be resources to provide direction in establishing positive programs for communities and states.
- Recognize that the same conditions that work for families and for schools also work for communities: Locations that are safe, supportive, and committed to respect and dignity for all people have less violence.
- Work with community leaders to identify the best strategies to move the community toward a safe environment. Policy makers should collaborate with police and legal affairs, the medical community, schools, and especially with community service agencies.
- Move beyond "tolerating differences" to celebrating diversity. Often sub-groups of community membership fail to reach out and appreciate the contributions diversity can bring to everyone's lives. When neighborhoods remain segregated and diversity of the community is not celebrated, there is greater opportunity for distrust and alienation of groups.

SUMMARY

The study presented in this chapter illustrates the importance of examining risk and protective factors at multiple levels of the ecological model to understand students' experiences of suicidal ideation and aggression. Maintaining positive relationships with family members, teachers, and peers were important protective factors. Most important, though, was the cumulative effect of these relationships.

REFERENCES

Ackard, D. M., Eisenberg, M. E., & Neumark-Sztainer, D. (2007). Long-term impact of adolescent dating violence on the behavioral and psychological health of male and female youth. *The Journal of Pediatrics, 151*(5), 476–481. doi: 10.1016/j.jpeds.2007.04.034

Bronfenbrenner, U. (1979). *The Ecology of Human Development: Experiments by Nature and Design*. Cambridge, MA: Harvard University Press.

Centers for Disease Control and Prevention. (2012). Youth Risk Behavior Surveillance—United States, 2011. *Morbidity and Mortality Weekly Report, Surveillance Summaries, 61*(4), 1–168.

Conyne, R. K., & Horne, A. M. (Eds.). (2013). *Prevention Practice Kit: Action Guides for Mental Health Professionals*. Thousand Oaks, CA: Sage.

De Luca, S. M., Wyman, P., & Warren, K. (2012). Latina adolescent suicide ideations and attempts: Associations with connectedness to parents, peers, and teachers. *Suicide and Life-Threatening Behavior, 42*(6), 672–683. doi: 10.1111/j.1943-278X.2012.00121.x

Espelage, D. L., & Horne, A. M. (2008). School violence and bullying prevention: From research-based explanations to empirically based solutions. In S. D. Brown & R. W. Lent (Eds.), *Handbook of Counseling Psychology* (4th ed., pp. 588–605). Hoboken, NJ: John Wiley and Sons.

Farrell, A. D., Kung, E. M., White, K. S., & Valois, R. F. (2000). The structure of self-reported aggression, drug use, and delinquent behaviors during early adolescence. *Journal of Clinical Child Psychology, 29*(2), 282–292. doi: 10.1207/S15374424jccp2902_13

Fekkes, M., Pijpers, F. I. M., & Verloove-Vanhorick, S. P. (2004). Bullying behavior and associations with psychosomatic complaints and depression in victims. *Journal of Pediatrics, 144*(1), 17–22. doi: 10.1016/j.jpeds.2003.09.025

Forehand, R., Biggar, H., & Kotchick, B. A. (1998). Cumulative risk across family stressors: Short- and long-term effects for adolescents. *Journal of Abnormal Child Psychology, 26*(2), 119–128. doi: 10.1023/a:1022669805492

Foshee, V. A. (1996). Gender differences in adolescent dating abuse prevalence, types and injuries. *Health Education Research, 11*(3), 275–286. doi: 10.1093/her/11.3.275

Gini, G., & Pozzoli, T. (2013). Bullied children and psychosomatic problems: A meta-analysis. *Pediatrics*. doi: 10.1542/peds.2013-0614

Gorman-Smith, D., Tolan, P. H., Zelli, A., & Huesmann, L. R. (1996). The relation of family functioning to violence among inner-city minority youths. *Journal of Family Psychology, 10*(2), 115–129. doi: 10.1037/0893-3200.10.2.115

Jessor, R., Turbin, M. S., Costa, F. M., Dong, Q., Zhang, H. C., & Wang, C. H. (2003). Adolescent problem behavior in China and the United States: A cross-national study of psychosocial protective factors. *Journal of Research on Adolescence, 13*(3), 329–360. doi: 10.1111/1532-7795.1303004

Kenny, M. E., Horne, A. M., Orpinas, P., & Reese, L. R. (Eds.). (2009). *Realizing Social Justice: The Challenge of Preventive Interventions*. Washington, DC: American Psychological Association.

Kiselica, M. S., Englar-Carlson, M., & Horne, A. M. (2008). *Counseling Troubled Boys: A Guidebook for Professionals*. New York: Routledge.

McNeely, C., & Falci, C. (2004). School connectedness and the transition into and out of health-risk behavior among adolescents: A comparison of social belonging and teacher support. *Journal of School Health, 74*(7), 284–292.

Miller-Johnson, S., Sullivan, T. N., Simon, T. R., & Multisite Violence Prevention Project. (2004). Evaluating the impact of interventions in the Multisite Violence Prevention Study: Samples, procedures, and measures. *American Journal of Preventive Medicine, 26*(1), 48–61. doi: 10.1016/j.amepre.2003.09.015

Nahapetyan, L., Orpinas, P., Holland, K. M., & Song, X. (2013). Longitudinal association of suicidal ideation and physical dating violence among high school students. *Journal of Youth & Adolescence*. doi: 10.1007/s10964-013-0006-6

O'Donnell, L., O'Donnell, C., Wardlaw, D. M., & Stueve, A. (2004). Risk and resiliency factors influencing suicidality among urban African American and Latino youth. *American Journal of Community Psychology*, *33*(1), 37–49.

Orpinas, P., & Horne, A. M. (2006). *Bullying Prevention: Creating a Positive School Climate and Developing Social Competence*. Washington, DC: American Psychological Association.

Roberts, R. E., Roberts, C. R., & Xing, Y. (2010). One-year incidence of suicide attempts and associated risk and protective factors among adolescents. *Archives of Suicide Research*, *14*(1), 66–78. doi: 10.1080/13811110903479078

Rutter, M., Maughan, B., Mortimore, P., Ouston, J., & Smith, A. (1979). *Fifteen Thousand Hours*. Cambridge, Massachusetts: Harvard University Press.

Rutter, P. A., & Behrendt, A. E. (2004). Adolescent suicide risk: Four psychosocial factors. *Adolescence*, *39*(154), 295–302.

Rutter, P. A., & Soucar, E. (2002). Youth suicide and sexual orientation. *Adolescence*, *37*(146), 289–299.

Trentacosta, C. J., Hyde, L. W., Shaw, D. S., Dishion, T. J., Gardner, F., & Wilson, M. (2008). The relations among cumulative risk, parenting, and behavior problems during early childhood. *Journal of Child Psychology & Psychiatry*, *49*(11), 1211–1219. doi : 10.1111/j.1469-7610.2008.01941.x

Vazsonyi, A. T., Chen, P., Young, M., Jenkins, D., Browder, S., Kahumoku, E., . . . Michaud, P.-A. (2008). A test of Jessor's Problem Behavior Theory in a Eurasian and a Western European developmental context. *Journal of Adolescent Health*, *43*(6), 555–564. doi: 10.1016/j.jadohealth.2008.06.013

Psychiatric Models of Bullying Involvement

The Impact of Perceived Psychiatric Illness on Victims, Bullies, and Bully-Victims

ANDREW EDMUND SLABY AND SAMANTHA PFLUM ■

In his book *Far from the Tree: Parents, Children and the Search for Identity*, Andrew Solomon (2012) delineates vertical and horizontal dimensions to individual identity. "Vertical" aspects of our identity include variables such as race, religion, ethnicity, social class, and education. "Horizontal" elements are those not shared by an individual's predominant subculture, including exceptional skills such as creativity or athleticism, identifying as a sexual or gender minority, or suffering from various medical and psychiatric conditions. Psychiatric disorders, in particular, distinguish a person as different from their family of origin and from the communities in which they live.

Throughout history, individuals identified as "different" have suffered varieties of physical and verbal abuse. Cultural identity, to some degree, has been maintained by labeling and rejecting those who differ from a society's predominant culture. In his book *Wayward Puritans*, Kai Erickson (1966) discusses how, in each century, cultures have consistently defined deviance to ensure adherence to "correct" societal standards. He illustrates his point by demonstrating that what may have been deviant at the beginning of the Pilgrim (seventeenth) century, such as kissing in public, was different from those crimes so punished at the end of that century (Erickson, 1966). Deviant forms of behavior are a necessary resource in society, providing a stark contrast between "normal" and "abnormal" social order (Erickson, 1966).

In contemporary society, bullying is analogous to stockade punishment in the seventeenth century. The bullying of people with psychiatric disorders is remarkably similar to the victimization of people with a minority sexual orientation, gender identity, or exceptional talent. Those who label and punish those with symptoms of psychiatric conditions often act out of fear that they may also be affected with such "abnormal" mental health states. In contrast to their identified victims, bullies utilize physical, verbal, emotional, and/or relational tactics to assert that they do not suffer from schizophrenia, depression, anxiety, mania, Tourette's syndrome, or some other "abnormality."

Bullying of the mentally ill, as well as the defining characteristics of bullies, victims, and bully-victims, is best understood according to the context in which bullying occurs. This chapter will examine how various psychiatric disorders may increase risk for bullying involvement, and will also address how bullying can exacerbate or lead to the onset of mental health symptoms. Characteristics of bullies, victims, and bully-victims in relation to psychiatric disorders will be described, along with current etiological theories about the impact of family functioning on bullying and psychiatric symptoms. This chapter will conclude with specific recommendations for mental health and medical providers, teachers, parents, and policy makers.

DEFINING DEVIANCE: PSYCHIATRIC ILLNESS PRECEDING PEER BULLYING

The majority of research on risk factors for bullying involvement is derived from studies of children, with few data available on the psychiatric status of the children at the time of study (Kumpulainen, Räsänen, & Puura, 2001). Other studies are longitudinal analyses of mental health and care-seeking that do not address psychiatric status as a precursor to bullying (Sourander et al., 2009). Incidence and prevalence figures vary by culture and by investigators' definitions of "bullying" (Card & Hodges, 2008), and few studies specify comparative rates for specific subpopulations, such as those suffering from a psychiatric disorder (Sourander et al., 2009). Research on bullying among young psychiatric patients is quite limited, and little differentiation exists between different forms of bullying or different psychiatric diagnoses.

It is apparent, however, that risk factors such as internalizing and externalizing symptoms suggest the possibility of either present psychiatric illness or demonstrable indicators of future psychopathology. The same could be said of the self-deprecation, poor social skills, and social isolation of victims, and the impulsivity, aggressiveness, and lack of empathy of bullies. Many psychiatric illnesses are either not apparent at an early age or are in a prodromal state, limiting the possibility for early intervention and treatment. Impairment of self-concept resulting from a nascent psychiatric disorder, when coupled with peer bullying, plays a critical role in casting a child as a victim of repeated bullying (Egan & Perry, 1998). The union of a budding psychiatric illness with peer bullying can contribute to the development of affective disorders (Kupersmidt & Khatri, 1995), pervasive anxiety, and suicidal ideation or behavior (Klomek, Marrocco, Kleinman, Schonfeld, & Gould, 2007).

In addition to occurring via direct physical or verbal attacks, peer bullying can manifest in an indirect manner. Relational bullying, cyber-bullying, and the destruction of property are pernicious forms of victimization that can differentially affect certain individuals (Arseneault et al., 2011; Cooper, Clements, & Holt, 2012;

Olweus & Limber, 2007). For instance, bullying that takes the form of the destruction of property may appear as repeated damage to obsessively placed objects by a person suffering from obsessive-compulsive disorder. Relational bullying may be particularly destructive for individuals lacking social support, a frequent correlate of depression and anxiety (Crawford & Manassis, 2011). The term *poly-victimization* has been used to refer to the exposure to different types of victimization at the hands of a variety of offenders. Once individuals become poly-victims, their risk for additional victimization increases (Finkelhor, Ormrod, Turner, & Holt, 2009). Poly-victimization can exacerbate existing or prodromal psychiatric conditions and can also contribute to the development of post-traumatic stress symptoms (Finkelhor et al., 2009).

Psychiatric Symptoms Predictive of Bullying Involvement

The relationship between childhood bullying and the development of psychiatric disorders is multifaceted and multi-determined. There appears to be a dose–response relationship between the frequency of childhood bullying and reported levels of psychiatric symptoms, with greater frequency of bullying being linked to exacerbations of psychiatric symptoms (Arseneault, Bowes, & Shakoor, 2010). Klomek and colleagues (2007) noted that more frequent involvement in bullying behavior (whether as a victim or as a bully) is linked to increased rates of depression, suicidal ideation, and suicide attempts. Compared to uninvolved youth, adolescents who were "frequently" victims of bullying were seven times more likely to be depressed; frequent bullies were three times more likely to be depressed (Klomek et al., 2007, p. 43). A similar pattern has been noted for suicidal ideation and suicide attempts, with frequent bullying victims reporting the highest rates of suicidal ideation and attempts (Klomek et al., 2007).

From a young age, psychiatric symptoms can be detected in youth who are involved with bullying (Kumpulainen et al., 2001). Cross-sectional studies in this domain have suggested that children who are anxious, depressed, or learning-disabled are at higher risk of being involved as victims (Crawford & Manassis, 2011; Kumpulainen et al., 2001; Kumpulainen, 2008; McCabe, Antony, Summerfeldt, Liss, & Swinson, 2003). Youth experiencing bullying report high levels of anxiety, and conversely, anxious children report higher rates of peer victimization (Crawford & Manassis, 2011). High levels of anxiety have been linked to poorer social skills in children, with anxiety predicting future social skills deficits (Crawford & Manassis, 2011). Victimization is significantly linked to generalized anxiety disorder and social phobia; victims of bullying are three times more likely than non-victims to have a formally diagnosed anxiety disorder (Crawford & Manassis, 2011). Additionally, 92% of adults diagnosed with social phobia, 50% with obsessive-compulsive disorder, and 35% with panic disorder recall being victimized when they were young (McCabe et al., 2003). Based on these findings, traditional treatments for childhood anxiety disorders, such as cognitive behavioral therapy, may indirectly reduce victimization by reducing symptoms of anxiety (Crawford & Manassis, 2011). When a child's anxiety is reduced through individual psychotherapy, he or she may develop greater social competence and peer acceptance. School-based intervention programs that target both individual and interpersonal factors are likely to be most effective in easing a child's anxiety and subsequently reducing victimization (Crawford & Manassis, 2011).

Bullies and bully-victims are more likely to exhibit symptoms of attention-deficit/hyperactivity disorder, oppositional defiant disorder, and conduct disorder. Bully-victim status in childhood has been found to predict both antisocial personality disorder and anxiety disorders in early adulthood (Copeland, Wolke, Angold, & Costello, 2013; Kumpulainen, 2008). Compared to uninvolved children, male bully-victims endorsing both bullying involvement and psychiatric symptoms had a fivefold risk for developing a full-blown psychiatric disorder in early adulthood (Kumpulainen, 2008). Additionally, bully-victims often endorse high rates of depression and behavioral disturbances (Kumpulainen, 2008). Bullies and bully-victims, in particular, may benefit from anger management and empathy training. These interventions can lessen a child's involvement in bullying and serve as a protective factor against the later development of severe psychiatric symptoms (Sahin, 2012). Empathy training, which incorporates lessons on kindness, understanding of feelings, and appreciation of differences, has also been shown to decrease bullying behaviors among a sample of sixth-grade students (Sahin, 2012).

Some studies have indicated a direct relationship between bullying and the later development of psychiatric disorders. In a prospective study of Finnish boys, Sourander and colleagues (2007) found that bullying perpetration among boys at age eight predicted the development of anxiety disorders in early adulthood. Children who bullied others were more likely than their uninvolved counterparts to develop antisocial personality characteristics, substance abuse, and depressive and anxiety disorders (Sourander et al., 2007). Compared to those not involved in bullying, children identified as bully-victims were five times more likely to develop an anxiety disorder and four times more likely to develop antisocial personality characteristics. Ten to fifteen years after bullying involvement, 28% of frequent perpetrators had developed a psychiatric disorder (Sourander et al., 2007). Importantly, bullies and victims with preexisting psychiatric symptoms were found to be at elevated risk for the later development of a full-blown psychiatric disorder (Sourander et al., 2007).

Bullying as a Catalyst for Later Psychiatric Illness

For youth at vulnerable developmental stages, budding psychiatric symptoms can be exacerbated by involvement in bullying. Klomek and colleagues (2013) noted that adolescents who bullied others and demonstrated concurrent suicide risk were most likely to experience psychiatric problems at a two-year follow-up. Suicide risk, as Klomek and colleagues defined it, included depression, substance use problems, suicidal ideation, and/or past suicide attempt(s), difficulties that were more frequently endorsed by bullying perpetrators (Klomek et al., 2013). For a young person with a developing psychiatric illness, "frequent bullying of others during high-school years increases the risk for later depression and suicidality above and beyond the other established risk factors of suicide" (Klomek et al., 2013, p. S41). Externalizing behavior, including bullying, is a significant correlate of depression and suicidality (Klomek et al., 2013). The complexity of the connection between bullying and psychiatric symptoms, particularly suicidality, underlies the importance of early psychological and programmatic intervention.

Children who are victimized in the early teenage years may be at greater risk for developing psychiatric problems later in life (Kumpulainen et al., 2001; Kumpulainen, 2008). Bullying has been associated with later reports of psychotic symptoms (Arseneault et al., 2011), paranoia, and bulimia nervosa in later years (Kumpulainen et al., 2001). Victimization by peers is strongly associated with youth reports of psychotic symptoms, which contributed to an increased risk of developing a psychotic illness later in life (Arseneault et al., 2011). Schreier and colleagues (2009) also noted that pre-adolescent victims of bullying are twice as likely as their non-bullied peers to develop psychotic symptoms in adolescence. Male victims were more depressed in later years, and male bully-victims were more likely to develop antisocial characteristics and anxiety disorders (Kumpulainen et al., 2001). Adolescent bullies were more likely to drink alcohol, be involved in physical fights, and demonstrate criminal behavior. Bullies, bully-victims, and victims were also more likely than their uninvolved peers to develop psychosomatic symptoms such as abdominal pain, backache, headache, impaired appetite, and bed-wetting (Gini & Pozzoli, 2009; Kumpulainen et al., 2001).

Suicidal ideation, impaired self-esteem, and heightened levels of depression have been found to endure once bullying has stopped (Arseneault et al., 2010). The experience of being bullied can lead to a distortion in how an individual perceives her or his personal experience beyond the time of being bullied. In some ways, this may result in what has been referred to in the psychoanalytic literature as a "paranoid pseudo-community" (Cameron, 1943). In this phenomenon, a person becomes paranoid and suspicious, behaving in a manner that pushes others away. This rejecting response from others would not have occurred had it not been for the symptom of paranoia, which was part of a psychiatric disorder the victim suffered that resulted in their being bullied. If, however, the paranoia engenders bullying, this former delusion becomes a reality. This reality then reaches a high intensity that is maintained even after bullying ceases. Individuals, particularly youth, who exhibit symptoms of paranoia are likely to be victimized by their peers. Bullying often derives from the desire to "fit in" and to conceal characteristics, such as paranoia, considered "unacceptable" by popular society. When one child bullies another, such behavior often derives from an individual's fear that they may exhibit psychiatric symptoms similar to those of their victim.

THE IMPACT OF BULLYING ON THE DEVELOPMENT OF PSYCHIATRIC SYMPTOMS

Risk Factors for Bullying and Associated Psychiatric Disorders

Victim-Specific Risk Factors

Studies of children have identified bullying victims as quieter and more passive, insecure, tearful, sensitive, physically weak, and submissive than their peers (Arseneault et al., 2010; Ball et al., 2008; Card & Hodges, 2008; Cooper et al., 2012; Copeland et al., 2013; Egan & Perry, 1998; Juvonen, Graham, & Schuster, 2003; Kaltiala-Heino, Rimpela, Marttunen, Rimpela, & Rantanen, 1999; Klomek et al., 2007; Kumpulainen, 2008; Luukkonen, Räsänen, Hakko, & Riala, 2010; Nansel et al., 2001; Smokowski & Kopasz, 2005; Turkel, 2007). Most victimized children also lack the social competencies necessary to establish membership within a peer group, such as a sense of humor, friendliness, and cooperativeness (Crawford & Manassis, 2011; Egan & Perry, 1998). Lower social status and poor social skills may have a bidirectional relationship with victimization (Copeland et al., 2013; Crawford & Manassis, 2011). With few protective friends, such youth are at increased risk for peer bullying. Social skills and friendship quality intersect such that poor social skills predict poor friendships (Crawford & Manassis, 2011). Compared to youth not involved in bullying, victims typically demonstrate lower self-esteem and self-regard (Arseneault, et al., 2010; Egan & Perry, 1998). Diagnoses of depression and anxiety, which often involve poor social skills, submissiveness, and low self-confidence, appear to make youth "easy targets" for peer bullying (Crawford & Manassis, 2011; Card & Hodges, 2008).

Bully-Specific Risk Factors

Bullies have been found to be destructive, aggressive, impulsive, dominating, and physically strong, with a low level of frustration tolerance and a strong dislike of school (Copeland et al., 2013; Nansel et al., 2001). The presence of externalizing behaviors (e.g., temper tantrums, irritability, aggressiveness, disobedience) increases the likelihood of being a bully or a bully-victim among both girls and boys (Nansel et al., 2001; Kim, Koh, & Leventhal, 2006; Luukkonen et al., 2010). Bullies are more likely to drink alcohol, use drugs, carry a weapon, have poor academic records, show less empathy for others, and have a greater need for dominance as children. Contemporary research indicates a correlation between childhood bullying behavior, symptoms of conduct disorder and, later in life, antisocial personality disorder (Copeland et al., 2013). Cross-sectional studies have indicated that bullies are more likely than their uninvolved peers to be diagnosed with attention-deficit/hyperactivity disorder (ADHD), a disorder characterized by low self-control and difficulty concentrating (Holmberg & Hjern, 2008; Unnever & Cornell, 2003). Some researchers have identified "popular aggressive" and "unpopular aggressive" bully subtypes (Farmer et al., 2010; Smokowski & Kopasz, 2005). Popular aggressive bullies associate with similarly popular peers and do not encounter social stigma or rejection as a result of their aggressive behavior. Unpopular aggressive bullies are generally rejected or ignored by other children, resorting to aggression to attract peer attention (Farmer et al., 2010; Smokowski & Kopasz, 2005).

Bully-Victim-Specific Risk Factors

Bully-victims are those who are both bullies and are bullied by others (Arseneault et al., 2010). As a group, bully-victims are often anxious, disobedient, hyperactive, impulsive, and aggressive, and tend to be more psychologically troubled than their peers (Arseneault et al., 2010; Copeland et al., 2013; Luukkonen et al., 2010). Some have been found to engage in more physical fights than nonaggressive victims or non-victims; they are also more likely to use alcohol or other drugs and to carry weapons (Nansel et al., 2001). Those who are both bullies and victims are generally found to be at the highest risk for depression (Klomek et al., 2007), self-harm, suicidal ideation, and suicide attempts (Hepburn, Azrael, Molnar, & Miller, 2012). Bully-victims often show symptoms of both internalizing and externalizing disorders (Arseneault et al., 2010), and report more long-term mental health problems than those solely identified as bullies or victims (Klomek et al., 2007).

Bullying and Suicide: Long-Term Risk

Bullying is a strong risk factor for the later development of suicidal ideation and behavior (Kim et al., 2006; Klomek et al., 2013). Compared to uninvolved youth, bullies, victims, and bully-victims are at greater risk for suicidal ideation, intentional (but non-suicidal) self-injury, suicidal behavior, and other-directed violence, particularly in adolescence (Cooper et al., 2012; Klomek et al., 2007; Hepburn et al., 2012; Centers for Disease Control and Prevention [CDC], 2011). This association holds even after taking race, ethnicity, gender, and immigration status into account (Hepburn et al., 2012). Among females, being bullied in childhood predicts suicide attempts up to 25 years after bullying has ceased (Klomek et al., 2007; Klomek, Sourander, & Gould, 2011). For all youth involved in bullying, the potential for suicidal ideation or behavior does not abate, but continues into adulthood. As adults, victims were more than twice as likely as uninvolved adults to attempt suicide later in life (Meltzer, Vostanis, Ford, Bebbington, & Dennis, 2011). The risk of self-directed violence subsequent to bullying appears to occur in a "dose"-related manner (Cooper et al., 2012), such that more frequent involvement in bullying exacerbates risk. The risk of suicide appears greatest for bully-victims, who play multiple roles in bullying (Hepburn et al., 2012).

THE IMPACT OF FAMILY DYNAMICS ON BULLYING INVOLVEMENT AND PSYCHIATRIC ILLNESS

Many extant studies on bullying are only descriptive in nature. More recently, however, longitudinal research has begun to identify the unique risk and protective factors linked to bullying and other forms of peer aggression. Some authors have emphasized the role of environmental factors that may serve to predispose youth to bullying involvement (Bowes, Maughan, Caspi, Moffitt, & Arseneault, 2010; Espelage, Bosworth, & Simon, 2000; Espelage, Low, Rao, Hong, & Little, 2013; Nickerson, Mele, & Osborne-Oliver, 2010). Warm and supportive family relationships are regarded as a protective factor in the management of stressful life events (Bowes et al., 2010; Nickerson et al., 2010). A supportive social network may minimize the development of behaviors that serve as magnets for bullies. While the resilience that is developed in supportive families may not protect individuals with psychiatric symptoms from being targeted, this resilience can alter the way a victim responds to his or her bully (Bowes et al., 2010). In addition, these youth are generally inoculated from the deleterious effects of bullying, such as self-deprecation, suicidal ideation, and suicidal behaviors (Bowes et al., 2010; Kumpulainen, 2008; Perkins, Craig, & Perkins, 2011; Rigby, Slee, & Martin, 2007).

Family Functionality

Cross-sectional research indicates that families of bullies and victims, compared to families of children not involved in bullying, are "less functional" and less supportive (Ball et al., 2008, p. 104). For children involved in or affected by bullying, punishment from caregivers is often physical or overly emotional, followed by a period of time in which the child is ignored (Roberts, 2000; Smokowski & Kopasz, 2005). Children who later become bullies learn that aggression is a "means to an end" (Smokowski & Kopasz, 2005, p. 103). Longitudinal studies indicate that such children are provided with less cognitive stimulation, less emotional support, and more television exposure (Ball et al., 2008). Families of bully-victims, in particular, are described as inconsistent and abusive. Such parents are often low in warmth and lacking in parental management skills, instead relying on hostile discipline tactics that are modeled by their children (Smokowski & Kopasz, 2005). Boys identified as bully-victims are more likely than uninvolved peers to "[experience] aggression, maternal hostility and restrictive discipline" (Ball et al., 2008, p. 104).

Family-Based Processes Linked to Bullying Involvement

Children who are involved in bullying may be products of a developmental process that begins with victimization, violence, or neglect within the family. These processes set the child up for victimization or bullying perpetration in other contexts, particularly among peers (Finkelhor et al., 2009). For victimized children, "emotional residues" from family-based maltreatment, such as hyper-arousal, fear, and passivity, may interfere with the development of age-appropriate friendships (Finkelhor et al., 2009, p. 317). These youth implicitly communicate their vulnerability to peers, which invites aggressive behavior and disrupts cognitive processes that can facilitate future avoidance of bullying (Perry, Hodges, & Egan, 2001). In families characterized by chaos and disorganization, children may be poorly supervised and roughly disciplined. With little supervision, youth can be subjected to considerable instability that places them at risk for victimization both inside and outside the home (Finkelhor et al., 2009). Their need for security, care, and attention may impair their judgment of who will be "safe" individuals outside the home, leading them to join unhealthy peer groups or to attach indiscriminately to classmates. Additionally, youth are at higher risk of peer victimization when their parents are incapacitated by mental illness, physical ailments, or substance abuse (Finkelhor et al., 2009). In these cases, it is likely that children are exposed to a variety of extraneous individuals, including extended-family members, friends, and caretakers. This ever-changing cast of characters can be confusing and disorienting for youth, reflecting a lack of consistency and permanence of caregivers (Finkelhor et al., 2009).

SUGGESTIONS FOR PROVIDERS, PARENTS, TEACHERS, AND POLICY MAKERS

Based on the information on bullying and psychiatric disorders presented in this chapter, we provide a number of recommendations intended to protect youth from the adverse effects of bullying or to minimize negative health outcomes in individuals with existing vulnerabilities.

For Mental Health and Medical Providers

- School-age children in mental health and medical settings should be screened for psychiatric symptoms related to bullying involvement. Symptom checklists can facilitate the screening process and can be adapted to use by students, parents, and teachers (Klomek et al., 2011). Such screening measures could be used to identify psychologically vulnerable populations, particularly those involved as victims, bullies, or bully-victims.
- Early assessment and identification of psychiatric symptoms is essential to improving mental health outcomes and reducing bullying among youth. Given the wide-reaching effects and persistent impact of bullying on mental health, early identification and treatment of problematic psychological symptoms (such as excessive worry, hopelessness, and thoughts of suicide) can help youth lead safer, healthier, and more productive lives.
- Youth who are prone to bullying involvement can benefit from social-skills training (Crawford & Manassis, 2011). Enhancement of their skills in friendship-development, resilience, and healthy coping can decrease symptoms of affective and anxiety disorders that can contribute to peer victimization.
- Empathy training and anger management skills have been found to be important ingredients in countering bullying (Sahin, 2012). Students who exhibit levels of empathy have been found to participate in more prosocial activities and to be less involved in physical and verbal violence.
- Individual, group, and family counseling by mental health professionals should be made available for youth involved in bullying (Juvonen et al., 2003). Bully-victims, in particular, are at considerable risk for the development of psychiatric illness in early adulthood and can benefit greatly from early intervention (Sourander et al., 2007).

For Parents and Teachers

- Be attuned to signs that a child may be suffering from in-school bullying (excessive worry, hopelessness, physical injury, withdrawal, talking about "not wanting to be there," etc.).
- Talk with children about what happens in school. A positive, supportive, and structured home environment can foster the development of resilience in potentially vulnerable youth. Youth with supportive families are often protected from the negative effects of bullying, including suicidality (Bowes et al., 2010; Kumpulainen, 2008; Perkins et al., 2011; Rigby et al., 2007).
- Bullying of vulnerable subpopulations, including youth with mental health diagnoses, should be specifically addressed in classroom discussions of bullying and peer relationships as well as in parent–teacher meetings and meetings with identified bullies, victims, and bully-victims (Lund, Blake, Ewing, & Banks, 2012).

- Prevention of bullying among youth with psychiatric disorders entails educating teachers, parents, students, and community members about the necessary supports for individuals with such symptoms or diagnoses. Youth with mental health problems require empathy, support, and validation, as well as significant protection from peer victimization (Perkins et al., 2011). Teachers should serve as appropriate role models for prosocial, cooperative classroom behavior.

For School Administrators and Policy Makers

- Coupled with school-based programs, community-wide anti-bullying programs are likely to be more effective than curriculum-specific interventions taught in schools alone (Bowllan, 2011; Frisen & Holmqvist, 2010). A positive scholastic and community climate increases bonding among students, emphasizes positive group communication, and fosters personal resilience.
- Bullying should be conceptualized as a systemic problem, one that requires intervention at multiple levels (individual, school, family, neighborhood, etc.).

CONCLUSION

The association among bullying, psychiatric symptoms, and psychiatric disorders is quite complex. Bullies, victims, and bully-victims have an increased incidence of psychological symptoms, including anxiety, depression, poor coping skills, social isolation, low self-esteem, and impulsivity (Copeland et al., 2013). Such symptoms can manifest before, during, and after actual bullying episodes. Some youth appear vulnerable because psychological impairment predisposes them to becoming targets of abuse. Others may withdraw and isolate themselves, reducing their opportunities for positive interactions with others. Bullying can enhance, precipitate, or aggravate psychiatric symptoms in individuals who are genetically predisposed to a major psychiatric disorder (Kim et al., 2006). In addition, suicidal ideation and/or behavior can result from persistent bullying, particularly in youth with nascent psychiatric conditions such as depression and anxiety (Cooper et al., 2012; Hepburn et al., 2012; Kaltiala-Heino et al., 1999; Kim et al., 2006; CDC, 2011).

In order to determine the degree to which psychological symptoms predate or are exacerbated by bullying, more prospective and longitudinal studies must be undertaken. Prospective studies can clarify the degree to which psychiatric symptoms precede or follow peer bullying, suggesting appropriate points for intervention. Longitudinal studies can also illuminate how bullying impacts later adult functioning. Additionally, further research can contribute to the development of new methods to teach coping mechanisms, engender resilience, and increase interpersonal effectiveness skills to counter bullying.

Sadness, apprehension, and anger are normal human emotions, particularly as experienced in response to stressful life events. The intensity of such symptoms is enhanced or attenuated by characteristics of our social matrices, as well as by historical and cultural factors. Although our labels of the psychiatrically ill have changed over the centuries, bullying continues to manifest as a punishment for being psychologically "different." The challenge to all of us, not just children and adolescents, is to move towards greater acceptance of differences in individual personality characteristics and psychological makeup. By embracing such differences, we foster an atmosphere of self- and other-respect that serves to counter the development of problematic psychological symptoms. Acknowledging and accepting individual differences also leaves greater room for the appreciation of ambiguity, which can frequently be a correlate of bullying.

In attempting to appear strong, the bully evinces his or her fragility. Bullies and bully-victims reveal their fear of losing control of their lives, as does a person experiencing symptoms of depression, anxiety, mania, or paranoia. Similarly, the fear of being out of control is a common factor in the human experience. The Roman playwright Terence once stated, *Homo sum, humani nihil a me alienum puto:* "I am a human being; I consider nothing that is human alien to me." In accepting Terence's words, we may be better able to empathize with those who are "different." In doing so, we may be able to accept not only who we are at the moment, but also all that we may become.

REFERENCES

Arseneault, L., Bowes, L., & Shakoor, S. (2010). Bullying victimization in youths and mental health problems: "Much ado about nothing"? *Psychological Medicine, 40,* 717–729. doi: 10.1017/S0033291709991383

Arseneault, L., Cannon, M., Fisher, H. L., Polanczyk, G., Moffitt, T. E., & Caspi, A. (2011). Childhood trauma and children's emerging psychotic symptoms: A genetically sensitive longitudinal cohort study. *The American Journal of Psychiatry, 168*(1), 65–72. doi:10.1176/appi.ajp.2010.10040567

Ball, H. A., Arseneault, L., Taylor, A., Maughan, B., Caspi, A., & Moffitt, T. E. (2008). Genetic and environmental influences on victims, bullies and bully-victims in childhood. *Journal of Child Psychology and Psychiatry, 49*(1), 104–112. doi: 10.1111/j.1469-7610.2007.01821.x

Bowes, L., Maughan, B., Caspi, A., Moffitt, T. E., & Arseneault, L. (2010). Families promote emotional and behavioural resilience to bullying: Evidence of an environmental effect. *Journal of Child Psychology and Psychiatry, 51*(7), 809–817. doi: 10.1111/j.1469-7610.2010.02216.x

Bowllan, N. M. (2011). Implementation and evaluation of a comprehensive, school-wide bullying prevention program in an urban/suburban middle school. *Journal of School Health, 81,* 167–173. doi: 10.1111/j.1746-1561.2010.00576.x

Cameron, N. (1943). The paranoid pseudo-community. *American Journal of Sociology, 49*(1), 32–38. doi: 10/1086/219306

Card, N. A., & Hodges, E. V. E. (2008). Peer victimization among schoolchildren: Correlations, causes, consequences, and considerations in assessment and intervention. *School Psychology Quarterly, 23*(4), 451–461. doi: 10.1037/a0012769

Centers for Disease Control and Prevention (2011). Bullying among middle school and high school students—Massachusetts, 2009. *Morbidity and Mortality Weekly Report, 60,* 465–471.

Cooper, G. D., Clements, P. T., & Holt, K. E. (2012). Examining childhood bullying and adolescent suicide: Implications for school nurses. *The Journal of School Nursing, 28*, 275–283. doi: 10.1177/1059840512438617

Copeland, W. E., Wolke, D., Angold, A., & Costello, E. J. (2013). Adult psychiatric outcomes of bullying and being bullied by peers in childhood and adolescence. *JAMA Psychiatry, 70*(4), 419–426. doi: 10.1001/jamapsychiatry.2013.504

Crawford, A. M., & Manassis, K. (2011). Anxiety, social skills, friendship quality, and peer victimization: An integrated model. *Journal of Anxiety Disorders, 25*, 924–931. doi: 10.1016/j.janxdis.2011.05.005

Egan, S. K., & Perry, D. G. (1998). Does low self-regard invite victimization? *Developmental Psychology, 34*(2), 299–309. doi: 10.1037/0012-1649.34.2.299

Erickson, K. T. (1966). *Wayward Puritans: A Study in the Sociology of Deviance.* Boston: Pearson/Allyn and Bacon.

Espelage, D. L., Bosworth, K., & Simon, T. R. (2000). Examining the social context of bullying behaviors in early adolescence. *Journal of Counseling and Development, 78*, 326–333. doi: 10.1002/j.1556-6676.2000.tb01914.x

Espelage, D. L., Low, S., Rao, M. A., Hong, J. S., & Little, T. D. (2013). Family violence, bullying, fighting, and substance use among adolescents: A longitudinal meditational model. *Journal of Research on Adolescence, 24*(2), 223–349. doi: 10.1111/jora.12060

Farmer, T. W., Petrin, R. A., Robertson, D. L., Fraser, M. W., Hall, C. M., Day, S. H., & Dadisman, K. (2010). Peer relations of bullies, bully-victims, and victims: The two social worlds of bullying in second-grade classrooms. *The Elementary School Journal, 110*, 364–392.

Finkelhor, D., Ormrod, R., Turner, H., & Holt, M. (2009). Pathways to poly-victimization. *Child Maltreatment, 14*(4), 316–329. doi: 10.1177/1077559509347012

Frisen, A., & Holmqvist, K. (2010). Adolescents' own suggestions for bullying interventions at age 13 and 16. *Scandinavian Journal of Psychology, 51*, 123–131. doi: 10.1111/j.1467-9450.2009.00733.x

Gini, G., & Pozzoli, T. (2009). Association between bullying and psychosomatic problems: A meta-analysis. *Pediatrics, 123*, 1059–1065. doi:10.1542/peds.2008-1215

Hepburn, L., Azrael, D., Molnar, B., & Miller, M. (2012) Bullying and suicidal behaviors among urban high school youth. *Journal of Adolescent Health, 51*, 93–95. doi:10.1016/j.jadohealth.2011.12.014

Holmberg, K., & Hjern, A. (2008). Bullying and attention-deficit-hyperactivity disorder in 10-year-olds in a Swedish community. *Developmental Medicine & Child Neurology, 50*, 134–138. doi: 10.1111/j.1469-8749.2007.02019.x

Juvonen, J., Graham, S., & Schuster, M. A. (2003). Bullying among young adolescents: The strong, the weak, and the troubled. *Pediatrics, 112*(6), 1231–1237. doi: 10.1542/peds.112.6.1231

Kaltiala-Heino, R., Rimpela, M., Marttunen, M., Rimpela, A., & Rantanen, P. (1999). Bullying, depression, and suicidal ideation in Finnish adolescents: School survey. *British Medical Journal, 319*, 348–351. doi: 10.1136/bmj.319.7206.348

Kim, Y. S., Koh, Y. J., & Leventhal, B. (2006). School bullying and suicidal risk in Korean middle school students. *Pediatrics, 115*, 357–363. doi: 10.1542/peds.2004-0902

Klomek, A. B., Kleinman, M., Altschuler, E., Marrocco, F., Amakawa, L., & Gould, M. S. (2013). Suicidal adolescents' experiences with bullying perpetration and victimization during high school as risk factors for later depression and suicidality. *Journal of Adolescent Health, 53*, S37–S42. doi:10.1016/j.jadohealth.2012.12.008

Klomek, A. B., Marrocco, F., Kleinman, M., Schonfeld, I. S., & Gould, M. S. (2007). Bullying, depression, and suicidality in adolescents. *Journal of the American Academy of Child and Adolescent Psychiatry, 46*(1), 40–49. doi:10.1097/01.chi.0000242237.84925.18

Klomek, A. B., Sourander, A., & Gould, M. S. (2011). Bullying and suicide: Detection and intervention. *Psychiatric Times, 28*(2), 1–6. Retrieved June 10, 2013 from http://www.psychiatrictimes.com/suicide/content/article/10168/1795797.

Kumpulainen, K. (2008). Psychiatric conditions associated with bullying. *International Journal of Adolescent Medical Health, 20*(2), 121–132. doi: 10.1515/IJAMH.2008.20.2.121

Kumpulainen, K., Rasanen, E., & Puura, K. (2001). Psychiatric disorders and the use of mental health services among children involved in bullying. *Aggressive Behavior, 27*, 102–110. doi: 10.1002/ab.3

Kupersmidt, J. B., & Khatri, P. (1995). Peer victimization and aggression as predictors of self-reported behavioral and emotional problems across adolescence. In N. R. Crick (Chair), *Recent Trends in the Study of Peer Victimization*. Symposium conducted at the biennial meeting of the Society for Research in Child Development, March 30–April 2, Indianapolis, IN.

Lund, E. M., Blake, J. J., Ewing, H. K., & Banks, C. S. (2012). School counselors' and school psychologists' bullying prevention and intervention strategies: A look into real-world practices. *Journal of School Violence, 11*(3), 246–265. doi: 10.1080/15388220.2012.682005

Luukkonen, A., Rasanen, P., Hakko, H., & Riala, K. (2010). Bullying behavior in relation to psychiatric disorders and physical health among adolescents: A clinical cohort of 508 underage inpatient adolescents in Northern Finland. *Psychiatry Research, 178*, 166–170. doi: 10.1016/j.psychres.2010.04.022

McCabe, R. E., Antony, M. M., Summerfeldt, L. J., Liss, A., & Swinson, R. P. (2003). Preliminary examination of the relationship between anxiety disorders in adults and self-reported history of teasing or bullying experiences. *Cognitive Behaviour Therapy, 32*, 187–193. doi: 10.1080/16506070310005051

Meltzer, H., Vostanis, P., Ford, T., Bebbington, P., & Dennis, M. S. (2011). Victims of bullying in childhood and suicide attempts in adulthood. *European Psychiatry, 26*(8) 498–503. doi: 10.1016/j.eurpsy.2010.11.006

Nansel, T. R., Overpeck, M., Pilla, R. S., Ruan, W. J., Simons-Morton, B., & Schiedt, P. (2001). Bullying behaviors among US youth: Prevalence and association with psychosocial adjustment. *Journal of the American Medical Association, 285*, 2094–2100. doi: 10.1001/jama.285.16.2094

Nickerson, A., Mele, D., & Osborne-Oliver, K. M. (2010). Parent-child relationships and bullying. In S. R. Jimerson, S. M. Swearer, & D. L. Espelage (Eds.), *Handbook of Bullying in Schools: An International Perspective* (pp. 187–197). New York: Routledge.

Olweus, D., & Limber, S. P. (2007). *Olweus Bullying Prevention Program: Teacher Guide*. Center City, MN: Hazelden Publishing.

Perkins, H. W., Craig, D. W., & Perkins, J. M. (2011). Using social norms to reduce bullying: A research intervention among adolescents in five middle schools. *Group Processes & Intergroup Relations, 14*(5), 703–722.

Perry, D. G., Hodges, E. V. E., & Egan, S. K. (2001). Determinants of chronic victimization by peers: A review and new model of family influence. In J. Juvonen & S. Graham

(Eds.), *Peer Harassment in School: The Plight of the Vulnerable and Victimized* (pp. 73–104). New York: Guilford.

Rigby, K., Slee, P. T., & Martin, G. (2007). Implications of inadequate parental bonding and peer victimization for adolescent mental health. *Journal of Adolescence, 30*, 801–812. doi: 10.1016/j.adolescence.2006.09.008

Roberts, W. B. (2000). The bully as victim. *Professional School Counseling, 4*, 148–156.

Sahin, M. (2012). An investigation into the efficiency of empathy training program on preventing bullying in primary schools. *Children and Youth Services Review, 34*, 1325–1330. doi: 10.1016/j.childyouth.2012.03.013

Schreier, A., Wolke, D., Thomas, K., Horwood, J., Hollins, C., Gunnell, D., Lewis, G.,... Harrison, G. (2009). Prospective study of peer victimization in childhood and psychotic symptoms in a nonclinical population at age 12 years. *Archives of General Psychiatry, 66*(5), 527–536. doi:10.1001/archgenpsychiatry.2009.23

Smokowski, P. R., & Kopasz, K. H. (2005). Bullying in school: An overview of types, effects, family characteristics, and intervention strategies. *Children & Schools, 27*(2), 101–110.

Solomon, A. (2012). *Far from the Tree: Parents, Children, and the Search for Identity.* New York: Scribner.

Sourander, A., Jensen, P., Ronning, J. A., Niemela, S., Helenius, H., Sillanmaki, L., Kumpulainen, K.,... Almqvist, F. (2007). What is the early adulthood outcome of boys who bully or are bullied in childhood? The Finnish "From a Boy to a Man" study. *Pediatrics, 120*(2), 397–404. doi: 10.1542/peds.2006-2704

Sourander, A., Ronning, J., Brunstein-Klomek, A., Gyllenberg, D., Kumpulainen, K., Niemelä, S.,... Almqvist, F. (2009). Childhood bullying behavior and later psychiatric hospital and psychopharmacologic treatment: Findings from the Finnish 1981 Birth Cohort study. *Archives of General Psychiatry, 66*, 1005–1012.

Turkel, A. R. (2007). Sugar and spice and puppy dogs' tails: The psychodynamics of bullying. *Journal of the American Academy of Psychoanalysis and Dynamic Psychiatry, 35*(2) 243–258. doi: 10.1521/jaap.2007.35.2.243

Unnever, J. D., & Cornell, D. G. (2003). Bullying, self-control, and ADHD. *Journal of Interpersonal Violence, 18*(2), 129–147. doi: 10.1177/0886260502238731

7

Cyber-bullying and Suicide

Is There a Link? What Are the Roles of Traditional Bullying and the Media?

SHERI BAUMAN ■

Although reports in the popular media may give the impression that cyber-bullying and suicide are rampant among youth, the fact is that cyber-bullying is less common than traditional bullying, and completed suicides are rare events, although tragic when they occur. The association between involvement in traditional bullying and suicidal behavior has been noted in multiple studies in the literature (Klomek, Sourander, & Gould, 2011), although most studies have been cross-sectional and thus cannot determine causality. It is important to extend this line of research to address cyber-bullying, and to determine how involvement in cyber-bullying is associated with suicidal behavior in young people. In this chapter, I examine what is known about the relationship between these behaviors in order to have a knowledge base from which to make recommendations for prevention and intervention.

SUICIDE THEORY

It is useful to consider a theory of suicidal behavior to explore how cyber-bullying experiences and their role in adolescent suicidal behaviors might be understood within the theory. The *interpersonal theory of suicide* (VanOrden, Witte, Cukrowicz, Braithwaite, Selby, & Joiner, 2010) proposes that there are two conditions (thwarted belongingness and perceived burdensomeness) that, when present, and accompanied by the capability for suicide (acquired via increased pain-tolerance or repeated exposure to increasingly painful or fearful stimuli), allow the individual to make a lethal or nearly lethal attempt. The theory proposes that suicide is a very difficult thing to do, and the ability to do it requires lowering the fear and increasing the capacity to take the action. More pertinent to this discussion, however, are the two conditions that set the stage. How might being victimized via cyber-bullying contribute to these conditions? The nature of technology is such that an act of cyber-bullying can be seen by an extremely large audience, meaning that victims may believe that their social world has been destroyed. Many young people use technology as a way to maintain relationships, but when cyber-bullying occurs, it may seem that those relationships have been irreparably damaged. These features may lead victims to believe they no longer belong. It may also be that vulnerable adolescents think seeking help from others would place an undue burden on them, particularly if they have had other problems; the problem seems insoluble and asking others to assist would ask too much of them. Then the perceived burdensomeness element is also present.

CHALLENGES

It is important to recognize at the outset of this discussion that there are particular challenges in this line of inquiry. Cyber-bullying research is hampered by inconsistencies in the definitions of the term and the ways it is measured, so that it is almost impossible to compare findings across studies (see Bauman, Cross, & Walker, 2013, for extended discussion of this topic). First, if the accepted definition of *bullying* (intentional, repetitive aggressive behavior characterized by an imbalance of power between the aggressor and the target) is applied to behavior using technology to transmit the aggression, few studies actually measure cyber-bullying. That is, digital communication is easily misunderstood, making intention to harm difficult to discern or even infer. Repetition may occur, not because the aggressor perpetrates repeated digital attacks against a target, but because the nature of the media is such that others may repeat the message (via forwarding, re-tweeting, etc.) and because the size of the audience can simulate repetition. Finally, the power imbalance is almost never addressed in the items used to assess cyber-bullying and victimization. Some might argue that the power imbalance is less salient in cyber-bullying because an individual with little physical or social power in the offline world may have superior technological skill and therefore assume power in the digital environment. In addition, the ability to conceal one's identity when perpetrating many forms of cyber-bullying means that the power imbalance may not be clear. Thus, because the three defining attributes of bullying are not always identifiable in cyber-bullying situations, it is likely that many studies are measuring cyber-*aggression* rather than cyber-*bullying*.

Second, different measures use different reference periods for reporting the behavior, so that findings are not always comparable. Some studies use the most recent two weeks; others use the previous few months, the school term, a year, or a lifetime. No studies to date have assessed the duration of the behavior, although frequency is generally measured. It is reasonable to assume that several incidents of cyber-bullying that occur over a relatively short duration (e.g., several days or weeks) would have a different impact than cyber-bullying that persists over months or years. A number of media interviews with victims (e.g., Casey Heynes; https://www.facebook.com/video/video.php?v=187413974635689) reveal that the victim had been targeted over a period of many years, which was a factor in the thoughts of suicide.

Finally, the wording of survey items, and whether or not a definition is provided (and attended to by the participant), leads to further challenges. For example, one study inquired how often the participant had been victimized via electronic communication meant "to bully, tease, or threaten you?" (Schneider, O'Donnell, Stueve, & Coulter, 2011). Teasing can be malicious, but it can also be good-natured and reciprocal among friends, and this item equates that behavior with more unambiguously harmful actions. Variation in types of questions is another confounding aspect of summarizing this body of literature.

Regarding suicidal behaviors, studies typically examine self-reported ideation, planning, and attempts. Only a few studies ask whether such attempts required medical intervention. Only one extant study examined completed suicides in an attempt to determine whether cyber-bullying was implicated as a proximal factor. Thus, the research linking cyber-bullying and suicide is also restricted by the use of self-reported data and shared method variance. The discussion of research in this chapter regarding the links between cyber-bullying and suicide must be interpreted with these caveats in mind.

CULTURAL AND MULTICULTURAL FACTORS

"Culture" typically refers to a range of beliefs, practices, history, and worldview shared by a group of individuals. Most often, racial and ethnic groups are the focus of multicultural discussions, but gender, sexual orientation, and disabilities are also important forms of cultural diversity. Although several studies have examined cultural factors as they relate to cyber-bullying or suicide, only a few studies have investigated them together. Unfortunately, none of the studies included students with disabilities as a population of interest.

Gender

A sample of 2,341 students in suburban New York high schools completed a survey about suicidal behaviors and peer victimization over two school years (2002 through 2004). Note that at that time, social networking sites had not yet appeared (Klomek, Marrocco, Kleinman, Schonfeld, & Gould, 2008). A single item was used to assess cyber-victimization: "Used email or Internet to be mean to you." For females, cyber-victimization was associated with serious suicidal ideation, regardless of the frequency of victimization, whereas only frequent victimization was associated with suicide attempts. For males, victimization was also associated with serious suicidal ideation, but there was only one male cyber-victim who reported a suicide attempt. Although this study was limited by the cross-sectional design and the time period in which it was conducted, it provided early evidence that, like traditional bullying, cyber-bullying involvement was associated with suicidal behaviors in adolescents.

Gender, Race, and Forms of Victimization

A later study used a sample of 1,963 students (41% white, 23% African American, 19% Hispanic/Latino, and 4.7% multiracial) in the sixth through eighth grades in the Midwestern United States (Patchin & Hinduja, 2010). The survey items on suicide referred to "ever," while the bullying items inquired about experiences in the previous 30 days. The suicide variable was an average of responses to four items, one of which described depressive symptoms, while the other three referred to suicide ideation, plans, and attempts. It could be that including depression in the suicide variable inflated the scores; although depression is associated with suicide, not all persons who are depressed consider or attempt suicide. Results indicated that Caucasian participants had lower suicidal ideation (their composite variable) scores than non-Caucasian participants. Increased odds for suicide attempts were found for all bullying variables (traditional victims, 1.7; traditional bullies, 2.1; cyber-bullying victims, 1.9, and cyber-bullying perpetrators, 1.5). This study showed that both aggressors and targets have increased risk for suicidal behaviors, and this occurs in youth of middle-school (junior high) age.

Sexual Orientation

Using a large sample of high school students (n = 20,406) in the Boston metropolitan area (75% white, 5.8% Hispanic), researchers analyzed self-report survey data collected in 2008 inquiring about participants' experiences in the previous 12 months (Schneider et al., 2011). School- and cyber-victimization were each assessed with a single item; suicidal behavior was assessed with items asking about suicidal thoughts, attempts, and attempts that required medical attention. Prevalence rates for victimization showed that 15.8% of students were victimized via technology, and 25.9% were victimized at school. Of the victims of cyber-bullying, 59.7% were also targeted at school, and 36.3% of school victims were also bullied in cyberspace. Only 6.4% of the sample were victims of cyber-bullying only, 9.4% were victims of both forms of bullying; and 15.5% were victimized only at school. It is notable that 18.3% of girls reported cyber-victimization (as did 13.2% of boys), while for school bullying, the rates for boys (26.6%) and girls (25.1%) were similar. However, girls were more likely than boys to be victims of both school- and cyber-bullying (11.1% vs. 7.6% for boys). Lesbian, gay, bisexual, and transgender (LGBT) participants were more likely to report both forms of victimization (33.1% vs. 14.5% for cyber, 42.3% vs. 24.8% for school). No racial or ethnic differences were found. Suicidal behavior was reported more often among students who were victimized in both school and cyberspace (15.2%); they were over five times more likely to report an attempt than non-victimized students. Those who were cyber-victims only (9.4%) and school victims only (4.2%) also were more likely to report an attempt than those who were not victimized at all (2.0%). The same pattern was detected for depressive symptoms, suicidal ideation, and self-injurious behavior. This study did not report on suicidal behavior for LGBT students in their sample.

Data from 17,366 middle and high school students' responses on the Dane County (Wisconsin) Youth Assessment were used to assess the risks of bullying, cyber-bullying, and suicidal behavior in LGBTQ (5.4%) and heterosexual youth (Sinclair, Bauman, Poteat, Koenig, & Russell, 2012). The sample was largely white (74%), with black (7%), bi- or multiracial (7%), Hispanic (5%), Asian (4%), other (2%), and Native American (1%) represented. The odds ratio for suicide was 4.15 for those who experienced cyber-victimization only, and 6.85 for those who experienced both cyber- and bias-based victimization. For suicide attempts, odds were 3.92 for cyber-victimization and no biased-based harassment, and 7.85 for those who experienced both cyber- and bias-based victimization.

Depression as a Mediator

Bauman, Toomey, and Walker (2013) examined Youth Risk Behavior Survey (YRBS) 2009 data from high school students in Arizona. The sample was weighted to be representative of the demographics in the state, with 46.5% of the sample identified as white, 24.1% as Hispanic/Latino, and 14.4% of multiple ethnicity including Hispanic. In this study, both perpetration and victimization by traditional and cyber forms of bullying were included; the reference period was the previous 12 months for all variables. Females were more likely to report all suicidal behaviors. For both cyber- and school-bullying, males were significantly more likely to report perpetrating those behaviors, although no gender difference was found for either form of victimization. The analysis of race/ethnic differences found no difference on any of the suicide variables nor on the bullying/victimization variables; except for the Hispanic/Latino group that reported significantly lower rates of bullying others in school.

Structural equation modeling (SEM) analyses were used to investigate whether depression mediated the relationship between the two forms of bullying and victimization and suicide attempts. Depression significantly predicted suicide attempts for both genders. Both forms of victimization predicted depression. However, for females, there was an association between school victimization and suicide attempts after accounting for depression. This association was not found for males. The indirect paths from traditional victimization were significant for both genders; for females, the proportion of variance in suicide attempts mediated by depression was 42.32%; for males, 60.28%. Traditional bullying perpetration was a significant predictor of depression for females but not for males. The direct path from traditional bullying to suicide was not significant after accounting for the mediation by depression. The findings were somewhat different for the cyber form: victimization predicted depression, but only for females. The direct association between cyber-victimization and suicide attempts was not significant after accounting for depression, and the indirect effect was significant only for females, accounting for 74.43% of variance in suicide attempts. Cyber-bullying others did not predict depression for either gender. For males only, there was a significant direct association between cyber-bullying others and suicide attempts.

Bullying, Cyber-Bullying, and Suicide Among Latina Adolescents

Since the 1960s, Hispanic females (Latinas) have been found to have the highest rates of depression and suicide attempts among all race/gender groups (Romero, Wiggs, Valencia, & Bauman, 2013). Using the Arizona YRBS survey for 2009, Romero and colleagues investigated the link between bullying involvement, both traditional and cyber, and suicide, in a population of 650 high school Latinas. In the sample, 11.6% had made a suicide attempt in the previous year; 23% were victimized at school, 26.3% were victimized electronically; 17.6% acknowledged bullying others at school, and 18.4% said they cyber-bullied others. It is unusual to see higher rates of cyber-involvement than traditional bullying. In regression equations, with depression controlled for, Latinas who were victimized at school were 1.5 times more likely to have made a suicide attempt in the previous year. None of the other bullying variables was a significant predictor of suicide attempts. For suicide ideation, again with depression controlled for, girls who were perpetrators of school bullying were 1.5 times more likely to have had suicidal thoughts than those who did not bully others at school, but none of the other bullying variables was a significant predictor. Finally, for suicide ideation, those who bullied others at school were 1.4 times more likely to have made a suicide plan. Unlike the previous studies, being involved with cyber-bullying was not a significant predictor of suicide attempts, but all bullying behaviors were significant predictors of depressive symptoms.

Cyber-Bullying, Traditional Bullying, and Suicide

Building on previous studies, Bonnano and Hymel (2013) studied the relative contribution of cyber-bullying involvement to suicidal ideation, and investigated whether that involvement contributes to the prediction of suicidal ideation over and above the contribution of traditional forms. Their sample consisted of 399 students in ninth and tenth grades in British Columbia, with Asian Canadians accounting for 62% of the sample; Caucasian, 22%; and mixed heritage, 6%. The researchers used a 10-item self-report measure to assess bullying and victimization in both traditional and cyber forms, and the Suicidal Ideation Questionnaire, a 15-item scale that inquires about suicidal thoughts in the previous month. Using hierarchical multiple regressions, the researchers determined that cyber-victimization and cyber-bullying others had a statistically significant association with suicide ideation. It is notable that physical and social bullying had no effect on the outcome variable. They also found that cyber bully-victims were about twice as likely to report suicidal ideation as were cyber-victims or cyber-bullies.

As part of a study of the relationships between traditional bullying, cyber-bullying, and a number of correlates, Kowalski and Limber (2013) asked their participants (931 students in grades 6–12 in a rural community; 95% white) a single item ("I wish I were dead") to tap suicidal ideation. Suicidal ideation was found to be highest among those who were both cyber-bullies and cyber-victims. Females who were classified as cyber-bullying victims or cyber-bullying perpetrators had higher scores than males on suicidal ideation, but male cyber-bully/victims' mean scores were higher than females'. All effects were small in magnitude. The authors importantly note that the involvement in bullying (traditional or cyber) explained only 4%–7% of the variance in suicidal ideation. This is a reminder that other factors must be considered when we are attempting to understand suicide.

Including Other Risky Behaviors

One final study was conducted in a Midwestern American state using YRBS items (Litwiller & Brausch, 2013). The 4,673 high school students in the sample were primarily white (89%), with other groups' representation at less than 2%, with the exception of the multiracial group (3.6%). In this study, variables describing risk factors (substance use, violent behavior, sexual behavior) were hypothesized to mediate the relationship between cyber-victimization and suicidal behaviors. The cyber-victimization items were created for this study; the suicide items were from the core YRBS items. Results showed that victimization by cyber-bullying had significant positive direct effects on substance use, violent behavior, and sexual behavior. The first two of these variables also had a significant positive direct effect on suicidal behavior; sexual behavior did not. Overall, the model with cyber-bullying as a predictor of suicidal behaviors explained 67% of the variance in the outcome variable. Indirect effects revealed that 48% of cyber-victimization's effect on suicidal behavior was mediated by substance use and violent behavior.

Completed Suicides

The studies above are limited to investigation of suicidal thoughts, plans, and attempts, all assessed via self-report. In one unique study, LeBlanc (2012) used media reports of completed suicides in which cyber-bullying was mentioned to assemble 41 cases (24 females, 17 of whom were between 13 and 18 years of age). All were from the United States, Canada, the United Kingdom, or Australia. In 12% of cases, the victim was identified as LGBT, and in another 12%, victimization was based on presumed homosexuality, although the data did not confirm that presumption. Interestingly, most of the suicides occurred in September and January—the beginning of school terms. The suicides occurred between 2003 and April 2012; 44% of cases occurred in the final 16 months of the range. Of the sample, 17% experienced online bullying only, while 78% were bullied online and at school. Thirty-two percent of the sample were reported to have had a mood disorder, and some depressive symptoms were mentioned in 15% more. Fewer than half of the deceased individuals were described as acting normally prior to the death. Formspring.me and/or Facebook.com were mentioned as the platforms for cyber-bullying in 21 cases, and text or video-messaging were implicated in an additional 14. This study suggests, as did some others, that cyber-bullying is more often coupled with traditional bullying, perhaps compounding the impact. In addition, social media were used for cyber-bullying in the majority of cases for which the platform was known.

To summarize, although the studies examining the relationships between cyber-bullying and victimization varied in their measures, sample composition, and analytical strategies, the findings almost all suggest that cyber-involvement, as either victim or aggressor, increases the risk for suicidal behavior in middle and high school youth. It is also clear that those who were victimized by both cyber-bullying and traditional bullying were more vulnerable to suicidal behaviors, as were bully-victims in both traditional and cyber-forms. Few gender and racial differences were detected, although it appears that females are more likely to engage in suicidal behaviors and to be cyber-victims. However, these findings must be considered cautiously, given the cross-sectional and self-report nature of the designs. In the next section, I will use what is known about cyber-bullying and suicidal behavior to situate these findings within theoretical frameworks.

A SYSTEMS PERSPECTIVE

Social-ecological theory (Espelage & Swearer, 2004, 2011) views the factors that are involved in bullying behaviors as a series of overlapping layers of influence, with the central layer being the individual, and concentric ovals radiating outward from the individual containing family, peers, school, community, and culture. The perspective should be considered from the outside in; the outer layers all contribute to the way in which individual characteristics are manifested. Johnson and Puplampu (2008) proposed that technology is a subsystem within the microsystem, acknowledging the importance of technology in development.

An important cultural influence on bullying and cyber-bullying—and perhaps on suicidal behaviors—is the school. In the school, the student interacts with peers, teachers and other educators, as well as with technology. The impact of the school on bullying has been well documented (see Espelage & Swearer, 2011, for coverage of individual, peer, classroom, and school climate characteristics that have been found to promote or discourage bullying). These factors are likely to have an impact on cyber-bullying as well; although most cyber-bullying takes place on personal devices, the interactions are most often with known peers, and as noted above, the majority of youth involved in cyber-bullying are also involved in traditional bullying. However, it is useful to focus on the role of educators with respect to cyber-bullying. Students rarely report cyber-bullying incidents to adults at school (Agatston, Kowalski, & Limber, 2007); Trachtenbroit (2011) found that the 361 educators in a large Southeastern school district who completed his survey did not have accurate information about cyber-bullying or suicide. This researcher determined the correct responses to his questions based on the "Indicators of School Crime & Safety: 2008" (Dinkes, Kemp, Baum, 2009). Educators underestimated the number of students affected by cyber-bullying, and overestimated the odds that a victim of cyber-bullying would attempt suicide. This finding speaks to the need to provide ongoing training to educators on both cyber-bullying and suicide.

MEDIA

One aspect of media that is particularly relevant to this discussion is the role of mass media in publicizing (some would say "sensationalizing") incidents of cyber-bullying that may be proximal factors in the suicide of an adolescent. Vulnerable youth who view extensive coverage of a victimized individual who takes his or her own life may perceive that not only has the person's torment ended, their names and story are widely known. This may make suicide seem to be a feasible solution to the problem. Media will undoubtedly continue to disseminate stories of suicides where cyber-bullying is seen as a contributor, but the research and practice communities could advocate for more sensitive media treatment. Somehow, the message must include alternative choices that would have given the deceased hope, and convey that cyber-bullying alone was not the cause of suicide, but that it may have been one of many factors with which the individual was struggling. The lack of balanced coverage may contribute to the inaccurate perceptions of educators regarding victims of cyber-bullying who attempt suicide.

Although young people embrace digital technology and all its platforms to increase social communication, they also take cues from the greater society about appropriate behaviors in this environment. Unfortunately, one need only peruse the comments on news stories, columns, blogs, and online videos, to realize that many of those remarks are disrespectful, demeaning, cruel, and malicious. The modeling by adults in cyberspace is not positive; young people may assume that such statements about and towards others are acceptable. The frequency with which one can see such cruel statements or view photos that intend to humiliate celebrities may suggest that these events are commonplace or normal; but young people have less experience managing and coping with such experiences, and vulnerable youth may see suicide as a way to end the humiliation. The social-ecological model reminds us that the outer layers have important influences on the more central layers.

With the proliferation of digital technology, and the rapid development of new and more powerful devices and platforms, our culture is enveloped in a technological context that extends to every area of life. Young people are proficient in the use of technology and conduct their social lives digitally. They do not distinguish between an "online" and "offline" reality, but see these worlds as one. There has also been a blurring of public and private information. This means that young people's relationships include digital communications via text and social media in essential ways. When one is victimized by cyber-bullying, the permanence of the content and the enormous audience that can view one's humiliation can exceed the coping capacity of even youth who generally are very successful. It is then that suicidal behavior may appear.

CONCLUSIONS, AND DIRECTIONS FOR FUTURE RESEARCH

The extant research, although still somewhat sparse, has demonstrated associations between cyber-bullying involvement and suicidal behavior in adolescents. It appears fairly clear that those who are victimized in both cyber and traditional contexts are at elevated risk, and those who are cyber bully-victims are also engaging in suicidal behaviors at higher rates. Females and LGBT youth are likely to be more vulnerable to both behaviors; other cultural factors have not yet been found to be associated with these phenomena.

It is reasonable to conclude, based on the literature to date, that there is an association between cyber-bullying involvement and suicidal behaviors in adolescents.

It would be helpful if prevention programs that address cyber-bullying included suicide-prevention components, and vice versa. In addition, depression may be the path by which victimization leads to suicidal behavior, and those who work with adolescents should routinely check them for depressive symptoms. If such symptoms are present, inquiring about the person's experiences with cyber-bullying and suicidal behaviors is imperative, and if a risk is detected, immediate evaluation should be arranged.

Future research should use more consistent practices to allow the studies to be comparable. Standard measures for both cyber-bullying/victimization and suicidal behaviors need to be accepted by the research community, and more careful evaluation and publication of psychometric properties of these measures is required. In addition, researchers should investigate coping strategies for cyber-bullying as a step towards developing relevant educational programs.

Most important, longitudinal studies with very large population-based samples are needed to better understand the causal relationship among the variables. Further studies of archival data on completed suicides would also be useful in understanding the links.

AVAILABLE RESOURCES

The following resources provide additional information for readers.

Websites

The American Foundation for Suicide Prevention (www.afsp.org) is an excellent source of information. The Cyber-bullying Research Center (www.cyber-bullying.us) and www.cyber-bullyhelp.org are useful sites. The latter includes links to a prevention curriculum designed for grades 6–12.

Books: Cyber-bullying

Bauman S. (2011). *Cyberbullying: What Counselors Need to Know.* Alexandria, VA: American Counseling Association.

Kowalski, R. M., Limber, S. P., & Agatston, P. W. (2012). *Cyberbullying: Bullying in the Digital Age* (2nd ed.). Hoboken, NJ: Wiley-Blackwell.

Books: Suicide

Joiner, T. (2007). *Why People Die by Suicide.* Cambridge, MA: Harvard University Press.

Joiner, T. (2011). *Myths About Suicide.* Cambridge, MA: Harvard University Press

Spirito, A., & Overholser, J. C. (2002). *Evaluating and Treating Adolescent Suicide Attempters: From Research to Practice.* Waltham, MA: Academic Press.

SUGGESTIONS

Medical Providers

- The research on suicide and bullying/cyber-bullying may not be known by medical providers (Cooper, Clements, & Holt, 2012). However, 90% of young people who committed suicide had seen a primary care physician within the past year (Tingley, 2013). Physicians have an opportunity for assessment and screening for mental health issues and suicidal thoughts and behaviors.
- Family physicians should recognize that some physical symptoms, particularly those linked to stress, might indicate that the patient is being victimized at school or online.
- Youth who have been victimized should be screened for depression and risk for suicide. If patients deny suicidal ideation, it may be useful to ask what *could* happen to cause them to think about suicide.
- School nurses are in a unique position to influence school policy and practices. They are also able to screen students who seek them out for medical attention. Students with frequent headaches, stomachaches, sleep problems, and the like should be assessed for involvement in bullying and/or cyber-bullying. If so, referral to appropriate services can be made.

Mental Health Providers

- Victims of cyber-bullying often exhibit symptoms of depression. When screening or treating an adolescent for depression, it would be useful to ask about victimization. If the student is being or has been victimized, the mental health provider needs to know what resources are available to assist the student with any technological actions that could be effective, and to help them ensure they are as protected as possible from future events.
- Other psychological symptoms (e.g., anxiety, social withdrawal) may also be linked to victimization. It is crucial that the mental health provider include experiences with cyber-bullying as part of an intake interview to ensure this influence on mental health is not overlooked.

Parents and Teachers

- Students are very reluctant to report cyber-victimization to adults; they fear adults will not understand, or overreact and restrict their access to technology. Thus, when inquiring about cyber-bullying, an indirect approach is recommended. Instead of saying, "Have you been cyber-bullied?" asking whether the student knows of any cyber-bullying within the friendship group or whether his or her school has had problems with cyber-bullying may produce a more informative interaction. Attending films or programs on the topic also provides an avenue to broach the topic in a less personal way, reducing defensiveness.
- Parents and teachers should work collaboratively to address the problems. Programs to prevent cyber-bullying should include the topic of suicide. Programs that raise awareness about suicide should include victimization by cyber-bullying as a potential trigger.

- Parents and teachers who are concerned about a particular student should refer her or him to a mental health practitioner for a timely assessment. Although suicide is a rare event in response to cyber-bullying, one does not want to ignore the possibility.

Policy Makers

Perhaps the most important policy issue related to cyber-bullying is the role of schools in incidents that occur or originate off-campus. Some state laws restrict schools to taking action only when school computers are used. Others states specify that when the action causes a substantial disruption to the educational process, schools may intervene. This uncertainty creates a dilemma for schools and can result in their ignoring serious cyber-incidents among students. A clear statement of schools' responsibility in dealing with cyber-bullying is needed.

REFERENCES

Agatston, P., Kowalski, R., & Limber, S. (2007). Students' perspectives on bullying. *Journal of Adolescent Health*, *41*, S59–S60. doi: 10.1016/j.jadohealth.2007.09.003

Bauman, S., Cross, D., & Walker, J. (2013). *Principles of Cyberbullying Research: Definition, Measures, and Methods*. New York: Routledge.

Bauman, S., Toomey, R., & Walker, J. (2013). Relations among bullying, cyberbullying and suicide in high school students. *Journal of Adolescence*, *36*, 341–360. http://dx.doi.org/10.1016/j.adolescence.2012.12.001

Bonnano, R. A., & Hymel, S. (2013). Cyber bullying and internalizing difficulties: Above and beyond the impact of traditional forms of bullying. *Journal of Youth & Adolescence*, *42*, 685–697. doi: 10.1007/s10964-013-9937-1

Cooper, G. D., Clements, P. T., & Holt, K. E. (2012). Examining childhood bullying and adolescent suicide: Implications for school nurses. *The Journal of School Nursing*, *28*, 275–283. doi: 10.1177/1059840512438617

Dinkes, R., Kemp, J., & Baum, K. (2009). *Indicators of School Crime and Safety: 2008* (NCES 2009-022/NCJ 226343). National Center for Education Statistics, US Department of Education, and Bureau of Justice Statistics, Office of Justice Programs, US Department of Justice. Washington, DC.

Espelage, D. L., & Swearer, S. (2004). *Bullying in American Schools*. New York: Routledge.

Espelage, D. L., & Swearer, S. (2011). *Bullying in North American Schools* (2nd ed.). New York: Routledge.

Johnson, G. M., & Puplampu, K. P. (2008). Internet use during childhood and the ecological techno-subsystem. *Canadian Journal of Learning and Technology*, *34*. Retrieved from http://www.cjlt.ca/index.php/cjlt/article/view/172.

Klomek, A. B., Marrocco, F., Kleinman, M., Schonfeld, I. S., & Gould, M. S. (2008). Peer victimization, depression, and suicidality in adolescents. *Suicide and Life-Threatening Behavior*, *38*, 166–180. doi: 10.1521/suli.2008.38.2.166

Klomek, A., Sourander, A., & Gould, M. S. (2011). Bullying and suicide: Detection and intervention. *Psychiatric Times*, *28*(2), 27–31. doi: 10.152/suli.2008.38.2.166

Kowalski, R., & Limber, S. (2013). Psychological, physical, and academic correlates of cyberbullying and traditional bullying. *Journal of Adolescent Health, 53*, S13–S20. doi:10.1016/j.jadohealth.2012.09.018

LeBlanc, J. C. (2012). Cyberbullying and suicide: A retrospective analysis of 22 cases. Paper presented at the American Academy of Pediatrics National Conference, October 20, 2012, New Orleans, LA.

Litwiller, B. J., & Brausch, A. M. (2013). Cyber bullying and physical bullying in adolescent suicide: The role of violent behavior and substance use. *Journal of Youth and Adolescence, 42*, 675–684. doi: 10.1007/s10964-013-9925-5

Patchin, J., & Hinduja, S. (2010). Bullying, cyberbullying, and suicide. *Archives of Suicide Research, 14*, 206–221. doi: 10.1080/13811118.2010.494133

Romero, A., Wiggs, C. B., Valencia, C., & Bauman, S. (2013). Latina teen suicide and bullying. *Hispanic Journal of Behavioral Sciences, 35*, 159–173. doi: 10.117/0739986312474237

Schneider, S. K., O'Donnell, L., Stueve, A., & Coulter, R. W. S. (2011). Cyberbullying, school bullying, and psychological distress: A regional census of high school students. *American Journal of Public Health, x*, e1–e7. doi: 10.2105/AJPH.2011.300308.

Sinclair, K. O., Bauman, S., Poteat, V. P., Koenig, B., & Russell, S. T. (2012). The association between cyber and bias-based harassment and academic, substance use and mental health problems. *Journal of Adolescent Health, 50*, 521–523. doi:10.1016/j.jadohealth,2011.09.009

Tingley, K. (2013). The suicide detective. *New York Times Magazine*, June 28. Retrieved from www.nytimes.com/2013/06/30/magazine/the-suicide-detective.

Trachtenbroit, M. L. B. (2011). Cyberbullying, school violence, and youth suicide. (Unpublished doctoral dissertation). Hattiesburg, MS: University of Southern Mississippi.

VanOrden, K. A., Witte, T. K., Cukrowicz, K. C., Braithwaite, S. R., Selby, E. A., & Joiner, T. E. (2010). The interpersonal theory of suicide. *Psychological Review, 117*, 575–600. doi: 10.1037/a0018697

PART THREE

Cultural Perspectives

8

The Connection Between Bullying and Suicide in Ethnic Minority Populations

TECETA THOMAS TORMALA, IULIA I. IVAN, REBECCA FLOYD, AND LEONARD C. BECKUM

Each year, millions of American children and teenagers suffer the pain, fear, and shame of ongoing bullying, aggression, and victimization from their peers. For a subset of these adolescents, the consequence of the emotional distress, increasing isolation from others, eroding self-image, and toll on the psyche is suicide (Espelage & Holt, 2013). Under-studied in the literature on adolescent bullying and suicide are the patterns across ethnic and racial groups, and the need for a more nuanced understanding of the association between peer victimization and suicidality is growing. People of color make up an increasing population within the United States; blacks, Latinos, American Indian/Alaska Natives, Asians/Pacific Islanders, and biracial/multiracial individuals currently make up 38% of the population, and projections place that proportion at 57% by 2050 (U.S. Census Bureau, 2012).

Central to an understanding of the connection between bullying and suicidality within communities of color is an attentiveness to the roles of social-ecological systems (Bronfenbrenner, 1977, 1994) and the intersection of social identities (Cole, 2009) with those behaviors. With these lenses, it is possible to attend to several things.

Ethnic and racial groups are differentially located within other social identity and contextual spheres (socioeconomic status [SES], level of acculturation, co-ethnic density; e.g., the suicidal ideation of a bullied Mexican adolescent might differ if her neighborhood is predominantly Mexican versus predominantly white [Wadsworth & Kubrin, 2007]).

The social experience of teens from the same ethnoracial background is influenced by and differs from one another based on their other social identities (gender, religion, citizenship status, language; e.g., the bullying experience of a black male teen is likely to be intensified when that teen is LGBT versus when he is heterosexual, and the attendant risk of suicide is higher [Hightow-Weidman et al., 2011]). The intersectional impact of an individual's characteristics and social identities on peer victimization and suicidality is shaped by interactions between and within various relevant in-groups (family, friends, school, community) and more broadly by the particular institutions, practices, and beliefs of the cultural group and broader society.

The connection between bullying and suicide in youth of color falls into three separate categories: differential bullying/victimization and suicide rates by ethnicity and race; racial bullying and peer discrimination; and individual and contextual factors prevalent in the lives of adolescents of color that predict likely differences in victimization, bullying, and suicide. All three facets are covered in the remainder of the chapter.

RACIAL AND ETHNIC DIFFERENCES IN BULLYING AND VICTIMIZATION, AND IN SUICIDALITY

The literature on the impact of race and ethnicity on bullying and peer victimization is spare and highly contradictory. Some studies demonstrate no racial and ethnic differences in bullying and victimization (Fitzpatrick, Dulin, & Piko, 2010), while others show that people of color are less likely to be victimized than whites (Wang, Iannotti, Luk, & Nansel, 2010). In other studies, researchers find that people of color are less likely to be bullies than whites are (Barboza et al., 2009), while others report that people of color are more likely to be bullies than whites are (Graham & Juvonen, 2002). At present, no consensus exists in the literature to suggest a simple pattern of youth bullying and victimization along ethnoracial lines in the United States.

Racial and ethnic differences exist in suicide, and patterns of suicide across adolescence are very different between ethnoracial groups in the United States. American Indians/Alaska Natives commit suicide at highly disproportionate rates compared to other groups—approximately 2.5 times the rate of the next-highest group, whites—followed by Latinos, blacks, and Asians/Pacific Islanders (Centers for Disease Control [CDC], 2010).

A SOCIAL-ECOLOGICAL ANALYSIS OF BULLYING AND SUICIDE IN YOUTH OF COLOR

When youth are bullied by their peers, this victimization is occurring within specific nested contexts for individuals, and it is the interactive effects of these contexts that serve as differential risk and protective factors related to bullying/victimization and to suicide across and within racial and ethnic groups.

Macrosystem

Macrosystem Within the United States

Some forms of bullying are directly related to societal-level stereotypes about particular group identities or intersectional identities: mocking about English-language ability to Latino or Asian immigrant youth (Mendez, Bauman, & Guillory, 2012), increased discrimination from black and Latino peers against Asian immigrants based on perceptions of teacher favoritism (attributed to the "model minority" stereotype) (Greene, Way, & Pahl, 2006).

Behaviors across racial and ethnic groups may be perceived differently from each other. Stereotypes about blacks include "aggressive," "violent," and "criminal" (Devine, 1989), and it is possible that bullying of a physical nature may be seen as normative within black or Latino youth, and thus be less likely than among other groups to be curtailed by school administrations. Conversely, school officials may over- or mislabel assertive, loud, or confrontational behavior as bullying when it is not, and disproportionately punish Latino and black students for being "bullies." Cultural meanings about what constitutes bullying and victimization vary (Smith, Cowie, Olafsson, & Liefooghe, 2002); it may be that the kinds of behaviors that are labeled as bullying by and about whites may not be categorized as such among other ethnoracial groups.

Macrosystems Within Groups of Color

Nested within the overall cultural macrosystem of the United States are the macrosystems of racial and ethnic groups. These are the ideologies, values, belief systems, norms, and patterns of behavior present within cultural groups.

Intragroup Norms and Expectations

Some within-group forms of bullying relate to an internal policing of group boundaries and normative behavior; an example is put-downs about whether someone is a "true" group member (e.g., "black enough," a "Real" American Indian or Mexican [Favor, 1999]) based on speech patterns, language, SES, academic achievement, or monoracial versus biracial identity. For blacks, Latinos, American Indians, and Asians, stigma around seeking help for distress may lower the likelihood that bullied teens will seek help outside of their family or trusted insiders (e.g., religious or spiritual figures in the community [Freedenthal & Stiffman, 2007]).

For Asian youth, cultural ideology supporting collectivism and group harmony can serve to suppress individual emotional expression (Tsai, Chentsova-Dutton, Freire-Bebeau, & Przymus, 2002). Asian American adolescents express greater difficulty with discussing personal problems with their parents than do whites (Rhee, Chang, & Rhee, 2003), which may impact the likelihood of their discussing victimization by peers. For black, Latino, and American Indian youth, cultural representations exist regarding particular attitudinal and behavioral norms that may be endorsed by group members themselves, and that are antithetical to help-seeking behavior for someone being victimized by peers: the "stoic Indian," the "tough black man or woman," the Latino who is high in *machismo*.

Exosystem

Barriers to Mental Health Treatment

Brown and Grumet (2009) detail a set of barriers to mental health treatment for low-income black adolescents related to mental health screening for negative psychological functioning and suicidal ideation; these include difficulty gaining access to schools, principal turnover, fear and mistrust of health providers and screenings, and the pervasive stigma of suicide and mental illness in the African American community. These factors are also likely to impede treatment for suicidality among low-SES Asians, Latinos, and American Indians.

Mesosystem

Parental Involvement in School

High parental involvement with teachers and school administrators has been shown to have positive effects on behavioral problems like aggression (Hill et al., 2004). Research has shown that parents of color tend to have lower levels of parental involvement in school than do white parents, for reasons including transportation issues, lack of time, language constraints, and feeling excluded by teachers (Lareau & Horvat, 1999). Parent involvement extends to discussions with teachers or school staff about warning signs regarding children being victimized, or exhibiting internalizing, externalizing, or suicidal behaviors.

Culture at Home versus Culture at School

For racial and ethnic minority groups, the clash between their culture of heritage and American culture in schools and among peers can increase suicidality. For foreign- and native-born Latinos, cultural assimilation and acculturative stress are risk factors for suicidality (Wadsworth & Kubrin, 2007). Joe and colleagues (2006) found that Caribbean men had the higher rates of suicidality compared to African American men. American Indian tribal groups with high pressures to acculturate have higher rates of suicide than those with low levels (Olson & Wahab, 2006). The stress that comes from the attempt to incorporate sometimes highly discrepant cultural beliefs, values, and behaviors can increase the risk of suicide in youth of color (Hovey & King, 1996).

Relatedly, the intergenerational conflict between increasingly acculturated children and their parents may prove detrimental to mental health, and heighten psychological distress and suicidality among bullied youth. Navigating between two very different cultures at home and outside of the home (e.g., school, peers, neighborhood) serves as a cause of family discord for immigrant youth—particularly for Latinas (Fortuna, Perez, Canino, Sribney, & Alegria, 2007)—that can lay a heavier burden on young people who are being bullied by peers. For Latinos and Asians in particular, expected obligations towards their family and family needs can foster overlooked personal difficulties (Zayas, Lester, Cabassa, & Fortuna, 2005).

Microsystem

Neighborhood

Exposure to violence is higher in black and Latino communities than in white communities (Truman & Planty, 2012), and violence and neighborhood crime are more likely to lead to aggression and bullying than safer neighborhoods (Cook, Williams, Guerra, Kim, & Sadek, 2010). Exposure to violence—both as a victim and as a witness—is associated with negative outcomes, including increased aggression and disorderly conduct, as well as internalizing outcomes like depression, anxiety, and post-traumatic stress (McDonald & Richmond, 2008), and suicidality (Lambert, Copeland-Linder, & Ialongo, 2008).

Another important neighborhood factor is ethnic neighborhood density, which serves as a protective factor. The suicide rates of immigrant Latinos are lower than of native-born counterparts in areas of high immigrant concentration, and the pattern reverses in areas of low immigrant concentration (Wadsworth & Kubrin, 2007).

Social Support and Family Discord

For youth of color, social support from relevant social networks—nuclear and extended family, religious network, neighborhood, and cultural community—may play an important role as a buffer between bullying and suicide. High social integration and support, as a result of large family and kin networks prevalent in communities of color, is an important protective factor against suicide risk (Compton, Thompson, & Kaslow, 2005), whereas family discord and conflict are risk factors (Lau, Jernewall, Zane, & Myers, 2002). Loneliness and lack of belonging are consequences of bullying and risk factors for suicide (Storch, Brassard, & Masia-Warner, 2003); it may be that for youth of color, the impact of those states would be buffered by extended family and kinship networks.

School Context

Research has shown that students who perceive teachers and other staff to be supportive are more willing to seek help for bullying or to cope with threats of aggression (Eliot, Cornell, Gregory, & Fan, 2010). Support and interest from teachers and peers has been shown to be associated with lower risks of bullying (Natvig, Albrektsen, & Qvarnstrøm, 2001). Black and Latino youth are more at risk than whites for experiencing less supportive environments from their teachers (Woolley & Bowen, 2007). These findings suggest that students of color are at particular risk of feeling unsupported in school, which may serve to heighten psychological distress from peer victimization.

Peer-Based Discrimination

Racial and ethnic minority adolescents are often the targets of prejudice and discrimination based on their cultural identity (Rosenbloom & Way, 2004), particularly Asian youth (Qin, Way, & Rana, 2008). Prejudice and discrimination based on ethnoracial background are associated with depression and hopelessness in people of color (Nyborg & Curry, 2003), which are factors that are associated with suicidality in youth (Cole, 1989). The stressors associated with ethnic and racial discrimination can exacerbate the effects of victimization on internalizing behaviors and beliefs, and this may be compounded by low SES status and being female (Peskin, Tortolero, Markham, Addy, & Baumler, 2007).

Youth Characteristics

Religiosity and Spirituality

Religiosity or spirituality are especially important protective factors for reducing the risk of suicide among blacks (Greening & Stoppelbein, 2002). Because of high centrality of spirituality and religiosity in ethnic culture among Asians and American Indians, it is likely to be relevant for those groups as well.

Expression of Psychological Distress

Language barriers serve as risk factors for help-seeking and increase the risk of suicide among immigrant Latino and Asian youth (Goldston et al., 2008). Depression has consistently been shown to be both a consequence of bullying and a risk factor for suicide (Klomek, Marrocco, Kleinman, Schonfeld, & Gould, 2007). Depression is experienced and expressed differently across racial and ethnic groups; in whites, it is commonly expressed verbally and emotionally as melancholia or depressed affect; while in blacks, it is often expressed as mood irritability, hostility, and agitation (Payne, 2012). In Asians, as with blacks, depression is often somaticized, experienced and manifested as headaches, backaches, stomachaches, or fatigue, rather than as sadness as it is commonly expressed in white populations (Tsai & Chentsova-Dutton, 2002). Students of color who are depressed because of peer victimization may not have their depression recognized by school nurses, counselors, teachers, or cross-ethnic peers.

POLICY SUGGESTIONS

Following are policy and practice suggestions relevant to different constituencies that are targeted to decrease the risks of bullying and suicide in ethnic minority populations.

Suggestions for Medical Providers

- *Cultural stereotypes*: Be aware of the influence of implicit bias on perceptions of and interactions with ethnically diverse patients; implicit prejudice can affect patients' willingness to disclose.
- *Treatment for psychological concerns*: Given the tendency among blacks, Asians, and Latinos to seek primary or emergency care over mental health providers for psychological issues, this difference may manifest in different trajectories of the link between bullying and suicide. Conduct routine psychosocial assessments.
- *Social networks*: Ask about the informal social networks and connections of patients of color. For many, disconnection from a broader family, ethnic, and/or religious context may signal a risk factor of suicidality among bullied teens.
- *Effects of stereotyping and discrimination*: Ask patients about experiences with bias; prejudice and discrimination have been shown to have negative short- and long-term health effects in people of color.
- *Cultural idioms of distress:* Note that depression—a known consequence of bullying and risk factor for suicide—is more likely to be expressed somatically for certain cultural groups, such as Asians and blacks.

Suggestions for Mental Health Providers

- *Intragroup norms and expectations*: Stigma about seeking treatment, mistrust of medical providers, and cultural mores about being tough may be barriers to seeking treatment for victimization. Identify these as possibilities in clients of color.

- *Barriers to access*: Significant disparities exist between whites and people of color in access to and effective treatment from mental health providers. Understand difficulties clients may have with transportation, insurance, and parental acceptance of treatment.
- *Acculturation, assimilation, and acculturative stress*: These factors may exacerbate the influence of being bullied for immigrants of color, and increase the risk of suicide. Ask about these factors for immigrant clients. Seek cultural consults when necessary.
- *Neighborhood effects.* The safety and security of an adolescent's neighborhood often has an impact on his or her psychological functioning and level of aggression. Ask clients about their neighborhood contexts.
- *Intersectionality*: Be aware that the experience of a bullied teen is mitigated by contextual and social identity factors: numerical minority versus majority status, SES, ethnic embeddedness, specific country/ethnicity/tribe of origin.

Suggestions for Parents and Teachers

- *Cultural meaning of bullying*: Bullying may have different connotations across ethnic and racial groups. Relatedly, teasing and playful aggression may be more negatively viewed when demonstrated by black and Latino teens. Take care not to use a one-size-fits-all definition across groups.
- *Media, technology, and cyberaggression:* Parents should be well-informed about and familiar with the ways technology can be used to facilitate bullying. Monitor and/or restrict children's access to forms of media or media expressions that may promote suicide.
- *Double-edged sword of close family ties*: Social support decreases the risk of suicide. However, cultural conflict between minority/immigrant youth and their parents can heighten psychological distress rather than alleviate it. Improve family functioning and stability.
- *Situational context*: The home and the classroom exert explicit and implicit effects on perceptions of and behavior towards others. Attend to whether students of color are numerical minorities or majorities.
- *Academic achievement*: Rather than being accepted as a socioeconomic or cultural norm, low or reduced academic achievement may signal social problems and risk for suicide.

Suggestions for Policy Makers

- *Honoring diversity*: Create a school norm of honoring diversity and cultural pluralism. Educate against bias and prejudice. Teach perspective-taking and social comparisons.
- *School climate*: Schools should have explicit and highly-visible policies that reinforce help-seeking behavior, discourage bullying and victimization, facilitate social cohesion, and encourage belonging and connectedness to the school.

- *Parent-school interactions*: Facilitate a warm, welcoming environment where parents of color feel invited to share thoughts and concerns with teachers and school officials.
- *Aggression within peer groups*: Adopt a zero-tolerance policy for aggression among all student groups. Encourage students from all groups to talk with teachers and school officials when they are victims of peer bullying.
- *Cultural competence*: Understand the population that is being served within a school or district. Facilitate cultural adaptations to anti-bullying and anti-suicide programs that are relevant to the student groups.

CONCLUDING REMARKS

Future research should explicitly measure race and ethnicity as predictor variables for bullying, victimization, and their influence on suicidality. Studies should look at peer aggression between whites and groups of color, and among groups of color. Important variables to attend to are immigration status, SES, gender, neighborhood and school demographics, and cultural meanings of bullying in different ethnoracial groups. It is imperative that the processes involved in bullying be understood across ethnic groups in the United States to more fully understand the life contexts and influences surrounding bullying and suicide, to be able to recognize warning signs, and ultimately to disrupt the connection between being victimized by peers and attempting suicide.

REFERENCES

Barboza, G. E., Schiamberg, L. B., Oehmke, J. Korzeniewski, S. J., Post, L. A., & Heraux, C. G. (2009). Individual characteristics and the multiple contexts of adolescent bullying: An ecological perspective. *Journal of Youth and Adolescence*, *38*, 101–121. doi: 10.1007/s10964-008-9271-1

Bronfenbrenner, U. (1977). Toward an experimental ecology of human development. *American Psychologist*, *32*, 513–531. 10.1037/0003-066X.32.7.513

Bronfenbrenner, U. (1994). Ecological models of human development. In T. Husen, & T. N. Postlethwaite (Eds.), *International Encyclopedia of Education* (2nd ed., pp. 1643–1647). New York: Elsevier Science.

Brown, M. M., & Grumet, J. G. (2009). School-based suicide prevention with African American youth in an urban setting. *Professional Psychology: Research and Practice*, *40*(2), 111–117. doi: 10.1037/a0012866.

Centers for Disease Control and Prevention (2010). *Welcome to WISQARS (Web-based Injury Statistics Query and Reporting System)*. Retrieved August 10, 2013, from Centers for Disease Control and Prevention, National Center for Injury Prevention and Control website: http://www.cdc.gov/injury/wisqars/index.html.

Cole, D. A. (1989). Psychopathology of adolescent suicide: Hopelessness, coping beliefs, and depression. *Journal of Abnormal Psychology*, *98*, 248–255. doi: 10.1037/0021-843X.98.3.248

Cole, E. R. (2009). Intersectionality and research in psychology. *American Psychologist, 64*, 170–180. doi: 10.1037/a0014564

Compton, M. T., Thompson, N. J., & Kaslow, N. J. (2005). Social environment factors associated with suicide attempts among low-income African Americans: The protective role of family relationships and social support. *Social Psychiatry and Psychiatric Epidemiology, 40*, 175–185. doi: 10.1007/s00127-005-0865-6

Cook, C. R., Williams, K. R., Guerra, N. G., Kim, T. E., & Sadek, S. (2010). Predictors of bullying and victimization in childhood and adolescence: A meta-analytic investigation. *School Psychology Quarterly, 25*, 65–83. doi: 10.1037/a0020149

Devine, P. G. (1989). Stereotypes and prejudice: Their automatic and controlled components. *Journal of Personality and Social Psychology, 56*, 5–18. doi: 10.1037/0022-3514.56.1.5

Eliot, M., Cornell, D., Gregory, A., & Fan, X. (2010). Supportive school climate and student willingness to seek help for bullying and threats of violence. *Journal of School Psychology, 48*, 533–553. doi: 10.1016/j.jsp.2010.07.001

Espelage, D. L., & Holt, M. K. (2013). Suicidal ideation and school bullying experiences after controlling for depression and delinquency. *Journal of Adolescent Health, 53*, S27–S31. doi: 10.1016/j.jadohealth.2012.09.017

Favor, J. M. (1999). *Authentic Blackness: The Folk in the New Negro Renaissance (New Americanists)*. Durham, NC: Duke University Press.

Fitzpatrick, K. M., Dulin, A., & Piko, B. (2010). Bullying and depressive symptomatology among low-income, African-American youth. *Journal of Youth and Adolescence, 39*, 634–645. doi: 10.1007/s10964-009-9426-8

Fortuna, L. R., Perez, D. J., Canino, G., Sribney, W., & Alegria, M. (2007). Prevalence and correlates of lifetime suicidal ideation and attempts among Latino subgroups in the United States. *Journal of Clinical Psychiatry, 68*, 572–581. doi: 10.4088/JCP.v68n0413

Freedenthal, S., & Stiffman, A. R. (2007). "They Might Think I Was Crazy": Young American Indians' reasons for not seeking help when suicidal. *Journal of Adolescent Research, 22*, 58–77. doi: 10.1177/0743558406295969

Goldston, D. B., Molock, S. D., Whitbeck, L. B., Murakami, J. L., Zayas, L. H., & Nagayama Hall, G. C. (2008). Cultural considerations in adolescent suicide prevention and psychosocial treatment. *American Psychologist, 63*, 14–31. doi: 10.1037/0003-066X.63.1.14

Graham, S., & Juvonen, J. (2002). Ethnicity, peer harassment, and adjustment in middle school: An exploratory study. *Journal of Early Adolescence, 22*, 173–199. doi: 10.1177/0272431602022002003

Greene, M. L., Way, N., & Pahl, K. (2006). Trajectories of perceived adult and peer discrimination among black, Latino, and Asian American adolescents: Patterns and psychological correlates. *Developmental Psychology, 42*, 218–238. doi: 10.1037/0012-1649.42.2.218

Greening, L., & Stoppelbein, L. (2002). Religiosity, attributional style, and social support as psychosocial buffers for African American and white adolescents' perceived risk for suicide. *Suicide and Life-Threatening Behavior, 32*, 404–417. doi: 10.1521/suli.32.4.404.22333

Hightow-Weidman, L. B., Phillips II, G., Jones, K. C., Outlaw, A. Y., Fields, S. D., & Smith, J. C. (2011). Racial and sexual identity-related maltreatment among minority

YMSM: Prevalence, perceptions, and the association with emotional distress. *AIDS Patient Care and STDs, 25*, S39–S45. doi: 1089/apc.2011.9877

Hill, N. E., Castellino, D. R., Lansford, J. E., Nowlin, P., Dodge, K. A., Bates, J. E., & Pettit, G. S. (2004). Parent academic involvement as related to school behavior, achievement, and aspirations: Demographic variations across adolescence. *Child Development, 75*, 1491–1509. doi: 10.1111/j.1467-8624.2004.00753.x

Hovey, J. D., & King, C. A. (1996). Acculturative stress, depression, and suicidal ideation among immigrant and second-generation Latino adolescents. *Journal of the American Academy of Child and Adolescent Psychiatry, 35*, 1183–1192. doi: 10.1097/00004583-199609000-00016

Joe, S., Baser, R., Breeden, G., Neighbors, H., & Jackson, J. (2006). Prevalence of and risk factors for lifetime suicide attempts among blacks in the United States. *Journal of the American Medical Association, 296*, 2112–2123. doi: 10.1001/jama.296.17.2112

Klomek, A. B., Marrocco, F., Kleinman, M., Schonfeld, I. S., & Gould, M. S. (2007). Bullying, depression, and suicidality in adolescents. *Journal of the American Academy of Child and Adolescent Psychiatry, 46*, 40–49. doi: 10.1097/01.chi.0000242237.84925.18

Lambert, S. F., Copeland-Linder, N., & Ialongo, N. S. (2008). Longitudinal associations between community violence exposure and suicidality. *Journal of Adolescent Health, 43*, 380–386. doi: 10.1016/j.jadohealth.2008.02.015

Lareau, A., & Horvat, E. M. (1999). Moments of social inclusion and exclusion: Race, class, and cultural capital in family-school relationships. *Sociology of Education, 72*, 37–53. doi: 10.2307/2673185

Lau, A. S., Jernewall, N. M., Zane, N., & Myers, H. F. (2002). Correlates of suicidal behaviors among Asian American outpatient youths. *Cultural Diversity and Ethnic Minority Psychology, 8*, 199–213. doi: 10.1037/1099-9809

McDonald, C. C., & Richmond, T. R. (2008). The relationship between community violence exposure and mental health symptoms in urban adolescents. *Journal of Psychiatric and Mental Health Nursing, 15*, 833–849. doi: 10.111/j.1365-2850.2008.01321.x

Mendez, J. J., Bauman, S., & Guillory, R. M. (2012). Bullying of Mexican immigrant students by Mexican American students: An examination of intracultural bullying. *Hispanic Journal of Behavioral Sciences, 34*, 279–304. doi: 10.1177/0739986311435970

Natvig, G. K., Albrektsen, G., & Qvarnstrøm, U. (2001). School-related stress experience as a risk factor for bullying behavior. *Journal of Youth and Adolescence, 30*, 561–575. doi: 10.1023/A:1010448604838

Nyborg, V. M., & Curry, J. F. (2003). The impact of perceived racism: Psychological symptoms among African American boys. *Journal of Clinical Child and Adolescent Psychology, 32*, 258–266. doi: 10.1207/S15374424JCCP3202_11

Olson, L. M., & Wahab, S. (2006). American Indians and suicide: A neglected area of research. *Trauma, Violence, and Abuse, 7*, 19–33. doi: 10.1177/1524838005283005

Payne, J. S. (2012). Influence of race and symptom expression on clinicians' depressive disorder identification in African American men. *Journal of the Society for Social Work and Research, 3*, 162–177. doi: 10.5243/jsswr.2012.11

Peskin, M. F., Tortolero, S. R., Markham, C. M., Addy, R. C., & Baumler, E. R. (2007). Bullying and victimization and internalizing symptoms among low-income black and Hispanic students. *Journal of Adolescent Health, 40*, 372–375. doi: 10.1016/j.jadohealth.2006.10.010

Qin, D. B., Way, N., & Rana, M. (2008). The "model minority" and their discontent: Examining peer discrimination and harassment of Chinese American immigrant youth. *New Directions for Child and Adolescent Development, 121*, 27–42. doi: 10.1002/cd.221

Rhee, S., Chang, J., & Rhee, J. (2003). Acculturation, communication patterns, and self-esteem among Asian and Caucasian American adolescents. *Adolescence, 38*, 749–768.

Rosenbloom, S. R., & Way, N. (2004). Experiences of discrimination among African American, Asian American, and Latino adolescents in an urban high school. *Youth and Society, 35*, 420–451. doi: 10.1177/0044118X03261479

Smith, P. K., Cowie, H., Olafsson, R. F., & Liefooghe, A. P.D. (2002). Definitions of bullying: A comparison of terms used, and age and gender differences, in a fourteen-country international comparison. *Child Development, 73*, 1119–1133. doi: 10.111/1467-8624.00461

Storch, E. A., Brassard, M. R., & Masia-Warner, C. L. (2003). The relationship of peer victimization to social anxiety and loneliness in adolescence. *Child Study Journal, 33*, 1–18.

Tsai, J. L., & Chentsova-Dutton, Y. (2002). Understanding depression across cultures. In I. Gotlib & C. Hammen (Eds.), *Handbook of Depression* (pp. 467–491). New York: Guilford Press.

Tsai, J. L., Chentsova-Dutton, Y., Freire-Bebeau, L., & Przymus, D. E. (2002). Emotional expression and physiology in European Americans and Hmong Americans. *Emotion, 2*, 380–397. doi: 10.1037/1528-3542.2.4.380

Truman, J. L., & Planty, M. (2012). *Criminal Victimization, 2011.* (U.S. Department of Justice, Bureau of Justice Statistics, BJS Bulletin). Retrieved from http://www.bjs.gov/content/pub/pdf.

U.S. Census Bureau (2012). 2012 national population projections: Summary tables. Percent distribution of the projected population by race and Hispanic origin for the United States: 2015 to 2060. Retrieved on August 10, 2013, from http://www.census.gov/population/projections/data/national/2012/summarytables.html.

Wadsworth, T., & Kubrin, C. E. (2007). Hispanic suicide in U.S. metropolitan areas: Examining the effects of immigration, assimilation, affluence, and disadvantage. *American Journal of Sociology, 112*, 1848–1885. doi: 10.1086/512711

Wang, J., Iannotti, R. J., Luk, J. W., & Nansel, T. R. (2010). Co-occurrence of victimization from five subtypes of bullying: Physical, verbal, social exclusion, spreading rumors, and cyber. *Journal of Pediatric Psychology, 35*, 1103–1112. doi: 10.1093/jpepsy/jsq048

Woolley, M. E., & Bowen, G. L. (2007). In the context of risk: Supportive adults and the school engagement of middle school students. *Family Relations, 56*, 92–104. doi: 10.1111/j.1741-3729.2007.00442.x

Zayas, L. H., Lester, R. J., Cabassa, L. J., & Fortuna, L. R. (2005). Why do so many Latina teens attempt suicide? A conceptual model for research. *American Journal of Orthopsychiatry, 75*, 275–287. doi: 10.1037/0002-9432.75.2.275

9

Cultural Competence and Prevention Programming

CYNTHIA HUDLEY

Violence against youth in America, whether self-directed or perpetrated by others, continues to be a serious social problem, with surprising variations by race/ethnicity and gender. In 2010, suicide was the fourth leading cause of death among all youth ages 10–14 and the third leading cause of death among those ages 15–19 (Centers for Disease Control and Prevention, 2013). Furthermore, in 2009, 28% of students in grades 6–12 reported that they experienced bullying at school or electronic (cyber) bullying (DeVoe & Bauer, 2011). Within these national figures, rates of suicide, bullying, and victimization differ by a variety of demographic indicators (e.g., race/ethnicity, social class, gender, sexual orientation). For example, suicide rates among ethnic minority adolescents, particularly males, have been increasing for the past decade, although white youth continue to show higher suicide rates overall (Balis & Postolache, 2008). Gender-nonconforming youth consider and attempt suicide at rates significantly higher than their peers (D'Augelli, Hershberger, & Pilkington, 2001). Data, while mixed, suggest that bullying and victimization are influenced by ecological factors that also vary by demographic and geographic variables. For example, some data suggest that while bullying may not vary significantly by race or ethnicity among adolescents (Hepburn, Azrael, Molnar, & Miller, 2012), victimization by peers is greater for ethnic minority and recent immigrant students (Peguero, 2012). Furthermore, victimization predicts the development of internalizing symptoms in early adolescence, and this is particularly true for all adolescent females and low-income adolescents (Zwierzynska, Wolke, & Lereya, 2013). Of perhaps the greatest concern, some self-report data indicate that any involvement with bullying (as bully, victim, or bully-victim) is a substantial and reliable predictor of suicidal ideation and suicide attempts (Hepburn et al., 2012),

The persistence of suicide and suicide attempts among adolescents is a continuing social problem to be addressed in order to stanch needless loss of life and emotional upheaval for both youth and their families. Those who experience bullying in any form are equally vulnerable to mental health difficulties related to social and personal adjustment, including heightened risk for suicidal ideation and suicide attempts. Youth violence-prevention programming to address these major mental health concerns must effectively integrate bullying and suicide prevention into comprehensive intervention packages (Lubell & Vetter, 2006) that include early identification, appropriate intervention, and continued follow-up. Most important for this discussion, a recent review of youth violence prevention programming suggests that bullying prevention programs, by far more prevalent that suicide prevention programs for adolescents, have shown limited effectiveness. However such programs demonstrate more effectiveness when they are attentive to a variety of ecological factors, including the racial and ethnic makeup of the school and community (Hong & Espelage, 2012). Such findings point to the significance of culturally competent intervention practice.

CULTURE AND PREVENTION PROGRAMS

A model of cultural competence that I have described to guide youth violence-prevention practice (Hudley, 2008; Hudley, 2011; Hudley & Taylor, 2006) adopts the definition of *culture* as a set of variable, loosely organized systems of meanings (e.g., beliefs, values, goals) that shape ways of living and are learned and shared by an identifiable group of people (Kitayama, 2002). These systems organize group members' psychological processes and behaviors (e.g., social norms, communication styles, rituals) to successfully adapt within a particular ecocultural niche. Why, one might ask, should culture so defined have an influence on prevention and intervention programming?

This view of culture is particularly valuable, as it links culture in meaningful ways to thought and behavior and suggests that prevention and intervention practice will have a far greater chance for success when framed and presented in ways that are appropriate to participants' cultural niches. Such culturally competent programming should increase the attractiveness and motivational impetus of prevention programs. Youth and communities must actually believe that intervention programming is relevant to their circumstances and capable of effecting real change if programs are to be successful and sustainable. There is compelling evidence that theory and practice developed in one cultural context may not apply successfully in another context. Such findings are not surprising once we understand culture as the system that organizes adaptation to a unique environment. Thus, prevention and intervention programs for youth bullying and suicide prevention will be most effective of they if they are framed in ecologically valid, culturally competent principles and practices.

A MODEL OF CULTURALLY COMPETENT INTERVENTION

The model that I have developed defines a series of principles that define cultural competence. Drawing on literature from the domains of mental health and multicultural education (Hudley & Taylor, 2006), this model of cultural competence comprises three elements:

1. The requisite self-knowledge, attitudes, and skills that allow youth-serving professionals to be effective with diverse populations of students. This

usage is similar to the existing definition of cultural competence in the mental health field. I use the term *culturally effective* to refer to this specific subdomain of cultural competence that addresses practitioner competence.

2. Intervention methods and programming that are responsive to and respectful of youths' cultures and communities. Curricula will present materials and strategies in ways that support participants' and families' cultural values and practices. I use the term *culturally responsive* to refer to this specific subdomain of cultural competence that refers to programmatic adequacy and appropriateness.
3. Program goals and desired outcomes that support participants' ability to successfully navigate their own ecocultural niche. This includes cultural pride, a positive sense of self, and the critical awareness to challenge inequality of all kinds. I use the term *culturally engaged* to refer to this specific subdomain of cultural competence that describes desired outcomes.

The culturally effective program leader is one with self-knowledge, the first component of cultural effectiveness. Self-knowledge comprises both an awareness of one's own culturally constructed worldview and the understanding that one's worldview is the product of prior life history and experience. Cultural effectiveness is virtually unattainable for program providers in the absence of self-knowledge. Self-knowledge is a precursor to understanding how participants' cultural systems organize behavior, and it makes visible the distorting power of one's own worldview. It is important to remember that an ethnic match per se is no assurance of matching worldviews between participant and client. Effective leaders understand and use culturally based interventions;, they are also able to translate general interventions into strategies that are appropriate for a given cultural group. Finally, culturally effective leaders must facilitate effective communication and interaction across cultural divides.

Culturally responsive methods and materials must empower students from non-dominant racial, ethnic, and social status groups to function successfully in their ecocultural niches as well as becoming skilled at navigating the dominant culture. Culturally responsive programming should make visible the existence of multiple cultural realms, the multiple and often competing demands that each context will exert, and the institutional bias that follows from the reality of cultural hegemony. To do this, program materials must develop critical thinking and analysis skills that will help students identify the bias inherent in culturally defined worldviews in a manner similar to the awareness that is necessary for a culturally effective leader. Culturally responsive materials teach students to respect and honor their own unique capacities, understand and honor the basic humanity in us all, and reject both interpersonal and intrapersonal violence based on individual behavior or characteristics. Specific activities for culturally responsive programming might include motivational speakers from various backgrounds drawn from the local community; a cultural history of the local neighborhoods; political organizing to address issues of crime victimization and social services; or cross-age mentoring in which youth are mentored by trained, caring members of the community and in turn mentor peers and younger students. In the process, youth develop leadership and organizational skills as well as a strong cultural identity, important tools that will support success in the mainstream culture.

The model makes it clear that culturally competent youth services must attend specifically to youth outcomes. Culturally effective leaders and culturally responsive programs provide the appropriate context; however, these elements are necessary, not sufficient. Therefore, cultural engagement is arguably the most important element in our model. Recall that culturally competent programs support each participant's capacity to navigate his or her own ecocultural niche successfully. For example, interdependence, communalism, and spirituality are all salient values of the traditional cultures of many non-dominant racial/ethnic communities in the United States (Hill, Soriano, Chen, & LaFromboise, 1994) that are explicitly in conflict with both interpersonal and intrapersonal violence. Commitment to and pride in these traditional values can also protect against the debilitating effects of racism and negative stereotypes, known risk factors for the development of antisocial behavior (Utsey, Chae, Brown, & Kelly, 2002).

With pride in and affirmation of their own cultural values as a base, youth are better prepared to develop bicultural competence. Bicultural competence comprises skills that allow participants to access the mainstream opportunity structure without feeling they are compromising their identity or "selling out." This "alternation model" of bicultural competence has shown a positive relationship with cognitive functioning, mental health, and self-esteem (LaFromboise, Coleman, & Gerton, 1993), all characteristics that militate against the hopelessness that can be a precursor of violent, antisocial, or suicidal behavior. This definition of cultural competence also incorporates a critical understanding of the role of culture in shaping one's beliefs, values, and behavior. Such understanding will lead participants to value their own unique personal characteristics, value cultural diversity, promote social interaction across cultural lines, and challenge acts of hatred and violence.

Elements of cultural engagement are subject to developmental processes (e.g., identity development); thus, the construct will take age-appropriate forms. We would expect cultural knowledge, attitudes, and bicultural competence to evolve as normative development progresses. For example, in childhood, participants may be developing an awareness of their own ethnic and cultural heritage, as well as distinguishing their cultural heritage from those of other groups. Cultural engagement at this age will take the form of increasing cultural knowledge and positive attitudes towards participants' own heritages as well as the heritages of groups other than their own. This form of cultural engagement should be effective in allaying or forestalling the development of negative attitudes toward one's own group or other groups and developing participants' critical reasoning concerning fairness and social justice.

By early adolescence, children of color in particular have typically formed a stable ethnic identity (Phinney, 1999) and have an awareness of the broader society's attitudes toward their particular sociocultural group. They will be ready to build on a foundation of cultural knowledge and critical thinking skills. Cultural engagement for this age group might take the form of involvement in cooperative activities (e.g., community improvement projects, peer mediation) to support justice and equality. As youth move through adolescence, cultural engagement should comprise bicultural competence, a developmental process that will occur throughout adolescence and beyond. Youth at this stage and beyond will increasingly master the capacity to function successfully in the milieu of the dominant cultural group and at the same time remain grounded in their home culture. Youth are thus buffered by a strong sense of positive identity. Building on experiences gained in school and community projects, cultural engagement will take the form of a progressively greater commitment to combat injustice, violence, and hatred of all kinds.

In closing, I would like to make explicit one final, important caveat concerning this model. Cultural competence is a developmental process that needs to be periodically revisited. Culture is a complex, evolving, living system that cannot be reified in a curriculum or training manual. Thus those who work in programs that serve youth must engage in ongoing processes of program- and self-evaluation to assure the relevance of particular program leaders and content to the culture(s) they are intended to serve.

REFERENCES

Balis, T. & Postolache, T. (2008). Ethnic differences in adolescent suicide in the United States. *International Journal of Child Health and Human Development, 1*, 281–296.

Centers for Disease Control and Prevention (2013). Youth violence: National statistics. Retrieved from the CDC website: http://www.cdc.gov/violenceprevention/youthviolence/stats_at-a_glance/national_stats.html.

D'Augelli, A. R., Hershberger, S. L., & Pilkington, N. W. (2001). Suicidality patterns and sexual orientation–related factors among lesbian, gay, and bisexual youths. *Suicide and Life-Threatening Behavior, 31*, 250–264. doi: 10.1521/suli.31.3.250.24246

DeVoe, J., & Bauer, L. (2011). Student victimization in U.S. schools: Results. From the *2009 School Crime Supplement to the National Crime Victimization Survey* (NCES 2012–314). U.S. Department of Education, National Center for Education Statistics. Washington, DC: U.S. Government Printing Office.

Hepburn, L., Azrael, D., Molnar, B., & Miller, M. (2012). Bullying and suicidal behaviors among urban high school youth. *Journal of Adolescent Health, 51*, 93–95. Available at http://dx.doi.org/10.1016/j.jadohealth.2011.12.014.

Hill, H., Soriano, F., Chen, S., & LaFromboise, T. (1994). Sociocultural factors in the etiology and prevention of violence among ethnic minority youth. In L. Eron, J. Gentry, & R. Schlegel (Eds.), *Reason to Hope: A Psychosocial Perspective on Violence and Youth* (pp. 59–97). Washington, DC: American Psychological Association.

Hong, J., & Espelage, D. (2012). A review of research on bullying and peer victimization in school: An ecological system analysis. *Aggression and Violent Behavior, 17*, 311–322. http://dx.doi.org/10.1016/j.avb.2012.03.003

Hudley, C. (2008). *You Did That on Purpose: Understanding and Changing Children's Aggression.* New Haven, CT: Yale University Press.

Hudley, C. (2011). Ethics and intervention programming. In A. Lemelle, W. Reed, & S. Taylor (Eds.), *Handbook of African American Health: Social and Behavioral Interventions* (pp. 35–44). New York: Springer.

Hudley, C., & Taylor, A. (2006). Cultural competence and youth violence prevention programming. In N. Guerra & E. Smith (Eds.), *Ethnicity, Culture, and Youth Violence Prevention Programming* (pp. 249–269). Washington, DC: American Psychological Association.

Kitayama, S. (2002) Culture and basic psychological processes—toward a system view of culture: Comment on Oyserman et al. (2002). *Psychological Bulletin*, *128*, 89–96. http://dx.doi.org/10.1037/0033-2909.128.1.89

LaFromboise, T., Coleman, H., & Gerton, J. (1993). Psychological impact of biculturalism: Evidence and theory. *Psychological Bulletin*, *114*, 395–412. http://dx.doi.org/10.1037/0033-2909.114.3.395

Lubell, K., & Vetter, J., 2006). Suicide and youth violence prevention: The promise of an integrated approach. *Aggression and Violent Behavior*, *11*, 167–175. http://dx.doi.org/10.1016/j.avb.2005.07.006

Peguero, A. (2012). Schools, bullying, and inequality: Intersecting factors and complexities with the stratification of youth victimization at school. *Sociology Compass*, *6/5*, 402–412. Available at http://dx.doi.org/10.1111/j.1751-9020.2012.00459.x.

Phinney, J. (1999). The structure of ethnic identity in young adolescents from diverse cultural groups. *Journal of Early Adolescence*, *19*, 301–322. Available at http://dx.doi.org/10.1177/0272431699019003001.

Utsey, S., Chae, M, Brown, C., & Kelly, D. (2002). Effect of ethnic group membership on ethnic identity, race-related stress and quality of life. *Cultural Diversity & Ethnic Minority Psychology*, *8*, 366–377.

Zwierzynska, K., Wolke, D., & Lereya, T. (2013). Peer victimization in childhood and internalizing problems in adolescence: A prospective longitudinal study. *Journal of Abnormal Child Psychology*, *41*, 309–323. doi: 10.1007/s10802-012-9678-8

10

Suicide Ideation Among Sexual Minority Youth

The Effects of Bullying and Possible Protective Factors

V. PAUL POTEAT AND IAN RIVERS ■

Sexual minority youth (i.e., lesbian, gay, bisexual, transgender, or questioning [LGBTQ]) continue to experience sizable physical and mental health disparities compared to their heterosexual peers. These range from anxiety, depression, suicidality, and lower self-esteem, to substance use (D'Augelli, Pilkington, & Hershberger, 2002; Friedman, Koeske, Silvestre, Korr, & Sites, 2006; Poteat, Aragon, Espelage, & Koenig, 2009). Such disparities have been connected to a range of precipitating factors such as higher rates of peer victimization or parental rejection (Doty, Willoughby, Lindahl, & Malik, 2010; Poteat, Mereish, DiGiovanni, & Koenig, 2011; Rivers, 2001; Ryan, Huebner, Diaz, & Sanchez, 2009). Among these disparities, suicidality remains especially concerning, whether ideation or attempts (Eisenberg & Resnick, 2006; Liu & Mustanski, 2012; Poteat et al., 2009; Rosario, Schrimshaw, & Hunter, 2005). The findings in the research literature underscore the continued need to identify factors that elevate suicidality risk. At the same time, recent advances have identified factors that buffer this risk (Eisenberg & Resnick, 2006; Goodenow, Szalacha, & Westheimer, 2006; Poteat et al., 2011). In this chapter, we review findings on suicidality among sexual minority youth while noting variability among subgroups of youth in this community; we consider a range of individual and contextual factors that underlie these disparities; and we note factors that attenuate suicidality risks among sexual minority youth. Finally, we note implications for future research, prevention, and intervention, as well as policies in this area.

SUICIDALITY RISK AMONG SEXUAL MINORITY YOUTH RELATIVE TO HETEROSEXUAL YOUTH

For this chapter, we focus our attention on suicidal ideation and attempted suicide among sexual minority youth. We also should note that there is a developing body of research on non-suicidal self-injury among sexual minorities, and it is important to acknowledge the shared purpose and concerns underpinning this research (House, Van Horn, Coppeans, & Stepleman, 2011; Sornberger, Smith, Toste, & Heath, 2013). Furthermore, some scholars have pointed to the need to distinguish between ideation and attempts, because prevalence rates and their associations with other factors may differ (Gilman, Cochran, Mays, Hughes, Ostrow, & Kessler, 2001). For instance, one study found that differences between sexual minorities and heterosexuals were distinct for suicidal ideation versus attempts: sexual orientation differences on ideation were more evident for females, and differences on attempts were more evident for males (Gilman et al., 2001). Most studies, however, have not made this distinction; therefore, researchers have tended to focus on factors that predict elevated risk on both ideation and attempts.

Reported rates of suicidal ideation and attempts among sexual minority youth vary depending on sampling approaches and how sexual orientation is operationalized. Nevertheless, research over the span of several decades has consistently shown that sexual minority youth report higher levels of suicidality than heterosexual youth, in terms of both ideation and attempts (Eisenberg & Resnick, 2006; Remafedi, French, Story, Resnick, & Blum, 1998; Russell & Toomey, 2012). A meta-analysis of multiple studies showed overall that lesbian, gay, and bisexual individuals were more than twice as likely to report suicide attempts (King et al., 2008). Further emphasizing the seriousness of suicidality during adolescence, emerging studies suggest that the discrepancy in rates of suicidality between sexual minorities and heterosexuals is more prominent during this period relative to adulthood, at least among males (Russell & Toomey, 2012).

Based on their shared experience of societal marginalization, there is justification and utility in examining suicidality among sexual minority youth collectively; yet this masks potential variability in their experiences. Specific studies have shown that suicide attempts are most elevated for gay and bisexual males (Garofalo, Wolf, Wissow, Woods, & Goodman, 1999). The meta-analysis by King and colleagues (2008) indicated that gay and bisexual males were more than four times as likely as heterosexuals to report suicide attempts in their lifetime. Further, Hatzenbuehler (2011) has shown that higher rates of suicide attempts among sexual minority youth were directly correlated with social-environmental factors (lack of sexual minority representation in the community, political conservatism, lack of gay-straight alliances or GSAs in schools, and the absence of non-discrimination and anti-bullying policies). Thus, suicidality disparities have been well established, and studies have now begun to identify some variability in levels of risk for sexual minority youth within the general population.

There are, however, areas in which we have limited knowledge. The majority of studies have focused on variability based upon gender. While this has highlighted differences between gay and lesbian youth, it has failed to give adequate attention to other groups, including bisexual and questioning youth as well as transgender youth. Several studies have shown distinct patterns of risk for these youth (Grossman

& D'Augelli, 2007; Poteat et al., 2009; Robinson & Espelage, 2011). Additionally, few theoretical frameworks have been offered to explain these distinct patterns. Furthermore, there has been limited attention given to differences among sexual minority youth based on other social identities (e.g., ability, race, socioeconomic status). Some emerging studies among adults have documented elevated suicidality risks among sexual minorities of color relative to white sexual minorities (Cochran, Mays, Alegria, Ortega, & Takeuchi, 2007) and elevated health risks more broadly (Balsam, Huang, Fieland, Simoni, & Walters, 2004; Greene, 2000), but attention to youth has been much more limited (Consolacion, Russell, & Sue, 2004; Poteat et al., 2011; Ryan et al., 2009).

THE CONNECTION BETWEEN BULLYING AND SUICIDALITY AMONG SEXUAL MINORITY YOUTH

It is important to consider how sexual orientation disparities in suicidality are a consequence of multiple underlying factors. Minority stress theory (Meyer, 2003) offers a model to understand the processes that lead to this disparity. Beyond the range of general life stressors experienced by sexual minorities, they also face unique and chronic stressors tied to their marginalized status in society. These stressors are both distal and proximal in nature. Distal stressors include external experiences such as discrimination, while proximal stressors represent internal psychological processes such as internalized homophobia or rejection sensitivity. Ecological systems theory (Bronfenbrenner, 1979) can be combined with minority stress theory to consider distal stressors as well as protective factors as various levels. Ecological systems theory situates individuals within social systems that range from the immediate microsystem (e.g., families, peers, schools) to the broader macrosystem (e.g., culture and societal values).

Stressors for sexual minority youth have been identified in many ecological systems. These include family rejection, concealment pressure across contexts, and peer harassment (Hershberger & D'Augelli, 1995; Lasser & Tharinger, 2003; Ryan et al., 2009; Poteat & Rivers, 2010). Given the focus of this text on bullying, we train our attention on this particular connection. We emphasize, however, that peer victimization is only one of the many forms of discrimination faced by sexual minority youth that contribute to an increased risk of suicide.

There is a strong connection between victimization and elevated suicidal ideation and attempts among sexual minority youth (Friedman et al., 2006; Goldblum et al., 2013; Poteat et al., 2011; Rivers 2001). Moreover, homophobic victimization is associated with exponentially higher levels of suicidal ideation and attempts, compared to victimization that is not homophobic or bias-based (Russell, Sinclair, Poteat, & Koenig, 2012). Russell and colleagues (2012) found that those who experienced general victimization absent of bias were 2.86 times as likely to report suicidal ideation in the past month and 2.46 times as likely to report having attempted suicide in the past year as non-victimized youth. In comparison, youth who had experienced homophobic victimization were 5.82 times as likely to report suicidal ideation and 5.80 times as likely to report having attempted suicide as non-victimized youth. This indicates the need to assess for the types of victimization that youth experience in order to more accurately determine risk. Although these findings have been based predominantly on single time-point studies, recent longitudinal findings offer stronger prospective evidence of this connection. Based on repeated assessments of victimization and suicidality among a diverse sample of sexual minority youth, Liu and Mustanski (2012) found that earlier reports of victimization by these youth predicted their ensuing levels of suicidality.

It is important to note that victimization often involves multiple individuals. In addition to the individual who may be considered the primary aggressor, other students often reinforce this individual, while still others observe the incident (Salmivalli, Lagerspetz, Björkqvist, Österman, & Kaukiainen, 1996). This dynamic also is evident for homophobic bullying and harassment (Poteat & Rivers, 2010). Sexual minority adults have reported that often they were victimized by groups of peers as opposed to single individuals (Rivers, 2001). This dynamic may partly explain why homophobic victimization is especially traumatic for sexual minority youth. Other findings indicate that witnessing the victimization of others is associated with elevated health risks (D'Augelli et al., 2002; Rivers, Poteat, Noret, & Ashurst, 2009), including suicidal ideation (Rivers & Noret, 2013). Sexual minority youth who observe the victimization of other sexual minority peers may experience secondary trauma or a heightened sense of vulnerability, which may contribute to increased risk of suicide.

There are other relevant ecological factors that further contextualize the association between victimization and suicidality. School climate, safety, and belonging are relevant in this regard. These factors represent a broader sense of isolation that is connected to victimization. Many sexual minority youth report feeling unsafe and unwelcome at school (Goodenow et al., 2006; Szalacha, 2003), which itself is associated with elevated suicidal ideation and attempts (Poteat et al., 2011). A diminished sense of belonging on this large a scale may explain its added significance in accounting for elevated reports of suicidal ideation and attempts. These findings underscore the need for practitioners to adopt more than an individualistic approach in their work with sexual minority youth; rather, a broader approach is needed to address how factors at the contextual level contribute to suicide risk among these youth. Indeed, researchers, practitioners, and policy advocates have emphasized the need for programs to promote safer and more welcoming schools for youth (Russell, Kosciw, Horn, & Saewyc, 2010).

PROTECTIVE FACTORS AND BUFFERS AGAINST SUICIDE RISK AMONG SEXUAL MINORITY YOUTH

Much of the research on sexual minority youth has focused on the basic documentation of health risks and sources of risk, with less attention being paid to protective factors and those that promote resilience. Nevertheless, studies are beginning to identify a range of individual and contextual factors that serve as sources of support and that mitigate risk for sexual minority youth. We provide a brief overview of some of these factors in relation to risk of suicide.

It is critical for sexual minority youth to receive support from multiple outlets. Family support and acceptance as well as adult support in general are associated with lower suicidal ideation and attempts (Eisenberg & Resnick, 2006; Goodenow et al., 2006; Poteat et al., 2011). Yet, there is mixed evidence as to whether parent, adult, or peer support directly attenuate the effects of victimization on levels of suicidality or psychological distress (Doty et al., 2010; Poteat et al., 2011). Ryan and colleagues (2009) have suggested that health professionals have a role to play with families in supporting the acceptance of sexual minority youth. Health professionals, such as nurse practitioners, often come into contact with sexual minority youth at a point of crisis where individual or family adjustment to a young person's "coming out" has not been positive. Where family acceptance is low, Ryan and colleagues found that 38.8% of youth reported suicidal thoughts in the past six months, with 56.8% having made at least one suicide attempt during their lifetime. By comparison, among youth in families with moderate acceptance, 22.9% reported suicidal thoughts in the past six months, and 36.1% had made at least one suicide attempt during their lifetime. Among those in families with high levels of acceptance, rates were 18.5% and 30.9%, respectively. Thus, it does seem that social support promotes the overall health and well-being of sexual minority youth and is associated with lower levels of suicidal ideation and suicide attempts. However, it is less clear whether these support structures have strong or consistent buffering effects for youth who experience victimization. Qualitative research on the long-term effects of homophobic bullying has found that adults who recalled having friendship networks and strong family or community ties outside school reported better mental health in later life and greater resilience than those who had few friends or links with community organizations in adolescence (Rivers, 2011). For sexual minority youth in particular, additional research is needed to identify forms of support that may be most beneficial. For example, the extent to which support mitigates the effects of victimization on suicide risk may vary according to the type of support provided (e.g., emotional, instrumental, or informational) and whether the support is sexual orientation–specific (i.e., support that directly affirms the sexual orientation of youth).

In terms of specific care for sexual minority youth in distress, Kreiss and Patterson (1997) discussed the role of primary-care providers in delivering dedicated frontline services in the community. Their assessment of the utilization of those services provided to these youth shows that, in addition to basic health care, dedicated services succeed where they offer a safe space for young people, have specialists trained in the health care of sexual minorities (including mental health care), and establish referral protocols to key service providers (e.g., emergency housing, law enforcement, counseling, and education). For sexual minority youth bullied at school, school counselors, psychologists and nurses often represent this frontline service and have to rely upon generic clinical skills when a young person comes to them in distress, unless specifically trained in sexual minority issues (Rivers, Duncan, & Besag, 2007). Additionally, other professionals who are regular visitors to the school environment, rather than permanent members of the faculty or staff, are sometimes approached by sexual minority youth for advice and guidance. Where support or a safe space is offered that allows these youth to disclose and talk through their issues and concerns, the likelihood of self-harm diminishes.

School-based support is incredibly important, and researchers have explored the role of structures and policies within schools that may promote the health of sexual minority youth. For example, several studies have considered the role and effects of gay-straight alliances (GSAs) in relation to this. Generally, findings indicate that sexual minority youth in schools with GSAs report lower risk on a range of health and academic indices than youth in schools without GSAs (Goodenow et al., 2006; Heck, Flentje, & Cochran, 2011; Poteat, Sinclair, DiGiovanni, Koenig, & Russell, 2013; Walls, Kane, & Wisneski, 2010). Notably, this includes lower reported suicidal ideation and attempts (Poteat et al., 2013). In addition, researchers have pointed to the importance of an inclusive curriculum that represents sexual minorities, anti-discrimination policies that specifically denote the protection of sexual minority youth, and anti-bullying programs that cover issues of diversity (Chesir-Teran & Hughes, 2009; Russell et al., 2010). These policies and practices have been linked to students' greater perceptions of safety and belonging at school (Russell et al., 2010), as well as to lower levels of suicide attempts (Hatzenbuehler, 2011).

Additionally, Ollis (2013) has advocated for professional learning or continuing professional development (CPD) for teachers and those working in schools. Targeted CPD addressing issues associated with gender-related and sexuality-related violence, including homophobia, have been shown to enhance teachers' personal and professional confidence in managing critical incidents as well as actively supporting the enforcement of anti-bullying and non-discrimination policies (Ollis, 2013). Additionally, using a theory-led framework to embed such learning can be useful in providing a social as well as policy-driven context to issues relevant to the well-being of sexual minority youth. For example, for nurse education, Morrissey and Rivers (1997) have suggested that the Mims-Swenson Sexual Health Model is useful in structuring professional learning. It is a four-stage process to learning wherein nurses first explore the ways in which attitudes and behaviors are molded by the social environment. They then move through a process of self-reflection in which their own levels of personal awareness are raised to an intermediate stage where they focus on ways of communicating effectively and non-judgmentally with service users. Finally, they reach an advanced stage in the learning process where they are able to integrate technical information with theory and policy and offer appropriately informed practice and referral.

Ollis (2013) and Morrissey and Rivers (1997) argue strongly that professional learning in both education and healthcare cannot be delivered effectively without the support of those in authority and a commitment to education on sexual minority issues. Morrissey and Rivers, for example, suggest that a 12-week course for health care professionals is essential to ensure that effective care is provided; while Ollis suggested that teachers need at least two days' training to fully understand the issues surrounding gender-related and sexuality-related violence.

CONCLUSION AND FUTURE DIRECTIONS

We have noted in this chapter that research over several decades has consistently shown that sexual minority youth report higher levels of suicidality than do heterosexual youth. However, this research has, to date, failed to pay adequate attention to the prevalence of suicide ideation as well as risk and protective factors among bisexual and questioning youth as well as transgender youth. Additionally, we have noted that few studies have applied solid theoretical frameworks to support our understanding of variability within the sexual minority youth community on suicide risk. Taking an ecological systems theory approach provides a useful meta-theoretical framework in which to understand the discrimination and victimization experienced by sexual minorities, and, when such a framework is coupled with Meyer's minority stress theory (2003), it is possible to construct a model wherein stressors such as family rejection, concealment pressure in various social contexts, and peer harassment can result in thoughts of suicide. Similarly, factors such as school climate, safety, and belonging have been found to be highly relevant to the narrative of suicide ideation. Positive school climates, together with family support and acceptance as well as adult support in general, are associated with lower suicide ideation and attempts. Currently, we do not understand fully how these various risk and protective factors interact. Additional research is needed to identify forms of support that may be most beneficial and that may lessen or mitigate the long-term harm caused by other systemic forms of discrimination. Such support may come from professionals who work with sexual minority youth and who have undertaken specialist training or professional development. Alternatively, providing sexual minority youth with supportive environments independent of their home or other community institutions that can act as stressors may have a positive impact upon youth well-being. Finally, there is a need for policy makers to acknowledge the diversity that exists within populations and communities and provide the resources and leadership to support minorities and tackle discrimination where and when it occurs.

Suggestions for Medical and Mental Health Providers

- Incorporate specialist training on sexual minority issues into professional learning and continuing professional development.
- Build a network of specialist advisory and referral agencies (including not-for-profit organizations) in the local area that offer clinical, educational, and social support interventions.
- Ensure training and refresher events are offered regularly for all staff.
- Monitor the number of sexual minority service users and adapt training to address local issues.
- Include sexual minority volunteers or advocates on steering groups and working parties to develop services.

Suggestions for Parents and Teachers

Parents

- Do not be afraid to talk to your child about her/his sexual minority identity.
- Express affection, validation, and support when a child "comes out."
- Seek advice from your local chapter of PFLAG or FFLAG.
- Be an advocate for your child whenever s/he faces discrimination or abuse.
- Engage with organizations and events that support sexual minority youth and families.
- Connect your child with local organizations and support groups.
- When faith is a relevant part of your child's life, make efforts to connect with affirming faith communities.

- Be active in communicating with your child about issues related to dating, healthy romantic relationships, and sexual health; make efforts to know your child's partner.
- Start saving for the wedding.

Teachers

- Ensure that sexual orientation and gender identity are included in non-discrimination and anti-bullying policies.
- Check the state board of education's policies on sexual orientation discrimination.
- Seek support from local LGBT agencies when you encounter homophobia or sexual minority youth experiencing harassment.
- Regularly audit your class and school to check that homophobic abuse is addressed.
- Consider introducing a gay-straight alliance in your school.

Suggestions for Policy Makers

- Advocate for non-discrimination and anti-bullying legislation, and the inclusion of clauses relating to sexual orientation and gender-identity discrimination.
- Work collaboratively with organizations that support sexual minority rights and inclusion, and seek their advice on legislative and policy issues.
- Challenge sexual orientation inequalities at the local, state, or national level.
- Advocate for better mental healthcare provision and targeted healthcare services for sexual minorities.
- Initiate efforts to include sexual orientation in national surveys of health and well-being.

REFERENCES

Balsam, K. F., Huang, B., Fieland, K. C., Simoni, J. M., & Walters, K. L. (2004). Culture, trauma, and wellness: A comparison of heterosexual and lesbian, gay, bisexual, and two-spirit Native Americans. *Cultural Diversity and Ethnic Minority Psychology, 10*, 287–301. doi: 10.1037/1099-9809.10.3.287

Bronfenbrenner, U. (1979). *The Ecology of Human Development*. Cambridge, MA: Harvard University Press.

Chesir-Teran, D., & Hughes, D. (2009). Heterosexism in high school and victimization among lesbian, gay, bisexual, and questioning youth. *Journal of Youth and Adolescence, 38*, 963–975. doi: 10.1007/s10964-008-9364-x

Cochran, S. D., Mays, V. M., Alegria, M., Ortega, A. N., & Takeuchi, D. (2007). Mental health and substance use disorders among Latino and Asian American lesbian, gay, and bisexual adults. *Journal of Consulting and Clinical Psychology, 75*, 785–794. doi: 10.1037/0022-006X.75.5.785

Consolacion, T. B., Russell, S. T., & Sue, S. (2004). Sex, race/ethnicity, and romantic attractions: Multiple minority status adolescents and mental health. *Cultural Diversity and Ethnic Minority Psychology, 10*, 200–214. doi: 10.1037/1099-9809.10.3.200

D'Augelli, A. R., Pilkington, N. W., & Hershberger, S. L. (2002). Incidence and mental health impact of sexual orientation victimization of lesbian, gay, and bisexual youths in high school. *School Psychology Quarterly, 17*, 148–167. doi: 10.1521/scpq.17.2.148.20854

Doty, N. D., Willoughby, B. L. B., Lindahl, K. M., & Malik, N. M. (2010). Sexuality related social support among lesbian, gay, and bisexual youth. *Journal of Youth and Adolescence, 39*, 1134–1147. doi: 10.1007/s10964-010-9566-X

Eisenberg, M. E., & Resnick, M. D. (2006). Suicidality among gay, lesbian, and bisexual youth: The role of protective factors. *Journal of Adolescent Health, 39*, 662–668. doi: 10.1016/j.jadohealth.200.04.024

Friedman, M. S., Koeske, G. F., Silvestre, A. J., Korr, W. S., & Sites, E. W. (2006). The impact of gender-role nonconforming behavior, bullying, and social support on suicidality among gay male youth. *Journal of Adolescent Health, 38*, 621–623. doi: 10.1016/j.jadohealth.2005.04.014

Garofalo, R., Wolf, R. C., Wissow, L. S., Woods, E. R., & Goodman, E. (1999). Sexual orientation and risk of suicide attempts among a representative sample of youth. *Archives of Pediatric& Adolescent Medicine, 153*, 487–493.

Gilman, S. E., Cochran, S. D., Mays, V. M., Hughes, M., Ostrow, D., & Kessler, R. C. (2001). Risk of psychiatric disorders among individuals reporting same-sex sexual partners in the National Comorbidity Survey. *American Journal of Public Health, 91*(6), 933–939. doi: 10.2105/AJPH.91.6.933

Goldblum, P., Testa, R. J., Pflum, S., Hendricks, M. L., Bradford, J., & Bongar, B. (2013). The relationship between gender-based victimization and suicide attempts in transgender people. *Professional Psychology: Research and Practice, 43*, 468–475. doi: 10.1037/a0029605

Goodenow, C., Szalacha, L., & Westheimer, K. (2006). School support groups, other school factors, and the safety of sexual minority adolescents. *Psychology in the Schools, 43*, 573–589. doi: 10.1002/pits.20173

Greene, B. (2000). African American lesbian and bisexual women. *Journal of Social Issues, 56*, 239–249. doi: 10.1111/0022-4537.00163

Grossman, A. H., & D'Augelli, A. R. (2007). Transgender youth and life-threatening behaviors. *Suicide and Life-Threatening Behaviors, 37*, 527–537. doi: 10.1521/suli.2007.37.5.527

Hatzenbuehler, M. L. (2011). The social environment and suicide attempts in lesbian, gay, and bisexual youth. *Pediatrics, 127*, 896–903. doi: 10.15421/peds.2010-3020

Heck, N. C., Flentje, A., & Cochran, B. N. (2011). Offsetting risks: High school gay-straight alliances and lesbian, gay, bisexual, and transgender (LGBT) youth. *School Psychology Quarterly, 26*, 161–174. doi: 10.1037/a0023226

Hershberger, S. L., & D'Augelli, A. R. (1995). The impact of victimization on the mental health and suicidality of lesbian, gay, and bisexual youths. *Developmental Psychology, 31*, 65–74. doi: 10.1037/0012-1649.31.1.65

House, A. S., Van Horn, E., Coppeans, C., & Stepleman, L. M. (2011). Interpersonal trauma and discriminatory events as predictors of suicidal and nonsuicidal self-injury in gay, lesbian, bisexual, and transgender persons. *Traumatology, 17*, 75–85. doi: 10.1177/1534765610395621

King, M., Semlyen, J., Tai, S. S., Killaspy, H., Osborn, D., Popelyuk, D., & Nazareth, I. (2008). A systematic review of mental disorder, suicide, and deliberate self harm in lesbian, gay and bisexual people. *BMC Psychiatry, 8*, 70. doi: 10.1186/1471–244X-8-70

Kreiss, J. L., & Patterson, D. L. (1997). Psychosocial issues in primary care of lesbian, gay, bisexual, and transgender youth. *Journal of Pediatric Health Care, 11*, 266–274. doi: 10.1016/S089-5245(97)90082-1

Lasser, J., & Tharinger, D. (2003). Visibility management in school and beyond: A qualitative study of gay, lesbian, and bisexual youth. *Journal of Adolescence, 26*, 233–244. doi: 10.1016/S0140–1971(02)00132-X

Liu, R. T., & Mustanski, B. (2012). Suicidal ideation and self-harm in lesbian, gay, bisexual, and transgender youth. *American Journal of Preventive Medicine, 42*, 221–228. doi: 10.1016/j.amepre.2011.10.023

Meyer, I. H. (2003). Prejudice, social stress, and mental health in lesbian, gay, and bisexual populations: Conceptual issues and research evidence. *Psychological Bulletin, 129*, 674–697. doi: 10.1037/0033-2909.1295.674

Morrissey, M. V., & Rivers, I. (1997). Applying the Mims-Swenson sexual health model to nurse education: Offering an alternative focus on sexuality and health care. *Nurse Education Today, 18*, 488–495. doi: 10.1016/S0260-6917(98)80175-5

Ollis, D. (2013). Planning and delivering intervention to promote gender and sexuality. In I. Rivers, & N. Duncan (Eds.), *Bullying: Experiences and Discourses of Sexuality and Gender* (pp. 145–161). London: Routledge.

Poteat, V. P., Aragon, S. R., Espelage, D. L., & Koenig, B. W. (2009). Psychosocial concerns of sexual minority youth: Complexity and caution in group differences. *Journal of Consulting and Clinical Psychology, 77*, 196–201. doi: 10.1037/a0014158

Poteat, V. P., Mereish, E. H., DiGiovanni, C. D., & Koenig, B. W. (2011). The effects of general and homophobic victimization on adolescents' psychosocial and educational concerns: The importance of intersecting identities and parent support. *Journal of Counseling Psychology, 58*, 597–609. doi: 10.1037/a0025095

Poteat, V. P., & Rivers, I. (2010). The use of homophobic language across bullying roles during adolescence. *Journal of Applied Developmental Psychology, 31*, 166–172. doi: 10.1016/j.appdev.2009.11.005

Poteat, V. P., Sinclair, K. O., DiGiovanni, C. D., Koenig, B. W., & Russell, S. T. (2013). Gay-straight alliances are associated with student health: A multi-school comparison of LGBTQ and heterosexual youth. *Journal of Research on Adolescence, 23*, 319–330. doi: 1111/j.1532-7795.2012.00832.x

Remafedi, G., French, S., Story, M., Resnick, M. D., & Blum, R. (1998). The relationship between suicide risk and sexual orientation: Results of a population-based study. *American Journal of Public Health, 88*, 57–60. doi: 10.2105/AJPH.88.1.57

Rivers, I. (2001). The bullying of sexual minorities at school: Its nature and long-term correlates. *Educational and Child Psychology, 18*, 32–46.

Rivers, I. (2011). *Homophobic Bullying: Research and Theoretical Perspectives.* New York: Oxford University Press.

Rivers, I., Duncan, N., & Besag, V. E. (2007). *Bullying: A Handbook for Educators and Parents.* Westport, CT: Praeger Publishers.

Rivers, I., Poteat, V. P., Noret, N., & Ashurst, N. (2009). Observing bullying at school: The mental health implications of witness status. *School Psychology Quarterly, 24*, 211–223. doi: 10.1037/a0018164

Rivers, I., & Noret, N. (2013). Potential suicide ideation and its association with observing bullying at school. *Journal of Adolescent Health, 53*, s32-s36. doi: 1016/j.jadohealth.2012.10.9

Robinson, J. P., & Espelage, D. L. (2011). Inequities in educational and psychological outcomes between LGBTQ and straight students in middle and high school. *Educational Researcher, 40*, 315–330. doi: 10.3102/0013189X11422112

Rosario, M., Schrimshaw, E. W., & Hunter, J. (2005). Psychological distress following suicidality among gay, lesbian, and bisexual youths: Role of social relationships. *Journal of Youth and Adolescence, 34*, 149–161. doi: 10.1007/s10964-005-3213-y

Russell, S. T., Kosciw, J., Horn, S., & Saewyc, E. (2010). Safe schools policy for LGBTQ students. *Society for Research in Child Development Social Policy Report, 24* (4), 3–17.

Russell, S. T., Sinclair, K. O., Poteat, V. P., & Koenig, B. W. (2012). Adolescent health and harassment based on discriminatory bias. *American Journal of Public Health, 102*, 493–495. doi: 10.2105/AJPH.2011.300430

Russell, S. T., & Toomey, R. B. (2012). Men's sexual orientation and suicide: Evidence for U.S. adolescent-specific risk. *Social Science and Medicine, 74*, 523–529. doi: 10.1016/j.socscimed.2010.07.038

Ryan, C., Huebner, D., Diaz, R. M., & Sanchez, J. (2009). Family rejection as a predictor of negative health outcomes in white and Latino lesbian, gay, and bisexual young adults. *Pediatrics, 123*, 346–352. doi: 10.1542/peds.2007-3524

Salmivalli, C., Lagerspetz, K., Björkqvist, K., Österman, K., & Kaukiainen, A. (1996). Bullying as a group process: Participant roles and their relations to social status within the group. *Aggressive Behavior, 22*, 1–15. doi: 10.1002/(SICI)1098-2337(1996)22:1<1::AID-AB1>3.0.CO;2-

Sornberger, M. J., Smith, N. G., Toste, J. R., & Heath, N. L. (2013). Nonsuicidal self-injury, coping strategies, and sexual orientation. *Journal of Clinical Psychology, 69*, 571–583. doi: 10.1002/jclp.21947

Szalacha, L. A. (2003). Safer sexual diversity climates: Lessons learned from an evaluation of Massachusetts Safe Schools Program for gay and lesbian students. *American Journal of Education, 110*, 58–88. doi: 10.1086/377673

Walls, N. E., Kane, S. B., & Wisneski, H. (2010). Gay-straight alliances and school experiences of sexual minority youth. *Youth and Society, 41*, 307–332. doi: 10.1177/004418X09334957

11

Suicide Risk Among Transgender and Gender-Nonconforming Youth

RYLAN J. TESTA AND MICHAEL L. HENDRICKS ■

As young people develop, they face pressures to exhibit socially desirable traits, behaviors, and identities in multiple domains, including gender. Youth who do not fit these expectations regarding gender are often subjected to negative social consequences, including bullying. In this chapter, we examine the prevalence of bullying experiences in transgender and gender-nonconforming (TGNC) youth, the prevalence of suicidality in these youth, and what the extant research says about the association between bullying and suicide in this population. We also examine how to address these patterns and support the development of healthy youth regardless of their gender identity or expression.

WHO ARE TRANSGENDER AND GENDER-NONCONFORMING YOUTH?

Essentially, TGNC youth comprise a fairly wide range of children and adolescents whose gender identity and/or expression of gender does not match the cultural expectation for the sex that was assigned to them at birth (Conron, Scout, & Austin, 2008; Meier & Labuski, 2013). While most individuals define their gender identity consistently with their assigned birth sex within the binary structure of male or female (Tobin et al., 2010), for some, gender identity and/or expression falls outside the gender binary (e.g., genderqueer, bigender, gender neutral; Kuper, Nussbaum & Mustanski, 2012). The amount of deviation tolerated varies by subculture and by sex assigned at birth, with some cultures evidencing societal acceptance and even reverence of diversity in gender identity and gender expression (Coleman, Colgan, & Gooren, 1992; Feinberg, 1996; Miller & Nichols, 2012; Schmidt, 2003). Among TGNC youth are those whose gender identity does not match their sex assigned at birth, referred to here as "transgender youth." For example, a person who was assigned male at birth might instead identify as a girl or trans woman or as a gender that is other than boy or man. For other TGNC youth, the primary deviation from the cultural norm may be in their expression of gender, rather than their gender identity. They might have interests or present themselves in appearance in ways that do not conform to cultural expectations for their sex assigned at birth. For example, a person who was assigned female at birth might dress and behave in ways considered masculine while still identifying as a girl.

While research on TGNC youth is currently in its infancy, it is evolving quickly (Coleman et al., 2011). The primary body of research falling into this domain is that focusing on transgender adolescents. Some literature also exists looking at gender-related victimization in lesbian, gay, and bisexual (LGB) adolescents. However, many of these studies unfortunately conflate sexual orientation with gender identity and expression. In addition, while research clearly shows that gender-nonconformity exists among heterosexual youth as well, this population of youth is very rarely studied with respect to their potential victimization. We will therefore focus much of our analysis and discussion on understanding how gender-nonconformity influences bullying and suicide, primarily for adolescents who identify as transgender (trans) or LGB, with recognition that our knowledge and recommendations are based on a currently limited and quickly evolving body of literature.

VICTIMIZATION OF TRANSGENDER AND GENDER-NONCONFORMING YOUTH

Young people do not always react negatively to a peer's gender-nonconformity. In many cases, their reactions may depend on just how far from the cultural expectation gender-presentation strays, along with other factors, such as the youth's sex assigned at birth, race/ethnicity, and age (Beemyn & Rankin, 2011). Nonetheless, studies suggest that, overall, TGNC youth face high rates of rejection and victimization, sometimes to serious degrees and with serious consequences. In their 2009 survey of 7,261 LGBT students (ages 13 through 18), the Gay, Lesbian, and Straight Education Network (GLSEN) found that 62.7% of respondents heard negative remarks about gender expression, 56.7% heard negative remarks about "not being masculine enough," and 39.7% heard negative remarks about "not being feminine enough" (Kosciw, Greytak, Diaz, & Bartkiewicz, 2010). This report also showed that trans students were more likely (76.3%) than LGB students (52.9%) to report feeling "unsafe at school because of their sexual or gender orientation" (Kosciw et al., 2010, p. 87). Goldblum and colleagues (2012) found that 44.8% of trans respondents reported having experienced hostility or insensitivity as a result of their gender identity or expression during high school, with 14.8% of these students reporting that the victimization was severe enough to prevent them from completing high school. Recent work by Nadal, Skolnik, and Wong (2012) noted that LGBT youth also reported being subjected to microaggressions—subtle forms of discrimination directed at members of minority groups.

Recent research has found that not all youth are at equal risk for victimization. Goldblum and colleagues (2012) found that in-school gender-based victimization was reported significantly more prevalently among the trans men (60.5%) than among trans women (38.8%). In addition, in this study, multiracial individuals (71.4%), African-Americans (53.1%), and those who classified their race as "other"

(50.0%) reported higher rates, compared to 38.2% of white respondents. Finally, Goldblum and colleagues (2012) found that a significantly higher percentage of individuals under age 45 (at the time of their participation in the study) reported having experienced gender-based victimization, compared to respondents ages 45 and older.

SUICIDALITY AMONG TRANSGENDER AND GENDER-NONCONFORMING YOUTH

Few studies have examined any association between gender-nonconformity itself and suicidality in youth or adults. Among these studies, findings have been mixed (D'Augelli et al., 2005; Fitzpatrick, Euton, Jones, & Schmidt, 2005; Friedman, Koeske, Silvestre, Korr, & Sites, 2006; Grossman & D'Augelli, 2007; Liu & Mustanski, 2012; Mustanski & Liu, 2013; Ploderl & Fartacek, 2009). What is clear is that trans people, and trans youth in particular, report alarming rates of suicidality. Recent research has revealed that between 38% and 83% of trans individuals have reported suicidal ideation (Goldblum et al., 2012; Grossman & D'Augelli, 2007; Testa et al., 2012; Xavier, Bobbin, Singer, & Budd, 2005), and approximately one-third of participants indicated a history of suicide attempts (Goldblum et al., 2012; Haas et al., 2011, Risser et al., 2005; Testa et al., 2012). Furthermore, among those who attempted suicide, the majority reported a history of multiple attempts across their lifespan (Goldblum et al., 2012; Testa et al., 2012). While multiple attempts have been associated with completed suicide in the general population, none of these studies on TGNC youth has evaluated completed suicide.[1]

Like victimization, suicidality has also been shown to vary based on demographics. Goldblum and colleagues (2012) found that suicide-attempt rates varied significantly by gender group, with trans men reporting the highest rates of suicide attempts, at 32.1%, while trans women reported a suicide-attempt rate of 26.5%. In addition, those in multiracial and "other" race categories reported the highest rates of attempt (57.1% and 60.0%, respectively), though Caucasian, African-American, and Latino/Latina respondents also reported high rates of suicide attempts (23.0%, 25.0%, and 28.6%, respectively). The Washington, D.C., Transgender Needs Assessment Survey (WTNAS), conducted by Xavier and colleagues (2005), also revealed that trans people of color are at increased risk for suicidality. Finally, both Goldblum and colleagues (2012) and Xavier and colleagues (2005) found that rates of suicidal ideation were highest among younger trans participants. Finally, while trans people of low and middle socioeconomic status (SES) had similar attempt rates (30.5% and 29.0%, respectively), those with high SES had a relatively much lower rate (9.1%; Goldblum et al., 2012).

THEORIES LINKING VICTIMIZATION AND SUICIDALITY AMONG TRANSGENDER AND GENDER-NONCONFORMING YOUTH

To better understand and explain the relationship between gender-based victimization and suicidality, Hendricks and Testa (2012) adapted Meyer's Minority Stress Model (2003) to specifically apply to the experiences of trans individuals, and wove into it key aspects of the Interpersonal Theory of Suicide developed by Joiner (2010). In this work, Hendricks and Testa described the primary pathways through which victimization of TGNC youth might lead to suicidality.

Drawing on Meyer's model, which was originally formulated to explain both the increased incidence of mental health symptoms and disorders found among lesbian, gay, and bisexual (LGB) people, several processes through which trans individuals are subjected to minority stress are delineated. First are the environmental and other external events that occur in the individual's life as a result of that person's minority status that create overt stress in the person's life. Examples would include discrimination and threats to the person's safety or security, such as bullying. The second set of processes involves the anticipation and expectation that the individual develops that external stressful events will occur. Anticipation of these events results in a heightened level of vigilance and further distress. As a result of this vigilance, trans people who are able to conceal their minority status may do so in order to protect themselves from psychological or physical harm. When this occurs, efforts to conceal their identity create additional distress. Third are the processes in which negative attitudes and prejudices from society are internalized. For LGB people, the epitome of this is internalized homophobia; for trans people, the epitome of this is internalized transphobia. This internalized sense of stigma can have direct negative effects on the individual's ability to cope with external stressful events and ultimately reduces the individual's resilience. Thus, when gender-based victimization occurs to self or others of one's minority identity status, one faces multiple processes of stress that increase the risk for mental health difficulties, including suicidality.

Hendricks and Testa (2012) incorporated the Interpersonal Theory of Suicide, developed by Joiner (2010), to offer a further explanation for the connection between gender-based victimization and suicide risk among trans people. Joiner's theory posits that completed suicide requires three components: perceived burdensomeness, thwarted belongingness, and the capability to enact lethal self-injury. "Burdensomeness" comprises liability (thinking that one would be more valuable dead than alive) and self-hate (Van Orden et al., 2010). Factors that contribute to self-hate include self-blame and low self-esteem. Hendricks and Testa (2012) highlighted how gender-related minority stress, including internalized transphobia and the anticipation of negative events, can lead to thoughts of self-hate and a related understanding of oneself as a burden to one's family or society. Thwarted belongingness is composed of two primary dimensions: loneliness or social disconnectedness, and an absence of reciprocal care or the lack of social support (Van Orden et al., 2010). Hendricks and Testa (2012) described how, for trans youth, loneliness may result from rejection by family members, friends, or peers who are unwilling to accept their trans status, and may be compounded by existing in a society that is generally not accepting of gender-nonconformity. In addition, even without exposure to overt rejection, discrimination, or violence, individuals who do not see people like themselves represented in their community or society may develop a sense of not belonging. Finally, Hendricks and Testa (2012) described how the capability for lethal self-harm may be acquired by many trans people, as this capability can develop as a result of repeated acts of abuse or assaults, or from any other repeated exposure to pain (Van Orden et al., 2010), such as exposure that has been shown to be experienced as a result of gender-based victimization.

The models developed by Meyer (2003) and Hendricks and Testa (2012) also address factors that lead to resilience in, respectively, LGB and trans populations. Specifically, these models name pride and participation in one's minority community as protective factors that buffer the individual against both external and internal minority stress factors. For example, trans individuals who identify with and engage with a trans community gain valuable social support to address minority stress while also developing a more positive concept of what it means to be a trans person.

RESEARCH LINKING VICTIMIZATION AND SUICIDALITY AMONG GENDER-NONCONFORMING YOUTH

Research has provided some preliminary support for these theories' implications that gender-related bullying would increase risk for suicide among TGNC youth. A study by Friedman and colleagues (2006) demonstrated that, among young adult gay men, there was an association between childhood femininity and suicidality, and that this relationship was mediated by experiences of bullying. In a sample of trans respondents, Goldblum and colleagues (2012) examined the relationship between having been subjected to hostility or insensitivity based on their gender identity or expression in school, and suicide attempts. They found that those in the overall sample who reported having been the victim of such gender-based hostility were approximately four times more likely to have made a suicide attempt than those who did not report being so victimized. Individuals who faced hostility had also made significantly more suicide attempts. This relationship was true for both trans men and trans women. A history of victimization and suicide attempts were both significantly more common among multiracial individuals. This highlights the crucial importance of the intersectionality of identities in understanding the experiences of TGNC youth. While no data have been collected on suicide completions in trans youth, in general, those who attempt suicide are at markedly higher risk for suicide completion than those who think about suicide but do not attempt it (Joiner, 2010; Van Orden et al., 2010).

Together, these studies add some support to the idea that bullying related to gender-nonconformity may increase the risk for suicide, and more clearly support a relationship between gender-related bullying and suicidal ideation and suicide attempt. However, since these studies were based on retrospective self-reports, causality could not be determined. Several other variables could explain the relationships found between victimization and suicidality. For instance, it is possible that individuals who were raised in social environments where they were exposed to bullying may also have been more likely to be rejected by parents and facing homelessness, or to face job discrimination and unemployment, and that these stressors were more predictive of suicidality than the experiences of bullying themselves. Another alternative explanation could be that study respondents experiencing long-standing depression or other mental health conditions have selective recall for prior negative events or a tendency to interpret experiences as more negative, as well as a higher incidence of suicidality. However, it is important to note that several studies have ruled out that gender-nonconformity itself is associated with suicidal ideation or suicide attempt among LGBT youth (Liu & Mustanski, 2012; Grossman & D'Augelli, 2007; Mustanski & Liu, 2013).

Finally, research has supported the idea that trans people's resilience is supported by identification and engagement with a trans community. A large survey of trans adults demonstrated that mere exposure to information that others like themselves exist has a strongly protective effect on TGNC youth, with those exposed to such knowledge before their own transition significantly less likely to report feeling suicidal when first identifying as trans, compared to those who did not have this prior awareness (Testa, Jimenez, & Rankin, in press). In two qualitative surveys, Singh, Hays, and Watson (2011) and Singh and McKleroy (2011) found that connecting with others like themselves was identified by TGNC participants as a resilience factor. Furthermore, Sánchez and Vilain (2009) found that "collective self-esteem," a concept defined as positive identification with one's social group, was a buffer against experiences of discrimination among self-identified male-to-female transsexuals. In youth specifically, Heck, Flentje, and Cochran (2011) found that LGBTQ adolescents who attend high schools with gay-straight alliance clubs had better mental health outcomes. Finally, Davis, Saltzburg, and Locke (2009) found that LGBT youth explicitly stated a desire for increased opportunities for interaction and support within the LGBT community, both from their LGBT-identified peers and older LGBT-identified adult role models. This factor was seen as beneficial and necessary for psychological and emotional well-being by the participants.

RESEARCH-BASED RECOMMENDATIONS

What Can Be Done in Schools?

With increased public attention to bullying and suicide over the past decade, interventions have been developed and evaluated and suggestions have been provided to schools, parents, and communities to attempt to address this problem. None of the programs or research found was designed primarily to address gender-related victimization. Among the several interventions that do include an LGBTQ focus, curricula often focus almost solely on sexuality and sexual identity. However, certain lessons from the research on these broader LGBTQ interventions are seen as applicable to addressing the issue of gender-related victimization.

From this literature, we have identified four areas, which we address here. First, it is important to decrease prejudicial attitudes and stigma among both youth and adults within a school or community. For students, research has shown that this can be done by providing curricula in schools that address issues of diversity, and that doing so can improve attitudes towards LGBTQ people and reduce bullying (Rogers, McRee, & Arntz, 2009). For example, a research study by GLSEN (2012) showed that an inclusive curriculum yielded lower levels of victimization related to LGBTQ identity. Furthermore, this was associated with lower levels of missed class days and an increase in the likelihood that students would confide in their teachers about LGBTQ issues. The inclusive curriculum comprised positive examples of LGBT people, histories, and events in class content. Similarly, research by Rogers, McRee, and Arntz (2009) found that participants who took a human sexuality class that was inclusive of LGB material reported significantly lower levels of homophobia at the conclusion of the course.

Second, it is important to promote resilience in TGNC youth through exposure to information, positive messages, role models, and peer support related to their gender identity and expression. In part, this can be addressed by providing gender-diversity training to the broad audience described above. In addition, providing a format for TGNC youth to have peer support is highly recommended. While research has demonstrated the positive effect of gay-straight alliances on LGBT youth, these organizations are advised to use a name that is more clearly inclusive to TGNC youth, and ensure that their environments are able to support gender as well as sexual diversity.

Third, it is important to train teachers and other school staff to understand gender diversity and to feel comfortable intervening in gender-related bullying. Research has found that teachers are less likely to intervene in harassment related to gender presentation than in other forms of bias, including race, religion, and disability (California Safe Schools Coalition, 2004). GLSEN's study showed that only 12.1% of LGBT students reported that teachers would intervene to stop negative gender-based remarks; in contrast, 55.8% felt that racist remarks would not be tolerated (Kosciw et al., 2010). Teachers' reaction to such events also has an impact on student behavior and overall school climate. For example, students who reported likelihood of witnessing a teacher intervene in LGBT bullying reported increased likelihood of intervening themselves (Wernick, Kulick, & Inglehart, 2012). In addition, inaction of teachers may lead students who have experienced bullying to hesitate reporting such incidents. GLSEN's report showed that the majority of LGBT students who were assaulted refused to report these events to parents or teachers (Kosciw et al., 2010). Training staff members, administrators, and teachers in the proper way to respond to gender-based victimization can enrich the learning environment for all students, including LGB and trans youth (Hong & Garbarino, 2012). School mental health workers must collaborate with administrators to promote a school climate that is safe and supportive for all students, particularly those targeted based on their gender minority status.

Fourth and finally, it is important for schools to arrange policy and school/community structure to discourage victimization of TGNC students. It has been shown that students feel safer and report less harassment in schools where specific groups are listed as protected by anti-bullying laws and policies (Hatzenbuehler, 2011; Kosciw et al., 2010). School personnel should be aware that gender-related harassment, including harassment based on perceived "failure to conform to stereotypical notions of masculinity and femininity," must be addressed in accordance with federal guidelines under Title IX (Office for Civil Rights, U.S. Department of Education, 2010, pp. 7–8). While no research has been done on the structure of school environments, many have also pointed out the importance of implicit learning of preferred gender norms through binary division of sports teams, bathrooms, locker rooms, and even "line-up" routines in schools. By changing these structural factors to create affirming educational environments, schools can both encourage broad embrace of gender diversity and encourage self-acceptance in TGNC youth.

What Can Be Done Outside of Schools?

While bullying most often occurs in schools, the people and environments of youths' lives outside of school are crucial influences on the extent to which victimization occurs and the effects of victimization on the mental health of TGNC youth. First, youth victimize TGNC peers because they learn through their culture that gender-nonconformity is a negative trait. In stark contrast, other current and historical cultures have valued gender-nonconformity, sometimes even believing that TGNC people had spiritual or healing roles to play in their society (Feinberg, 1996). In mainstream Western cultures, negative messages regarding gender-nonconformity are learned not only at school, but in the home, through the media, in religious contexts, and in the way communities are structured, healthcare is provided, and policies are crafted. Similarly, across these contexts there are often few positive messages, images, and role models speaking to the value of gender-nonconformity and TGNC people. Attitude change at a societal level will therefore require action at multiple levels and by all parties to reduce the negative and increase the positive messages youth receive about gender-nonconformity. While broad attitude change can seem like a daunting task, the progress of the civil rights and gay rights movements demonstrates how real change can occur when enough voices are heard. Ultimately such attitude change will be necessary to end victimization of TGNC youth.

However, there are many things we can do to positively affect outcomes for TGNC youth before societal changes come to fruition. Put simply, actors at all levels, including family, clergy, policy-makers, and providers, can help TGNC youth develop resilience. As discussed above, key aspects of resilience for TGNC youth include developing a sense of pride and connecting with others who share their identity and experience, as well as having acceptance and identity affirmation for LGBTQ youth (Ryan, Russell, Huebner, Diaz, & Sanchez, 2010). Youth should therefore be provided access to positive information, peers, and role models that reflect their own identities. In the past, such resources were not easily accessible to people in certain communities. However, with technology increasing access to resources and to other people on a global scale, ample resources and people now exist online to which youth can be steered. In addition, parents, providers, clergy, and others who interact with youth can be significant sources of affirmation and acceptance by doing simple things like asking for and endorsing a youth's request for which pronouns and name to use, clothing to wear, and activities in which to engage.

Considering the high percentage of TGNC youth who report a history of suicide attempts, it is important for all to be attuned to warning signs and be aware of appropriate steps to take should a youth appear at risk for suicidal behavior. Youth who are TGNC and in distress need access to service providers and settings that are accepting and affirming of their identities, prepared to discuss the effects of gender-related victimization and minority stress on their mental health, and able to provide developmentally appropriate resources to support identity development, pride, and connection with others like themselves. The American Counseling Association (Association for Lesbian, Gay, Bisexual & Transgender Issues in Counseling [ALGBTIC], 2009) has developed *Competencies for Counseling with Transgender Clients*, in which they advocate an approach that is strength-based, multiculturally informed, and derived from feminist theories and social justice. Hendricks and Testa (2012) and Goldblum and colleagues (2012) provide further recommendations and resources for mental health clinicians working with TGNC people and TGNC youth. Work with families may be particularly important, as many TGNC youth experience negative treatment at home that further exacerbates their distress (Ryan et al., 2010). Programs such as the Family Acceptance Project in

San Francisco (Family Acceptance Project, 2013) help families better understand, accept, and protect their children.

Finally, all interventions to address the high rates of bullying and suicidality among TGNC youth should be evidence-based. To date, it seems that more effort has been expended on documenting the problem than on developing interventions, with potentially harmful consequences. For example, the "It Gets Better" campaign, initiated by American author Dan Savage, has been both praised and criticized for its possible stimulus effect that can yield "copycat" suicide behavior. The American Foundation for Suicide Prevention, in partnership with the Gay and Lesbian Medical Association, met in November 2007 to promote improved understanding of how to reduce suicide risk and behavior in the LGBT population (Haas et al., 2011) and provided recommendations for media campaigns increase access to services and calls to expand culturally appropriate mental health and substance abuse programs for LGBT populations (Haas et al., 2011).

SUMMARY OF RECOMMENDATIONS

Suggestions for Healthcare Providers (Particularly Mental Health)

- Promote TGNC youths' resilience by facilitating access to TGNC peers and role models.
- Educate yourself about how to provide culturally competent services for TGNC youth by accessing resources, such as the World Professional Association of Transgender Health's *Standards of Care Version 7* (Coleman et al., 2011) and the American Counseling Association's *Competencies for Counseling with Transgender Clients* (ALGBTIC, 2009).
- Assess TGNC youths' exposure, including prior discrimination or victimization, expectations of future victimization or rejection, internalized transphobia, and expressions of resilience, and take necessary steps to minimize future occurrence of these stressors.
- Be aware of what resources exist in the youths' communities for TGNC youth who are experiencing minority stress and/or suicidality.
- Communicate acceptance of TGNC youths' identities and expressions, and respect for each youth's unique strengths.
- Make structural changes in your facility, by, for example, ensuring that intake forms and restrooms allow for gender diversity.
- Recognize the limits of your training and your beliefs and attitudes about gender-nonconformity and refer out when appropriate.

Suggestions for Parents and Teachers

- Provide educational curricula that teach all students to value people with diverse gender identities and expressions.
- Facilitate TGNC youths' access to TGNC peers and role models.
- Educate yourselves and other adults in your community about gender diversity.
- Train and empower all school staff to feel comfortable intervening in gender-related bullying.

- Develop and enforce school policies, with awareness of Title IX, to protect TGNC youth and respond to gender-based victimization.
- Make structural changes in school environments to represent gender diversity as a normal, respected identity by having gender-neutral bathrooms, locker-rooms, sports, and group work options, as well as curricula and texts that represent gender diversity.
- Be sensitive to the unique stressors for TGNC youth and the related increased risk for suicidality, and encourage accessing culturally competent mental health resources when appropriate.
- Communicate acceptance of TGNC youths' identities and expressions, and respect for each youth's unique strengths.

Suggestions for Policy Makers

- Create and support policies that will promote school environments that are comfortable safe spaces for TGNC youth.
- Develop and support policies that will increase access to culturally competent mental health resources for TGNC youth who are experiencing distress.
- Ensure that non-discrimination policies include protections for TGNC people at the broadest levels of society, such that TGNC youth can have less negative expectations about their futures, and TGNC adults can become more accessible as role models to TGNC youth.
- Encourage ongoing funding for programs of intervention and research that focus on TGNC youth.

NOTE

1. A very few studies have found elevated rates of completed suicide among adult transsexuals (see Dhejne et al., 201;1 van Kesteren, Asscheman, Megens, & Gooren, 1997).

REFERENCES

Association of Lesbian, Gay, Bisexual, and Transgender Issues in Counseling (ALGBTIC) (2009). *Competencies for Counseling with Transgender Clients*. Alexandria, VA: ALGBTIC.

Beemyn, G., & Rankin, S. (2011). *The Lives of Transgender People*. New York: Columbia University Press.

California Safe Schools Coalition and 4-H Center for Youth Development, University of California, Davis. *Consequences of Harassment Based on Actual or Perceived Sexual Orientation and Gender Non-Conformity and Steps for Making Schools Safer*. 2004. http://www.calendow.org/uploadedFiles/safe_place_to_learn.pdf

Coleman, E., Bockting, W., Botzer, M., Cohen-Kettenis, P., DeCuypere, G., Feldman, J., ... Zucker, K. (2011). Standards of care for the health of transsexual, transgender, and gender-nonconforming people, 7th version. *International Journal of Transgenderism*, *13*(4), 165–232. doi:10.1080/15532739.2011.700873

Coleman, E., Colgan, P., & Gooren, L. (1992). Male crossgender behavior in Myanmar (Burma): A description of the acault. *Archives of Sexual Behavior, 21*(3), 313–321. doi:10.1007/BF01542999

Conron, K. J., Scout, & Austin, S. B. (2008). "Everyone has a right to, like, check their box": Findings on a measure of gender identity from a cognitive testing study of adolescents. *Journal of LGBT Health Research, 4*, 1–9. doi:10.1080/15574090802412572

D'Augelli, A. R., Grossman, A. H., Salter, N. P., Vasey, J. J., Starks, M. T., & Sinclair, K. O. (2005). Predicting the suicide attempts of lesbian, gay, and bisexual youth. *Suicide and Life-Threatening Behavior, 35*(6), 646–660. doi: 10.1521/suli.2005.35.6.646

Davis, T. S., Saltzburg, S., & Locke, C. R. (2009). Supporting the emotional and psychological well being of sexual minority youth: Youth ideas for action. *Children and Youth Services Review, 31*(9), 1030–1041. doi: 10.1016/j.childyouth.2009.05.003

Dhejne, C., Lichtenstein, P., Boman, M., Johansson, A. L. V., Långström, N., & Landén, M. (2011). Long-term follow-up of transsexual persons undergoing sex reassignment surgery: Cohort study in Sweden. *PLoS One, 6*, e16885.

Family Acceptance Project (2013). Retrieved June 30, 2013 from http://familyproject.sfsu.edu.

Feinberg, L. (1996). *Transgender Warriors: Making History from Joan of Arc to Dennis Rodman;[with a New Afterword]*. Beacon Press, Boston.

Fitzpatrick, K. K., Euton, S. J., Jones, J. N., & Schmidt, N. B. (2005). Gender role, sexual orientation and suicide risk. *Journal of Affective Disorders, 87*(1), 35–42. doi:10.1016/j.jad.2005.02.020

Friedman, M. S., Koeske, G. F., Silvestre, A. J., Korr, W. S., & Sites, E. W. (2006). The impact of gender-role nonconforming behavior, bullying, and social support on suicidality among gay male youth. *Journal of Adolescent Health, 38*(5), 621–623. doi:10.1016/j.jadohealth.2005.04.014

Gay, Lesbian, and Straight Education Network (GLSEN) (2012). *Teaching Respect: LGBT-Inclusive Curriculum and School Violence (Research Brief)*. New York: GLSEN.

Goldblum, P., Testa, R. J., Pflum, S., Hendricks, M., Bradford, J., & Bongar, B. (2012). In-school gender-based victimization and suicide attempts in transgender individuals. *Professional Psychology: Research and Practice*, 43, 468–475. doi: 10.1037/a0029605

Grossman, A. H., & D'Augelli, A. R. (2007). Transgender youth and life-threatening behaviors. *Suicide and Life-Threatening Behavior, 37*(5), 527–537. doi: 10.1521/suli.2007.37.5.527

Haas, A. P., Eliason, M., Mays, V. M., Mathy, R. M., Cochran, S. D., D'Augelli, A. R.,... Clayton, P. J. (2011). Suicide and suicide risk in lesbian, gay, bisexual, and transgender populations: Review and recommendations. *Journal of Homosexuality, 58*(1), 10–51. doi: 10.1080/00918369.2011.534038

Hatzenbuehler, M. L. (2011). The social environment and suicide attempts in lesbian, gay, and bisexual youth. *Pediatrics, 127*(5), 896–903. doi: 10.1542/peds.2010-3020

Heck, N. C., Flentje, A., & Cochran, B. N. (2011). Offsetting risks: High school gay-straight alliances and lesbian, gay, bisexual, and transgender (LGBT) youth. *School Psychology Quarterly, 26*(2), 161. doi: 10.1037/a0023226

Hendricks, M. L., & Testa, R. J. (2012). A conceptual framework for clinical work with transgender and gender-nonconforming clients: An adaptation of the Minority Stress Model. *Professional Psychology: Research and Practice, 43*(5), 460. doi:10.1037/a0029597

Hong, J. S., & Garbarino, J. (2012). Risk and protective factors for homophobic bullying in schools: An application of the social-ecological framework. *Educational Psychology Review, 24*(2), 271–285. doi: 10.1007/s10648-012-9194-y

Joiner, T. (2010). *Myths About Suicide*. Boston: Harvard University.

Kosciw, J. G., Greytak, E. A., Diaz, E. M., & Bartkiewicz, M. J. (2010). *The 2009 National School Climate Survey: The Experiences of Lesbian, Gay, Bisexual and Transgender Youth in Our Nation's Schools*. New York: Gay, Lesbian, and Straight Education Network.

Kuper, L. E., Nussbaum, R., & Mustanski, B. (2012). Exploring the diversity of gender and sexual orientation identities in an online sample of transgender individuals. *Journal of Sex Research, 49*, 244–254. doi:10.1080/00224499.2011.596954

Liu, R. T., & Mustanski, B. (2012). Suicidal ideation and self-harm in lesbian, gay, bisexual, and transgender youth. *American Journal of Preventive Medicine, 42*(3), 221–228. doi: 10.1016/j.amepre.2011.10.023

Meier, S. C., & Labuski, C. M. (2013). The demographics of the transgender population. In A. K. Baumle (Ed.), *International Handbook of the Demography of Sexuality* (pp. 289–327). New York: Springer.

Meyer, I. H. (2003). Prejudice, social stress, and mental health in lesbian, gay, and bisexual populations: Conceptual issues and research evidence. *Psychological Bulletin, 129*(5), 674–697. doi:10.1037/0033-2909.129.5.674

Miller, J., & Nichols, A. (2012). Identity, sexuality and commercial sex among Sri Lankan nachchi. *Sexualities, 15*(5–6), 554–569. doi:10.1177/1363460712446120

Mustanski, B., & Liu, R. T. (2013). A longitudinal study of predictors of suicide attempts among lesbian, gay, bisexual, and transgender youth. *Archives of Sexual Behavior, 42*(3), 437–448. doi: 10.1007/s10508-012-0013-9

Nadal, K. L., Skolnik, A., & Wong, Y. (2012). Interpersonal and systemic microaggressions toward transgender people: Implications for counseling. *Journal of LGBT Issues in Counseling, 6*(1), 55–82. doi:10.1080/15538605.2012.648583

Office for Civil Rights, U.S. Department of Education (2010). "Dear Colleague" letter. Washington, DC: OCR, USDOE. Retrieved June 30, 2013 from http://www2.ed.gov/about/offices/list/ocr/letters/colleague-201010.html.

Plöderl, M., & Fartacek, R. (2009). Childhood gender-nonconformity and harassment as predictors of suicidality among gay, lesbian, bisexual, and heterosexual Austrians. *Archives of Sexual Behavior, 38*(3), 400–410. doi: 10.1007/s10508-007-9244-6

Risser, J. M. H., Shelton, A., McCurdy, S., Atkinson, J., Padgett, P., Useche, B., . . . Williams, M. (2005). Sex, drugs, violence, and HIV status among male-to-female transgender person in Houston, Texas. *International Journal of Transgenderism, 8*(2–3), 67–74. doi: 10.1300/j485v08n02_07

Rogers, A., McRee, N., & Arntz, D. L. (2009). Using a college human sexuality course to combat homophobia. *Sex Education, 9*(3), 211–225. doi: 10/1080/14681810903059052

Ryan, C., Russell, S. T., Huebner, D., Diaz, R., & Sanchez, J. (2010). Family acceptance in adolescence and the health of LGBT young adults. *Journal of Child and Adolescent Psychiatric Nursing, 23*(4), 205–213. doi: 10.1111/j.1744-6171.2010.00246.x

Sánchez, F. J., & Vilain, E. (2009). Collective self-esteem as a coping resource for male-to-female transsexuals. *Journal of Counseling Psychology, 56*(1), 202. doi: 10.1037/a0014573

Schmidt, J. (2003). Paradise lost? Social change and Fa'afafine in Samoa. *Current Sociology, 51*, 417–432. doi: 10.1177/0011392103051003014

Singh, A. A., Hays, D. G., & Watson, L. S. (2011). Strength in the face of adversity: Resilience strategies of transgender individuals. *Journal of Counseling & Development*, 89, 20–27.

Singh, A. A., & McKleroy, V. S. (2011). "Just getting out of bed is a revolutionary act": The resilience of transgender people of color who have survived traumatic life events. *Traumatology, 17*(2), 34–44. doi: 10.1177/1534765610369261

Testa, R. J., Jimenez, C. L., & Rankin, S. (2014). Risk and resilience during transgender identity development: The effects of awareness of and engagement with other transgender people on affect. *Journal of Gay and Lesbian Mental Health, 18*(1), 34–56.

Testa, R. J., Sciacca, L. M., Wang, F., Hendricks, M., Goldblum, P., Bradford, J., & Bongar, B. (2012). Effects of violence on transgender people. *Professional Psychology: Research and Practice, 43*, 452–459. doi: 10.1037/a0029604

Tobin, D. D., Menon, M., Spatta, B. C., Hodges, E. V. E., & Perry, D. G. (2010). The intrapsychics of gender: A model of self-socialization. *Psychological Review, 117*, 601–622. doi:10.0137/a0018936

van Kesteren, P. J. M., Asscheman, H., Megens, J. O. J., & Gooren, L. J. G. (1997). Mortality and morbidity in transsexual subjects treated with cross-sex hormones. *Clinical Endocrinology, 47*, 337–342. doi: 10.1046/j.1365-2265.1997.2601068.x

Van Orden, K. A., Witte, T. K., Cukrowicz, K. C., Braithwaite, S. R., Selby, E. A., & Joiner T. E. Jr., (2010). The interpersonal theory of suicide. *Psychological Review, 117*(2), 575. doi: 10.1037/a0018697

Wernick, L. J., Kulick, A., & Inglehart, M. H. (2012). Factors predicting student intervention when witnessing anti-LGBTQ harassment: The influence of peers, teachers, and climate. *Children and Youth Services Review 35*, 296–301. doi: 10.1016/j.childyouth.2012.11.003

Xavier, J., Bobbin, M., Singer, B. & Budd, E. (2005). A needs assessment of transgendered people of color living in Washington, DC. *International Journal of Transgenderism, 8*(2–3), 31–47. doi: 10.1300/J485v08n02_04

12

The Relation Between Suicidal Ideation and Bullying Victimization in a National Sample of Transgender and Non-Transgender Adolescents

MICHELE L. YBARRA, KIMBERLY J. MITCHELL, AND JOSEPH KOSCIW ■

As the third most common cause of death among adolescents in the United States (Centers for Disease Control and Prevention [CDC], 2012), suicide is a significant public health issue (CDC, 2010). Suicidal ideation is a precursor to suicidal behavior, making it an important intervention target (Herba, Ferdinand, van der Ende, & Verhulst, 2007; Kerr, 2008; Lewinsohn, Rohde, & Seeley, 1994; Reinherz, Tanner, Berger, Beardslee, & Fitzmaurice, 2006).

Linkages between suicidal ideation and peer victimization have been noted in general community samples of youth (Brunstein-Klomek et al., 2007; Hinduja & Patchin, 2010; Klomek et al., 2008), as well as among LGB youth, specifically (Anhalt & Morris, 1998; Fergusson, Horwood, & Beautrais, 1999; Kann et al., 2011; McDaniel, Purcell, & D'Augelli, 2001; Remafedi, French, Story, Resnick, & Blum, 1998; Russell & Joyner, 2001), but little is known about linkages among transgender youth. Some of the nascent literature on bullying and peer victimization has shown that gender minority youth, such as those who identify as transgender or outside the gender binary of male/female, may have a higher incidence of victimization than their cisgender peers.[1] Compared to non-transgender youth, transgender youth are more likely to be physically harassed and assaulted—often because of their gender expression (Greytak, Kosciw, & Diaz, 2009; Grossman & D'Augelli, 2006; Kosciw, Greytak, Bartkiewicz, Boesen, & Palmer, 2012; McGuire, Anderson, Toomey, & Russell, 2010). Transgender teens also report elevated rates of generalized peer victimization and bully victimization compared to their cisgender peers (Ybarra, Mitchell, Palmer, & Resiner, 2014).

There is some evidence about the relation between experiences of violence and suicidal ideation among transgender adults. Findings from the Virginia Transgender Health Initiative Survey suggest that transgender adults who had experienced physical and/or sexual violence "since the time [they] were 13" were more likely to report a history of suicide attempts than were their non-victimized peers (Testa, Sciacca, Wang, & Hendricks, 2012). Almost all of these victims noted that the physical (98%) or sexual (89%) violence was primarily a result of their gender identity or expression. These adults were asked to report retrospectively on their in-school gender-based victimization. Those who reported violence in school were about four times more likely to have attempted suicide than those who had not experienced such violence (Goldblum et al., 2012).

Transgender people face more mental health disparities than non-transgender youth, and are more likely to report challenges such as suicidal ideation for several reasons. First, the stigma one experiences because he or she is gender nonconforming can compound the typical everyday stress experienced by most individuals (Hendricks & Testa, 2012; Meyer, 2003) regardless of their gender identity. Second, gender minority individuals may internalize the prejudice and rejection from society and attribute its cause to their gender identity (internalized transphobia) (Hendricks & Testa, 2012), a core part of their self. This internalized stigma could indeed be the most damaging from a mental health perspective. This minority stress theory has been applied to sexual minority individuals, and there may be similar processes for gender minority individuals as well. Third, the anticipation or expectation of violence may result in mental health disparities (Hendricks & Testa, 2012; Meyer, 2003); two out of three transgender youth report feeling unsafe at school because of how they express their gender (65%; Greytak et al., 2009). Thus, some transgender youth who are open about their gender identity status may move through their school day fearing the violence that they have come to expect; and others may struggle with how open to be about their identity out of fear for their personal safety. Fourth, actual experiences of gender-related victimization could undoubtedly affect individual psychological well-being.

In sum, existing research suggests that transgender youth may be both more likely to be bullied and also to report suicidal ideation. Although there are reasons to believe there may be direct linkages between bullying and suicidal ideation for transgender youth, this has yet to be empirically tested. It also seems possible that other factors may explain observed associations between gender identity and suicidal ideation, and it is these other influential factors that need to be addressed to buffer transgender youth from further harm.

METHOD

Data for the Teen Health and Technology (THT) study were collected online between August 2010 and January 2011 from 5,907 13–18 year olds in the United

States. The survey protocol was reviewed and approved by the Chesapeake Institutional Review Board (IRB), the University of New Hampshire IRB, and the Gay, Lesbian and Straight Education Network (GLSEN) Research Ethics Review Committee.

THT was designed to provide a general population sample of adolescents but allow for comparisons related to sexual orientation and gender identity by employing an oversample of LGBT-identified youth. Participants were recruited: (1) from the Harris Poll Online (HPOL) opt-in panel (n = 3,989 respondents); and (2) through referrals from GLSEN (n = 1,918 respondents). HPOL email invitations referred to a survey about "online experiences." GLSEN sent invitations to their members' list. The text referred to a survey about "health and the Internet"; and noted that they were particularly interested in hearing from LGBT youth. The invitations did not mention bullying or suicide.

The response rate for the HPOL sample was calculated as the number of individuals who started the survey divided by the number of email invitations sent, minus any email invitations that were returned as undeliverable. The HPOL sample survey response rate, 7.2%, was within the range of other recent surveys (Lenhart, Purcell, Smith, & Zickuhr, 2010; Mitchell & Jones, 2011). The response rate for the GLSEN sample could not be calculated as the denominator (i.e., the number of youth who saw the invitation is indeterminable).

Procedure

A waiver of parental consent was granted by the IRBs. The survey was self-administered online. Qualified respondents were: (1) United States residents; (2) 13–18 years old; (3) in fifth grade or above; and (4) provided informed assent. The median survey length was 23 minutes for HPOL respondents and 34 minutes for GLSEN respondents. The survey length was longer for participants who identified as LGBT because they had additional LGBT-specific questions.

Measures

Bullying is defined as a specific form of peer victimization that occurs repeatedly and is perpetrated by someone who has more power than the perpetrator (Olweus, 1993). Recent data suggest that it is important to be clear about the measurement of peer victimization used in the study, and when possible, to stratify youth by bullying and non-bullying victimization (Ybarra, Espelage, & Mitchell, 2014) to discern how these different forms of peer victimization may relate to suicidal ideation. First, youth were asked: "Bullying can happen anywhere, like at school, at home, or other places you hang out. In the past 12 months, how often were you bullied or harassed by someone about your same age...?" Next, youth were asked about different types of bullying: "In the past 12 months, how often have others about your age bullied or harassed you by...? These are things that happen in-person, on the phone, online, or by text message." For both questions, response options ranged from "Never" to "Every day/almost every day." Seven types were queried (e.g., threatening or aggressive comments).

Youth who indicated they had been bullied at least once in some way or through some mode were asked a dichotomous ("Yes" or "No") follow-up question about differential power (Ybarra, boyd, Korchmaros, & Oppenheim, 2012): "Thinking just about the past 12 months, were you ever bullied or harassed by someone who had more power or strength than you? This could be because the person was bigger than you, had more friends, was more popular, or had more power than you in another way." They also were asked whether the bullying had happened repeatedly.

Based on their answers, youth were categorized into one of three exclusive groups: (1) a victim of bullying (i.e., it happened intensely—either monthly or more often, or repeatedly—and by someone with more power than them); (2) a victim of non-bullying generalized peer victimization (i.e., victimized at least once, but not necessarily repeatedly, or by someone with more power than them); or (3) no peer victimization.

Suicidal ideation was measured with an item from the revised version of the Center for Epidemiologic Studies Depression scale Revised (CESD-R; Eaton, Muntaner, Smith, Tien, & Ybarra, 2004): "I wished I were dead." Youth who reported these feelings for at least one or two days in the last week were compared to youth who felt this not at all, or less than one day in the preceding week.

Gender was queried directly after the question about biological sex by asking: "What is your gender? Your gender is how you feel inside and can be the same as or different than the answer you gave above." Response options were: "Male," "Female," "Transgender," and "Other." Youth who reported their biological sex to be different from their gender and did not indicate that their gender was transgender, were asked a follow-up question: "Are you of transgender experience?" ("Yes" or "No"). Based upon their responses, youth were coded into one of five categories: (1) cisgender male (i.e., biological sex and gender were both male), (2) cisgender female (i.e., biological sex and gender were both female), (3) transgender (i.e., identified their gender as transgender), (4) gender-nonconforming (i.e., more than one gender, but did not identify their gender as transgender; different biological sex and gender, but did not identify their gender as transgender), and (5) other (i.e., identified their gender as "other").

Covariates

To understand the relation between peer victimization and suicidal ideation, other influential factors that may explain the association need to be taken into account. Based on the literature on the general population of adolescents, these included major depressive disorder, alcohol and drug use, low self-esteem, and poor social and family support; age; race; and poor parent–child relationships and living in poverty.

Weighting and Data Management

First, the HPOL sample was weighted to known demographics of 13–18-year-olds based on the 2009 Current Population Survey (CPS) (United States' Census Bureau, 2009). Next, a demographic profile was created for LGBT teens in the HPOL sample and was applied to the GLSEN-recruited LGBT teens. Then a propensity score was created to adjust for behavioral and attitudinal differences between the two groups.

Finally, a postweight was applied so that GLSEN and HPOL LGBT teens each accounted for 50% of the combined total LGBT population, and extreme weights were trimmed to avoid undue influence on estimates (Potter, 1990).

Respondents who declined to answer more than 20% of the survey, or those who did not meet valid data requirements (e.g., survey length was less than five minutes) were excluded. As a result, 365 surveys were dropped. The final analytical sample size was 5,542 youth. Missing data were imputed using the "impute" command in Stata (StataCorp, 2009). Greater detail about the weighting and measures is available (GLSEN Center for Innovative Public Health Research, & Crimes Against Children Research Center, 2013).

Data Analyses

To understand how observed associations behaved within the context of other influential factors, multivariable logistical regression models were estimated. First, gender identity was entered into the model (Model 1). Next, peer victimization was added to determine how well this explained observed associations between suicidal ideation and gender identity (Model 2). Finally, additional factors known to predict suicidal ideation (e.g., alcohol use) were added to observe their further impact on the association between suicidal ideation and gender identity (Model 3). Gender identity was tested as an effect-modifier of victimization experience and suicidal ideation. All reported analyses are based on weighted data.

RESULTS

In this national online study of 5,542 youth 13–18 years of age, 3.4% of youth self-identified as transgender, 3.6% as gender-nonconforming, and an additional 0.9% as other gender. Rates of past-year bullying and generalized peer victimization differed significantly by gender: 48% of transgender youth reported being bullied and 38% reported generalized peer victimization, compared to 44% and 42%, respectively, of gender-nonconforming youth; 55% and 37% of youth of "other" gender; 21% and 47% of cisgender males; and 25% and 43% of cisgender females ($p < 0.001$). Similar differences were noted in rates of past-week suicidal ideation: 41%–53% of non-cisgender youth reported recently wishing to be dead, compared to 21% of cisgender females and 13% of cisgender males ($p < 0.001$).

Interaction terms for gender identity and bullying were entered into a logistical regression model predicting the odds of suicidal ideation. The interaction did not significantly contribute to the overall logistical regression model ($p = 0.19$). Thus, stratified models were not estimated.

As shown in Table 12.1, the relative odds of recent suicidal ideation were significantly higher for all non-cisgender male youth compared to cisgender male youth, including cisgender female youth (Model 1). These associations were attenuated by 22% or more with the inclusion of peer victimization for all youth except for cisgender females (Model 2). Once other influential factors were taken into account (Model 3), the odds of suicidal ideation for cisgender female and other gender

Table 12.1. Relative Odds of Recent Suicidal Ideation given Past-Year Peer Victimization and Gender Identity ($N = 5542$)

Personal characteristics	**Model 1: Gender identity**		**Model 2: + Peer victimization**		**Model 3: + Additional explanatory factors**	
	aOR (95% CI)	**p-value**	**aOR (95% CI)**	**p-value**	**aOR (95% CI)**	**p-value**
Gender identity						
Cisgender male	1.0 (RG)		1.0 (RG)		1.0 (RG)	
Cisgender female	1.78 (1.40, 2.27)	< 0.001	1.71 (1.34, 2.18)	< 0.001	1.04 (0.77, 1.41)	0.79
Transgender	7.68 (4.37, 13.49)	< 0.001	5.83 (3.22, 10.54)	< 0.001	1.71 (0.94, 3.11)	0.08
Gender nonconforming	6.81 (3.82, 12.12)	< 0.001	5.30 (2.95, 9.52)	< 0.001	3.03 (1.16, 7.94)	0.02
Other gender	4.57 (1.81, 11.53)	0.001	2.98 (0.97, 9.11)	0.06	0.86 (0.30, 2.44)	0.78
Peer victimization						
No victimization						
Generalized peer victimization			1.93 (1.43, 2.60)	< 0.001	1.55 (1.06, 2.28)	0.025
Bully victimization			4.88 (3.54, 6.71)	< 0.001	2.07 (1.29, 3.30)	0.002
Psychosocial characteristics						
Depressive symptomatology					1.20 (1.17, 1.22)	< 0.001
High in-person social support					0.80 (0.53, 1.21)	0.29
Alcohol use					1.15 (0.96, 1.37)	0.12
Poor caregiver monitoring in-person					1.06 (0.72, 1.57)	0.77
Poor caregiver monitoring via technology					1.21 (0.79, 1.86)	0.38
Highly coercive parental discipline					2.15 (1.38, 3.36)	0.001
Poor caregiver–child emotional bond					1.52 (1.03, 2.25)	0.03
High self-esteem					0.18 (0.09, 0.33)	< 0.001

(continued)

Table 12.1 Continued

Personal characteristics	Model 1: Gender identity		Model 2: + Peer victimization		Model 3: + Additional explanatory factors	
	aOR (95% CI)	p-value	aOR (95% CI)	p-value	aOR (95% CI)	p-value
Demographic characteristics						
Low income					0.99 (0.72, 1.36)	0.96
Age					0.96 (0.87, 1.07)	0.46
Hispanic ethnicity					0.86 (0.56, 1.33)	0.51
Race						
White						
Black/African American					1.37 (0.84, 2.22)	0.21
Native American/Alaska Native					3.01 (0.86, 10.53)	0.09
All other					1.43 (0.96, 2.15)	0.08
Urbanicity						
Urban/city						
Suburban					0.89 (0.61, 1.30)	0.55
Small town/rural					0.91 (0.65, 1.28)	0.58
Low caregiver education (high school or less)					1.26 (0.90, 1.77)	0.18
Process indicators						
Not alone when completing the survey	0.88 (0.42, 1.85)	0.75	1.27 (1.01, 1.59)	0.04	1.19 (0.90, 1.59)	0.22
Not honest in answering survey questions	1.23 (0.99, 1.54)	0.07	0.96 (0.47, 1.98)	0.92	0.77 (0.34, 1.74)	0.54

youth were no longer statistically or clinically significant. The odds for transgender youth were reduced 71%, and were borderline significant (adjusted odds ratio (aOR) = 1.71, $p = 0.08$). The odds for gender-nonconforming youth were reduced by 43%.

As shown in Model 2, compared to youth who had not experienced victimization, youth who experienced generalized peer victimization were nearly twice as likely, and youth who experienced bullying victimization were nearly five times more likely, to report suicidal ideation. Once other influential factors were taken into consideration (Model 3), the relative odds of suicidal ideation were reduced by 20% for victims of generalized peer aggression and by 58% of youth who were victims of bullying.

DISCUSSION

Gender minority youth are significantly more likely to report recent suicidal ideation in this national survey of adolescents. Much of the elevated odds is explained by victimization experiences as well as other concurrent psychosocial challenges, however. Professionals working with transgender youth need to be particularly mindful about the high rates of bullying and victimization among these youth, and the potential overlaps these experiences can have with negative psychosocial outcomes, such as suicidal ideation.

Findings provide support for the application of the minority stress model to gender minority youth, as it has been for sexual minority youth. Although victimization experiences partially attenuated the odds of suicidal ideation for youth of a non-cisgender identity, they were nearly wholly accounted for by psychosocial factors. Given this, further research is needed that examines the pathways from victimization and discrimination experiences to other psychosocial factors that then may predict suicidal ideation.

Aside from well-being (self-esteem and depression), the only other contextual variables that were significantly associated with suicidal ideation were those that reflected family relationships (i.e., coercive discipline and poor emotional bond). Given the high rate of homelessness among the LGBT youth population (Hunter, 2008)—often because of poor family relationships—and the significance of these family items in our analyses, it seems crucial for adolescent health professionals to identify concrete ways in which non-traditional families and supports can be built around transgender youth to compensate for the lack of positive caregiver–child relationships. Future research could also examine whether family relationships moderate the effect of victimization on ideation.

In the present study, gender-nonconforming youth have persistently significant and elevated odds for suicidal ideation as compared to their peers, even when other influential factors are taken into account. It may be that not being transgender *or* cisgender may result in a similar lack of community, as has been posited for bisexual youth (Espelage, Aragon, Birkett, & Koenig, 2008; Robinson & Espelage, 2011; Ybarra, Mitchell, Kosciw, & Korchmaros, under review). It may also signify additional psychological or emotional stressors among these youth who actively choose to identify outside the norm of societal conventions and also do not identify as transgender.

Findings should be interpreted within the limitations of the study. First, stress and discrimination could possibly explain the remainder of the elevated odds of suicidal ideation for non-cisgender youth. Neither measure was included in the study, however, so this hypothesis cannot be evaluated. Second, the single item for suicidal ideation is crude. Moreover, because the item was from a larger depression scale, it is possible that the measure of suicidal ideation and the measure of depression were more highly related than they would have been if they were from separate scales. Lastly, it would have been optimal to stratify the transgender group by male and female, as we did with the cisgender group. Because only 18 youth were transgender female, however, we lacked the sample size to support stable estimates.

CONCLUSION

The current study adds to the growing literature documenting the concerning linkages between peer victimization and suicidal ideation. Similar to sexuality minority youth, this relation appears to be particularly strong for gender minority youth. Much of the relation is explained by other, concomitant factors. If we are to affect the rates of mental health challenge, particularly suicidal ideation, more needs to be done to reduce the rates of victimization, particularly heterosexist aggression.

Suggestions for Providers, Teachers, Parents, and Policy Makers

- Require cultural competency training for professionals working with youth to ensure appropriate understanding of transgender youth.
- Recognize that gender-nonconforming youth who do not self-identify as being transgender may be in particular need of non-judgemental support to address suicidal ideation.
- Understand that suicidal ideation among transgender youth is often not about their gender identity specifically, but about the challenges that they are facing more generally, including poor caregiver–child relationships, low self-esteem, and depressive symptomatology.

ACKNOWLEDGMENTS

The project described was supported by Award Number R01 HD057191 from the National Institute of Child Health and Human Development. The content is solely the responsibility of the authors and does not necessarily represent the official views of the National Institute of Child Health and Human Development or of the National Institutes of Health. We would like to thank the entire study team from the Center for Innovative Public Health Research, the University of New Hampshire, the Gay Lesbian Straight Education Network, Labtrobe University, and Harris Interactive, who contributed to the planning and implementation of the study. Finally, we thank the study participants for their time and willingness to participate in this study.

NOTE

1. Cisgender refers to someone whose biological sex is the same as one's gender identity. Gender identity is the knowledge of oneself as being male or female. Transgender youth have a gender that is different than their biological sex. This is separate from one's sexual orientation, which relates to sexual attraction (e.g., homosexual, heterosexual, bisexual, etc.).

REFERENCES

Anhalt, K., & Morris, T. L. (1998). Developmental and adjustment issues of gay, lesbian, and bisexual adolescents: a review of the empirical literature. *Clinical Child and Family Psychology Review, 1*(4), 215–230. doi: 10.1023/A:1022660101392

Brunstein-Klomek, A., Marrocco, F., Kleinman, M., Schonfeld, I. S., & Gould, M. S. (2007). Bullying, depression, and suicidality in adolescents. *Journal of the American Academy of Child and Adolescent Psychiatry, 46*(1), 40–49. doi: 10.1097/01.chi.0000242237.84925.18

Centers for Disease Control and Prevention (2010). *Understanding Suicide Fact Sheet.* Atlanta, GA: Centers for Disease Control and Prevention, National Center for Injury Prevention and Control. Retrieved May 25, 2014, from http://www.cdc.gov/ViolencePrevention/pdf/Suicide-FactSheet-a.pdf.

Centers for Disease Control and Prevention (2012). Suicide prevention: Youth suicide. Retrieved May 22, 2014, from http://www.cdc.gov/ViolencePrevention/suicide/youth_suicide.html.

Eaton, W. W., Muntaner, C., Smith, C., Tien, A., & Ybarra, M. L. (2004). Center for Epidemiologic Studies Depression Scale: Review and revision (CESD and CESD-R). In M. E. Maruish (Ed.), *The Use of Psychological Testing for Treatment Planning and Outcomes Assessment* (3rd ed., pp. 363–377). Mahwah, NJ: Lawrence Erlbaum.

Espelage, D. L., Aragon, S. R., Birkett, M., & Koenig, B. W. (2008). Homophobic teasing, psychological outcomes, and sexual orientation among high school students: What influence do parents and schools have? *School Psychology Review, 37*(2), 202–216.

Fergusson, D. M., Horwood, L. J., & Beautrais, A. L. (1999). Is sexual orientation related to mental health problems and suicidality in young people? *Archives of General Psychiatry, 56*(10), 876–880. doi: 10.1001/archpsyc.56.10.876

Gay Straight Lesbian Education Network, Center for Innovative Public Health Research, & Crimes against Children Research Center. (2013). Out online: The experiences of lesbian, gay, bisexual and transgender youth on the Internet. New York: Gay, Lesbian and Straight Education Network. Retrieved May 25, 2014, from http://glsen.org/sites/default/files/Out%20Online%20FINAL.pdf

Goldblum, P., Testa, R. J., Pflum, S., Hendricks, M. L., Bradford, J., & Bongar, B. (2012). The relationship between gender-based victimization and suicide attempts in transgender people. *Professional Psychology: Research and Practice, 43*(5), 468–475. doi: 10.1037/a0029605

Greytak, E. A., Kosciw, J. G., & Diaz, E. M. (2009). Harsh realities: The experience of transgender youth in our nation's schools. New York: Gay, Lesbian and Straight Education Network. Retrieved May 25, 2014, from http://glsen.org/sites/default/files/Harsh%20Realities.pdf.

Grossman, A. H., & D'Augelli, A. R. (2006). Transgender youth: Invisible and vulnerable. *Journal of Homosexuality, 51*(1), 111–128. doi: 10.1300/J082v51n01_06

Hendricks, M. L., & Testa, R. J. (2012). A conceptual framework for clinical work with transgender and gender nonconforming clients: An adaptation of the Minority Stress Model. *Professional Psychology: Research and Practice, 43*(5), 460–467. doi: 10.1037/a0029597

Herba, C. M., Ferdinand, R. F., van der Ende, J. A. N., & Verhulst, F. C. (2007). Long-term associations of childhood suicide ideation. *Journal of the American Academy of Child and Adolescent Psychiatry, 46*(11), 1473–1481. doi: 10.1097/chi.0b013e318149e66f

Hinduja, S., & Patchin, J. W. (2010). Bullying, cyberbullying, and suicide. *Archives of Suicide Research, 14*(3), 206–221. doi: 10.1080/13811118.2010.494133

Hunter, E. (2008). What's good for the gays is good for the gander: Making homeless youth housing safer for lesbian, gay, bisexual, and transgender youth. *Family Court Review, 46*(3), 543–557. doi: 10.1111/j.1744-1617.2008.00220.x

Kann, L., Olsen, E. O., McManus, T., Kinchen, S., Chyen, D., Harris, W. A., . . . Centers for Disease Control and Prevention (CDC). (2011). Sexual identity, sex of sexual contacts, and health-risk behaviors among students in grades 9–12—youth risk behavior surveillance, selected sites, United States, 2001–2009. *Morbidity & Mortality Weekly Review Surveillance Summary, 60*(7), 1–133.

Kerr, D. C. R. (2008). Replicated prediction of men's suicide attempt history from parent reports in late childhood. *Journal of the American Academy of Child and Adolescent Psychiatry, 47*(7), 834–835. doi: 10.1097/CHI.0b013e31817395e4

Klomek, A. B., Marrocco, F., Kleinman, M., Schonfeld, I. S., & Gould, M. S. (2008). Peer victimization, depression, and suicidality in adolescents. *Suicide & Life-Threatening Behavior, 38*(2), 166–180. doi: 10.1521/suli.2008.38.2.166

Kosciw, J. G., Greytak, E. A., Bartkiewicz, M. J., Boesen, M. J., & Palmer, N. A. (2012). The 2011 National School Climate Survey: The experiences of lesbian, gay, bisexual, and transgender youth in our nation's schools. New York: Gay, Lesbian and Straight Education Network. Retrieved May 25, 2014, from http://glsen.org/sites/default/files/2011%20National%20School%20Climate%20Survey%20Full%20Report.pdf.

Lenhart, A., Purcell, K., Smith, A., & Zickuhr, K. (2010). Social media and young adults. Washington, DC: Pew Internet & American Life Project. Retrieved May 22, 2014, from http://www.pewinternet.org/Reports/2010/Social-Media-and-Young-Adults.aspx.

Lewinsohn, P. M., Rohde, P., & Seeley, J. R. (1994). Psychosocial risk factors for future adolescent suicide attempts. *Journal of Consulting and Clinical Psychology, 62*(2), 297–305. doi: 10.1037/0022-006X.62.2.297

McDaniel, J. S., Purcell, D., & D'Augelli, A. R. (2001). The relationship between sexual orientation and risk for suicide: Research findings and future directions for research and prevention. *Suicide and Life-Threatening Behavior, 31*(s1), 84–105. doi: 10.1521/suli.31.1.5.84.24224

McGuire, J. K., Anderson, C. R., Toomey, R. B., & Russell, S. T. (2010). School climate for transgender youth: A mixed method investigation of student experiences and school responses. *Journal of Youth and Adolescence, 39*(10), 1175–1188. doi: 10.1007/s10964-010-9540-7

Meyer, I. H. (2003). Prejudice, social stress, and mental health in lesbian, gay, and bisexual populations: conceptual issues and research evidence. *Psychological Bulletin, 129*(5), 674–697. doi: 10.1037/0033-2909.129.5.674

Mitchell, K. J., & Jones, L. M. (2011). Youth Internet Safety (YISS) Study: Methodology report. Durham, NH: Crimes Against Children Research Center, University of New Hampshire. Retrieved May 22, 2014, from http://www.unh.edu/ccrc/pdf/YISS_Methods_Report_final.pdf.

Olweus, D. (1993). *Bullying at School.* Oxford, England: Blackwell Publishing.

Potter, F. (1990). A study of procedures to identify and trim extreme sampling weights. Proceedings of the Section on Survey Research Methods, American Statistical Association. Retrieved May 22, 2014, from http://www.amstat.org/sections/srms/Proceedings/papers/1990_034.pdf.

Reinherz, H. Z., Tanner, J. L., Berger, S. R., Beardslee, W. R., & Fitzmaurice, G. M. (2006). Adolescent suicidal ideation as predictive of psychopathology, suicidal behavior, and compromised functioning at age 30. *American Journal of Psychiatry, 163*(7), 1226–1232. doi: 10.1176/appi.ajp.163.7.1226

Remafedi, G., French, S., Story, M., Resnick, M. D., & Blum, R. (1998). The relationship between suicide risk and sexual orientation: results of a population-based study. *American Journal of Public Health, 88*(1), 57–60. doi: 10.2105/AJPH.88.1.57

Robinson, J. P., & Espelage, D. L. (2011). Inequities in educational and psychological outcomes between LGBTQ and straight students in middle and high school. *Educational Researcher, 40*(7), 315–330. doi: 10.3102/0013189x11422112

Russell, S. T., & Joyner, K. (2001). Adolescent sexual orientation and suicide risk: Evidence from a national study. *American Journal of Public Health, 91*(8), 1276–1281. doi: 10.2105/ajph.91.8.1276

StataCorp. (2009). Stata Statistical Software (Release 11) [Computer program]. College Station, TX: StataCorp LP.

Testa, R. J., Sciacca, L. M., Wang, F., & Hendricks, M. L. (2012). Effects of violence on transgender people. *Professional Psychology: Research and Practice, 43*(5), 452–459. doi: 10.1037/a0029604

United States' Census Bureau. (2009). Current population survey: population estimates, vintage 2009, national tables. Retrieved M ay 22, 2014, from http://www.census.gov/popest/data/historical/2000s/vintage_2009/index.html.

Ybarra, M., Mitchell, K., Palmer, N., & Resiner, S. (under review). The influence of social support in explaining the odds of victimization online and offline in a national sample of LGBT and non-LGBT youth.

Ybarra, M. L., Boyd, D., Korchmaros, J. D., & Oppenheim, J. K. (2012). Defining and measuring cyberbullying within the larger context of bullying victimization. *Journal of Adolescent Health, 51*(1), 53–58. doi: 10.1016/j.jadohealth.2011.12.031

Ybarra, M. L., Espelage, D. L., & Mitchell, K. J. (2014). Differentiating youth who are bullied from other victims of peer-aggression: the importance of differential power and repetition. *Journal of Adolescent Health.* pii: S1054-139X(14)00089-5. doi: 10.1016/j.jadohealth.2014.02.009

Ybarra, M. L., Mitchell, K. J., Kosciw, J., & Korchmaros, J. D. (under review). Bullying victimization and suicidal ideation in a national sample of LGB and heterosexual youth. *Prevention Science.*

PART FOUR

Explanatory Models

13

Social-Psychological Model of Adolescent Suicide

CHRISTOPHER D. CORONA, DAVID A. JOBES, AND ALAN L. BERMAN ■

To underscore the growing public health concern over bullying and suicidal behavior among adolescents, the Centers for Disease Control and Prevention convened a panel in 2010 to directly address the interplay between bullying (which includes victims of bullying, perpetrators, and victims who also bully) and suicidal behavior (which can manifest as expressed suicide ideation, a suicide attempt, or death by suicide; Hertz, Donato, & Wright, 2013). One goal of the panel was to begin a discussion that will eventually lead to a better understanding of the ways in which these phenomena interact, hence, ideally, paving the way for interventions that reduce the incidence of both bullying among youth and associated suicidal behaviors.

The effort to understand this unique interaction begins with a thorough understanding of suicidal behavior among adolescents. Thus, the present chapter will discuss adolescent suicide, focusing on important psychosocial perspectives for suicidal behavior and contextualizing these theories within adolescent psychology. A proposed developmental pathway linking bullying with suicidal behavior will then be discussed. Finally, recommendations will be provided to health providers, educators, parents, and policy makers that can potentially guide the discussion as we continue to develop an understanding of the relationship between bullying and suicide.

AN EPIDEMIOLOGICAL PERSPECTIVE

In 2010, there were 4,600 suicides in the United States among 15–24-year-olds, making it the third leading cause of death in this age group (Centers for Disease Control and Prevention, 2012a). Eighty-one percent of these suicides were males. Despite the higher rate of completed suicides among youth males, a plethora of data show that female youth attempt suicide at a higher rate than male youth (Berman, Jobes, & Silverman, 2006). Moreover, a recent survey indicated that, among ninth- to twelfth-grade students in public and private schools nationwide, 16% reported suicidal ideation in the year prior to the survey, 13% reported making a plan to complete suicide, and 8% reported making a suicide attempt (Murphy, Xu, & Kochanek, 2013). Approximately 157,000 youth in this sample reported receiving medical care for self-inflicted injuries.

Cultural variations also exist with regard to adolescent suicide. Native American and Alaskan Native youth currently have the highest rate of suicide-related deaths (Centers for Disease Control and Prevention, 2012a). A recent survey also indicated that Hispanic youth in public and private schools nationwide are more likely to report making a suicide attempt than their non-Hispanic peers (Murphy et al., 2013).

Recent studies have estimated that the percentage of adolescents who experience bullying behavior (including those who bully and those who are victims) falls between 20% and 56%, with widely varying estimates of the extent to which this behavior occurs online (Borowsky, Taliaferro, & McMorris, 2013; Centers for Disease Control and Prevention, 2012a; Kowalski & Limber, 2013). Hertz and colleagues (2013) extrapolated these estimates to a modern classroom of 30 students that, then, would contain between 6 and 17 students that are involved in bullying as a perpetrator, a victim, or a bully-victim. The prevalence of both bullying and suicidal behaviors among youth underscores the significance of these problems. To begin to integrate the understanding of these phenomena, a discussion of the social-psychological underpinnings of adolescent suicidal behavior follows.

SOCIAL-PSYCHOLOGICAL PERSPECTIVES

As Berman and colleagues (2006) discussed, numerous attempts have been made over the years to explain suicidal behavior from perspectives inclusive of psychoanalytic and cognitive-behavioral theory as well as biological, developmental, and social psychology. The discussion that follows is not exhaustive in terms of these perspectives, but includes the psychosocial perspectives that the authors feel are most relevant to the current discussion of bullying and suicide.

The family system can be very influential in the life of an adolescent, and pathogenic family dynamics have been implicated as risk factors for suicidal behavior. Wagner, Silverman, and Martin (2003) discussed research suggesting that problems in the family system such as low adaptability and cohesion are associated with non-fatal suicidal behavior such as ideation and attempts. Sheftall, Mathias, Furr, and Dougherty (2013) supported this discussion with a study examining the relationship between suicide attempts and parental attachment, family adaptability and cohesion in a sample of 262 adolescent psychiatric inpatients. Those with a history of making a suicide attempt rated the quality of their maternal and paternal attachments significantly lower than those with no history of making a suicide attempt. Emotional bonding (cohesion) and the ability of the family to change structure, roles, and rules in response to stress (adaptability) were also rated significantly lower by those with a history of making a suicide attempt. Sheftall and colleagues argued that early family attachment quality and dynamics set the stage for how one views and behaves in relationships moving forward, and that negative experiences early in life could be precursors to suicide risk factors such as social disconnection and a lack of support.

Wagner (1997) and Wagner and colleagues (2003) also discussed research suggesting that child maltreatment such as physical and sexual abuse is strongly associated with both fatal and non-fatal suicidal behavior, and other researchers have attempted to further understand the mechanisms involved in this relationship. Bedi and colleagues (2011) used family survey data from over 2,500 respondents to examine the effects of childhood sexual abuse (CSA) on the development of depression, post-traumatic stress disorder (PTSD), and suicidal behavior, including ideation, plans, and attempts. While the researchers found that a history of CSA is significantly associated with increased risk of suicidal behavior, they found this association to be reduced after controlling for depression and PTSD. These findings suggest that depression and PTSD partially account for the relationship between CSA and suicidal behavior. Soylu and Alpaslan (2012) reviewed forensic and social worker reports for 106 sexually abused children between the ages of 12 and 18. Suicidal ideation developed in over 60% of the cases studied, and 24.5% involved a suicide attempt. The researchers also found that the rate of suicidal ideation and attempts was higher in cases where PTSD developed after the abuse, the abuser was someone known to the victim, or the victim was repeatedly exposed to abuse. These findings highlight, not only the relationship between childhood abuse and suicidal behavior, but also the factors involved that can mediate this relationship.

Jobes (1995, 2000) sought to further understand the role of relationships both inside and outside the family system as it pertains to the development of suicidal behavior. He ultimately argued that the suicidal mind essentially exists at some point on a continuum between intrapsychic (self-oriented) and interpsychic (relationally oriented) conflict. Those with intrapsychic suicidality are characterized by negative perceptions of the self as well as feelings of failure and hopelessness. Those with interpsychic suicidality struggle with interpersonal strife as well as feelings of loneliness and disconnection from others. Jobes also argued that those with different suicidal motivations could present different risk profiles, with relationally oriented suicidality being protective against suicidal behavior, and self-focused suicidality being facilitative.

Stone (2011) and Lento, Ellis, and Jobes (2013) examined the intrapsychic versus interpsychic conceptualization of suicide empirically. Stone studied 108 inpatients hospitalized for suicidal behavior and receiving intensive, suicide-focused treatment. Based on qualitative data provided in response to questions related to their suicidal thinking, these patients were classified as either self oriented or relationally oriented. These inpatients also provided ratings of their wish to live and their wish to die. Stone found that those with relationally oriented suicidal thinking had stronger wishes to live in comparison to their wishes to die. In other words, the relational nature of their suicidality was in and of itself protective. Lento and colleagues studied 32 suicidal inpatients who received an average of 11.81 sessions of suicide-focused psychotherapeutic treatment. Patients with more of a self than relational orientation to their suicidality had higher ratings of depression, hopelessness, and suicidal ideation at the start of treatment. Over the course of treatment, these patients resolved their suicidal ideation at a slower rate that did patients whose relationship to suicidality was equally self- and relationally focused. These findings provide support for the arguments that the interpersonal context for suicidal behavior can be individualized, and that risk assessment and treatment implications can vary based on context.

THE INTERPERSONAL THEORY OF SUICIDE

Thomas Joiner's interpersonal theory of suicide (2005) argues that death by suicide requires the interaction of three constructs within an individual: thwarted belongingness, perceived burdensomeness, and acquired capability. The concept of thwarted belongingness can be traced to a theory proposed by Baumeister and Leary (1995) arguing that all people share a common need to belong. Joiner's theory posits that the desire for suicide will develop if this fundamental need is not met. This notion builds upon earlier social-psychological conceptualizations in that it isolates the specific interpersonal mechanism at play in suicidal behavior (Van Orden et al., 2010). It also addresses social interaction on a deeper level than merely the presence of relationships, and concerns the nature of those relationships. In other words, a true sense of belonging manifests in the quality of relationships in one's life, not the quantity. Joiner argues that suicidal desire can manifest as a response to the consistent and pervasive feeling that one does not belong.

Perceived burdensomeness involves feelings of self-hatred and of being a liability to others (Joiner, 2005). Such feelings of burdensomeness have traditionally been tied to family-related issues such as conflict, illness, and unemployment (Richman, 1986; Sabbath, 1969; Van Orden et al., 2010). However, Joiner expands the reach of this construct to include the relationships that exist outside of the family structure. In other words (and this is arguably relevant to adolescent interactions), feelings of burdensomeness can also be involved in peer interactions. Again, Joiner argues that consistent and pervasive feelings of being a burden to others will lead to the development of a desire for suicide.

Though not necessarily social in nature, the third pillar of Joiner's interpersonal theory of suicide is nonetheless important to discuss. The innate human survival instinct is powerful and steadfast, but is obviously overcome in individuals who die by suicide. What is it that sets apart those who ultimately die by suicide from those who desire suicide but never make an attempt? Joiner argues that it is the "acquired ability to enact lethal self-injury" (2005, p. 22). He acknowledges the difficulty of overcoming the human disposition for survival, and argues that one can actually become habituated to and comfortable with the idea of self-harm. More specifically, repeated and prolonged exposure to "painful and provocative stimuli" will eventually lower one's fear of self-harm and raise the risk of making a serious suicide attempt (Van Orden et al., 2010, p. 587). Such stimuli include risky behaviors such as substance abuse, violence, and thrill-seeking behavior (Joiner, 2005).

Empirical support for the interpersonal theory of suicide was found in a study conducted by Van Orden, Witte, Gordon, Bender, and Joiner (2008) that examined suicidal behavior in a college counseling center sample. After controlling for age, gender, and depressive symptomatology, the researchers found that perceived burdensomeness alone predicted the presence of suicidal ideation, while thwarted belongingness alone did not. However, the researchers found that the interaction between perceived burdensomeness and thwarted belongingness was the most significant predictor of suicidal ideation, indicating that the presence of both social constructs is related to suicidal risk.

The relationship between socialization and suicide is complex and exists both inside and outside of the family system. Jobes argues that relationally focused suicidality is more protective than suicidality focused solely on the self; however, Joiner asserts that the context for developing suicidal behavior is inherently social. While existing and current research continues to highlight the role of social factors in the development of suicidal behavior, future research should continue to examine the complexity of this relationship (especially as it pertains to the unique social challenges faced by adolescents).

THE ADOLESCENT CONTEXT

When discussing suicide among adolescents, it is important to address the developmental realities and challenges that are unique to this phase of life. From the turn of the twentieth century, scholars have been characterizing adolescence as a uniquely trying time and attempting to explain these challenges from a psychological perspective. Hall (1904) proposed a "storm and stress" model arguing that adolescence is an inherently tumultuous phase characterized by interpersonal conflict, mood fluctuations, and reckless behavior. Since Hall, other theorists have posited that adolescence might not be as bleak and distressing as once believed. Studies have provided evidence that many adolescents enjoy their lives, engage in fulfilling relationships, and look forward to the future (Offer, 1987; Offer & Schonert-Reichl, 1992). These seemingly contradictory viewpoints have paved the way for a less polarized understanding of adolescence as a time that is often (but not necessarily) characterized by distress (Berman et al., 2006). It has been argued that such distress can include interpersonal conflicts, mood fluctuations, and reckless behavior, as mentioned earlier, and also that it can be shaped by biological and cultural factors (Arnett, 1999; Buchanan et al., 1990).

Generalities aside, it has been argued that today's youth are growing up in a post–September 11th world that is shaping their psychology in unique and heretofore unseen ways (Taffel, 2001). Berman and colleagues (2006) have asked whether voluminous and routine exposure to provocative stimuli (e.g., violence, sex, substance abuse, and extravagance) through the media and through a rapidly evolving (and arguably less private) online culture is creating levels of awareness, pressure, and vulnerability that are unprecedented. Gross and Levin (1987) emphasized the especially significant amount of formative learning in a variety of contexts that occurs during the adolescent years, and posited that this influences the unique ways in which different adolescents respond to and behave in their world. It is worth asking how such a formative developmental phase that has recently seen an influx of uniquely provocative stimuli contributes to the ways in which adolescents conceptualize death and suicide.

ADOLESCENT PERCEPTIONS OF DEATH AND SUICIDE

While this is a difficult question to answer, some have tried to address it theoretically and empirically. Berman and colleagues (2006) argue that, during adolescence, curiosity about death becomes more profound as various physical, social, and personal forces interact. More specifically, they contend that this developing formulation can lead to the beginning of more existential contemplations about the meaning of life and death. Ideally, these contemplations take shape in a way that allows the adolescent to visualize goals in life and fosters hope of reaching those goals. Allen (1987), however, argues that such a formative phase in the creation of life and death concepts can be a double-edged sword. While a budding sense of meaning and purpose in life can present itself, he argues that an underdeveloped appreciation of the permanence of death is also possible. This can manifest as a misunderstanding of the notion of nonexistence and of the fact that one cannot return from death. Should healthy senses of hope and appreciation for death not develop concurrently, one could be especially at risk for suicidal behavior (Berman et al., 2006).

Baron and Byrne (1984) posited a relatively recent desensitization effect whereby increased exposure to suicidal behavior through movies and television has resulted in a less aversive reaction among adolescents to suicide in general. Considering this theory in conjunction with an increased number of avenues for exposure (especially inclusive of the media and Internet), Berman and colleagues (2006) have argued that suicide could be reinforced in this age group as a viable option for coping with distressing situations. Such reinforcement can also come from within one's peer group, and Joiner (2003) addressed the potential for suicidal behavior to cluster among peers. Results from a study conducted among college roommates suggested that "assortative relating" and shared stress contribute jointly to the phenomenon of clustering. "Assortative relating" is the tendency for individuals who share similar characteristics (including suicide risk factors) to form relationships with each other, and shared stress occurs when vulnerable individuals are exposed as a group to a serious stressor that has the potential to fuel suicidality. Joiner also argues that similar occurrences of assortative relating and shared stress have been found in other documented suicide clusters (Haw, 1994).

From a cognitive perspective, Orbach, Kedem, Gorchover, Apter, and Tyano (1993) found differences between suicidal and non-suicidal adolescents with regard to the ways in which they processed fears of death. Specifically, suicidal adolescents experienced fear of death as facilitative of suicidal behavior, whereas non-suicidal adolescents experienced fear of death as preventive. Similarly, Renberg and Jacobsson (2003) conducted a population-level study in Sweden, and found that those with a history of suicidal behavior had more permissive attitudes towards suicide in general.

In summary, it can be argued that adolescence is a phase characterized by profound personal and social change, powerful and diverse stimuli, and maturational dynamics that shape entry into adulthood. These influences can have a profound effect on the ways in which adolescents interact with and interpret their environment, and understanding this relationship is a key component in the effort to prevent suicidal behavior in this demographic.

TOWARDS A DEVELOPMENTAL PATHWAY

As a supplement to a brief review of select literature describing the psychosocial correlates of suicidal behavior, we posit a developmental model that attempts to trace the path of potential psychosocial events that can be experienced by adolescents, beginning with a vulnerability to bullying and ending with suicidal behavior. Literature suggests that certain individuals are inherently more vulnerable to bullying (i.e., those who do not identify as heterosexual, those with intellectual and developmental disabilities, those with mental disorders, and those with abnormal body weights). These individuals are thus more likely to be victimized by those with a need to exert power over others, who often emerge from the same population of vulnerable youth (Borowsky et al., 2013). There is also evidence to support the claim that victims experience heightened levels of psychosocial sequelae (i.e., depression, anxiety, and social disconnection) that are risk factors for suicidal behavior.

Vulnerability

Those identifying as gay, lesbian, bisexual, or transgendered are especially vulnerable to bullying from peers (Berlan, Corliss, Field, Goodman, & Bryn Austin, 2010; Williams, Connolly, Pepler, & Craig, 2003). Further investigating this vulnerability, Patrick, Bell, Huang, Lazarakis, and Edwards (2013) conducted a study suggesting that the consequences of bullying because of sexual orientation are of greater magnitude than those of bullying for other reasons. The researchers analyzed data from over 27,000 eighth-, tenth-, and twelfth-graders collected using the Washington State Healthy Young Survey. Those being bullied reported lower quality of life scores and increased risk for depression and suicidal ideation, with the strongest correlates found among those bullied because of their sexual orientation. While the extent to which risk in this population can be directly attributed to bullying because of sexual orientation remains unclear, these findings highlight the vulnerability inherent among those with a non-heterosexual orientation.

Fisher, Moskowitz, and Hodapp (2012) examined vulnerability among those with intellectual and developmental disabilities, including genetic disorders, autism spectrum disorders, psychiatric disorders, cerebral palsy, attention-deficit hyperactivity disorder, and hearing impairments. The researchers surveyed caregivers of 146 disabled adults regarding victimization, including theft, teasing, and abuse. Findings suggested that even those with intellectual and developmental disabilities who are higher functioning and more aware of risky situations were victimized at rates similar to those with lower functioning and less able to gauge risk. Regardless of their level of functionality, those with intellectual and developmental disabilities are at increased risk of exploitation and abuse (Nettelbeck & Wilson, 2002; Petersilia, 2001; Sullivan & Knutson, 2000).

Literature also suggests a relationship between body weight and vulnerability to victimization. Reulbach and colleagues (2013) analyzed data drawn from over 8,500 nine-year-olds from 910 primary schools in Ireland. Those with body mass indices in either the "overweight" or "obese" classification were significantly more likely to experience bullying than those in other weight classifications. Additionally, self-perception of being skinny or very skinny was significantly associated with bullying. Brixval, Rayce, Rasmussen, Holstein, and Due (2012) conducted a similar study among over 4,700 11-, 13-, and 15-year-olds in Denmark. Overweight and obese students were significantly more exposed to bullying than normal-weight students, and the researchers found that this relationship was mediated by body image. In other words, the risk for bullying increased as students' perceptions of their body weight strayed further from what they believed to be normal. Though there are probably other demographics also at increased risk for bullying, the literature presented here suggests heightened vulnerability among those who do not identify as heterosexual, those with intellectual and developmental disabilities, those with mental disorders, and those with body mass indices that fall outside the normal range.

Power

Power differentials between perpetrators of bullying and their targets have been discussed as key characteristics of this type of victimization (Besag, 1989; Olweus, 1993; Olweus, 1996). To further understand the complex role that power plays in bullying, Vaillancourt, Hymel, and McDougall (2003) conducted a study among 555 students aged 11–17 years from elementary and secondary schools in Canada. The researchers argued that bullies use two primary forms of power (explicit and implicit) as described by LaFreniere and Charlesworth (1983). Explicit social power is expressed openly and with force, thereby using intimidation to elicit fear and submission. Implicit social power depends on acceptance by peers, and is gained by demonstrating competence and achieving status. Vaillancourt and colleagues hypothesized that two types of bullies would be identified based on their use of power: those who use explicit power and are thus disliked by their peers, and those who use implicit power and are thus popular among their peers. The researchers were also interested in whether these different types of bullies would demonstrate differences in their self-perceptions of social status and mental health.

Using peer assessment and self-report measures, the researchers found that many of the bullies identified in their study did not fit the stereotype of a psychologically maladjusted and socially marginalized student. Over half of those identified as bullies were perceived by others as powerful and popular, and these perceptions seemed to be influenced by both explicit and implicit power. Most bullies were perceived to be physically and relationally aggressive, and some were also perceived to possess valuable social assets such as wealth, attractiveness, athletic competence, and leadership skills. The researchers also categorized bullies based on their level of perceived power (high, moderate, and low), and found that the most powerful bullies seemed to wield the most implicit power and were thus popular among their peers.

In general, those identified as powerful bullies in this study reported higher levels of general self-worth, less loneliness, and feeling better integrated within their peer group. Notably, there was no significant relationship between being identified as a powerful bully and depression, thus raising the question of whether bullying can in some way protect perpetrators from depression. While the mediating mechanisms between the use of power and the positive outcomes reported for bullies in this study were not addressed, these results begin to shed light on motivating factors for those who bully and the ways in which bullying behavior can be reinforced by the environment.

VICTIMIZATION

The exertion of power and influence over others by means of victimization can cause a host of negative psychosocial sequelae. Hawker and Boulton (2000) conducted a meta-analysis of cross sectional studies published between 1978 and 1997 that examined associations between victimization and psychosocial maladjustment. The 23 studies analyzed included over 5,000 children. The researchers classified victimization into five categories (indirect, relational, physical, verbal, and generic), and examined psychosocial maladjustment in the form of depression, loneliness, generalized and social anxiety, and self-perceptions of global and social self-worth. Moderately significant effect sizes were found correlating victimization positively with depression, loneliness, and anxiety. Negative correlations were found between victimization and self-perceptions of global and social self-worth. Effect sizes ranged from .19 (anxiety) to .29 (depression), with the strongest correlations found between victimization, loneliness, and depression.

Reijntjes, Kamphuis, Prinzie, and Telch (2010) conducted a similar meta-analysis examining over 12,000 children in 15 studies; however, only prospective studies that followed children over two or more time points were included. This allowed researchers to control for baseline psychosocial maladjustment among victims, thus more rigorously examining this relationship. Experiences of victimization were classified into four categories (peer victimization, peer harassment, peer aggression, and bullying); and internalizing problems, including depression, anxiety, withdrawal, loneliness, and somatic complaints, were examined. After controlling for baseline internalizing problems, researchers found that victimization was associated with increases in internalizing problems at follow-up. As with results found by Hawker and Bolton (2000), the largest effect sizes in this analysis were seen with depression (.41) and loneliness (.29). It is notable that both meta-analyses examining the relationship between victimization and psychosocial maladjustment identified depression and loneliness as the strongest correlates. These findings are supported by research implicating the role of social disconnection and depression in the development of the desire for suicide (Brown, Beck, Steer, & Grisham, 2000; Joiner, 2005; Van Orden et al., 2010).

Future Directions and Recommendations

The literature discussed thus far suggests that interpersonal dynamics are especially important when examining the relationship between bullying and suicide among youth. However, this interaction exists at multiple levels and is not yet fully understood. The pathway proposed in this chapter is not exhaustive and only minimally addresses the psychosocial experiences of perpetrators; however, the authors feel it is a solid foundation upon which we can begin to understand bullying as a precipitant of suicidal behavior. Accordingly, the following recommendations are provided as the effort to learn more about the interaction between bullying and suicidal behavior continues.

Medical and Mental Health Providers

- It is imperative that those in the provider community familiarize themselves both with emerging literature on suicidal behavior (especially with respect to adolescents) and with evolving best practices related to treating suicidal clients. The field of suicidology is growing at an incredibly rapid rate, and an effort needs to be made by those in provider roles to become educated about emerging trends in the identification and treatment of suicidal individuals. Additionally, the Substance Abuse and

Mental Health Services Administration provides a National Registry of Evidence-Based Programs and Practices (http://www.nrepp.samhsa.gov). Providers are encouraged both to consult this registry in an effort to familiarize themselves with the options available for treating suicidal clients and to seek training in any evidence-based practice they feel is necessary or relevant to their current scope of care.
- As Berman and colleagues (2006) have discussed, providers themselves are "not immune to labeling their clients or participating in interactive dynamics that may be pathogenic" (p. 74). Though valid and understandable, the intense pain and struggle experienced by suicidal clients can indeed be exhausting, frightening, and even frustrating for those responsible for their care. Providers are encouraged to exercise patience and professionalism with this population, and to seek out support services (such as professional consultation and self-care activities) that will enable them to continue to practice therapeutically with suicidal clients.

Parents and Teachers

- Educators and parents enjoy frequent interactions with adolescents, which puts them at the front lines of the battle to minimize bullying and its effects on suicidal behavior. Those who occupy these special positions are encouraged to educate themselves about the realities of bullying and suicidal behavior. Both the American Foundation for Suicide Prevention and the website www.stopbullying.gov provide a wealth of information that can help educators and parents identify bullying and suicidal behavior as well as intervene in an effective manner. Educators are encouraged to implement initiatives aimed at minimizing both the incidence of bullying in school and the negative effects of bullying that do occur. Both parents and educators are encouraged to become familiar with and provide response options for suicidal behavior that include contacting hotlines or accessing mental health care.
- Like providers, educators and parents are not immune from the labeling and stigmatization that can follow the identification of suicidal behaviors. Such reactions have the potential to intensify negative self-directed feelings experienced by suicidal individuals as well as behavioral reactions to those feelings (Berman et al., 2006). It is recommended that educators and parents acknowledge and validate the struggles of suicidal adolescents and create a safe environment within which help-seeking behavior is encouraged and reinforced.

Policy Makers

- Continue to fund research that investigates suicide, bullying, and their interaction. This chapter has highlighted the notion that suicide and bullying are affected by factors existing at multiple levels of an individual's interaction with the world, including his or her biological makeup, internal psychological experiences, and external social interactions. This is closely aligned with Bronfenbrenner (1977) and his belief that understanding individual experiences necessitates understanding the myriad interactions that contextualize an individual's life. Thus, while we have an empirical foundation that highlights risk factors associated with suicide and bullying, there is a need for continuing heuristic examination that attempts to discover the ways in which these constructs interact.

- It is important to note that the literature to date in these fields has not sufficiently addressed the roles that culture (specifically related to race and ethnicity) and sexual orientation play in the development of suicidal behavior as a response to bullying. Given the pervasive and influential nature of these constructs and their impact on social interaction, further elucidating any trends that exist across cultures and across different sexual orientations with respect to bullying and suicide is imperative.
- A central component of the Centers for Disease Control and Prevention's Strategic Direction for Suicide Prevention is fostering connectedness between youth and their family, school, and community environments (Centers for Disease Control and Prevention, 2012b). Programs such as Sources of Strength (Wyman et al., 2010) and Tennessee Lives Count (Hertz et al., 2013) have shown promise with regard to helping youth feel more connected to those around them and reducing the stigma associated with suicidal behavior. Funding support should be provided in an effort to assess the effectiveness and feasibility of interventions of this nature. Funding support should also be provided to initiatives that have demonstrated the potential for implementation and effectiveness within communities at risk, especially with regard to vulnerable populations such as those with intellectual or developmental disabilities, abnormal body weights, psychiatric disorders, and non-heterosexual orientations.

REFERENCES

Allen, B. P. (1987). Youth suicide. *Adolescence, 22*, 271–290.

Arnett, J. J. (1999). Adolescent storm and stress, reconsidered. *American Psychologist, 54*(5), 317–326.

Baron, R. A., & Byrne, D. E. (1984). *Social Psychology: Understanding Human Interaction* (4th ed.). Newton, MA: Allyn & Bacon.

Baumeister, R. F., & Leary, M. R. (1995). The need to belong: Desire for interpersonal attachments as a fundamental human motivation. *Psychological Bulletin, 117*(3), 497.

Bedi, S., Nelson, E. C., Lynskey, M. T., Mc Cutcheon, V. V., Heath, A. C., Madden, P. A. F., & Martin, N. G. (2011). Risk for suicidal thoughts and behavior after childhood sexual abuse in women and men. *Suicide and Life-Threatening Behavior, 41*(4), 406–415.

Berman, A. L., Jobes, D. A., & Silverman, M. M. (2006). *Adolescent Suicide: Assessment and Intervention* (2nd ed.). Washington, DC: American Psychological Association.

Berlan, E. D., Corliss, H. L., Field, A. E., Goodman, E., & Bryn Austin, S. (2010). Sexual orientation and bullying among adolescents in the Growing Up Today study. *Journal of Adolescent Health, 46*(4), 366–371.

Besag, V. E. (1989). *Bullies and Victims in Schools*. Philadelphia: Open University Press.

Borowsky, I. W., Taliaferro, L. A., & McMorris, B. J. (2013). Suicidal thinking and behavior among youth involved in verbal and social bullying: Risk and protective factors. *Journal of Adolescent Health, 53*(1), S4-S12.

Brixval, C. S., Rayce, S. L., Rasmussen, M., Holstein, B. E., & Due, P. (2012). Overweight, body image and bullying—an epidemiological study of 11- to 15-year-olds. *The European Journal of Public Health, 22*(1), 126–130.

Bronfenbrenner, U. (1977). Toward an experimental ecology of human development. *American Psychologist, 32*(7), 513–531.

Brown, G. K., Beck, A. T., Steer, R. A., & Grisham, J. R. (2000). Risk factors for suicide in psychiatric outpatients: A 20-year prospective study. *Journal of Consulting and Clinical Psychology, 68*(3), 371–377.

Buchanan, C. M., Eccles, J. S., Flanagan, C., Midgley, C., Feldlaufer, H., & Harold, R. D. (1990). Parents' and teachers' beliefs about adolescents: Effects of sex and experience. *Journal of Youth and Adolescence, 19*(4), 363–394.

Centers for Disease Control and Prevention. (2012a). Youth Risk Behavior Surveillance—United States, 2011. *Morbidity and Mortality Weekly Report Surveillance Summaries, 61*, no. SS 4. Retrieved July 7, 2013, from http://www.cdc.gov/mmwr/pdf/ss/ss6104.pdf.

Centers for Disease Control and Prevention (2012b). Promoting individual, family, and community connectedness to prevent suicidal behavior. Retrieved July 7, 2013, from http://www.cdc.gov/ViolencePrevention/pdf/Suicide_Strategic_Direction_Full_Version-a.pdf.

Fisher, M. H., Moskowitz, A. L., & Hodapp, R. M. (2012). Vulnerability and experiences related to social victimization among individuals with intellectual and developmental disabilities. *Journal of Mental Health Research in Intellectual Disabilities, 5*(1), 32–48.

Gross, A. M., & Levin, R. B. (1987). Learning. In V. B. Van Hasselt & M. Hersen (Eds.), *Handbook of Adolescent Psychology* (pp. 77–90). New York: Pergamon Press.

Hall, G. S. (1904). *Adolescence: Its Psychology and Its Relation to Physiology, Anthropology, Sociology, Sex, Crime, Religion, and Education* (Vols. 1–2). Englewood Cliffs, NJ: Prentice Hall.

Haw, C. M. (1994). A cluster of suicides at a London psychiatric unit. *Suicide and Life-Threatening Behavior, 24*(3), 256–266.

Hawker, D. S. J., & Boulton, M. J. (2000). Twenty years' research on peer victimization and psychosocial maladjustment: A meta-analytic review of cross-sectional studies. *Journal of Child Psychology and Psychiatry, 41*(4), 441–455.

Hertz, M. F., Donato, I., & Wright, J. (2013). Bullying and suicide: A public health approach. *Journal of Adolescent Health, 53*(1), S1–S3.

Jobes, D. A. (1995). The challenge and the promise of clinical suicidology. *Suicide and Life-Threatening Behavior, 25*(4), 437–449.

Jobes, D. A. (2000). Collaborating to prevent suicide: A clinical-research perspective. *Suicide and Life-Threatening Behavior, 30*(1), 8–17.

Joiner, T. (2003). Contagion of suicidal symptoms as a function of assortative relating and shared relationship stress in college roommates. *Journal of Adolescence, 26*(4), 495–504.

Joiner, T. (2005). *Why People Die by Suicide*. Cambridge, MA: Harvard University Press.

Kowalski, R. M., & Limber, S. P. (2013). Psychological, physical, and academic correlates of cyberbullying and traditional bullying. *Journal of Adolescent Health, 53*(1), S13–S20.

LaFreniere, P., & Charlesworth, W. R. (1983). Dominance, attention, and affiliation in a preschool group: A nine-month longitudinal study. *Ethology and Sociobiology, 4*(2), 55–67.

Lento, R. M., Ellis, T. E., & Jobes, D. A. (2013). Self vs. relational suicidal orientation: Implications for treatment course and outcome. Paper session presented April, 26th at the 46th Annual Conference of the American Association of Suicidology, Austin, TX.

Murphy, S. L., Xu, J., & Kochanek, K. D. (2013). Death: Final data for 2010. *National Vital Statistics Report, 61*, no. 4. Retrieved July 7, 2013, from http://www.cdc.gov/nchs/data/nvsr/nvsr61/nvsr61_04.pdf.

Nettelbeck, T., & Wilson, C. (2002). Personal vulnerability to victimization of people with mental retardation. *Trauma, Violence, & Abuse, 3*(4), 289–306.

Offer, D. (1987). In defense of adolescents. *Journal of the American Medical Association, 257*(24), 3407–3408.

Offer, D., & Schonert-Reichl, K. A. (1992). Debunking the myths of adolescence: Findings from recent research. *Journal of the American Academy of Child & Adolescent Psychiatry, 31*(6), 1003–1014.

Olweus, D. (1993). *Bullying at School: What We Know and What We Can Do.* Oxford, England: Wiley-Blackwell.

Olweus, D. (1996). Bullying at school: Knowledge base and an effective intervention program. *Annals of the New York Academy of Sciences, 794*(1), 265–276.

Orbach, I., Kedem, P., Gorchover, O., Apter, A., & Tyano, S. (1993). Fears of death in suicidal and nonsuicidal adolescents. *Journal of Abnormal Psychology, 102*(4), 553.

Patrick, D. L., Bell, J. F., Huang, J. Y., Lazarakis, N. C., & Edwards, T. C. (2013). Bullying and quality of life in youths perceived as gay, lesbian, or bisexual in Washington State, 2010. *American Journal of Public Health, 103*(7), 1255–1261.

Petersilia, J. R. (2001). Crime victims with developmental disabilities: A review essay. *Criminal Justice and Behavior, 28*(6), 655–694.

Reijntjes, A., Kamphuis, J. H., Prinzie, P., & Telch, M. J. (2010). Peer victimization and internalizing problems in children: A meta-analysis of longitudinal studies. *Child Abuse & Neglect, 34*(4), 244–252.

Renberg, E. S., & Jacobsson, L. (2003). Development of a questionnaire on attitudes towards suicide (ATTS) and its application in a Swedish population. *Suicide and Life-Threatening Behavior, 33*(1), 52–64.

Reulbach, U., Ladewig, E. L., Nixon, E., O'Moore, M., Williams, J., & O'Dowd, T. (2013). Weight, body image and bullying in 9-year-old children. *Journal of Paediatrics and Child Health, 49*(4), E288–E293.

Richman, J. (1986). *Family Therapy for Suicidal People.* New York: Springer Publishing Company.

Sabbath, J. C. (1969). The suicidal adolescent—the expendable child. *Journal of the American Academy of Child Psychiatry, 8*(2), 272–285.

Sheftall, A. H., Mathias, C. W., Furr, R. M., & Dougherty, D. M. (2013). Adolescent attachment security, family functioning, and suicide attempts. *Attachment & Human Development, 15*(4), 368–383.

Soylu, N., & Alpaslan, A. H. (2012). Suicidal behavior and associated factors in sexually abused adolescents. *Children and Youth Services Review, 35*(2), 253–257.

Stone, G. (2011). Self-orientation and relational-orientation in suicidal risk: Possible facilitative and protective aspects. (Unpublished doctoral dissertation.) The Catholic University of America, Washington, DC.

Sullivan, P. M., & Knutson, J. F. (2000). Maltreatment and disabilities: A population-based epidemiological study. *Child Abuse & Neglect, 24*(10), 1257–1273.

Taffel, R. (2001). The wall of silence: Therapists must finally recognize that the world of today's adolescents has changed profoundly, and that our approaches with them and their families need to catch up. *Psychotherapy Networker, 25*(3), 52–58.

Van Orden, K. A., Witte, T. K., Gordon, K. H., Bender, T. W., & Joiner, T. E., Jr. (2008). Suicidal desire and the capability for suicide: Tests of the interpersonal-psychological theory of suicidal behavior among adults. *Journal of Consulting and Clinical Psychology, 76*(1), 72–83.

Van Orden, K. A., Witte, T. K., Cukrowicz, K. C., Braithwaite, S. R., Selby, E. A., & Joiner T. E. Jr., (2010). The interpersonal theory of suicide. *Psychological Review, 117*(2), 575–600.

Vaillancourt, T., Hymel, S., & McDougall, P. (2003). Bullying is power: Implications for school-based intervention strategies. *Journal of Applied School Psychology, 19*(2), 157–176.

Wagner, B. M., Silverman, M. A. C., & Martin, C. E. (2003). Family factors in youth suicidal behaviors. *American Behavioral Scientist, 46*(9), 1171–1191.

Wagner, B. M. (1997). Family risk factors for child and adolescent suicidal behavior. *Psychological Bulletin, 121*(2), 246–298.

Williams, T., Connolly, J., Pepler, D., & Craig, W. (2003). Questioning and sexual minority adolescents: High school experiences of bullying, sexual harassment and physical abuse. *Canadian Journal of Community Mental Health, 22*(2), 47–58.

Wyman, P. A., Brown, C. H., LoMurray, M., Schmeelk-Cone, K., Petrova, M., Yu, Q.,... Wang, W. (2010). An outcome evaluation of the Sources of Strength suicide prevention program delivered by adolescent peer leaders in high schools. *American Journal of Public Health, 100*(9), 1653–1661.

14

Bullying as a Sociocultural Pathway to Suicide

JOYCE CHU, JOHNSON MA, BRUCE BONGAR, AND PETER GOLDBLUM ■

Prevalent explanatory models of suicide and media portrayal tend to conceptualize suicide as an individual act or mental health–related event. However, many theorists and recent findings have shown that suicide can and should be regarded as a sociocultural phenomenon, understood within the sociocultural context in which the suicidal risk and acts are embedded. This chapter aims to move beyond popular belief that portrays suicide as an individual act or a mental illness–related event and presents readers with evidence and an understanding of sociocultural explanations for suicidal behaviors among youth. We first review sociocultural theories of suicide that explain why the act of suicide can be viewed as a socioculturally driven choice. Second, we show how problems associated with social structures can lead to suicide. Third, we discuss specific sociocultural stressors that put youth at risk for suicide. Finally, we illuminate how an understanding of the sociocultural underpinnings of suicide explains the link between bullying and suicide risk, thus providing invaluable directions and implications for prevention of suicide among youth who are bullied.

SUICIDE AS A SOCIOCULTURAL PHENOMENON

An array of predominant theories has looked at an individual's cognitions, motivations, emotions, or biology as explanations for a suicidal act. For example, psychodynamic theories propose that suicide is caused by unconscious drives and desires to escape from psychological pain (Menninger, 1938; Shneidman, 1998). Contemporary cognitive behavioral theories propose that suicide is precipitated by hopelessness, which is associated with maladaptive thoughts, defective problem-solving strategies, and emotion dysregulation (Wenzel & Beck, 2008; Linehan, 1993). Biological theories suggest that suicidal behavior results from the concurrent presence of a predispositional vulnerability and an activating psychosocial stressor (Mann, 2003).

Common to many of these theories is the portrayal of suicide as related to mental illness. Many studies have investigated the link between suicide and psychiatric disorders such as depressive, psychotic, or bipolar disorders, finding that most—approximately 90%—of suicidal individuals across age groups have a mental illness (Mościcki, 1997). As a result, mental illness is commonly used as a primary indicator to screen for suicide risk (e.g., Bajaj et al., 2008).

Though the psychodynamic, cognitive behavioral, biological, and psychiatric explanations for suicide have been useful for understanding how factors within an individual can result in suicide, they underemphasize the influence of the sociocultural system where individuals and risk factors are embedded (Wagner, 1997). Many theoretical and research scholars have instead suggested that suicide can be a culturally and socially driven phenomenon unrelated to mental illness. The ecological model in particular lends greater understanding of the complex dynamic between personal, interpersonal, and sociocultural factors that influence adolescents' suicidal behaviors (Ayyash-Abdo, 2002). According to Bronfenbrenner's ecological model (1979), human development in its broadest sense (including suicidal behaviors) is constantly shaped and influenced by the ongoing interaction between the individual and the environment. The ecological environment is defined as a nested structure where the individual is placed within multiple levels of sociocultural systems. *Microsystems* refer to the immediate settings where the individual is exposed to a pattern of activities, role acquisition, and interpersonal relations. Some of a child's primary microsystems are commonly identified as home, school, religious institution, and peer group. The *mesosystem* is developed when the individual child moves into new settings and engages in multiple activities in multiple interconnected microsystems. These microsystems, in turn, are interrelated with *exosystems* (e.g., parents' places of work, sibling's involvement in school, and parents' social network, etc.) where the individual child is not necessarily an active participant. All of these systems are embedded in the *macrosystem*, or culture, where the individual child lives. The model ends with the *chronosystem*, which refers to the patterning of environmental events and life transitions experienced by the individual. Bronfenbrenner (1979) contends that changes that take place in any given system in the ecological model affect the individual and multi-systems as a whole.

Suicidal behaviors in particular have been discussed as products of a complex interplay between multiple ecological systems (Leach & Leong, 2008). In particular, an act of suicide cannot be simply attributed to any single risk factor (i.e., depression, sexual orientation, or bullying) without taking into account numerous contextual factors (i.e., lack of communication between parents and teaching staffs, discrimination, and poverty). Leenaars (2008) specifically suggested that suicidal behaviors can be best understood from exploring the intersection between different levels of sociocultural systems that are embedded within one's ecological system.

Various social science studies have illuminated compelling evidence of suicide as a sociocultural phenomenon. Lester (2008), for example, highlights how differential suicide rates across gender, social class, ethnicity, and nations throughout the world indicate the role of culture in shaping the meaning of suicide in any given society. Indeed, in Papua–New Guinea, the act of suicide has been found to be a socioculturally driven behavior (Counts, 1988). Counts (1988) recounted one example where a betrothed woman was rejected and treated poorly by her future family members. Suicide was chosen by this woman as a culturally powerful act that would impose social and political sanctions on the family members who maltreated her, effectively shaming and wielding power over the surviving kin.

Consistent with the idea that suicide can be driven by environmental influences, Chu, Chi, Chen, and Leino (2014) examined epidemiological data and found evidence of a predominantly sociocultural suicide subtype. In contrast to previous research that related suicide to mental illness in about 90% of suicidal individuals (Mościcki, 1997), Chu and colleagues found that approximately half of the suicides in an Asian American sample were characterized by sociocultural factors such as acculturation, chronic illness, family conflict, or perceived discrimination. While mental illness remains a valid risk factor for suicide, this study highlighted the heterogeneity of suicide in different ethnic minority groups, and the importance of suicide as a sociocultural phenomenon embedded in the context of an ecological model.

With the understanding that suicide can be a sociocultural phenomenon, we now turn to a review of theories and research that illuminate the specific mechanisms by which sociocultural pressures can result in suicide among youth populations. In particular, we discuss cultural meanings theories, problems with social structures, and sociocultural stressors that explain how sociocultural factors such as bullying can precipitate suicide.

SOCIOCULTURAL EXPLANATIONS FOR WHY YOUTH COMMIT SUICIDE

Cultural Meanings That Beget Suicide as a Socioculturally Driven Choice

Theories of cultural *meanings* related to suicide explain why someone who experiences a life stressor may become at risk for suicide, or why some with suicidal ideation and risk go on to attempt or complete suicide and others do not. (e.g., Chu, Goldblum, Floyd, & Bongar, 2010; Lester, 2008; Lester, 2011; Stice & Canetto, 2008). Lester (2011) emphasizes the importance of distinguishing between individual meanings of suicide (individual motive to commit suicide) and the cultural meanings of suicide—cultural normative values and beliefs assigned to suicidal behaviors—that influence a person to consider suicide. Indeed, according to the Cultural Theory and Model of Suicide (Chu et al., 2010), people ascribe cultural *meanings* to experienced life-stressors and events that can either exacerbate or alleviate the emotional suffering, leading one down the path towards rather than away from suicidal behaviors. Similarly, the cultural meaning that one ascribes to the act of suicide itself determines whether one crosses the threshold to perform a suicidal act. Such cultural meanings are socioculturally determined; for example, an individual whose culture associates job loss with shame for his entire family may consider suicide, particularly if he understands suicide as a culturally appropriate way to alleviate such shame. These cultural meanings are encapsulated within *cultural sanctions*, defined as a cultural context's messages of approval or disapproval that determine the acceptability of suicide as an option and the shame and stigma associated with certain life events (Chu et al., 2010).

The cultural-scripts theory proposed by Stice and Canetto (2008) also explains how cultural meanings of an event or of suicide may define social conditions under which suicide becomes a socially permissible solution. Cultural beliefs about acceptable conditions for suicide can become a set of social guidelines, analogous to a script, which tell people how to behave under certain situations. For instance, among older Caucasian adults, chronic physical illness is commonly perceived as the most socially justifiable reason for committing suicide, to end pain and suffering (Stice & Canetto, 2008). Gender differences also exist, with men more likely to endorse financial hardship as an acceptable reason for suicide, and women more likely to view romantic-relationship problems as a reason for suicide (McAndrew & Garrison, 2007).

In the context of adolescent development, specific cultural meanings and sanctions are ascribed to certain adolescent behaviors and social situations that influence the development of suicidal risk. Social membership and acceptance carries significant cultural meaning for adolescents (Espelage, 2002). When youth are excluded or ridiculed by their peer group, they may perceive this event as catastrophic for their self-worth, leading to distress, a sense of a foreshortened future, and ultimately, suicidal ideation and behaviors.

An examination of news reports, literature, and media portrayals of suicide illuminates the ways in which cultural meanings of suicide and life events can shape suicide behaviors among adolescents. In *Dead Poets Society*, a classic 1989 American movie, the 17-year-old protagonist takes his own life as an act of rebellion against his authoritarian father's control and as a personal lament over his foreshortened sense of the future. Messages depicted in popular culture also appear in real life. In 2009, four American high school students from the same high school in Palo Alto, California, killed themselves at different times in a six-month span by jumping in front of a local train (Netter, 2009). Though there was no clear link between these students or definitive answers as to the reasons for their suicides, Canetto's cultural-script theory (2008) may inspire speculation that, by these young people, their suicides may have been viewed as a socially acceptable solution to suffering among a group of troubled adolescents. Furthermore, these vulnerable youth may have become susceptible to the social phenomenon of "suicide contagion" (Gould, 1990), wherein exposure to suicide via fellow peers, media, or news reports may increase the likelihood of attempting suicide in real life (Gould, Jamieson, & Romer, 2003).

Problems with Sociocultural Structure That Can Lead to Suicide

Deficits within the structures of one's sociocultural context can also explain the occurrence of suicide. Durkheim (1951) defined "social structures" as human institutions created by society (e.g., marriage, family). According to Durkheim's social theory of suicide (1951), suicide can be categorized into four subtypes related to problems with integration and moral regulation within one's social structure. An *egoistic suicide* occurs when one's society fails to integrate him or her into the social system; this social disintegration is characterized by a sense of not belonging, antipathy, and meaninglessness in the absence of proper social structure. *Altruistic suicide*, in contrast, occurs when a society values extreme social integration and the needs of the group over the individual, compelling one to engage in self-destructive behaviors for the greater social good. Soldiers, who are expected to sacrifice for patriotic reasons, exemplify altruistic suicide.

On the dimensions of moral regulation, *anomic suicide* occurs when there is a lack of clear moral guidelines and rules. This type of moral confusion often takes place in major cultural shifts when the social order becomes dysregulated. *Fatalistic suicide,* on the other hand, occurs when internal passions are overruled by strict societal orders and regulations that are often characteristic of an oppressive society. Individuals who experience oppression may see little hope for self-expression and view suicide as an escape from a life controlled by others.

In essence, Durkheim (1951) pointed out that suicide is a product of interaction between the individual and structures in the social context, rather than a purely individual act motivated by isolated risk factors. Other social science researchers have also hypothesized that suicide is influenced by the concept of modern individualism, which promotes self autonomy at the expense of social connectedness and sense of belonging. Eckersley and Dear (2002) found a strong positive relationship between male youth suicide rates in developed nations and subjective endorsement of cultural variables of individualism. This relationship between individualism and suicide was discussed within the context of Durkheim's theory in which suicide is viewed as a result of low social integration and moral dysregulation in a society.

Sociocultural Stressors That Put Youth at Risk for Suicide

In addition to existing sociocultural theories of suicide, it is important to discuss the impact of specific sociocultural stressors that increase suicide risk. According to the Cultural Model of Suicide (Chu et al., 2010), three categories of sociocultural stressors are directly associated with elevated suicidal risk: minority stress, social discord, and culturally sanctioned events.

"Minority stress" (see Chapter 15, by Meyer, Frost, and Nezhad, in this volume) refers to the unique stresses experienced by cultural minority groups as a result of their age, gender, ethnicity, sexual orientation, religious beliefs, or socioeconomic status. Meyer (1995) conceptualizes minority stress in terms of three types of stressors: internalized negative societal attitudes towards the minority member; subjective expectation of rejection and discrimination; and actual experience of chronic discrimination and violence (Meyer, Schwartz, & Frost, 2008). Consequently, the experience of minority stress through ongoing discrimination and societal injustice may increase the likelihood of internalizing a negative self-image and low self-esteem (Meyer, 2003). For instance, research has found that youth who identify as lesbian, gay, or bisexual are more likely to experience bullying at school, which is strongly related to increased suicide risk (Hong, Espelage, & Kral, 2011).

In terms of social discord, family conflict and peer rejection are commonly identified as risk factors for suicidal behaviors among youth (Amital & Apter, 2012; Prinstein, Boergers, Spirito, Little, & Grapentine, 2000), with different cultural minority groups experiencing different forms of social discord. For example, increased suicidality among lesbian, gay, bisexual, transgender, and questioning (LGBTQ) youth can be attributed to the experiences of family rejection (Ryan, Huebner, Diaz, & Sanchez, 2009), and alienation from personal friends and community (Hershberger, Pilkington, & D'Augelli, 1997). In contrast, suicide among Asian and Latino American youth is related predominantly to family and intergenerational conflict (Lau, Jernewall, Zane, & Myers, 2002; Locke & Newcomb, 2005), and poor extended community networks and family troubles appear to be predictive of suicide risk among African American youth (Summerville, Kaslow, Abbate, & Cronan, 1994).

Culturally sanctioned events include stressors associated with feelings of shame and rejection that are deemed justifiable reasons for suicide (Chu et al., 2010). An adolescent during puberty may be particularly sensitive to life events that she perceives as shameful or embarrassing. Literature has lent support to the hypothesis that adolescents can become uniquely vulnerable to social stress because of hormonal changes and brain development (Marceau, Dorn, & Susman, 2012). In addition, an under-developed prefrontal cortex in adolescence is associated with cognitive processing errors, immature impulse control, and heightened responsiveness to external socioemotional stimuli (Luna, Padmanabhan, & O'Hearn, 2010). As such, stressful events that may be perceived as insignificant by adults may be perceived as devastating by an adolescent. In the extreme case, a teen victim of assault may become overwhelmed by shame and engage in self-destructive behaviors before seeking help. For instance, 15-year-old Audrie Pott, a sexual assault victim, committed suicide on October of 2012 after she learned that pictures of her in the alleged assault were being distributed via Internet (Associated Press, 2013).

BULLYING AS A SOCIOCULTURAL PATHWAY TO SUICIDE

The sociocultural theories, models, and studies discussed in this chapter provide a foundation for understanding how the experience of bullying may be linked to suicide via social and cultural pathways. For example, bullying may infiltrate multiple levels of one's ecological system—the school, social communities, media, or larger community members—that can influence suicide in an integrated and interactive fashion (Bronfenbrenner, 1979). From the perspective of Durkheim's social theory of suicide (1951), bullying may exemplify the extreme isolation resulting from failure to integrate an individual into one's social system (egoistic suicide), or the need to escape a life controlled by others in an oppressive situation (fatalistic suicide).

Bullying may also lay the foundation for a sociocultural subtype of suicide. Just as Chu and colleagues (2014) found that sociocultural factors such as discrimination typified half of suicidal individuals among an Asian American cultural minority group, bullying may characterize a subgroup of individuals for whom suicide may appear to be an acceptable action.

Chu and colleagues' (2010) Cultural Model of Suicide, reprinted in Figure 14.1, places bullying along a pathway to suicide, showing how sociocultural influences interplay to precipitate suicide in response to the experience of bullying. As depicted in Figure 14.1 (point A), bullying may be best understood as a specific sociocultural life-stressor that initiates the path to suicidal ideation and behaviors. The World Health Organization (2002) defines bullying behavior as "the intentional use of physical and psychological force or power, threatened or actual, against oneself, another person, or against a group or community that either results in or has a high likelihood of resulting in injury, death, psychological harm, mal-development,

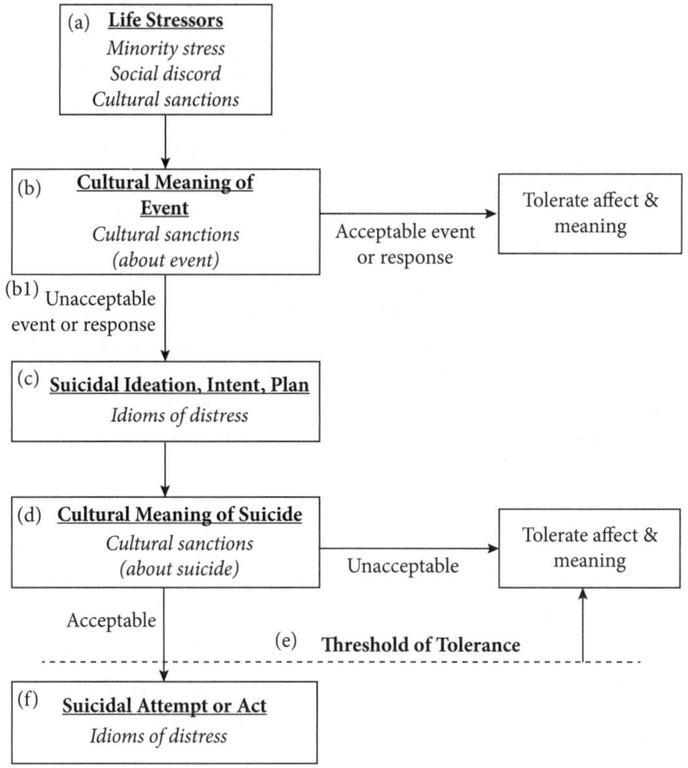

Figure 14.1 The Cultural Model of Suicide.

Reprinted from Chu et al. (2010), with kind permission of Elsevier.

or deprivation." The targeted individual is commonly attacked for his behaviors, appearance, ethnicity, and/or sexual orientation, leading to higher risk of suicide. Pursuant to these definitions, bullying can create the social discord or minority stress (when victimized because of one's cultural minority identity) that can initiate elevated suicide risk and behaviors (as defined by Chu et al., 2010).

Theories around cultural meanings (Chu et al., 2010; Lester, 2008; Lester, 2011; Stice & Canetto, 2008) provide a further basis for understanding whether one who is bullied moves further down the sociocultural path to suicidal behaviors (Figure 14.1). When one is a victim of bullying, cultural practice may ascribe the meanings of shame, loss of face, isolation, or lack of worth to the position of being a victim of bullying (Figure 14.1, point B). Individuals applying these negative cultural meanings would experience bullying as an unacceptable event (point B1) and potentially express suicidal ideation, intention, or plan as a result (point C). Cultural meaning may also portray suicide as a socially acceptable response relieving shame, or escaping a socially isolating situation, for someone who has been bullied (point D). In the face of these cultural meanings, one who has been bullied may cross the threshold of tolerance (point E) and attempt or complete suicide (point F). Overall, Chu and colleagues' (2010) Cultural Model of Suicide, along with Stice and Canetto's (2008) cultural script approach, show how sociocultural messages and stories of suicide among victims of bullying may create a blueprint for a sanctioned path between bullying and suicide.

IMPLICATIONS FOR BULLYING AND SUICIDE PREVENTION

Prevention of adolescent suicide and bullying is a public health issue that calls for community approach (Srabstein et al., 2008) in the context of the social-ecological system. Key to the application of sociocultural understandings of bullying and suicide are conceptualizations of bullying as sources of minority stress, social isolation, social oppression, or social discord. Cultural scripts related to suicide connect these sociocultural experiences of bullying to cultural meanings (e.g., a need to escape from social structures of one's society, a need to absolve shame, a need to reclaim power in one's social environment, etc.) that ultimately result in elevated suicide risk, behaviors, or completions. These cultural considerations for bullying and suicide are firmly embedded in multiple contexts of one's ecological system. Therefore, we center our discussion of implications for suicide prevention around the micro-, meso-, exo-, and macro-systems in which adolescents live.

Micro- and Mesosystem-Level Interventions: Families and Schools

At microsystem and mesosystem levels, families and schools are the primary targeted systems for bullying and suicide prevention and intervention. Researchers have recommended that school officials conduct ongoing assessment to evaluate whether the culture of bullying is unintentionally supported by the school administration and staff (Swearer & Espelage, 2004). Teachers' beliefs about bullying create a sociocultural environment that defines cultural scripts and meanings around bullying, and influences peer victimization and inclinations of students to intervene (or not) when witnessing bullying (Hektner & Swenson, 2011). Results of school-wide assessments can inform interventions that include both education and skill-building components to produce changes in attitudes and behaviors (Ayyash-Abdo, 2002; see Limber, Chapter 17).

In particular, classroom education components of school-based interventions are designed to reduce suicide and bullying by raising students' awareness of bullying behaviors, educating bullying victims about coping strategies, and offering resources to bullying victims (Kalafat & Elias, 1994). Such curricula aim to create sociocultural environments with decreased bullying-related minority stresses, social isolation, and social discord. Despite mixed results in actual reduction of bullying and suicidal behaviors, such interventions appear to be more effective in primary than secondary school (Smith & Ananiadou, 2003). These differential outcomes related to age highlight the importance of early intervention in elementary school where bullying behaviors begin to surface (Espelage & Horne, 2008; see Welcoming Schools, Chapter 19).

Skill-building curricular components, on the other hand, involve teaching social skills that are developmentally and culturally appropriate for pre-identified at-risk youth to overcome socially challenging situations like rejection, teasing, and bullying—defined as ecologically valid social skills (Laugeson, Frankel, Mogil, & Dillon, 2009). The ecologically valid social skills intervention helps at-risk youth learn socially acceptable manners and communication skills that have been found to improve self-esteem and peer interactions. The effectiveness of such interventions depends on parents' direct participation and their reinforcement of the social skills at home (Laugeson et al., 2009). Literature has shown that equipping parents with effective parenting skills is an effective prevention strategy in managing early-childhood conduct problems and reducing bullying behaviors (Burkhart, Knox, & Brockmyer, 2013).

Bullying is a group process rather than individual act, and it typically involves peers in victimization and perpetration (Hong & Espelage, 2012). In addition to the actual perpetrator, bystanders—individuals who observe without intervening—contribute to sociocultural contexts conducive to bullying behaviors (Espelage, 2012). Silent participation by the bystander may signify permission and tacit approval of bullying that can foster negative peer relationships and a school culture of apathy (Twemlow, 2004). Thus, school-based interventions should be supplemented by efforts to cultivate friendships and positive peer relations as protective factors against bullying victimization (Demaray & Malecki, 2003). In an effort to foster a pro-social culture among youth within schools, several Canadian provinces have implemented school-based violence-prevention programs to reduce youth violence by increasing empathy and socio-emotional competency via classroom observation of mother–infant interactions, with some evidence of success up to three years after program completion (Santos, Chartier, Whalen, Chateau, & Boyd, 2011). Although more research on the effectiveness of early empathy education as violence prevention is still needed, cultivating a culture of empathy to counter a social culture of bullying is promising for parents and schools. Ultimately, changing the cultural context at the micro- and mesosystem levels within families, at school, and among peers can shift some of the sociocultural influences that create pathways from bullying to suicide.

Exosystem Community-Level Interventions

At the exosystem level, community members who are in regular contact with youth, regardless of their professions, should be incorporated into prevention and intervention strategies to raise the community's capacity to combat suicide and bullying (Krug, Mercy, Dahlberg, & Zwi, 2002). Evidence-based suicide-prevention training programs such as Question-Persuade-Refer (QPR) have been developed to support and train lay people and organizations about signs of suicidal risk (QPR Institute, 2011). The QPR model is founded on the idea of a "gatekeeper," or someone in the position to recognize warning signs of potential suicide crisis. Additional community-level anti-bullying and suicide-prevention programs such as the It Gets Better Project (2010), the Trevor Project (2013), or the Bully Project (2012) have been developed and provided online for easy public access, though limited data about their effectiveness currently exist (see Bliss et al., Chapter 22).

Together, these efforts at changing the sociocultural context at the micro-, meso-, and exosystem levels can ultimately change the macrosystem culture to prevent suicide as a response to bullying victimization. With an understanding that sociocultural precipitants, scripts, and meanings create a pathway from bullying to suicide, interventions targeted at the family, school administration and staff, peers, and community can address the problem of suicidal risk among youth who have been bullied.

CONCLUSION

Adolescence is marked by rapid physical and psychological developmental changes that are continuously shaped by culture and society. As our society tends to favor the individualistic and simplistic explanations of suicide, complex interactions between individuals and their social environments are often overlooked or underappreciated. The various sociocultural explanations in this chapter have established that suicide and bullying are embedded sociocultural phenomena that can be attributed to the interplay between multiple factors in multiple social systems.

Bullying can lead to elevated suicidal behaviors via several sociocultural pathways. Bullying can create the social discord or minority stress associated with elevated suicide risk and behaviors. It may also result in the type of failed integration into one's social system or need to escape an oppressive social situation that have been advanced as explanations of what precipitates suicide. When cultural meanings of shame or low worth are ascribed to being a victim of bullying, suicide may be seen by youth as a culturally sanctioned solution "scripted" in response to the experience of being bullied. A predominant pathway from bullying to suicide is represented by Chu and colleagues' (2010) Cultural Model of Suicide (Figure 14.1). Ultimately, with multiple sociocultural pathways between bullying and suicide, bullying may be conceptualized as a sociocultural suicide subtype.

Overall, bullying and suicide should be viewed through a sociocultural lens; efforts should be made to understand the social and cultural factors that precipitate bullying and create an environment conducive to suicide. Interdisciplinary collaboration between academia, schools, families, communities, and professionals of different specializations is needed for research and interventions that can account for the social and cultural factors that contribute to youth suicide

Recommendations

Parents and Educators

1. Schools can promote anti-bullying culture by targeting three key areas: (a) Train teaching staff to be sensitive in detecting bullying behavior and be competent to intervene; (b) reduce the bystander effect in bullying by promoting "Good Samaritan" behaviors via teaching, role modeling, and acknowledgement; (c) implement social skills training programs that are developmentally and culturally appropriate for youth at risk for social isolation and bullying.
2. Family- and school-based interventions should be tailored to the cultural meanings ascribed to bullying behavior or suicidal behavior, and the specific contextual factors that facilitate suicidal behaviors as a consequence of bullying.
3. Parents can acquire effective parenting skills through training to minimize children's violent behaviors in school.
4. Interactions and communications between schools and parents can be strengthened through the use of Internet technology when at-risk youth are being identified.

Medical and Mental Health Providers

1. Future or practicing clinicians can become informed about the cultural perspectives related to bullying, violence, and suicide through graduate training or professional development.
2. Risk assessment for suicide should incorporate cultural issues that are salient to the youth population, especially ethnic and sexual minority youth.
3. More research is needed to study the effectiveness of anti-bullying and suicide intervention for youth populations of minority status.

Community and Policy Makers

1. Policy makers at various levels of community or governmental services can shape cultural norms and beliefs towards bullying by developing culturally sensitive policies and practices.
2. Media reports of bullying and suicide may include resources and service information (local or regional) to promote help-seeking behavior among victims of bullying at risk of suicide.
3. Community-based agencies or religious organizations can collaborate to promote anti-bullying and suicide prevention through public events such as community resource fairs that are free and accessible to all community members.

REFERENCES

Amital, M., & Apter, A. (2012). Social aspects of suicidal behavior and prevention in early life: a review. *International Journal of Environmental Research and Public Health, 9*, 985–994. doi: 10.3390/ijerph9030985

Associated Press, The (2013 April 12). Three U.S. teens arrested for sexual battery after girl's suicide. Retrieved May 28, 2014, from http://www.cbc.ca/news/world/story/2013/04/12/us-teens-arrested-girl-suicide.html.

Ayyash-Abdo, H. (2002). Adolescent suicide: An ecological approach. *Psychology in the School, 39*(4), 459–475. doi: 10.1002/pits.10042

Bajaj, P., Borreani, E., Ghosh, P., Methuen, C., Patel, M., & Crawford, M. J. (2008). Screening for suicidal thoughts in primary care: the views of patients and general practitioners. *Mental Health In Family Medicine, 5*(4), 229–235.

Bronfenbrenner, U. (1979). *The ecology of human development.* Boston, MA: Harvard University Press.

Bully Project, The (2012). Retrieved November 12, 2013, from http://www.thebullyproject.com/.

Burkhart, K. M., Knox, M., & Brockmyer, J. (2013). Pilot evaluation of the ACT Raising Safe Kids Program on children's bullying behavior. *Journal of Child and Family Studies, 22*, 942–951. doi:10.1007/s10826-012-9656-3

Chu, J. P., Goldblum, P., Floyd, R., & Bongar, B. (2010). The cultural theory and model of suicide. *Applied and Preventive Psychology, 14*, 25–40.

Chu, J., Chi, K., Chen, K., & Leino, A. (2014). Ethnic variations in suicidal ideation and behaviors: A prominent subtype marked by non-psychiatric factors among Asian Americans. *Journal of Clinical Psychology.*

Counts, D. A. (1988). Ambiguity in the interpretation of suicide. In D. Lester (Ed.), *Why Women Kill Themselves* (pp. 87–109). Springfield, IL: Charles Thomas.

Demaray, M. K., & Malecki, C. K. (2003). Perceptions of the frequency and importance of social support by students classified as victims, bullies and bully/victims in an urban middle school. *School Psychology Review, 32*, 471–489.

Durkheim, E. (1951). *Suicide: A Study in Sociology*. London: Routledge and Kegan Paul.

Espelage, D. L. (2002). Bullying in early adolescence: The role of the peer group. (Report No. EDO-PS-02-16). Champaign, IL: Clearinghouse on Elementary and Early Childhood Education (ERIC Document Reproduction Service No. ED-99-CO-0020).

Espelage, D., & Horne, A. (2008). School violence and bullying prevention: From research based explanations to empirically based solutions. In S. Brown & R. Lent (Eds.), *Handbook of Counseling Psychology* (4th ed., pp. 588–606). Hoboken, NJ: John Wiley and Sons.

Gould, M. S. (1990). Suicide clusters and media exposure. In S. J. Blumenthal & D. J. Kupfer (Eds.), *Suicide Over the Life Cycle: Risk Factors, Assessment, and Treatment of Suicidal Patients* (pp. 517–532). Washington, DC: American Psychiatric Press.

Gould, M., Jamieson, P., & Romer, D. (2003). Media contagion and suicide among the young. *American Behavioral Scientist, 46*(9), 1269–1284. doi: 10.1177/0002764202250670

Hektner, J. M., & Swenson, C. A. (2012). Links from teacher beliefs to peer victimization and bystander intervention: tests of mediating processes. *The Journal of Early Adolescence, 32*(4), 516–536. doi: 10.1177/0272431611402502

Hershberger, S. L., Pilkington, N. W., & D'Augelli, A. R. (1997). Predictors of suicide attempts among gay, lesbian, and bisexual youth. *Journal of Adolescent Research, 12*(4), 477–497.

Hong, J. S., & Espelage, D. L. (2012). A review of research on bullying and peer victimization in school: An ecological systems analysis. *Aggression and Violent Behavior, 17*, 311–322. doi:10.1016/j.avb.2012.03.003

Hong, J. S., Espelage, D. L., & Kral, M. J. (2011). Understanding suicide among sexual minority youth in America: An ecological systems analysis. *Journal of Adolescence, 34*, 885–894.

It Gets Better Project (2010). Retrieved November 12, 2013, from http://www.itgetsbetter.org/.

Kalafat, J., & Elias, M. (1994). An evaluation of a school-based suicide awareness intervention. *Suicide and Life-Threatening Behavior, 22*, 315–321.

Krug, E. G., Mercy, J., Dahlberg, L. L., & Zwi, A. B. (2002). The world report on violence and health. *The Lancet, 360*, 1083–1088.

Lau, A. S., Jernewall, N. M., Zane, N., & Myers, H. F. (2002). Correlates of suicidal behaviors among Asian American outpatient youths. *Cultural Diversity and Ethnic Minority Psychology, 8*(3), 199–213.

Laugeson, E. A., Frankel, F., Mogil, C., & Dillon, A. R. (2009). Parent assisted social skills training to improve friendship in teens with Autism Spectrum Disorder. *Journal of Autism and Developmental Disabilities, 39*, 596–606.

Leenaars, A. A. (2008). Suicide: a cross-cultural theory. In F. T. L. Leong & M. M. Leach (Eds.), *Suicide Among Racial and Ethnic Minority Groups* (pp. 13–38). New York: Routledge.

Leong, F. T. L., & Leach, M. M. (Eds.). (2008). *Suicide Among Racial and Ethnic Minority Groups*. New York: Routledge.

Lester, D. (2008). Suicide and culture. *World Cultural Psychiatric Research Review, 3*(2), 51–68.

Lester, D. (2011). The cultural meaning of suicide: what does that mean? *Journal of Death and Dying, 64*(1), 83–94.

Linehan, M. M. (1993). *Cognitive-Behavioral Treatment of Borderline Personality Disorder.* New York: Guilford.

Locke, T. F., & Newcomb, M. D. (2005). Psychosocial predictors and correlates of suicidality in teenage Latino males. *Hispanic Journal of Behavioral Sciences, 27*(3), 319–336.

Luna, B., Padmanabhan, A., & O'Hearn, K. (2010). What has fMRI told us about the development of cognitive control through adolescence? *Brain and Cognition, 72*(1), 101–113. doi: 10.1016/j.bandc.2009.08.005.

Mann, J.J. (2003). Neurobiology of suicidal behavious. *Nature Reviews Neuroscience, 4*(10), 819–828.Marceau, K., Dorn, L. D., & Susman, E. J. (2012). Stress and puberty-related hormone reactivity, negative emotionality, and parent-adolescent relationships. *Psychoneuroendocrinology, 37,* 1286–1298.

McAndrew, F. T., & Garrison, A. J. (2007). Beliefs about gender differences in methods and causes of suicide. *Archives of Suicide Research, 11*(3), 271–279. doi: 10.1080/13811110701403940

Menninger, K. A. (1938). *Man Against Himself.* New York: Harcourt, Brace and Company.

Meyer, I. H. (1995). Minority stress and mental health in gay men. *Journal of Health and Social Behavior, 36*(1), 38–56.

Meyer, I. H. (2003). Prejudice, social stress, and mental health in lesbian, gay, and bisexual populations: conceptual issues and research evidence. *Psychological Bulletin, 129*(5), 674–697.

Meyer, I. H., Schwartz, S., & Frost, D. M. (2008). Social patterning of stress and coping: Does disadvantaged status confer excess exposure and fewer coping resources? *Social Science & Medicine, 67,* 368–379.

Mościcki, E. (1997). Identification of suicide risk factors using epidemiologic studies. *The Psychiatric Clinics of North America, 20*(3), 499–517.

Netter, S. (2009 October 21). Teen train suicide cluster shakes affluent California town. *ABC News.* Retrieved May 28, 2014, from http://abcnews.go.com/US/palo-alto-struggles-rash-teen-train-suicides/story?id=8881813#.Ucfw4fk3tcx.

Prinstein, M. J., Boergers, J., Spirito, A., Little, T. D., & Grapentine, W. L. (2000). Peer functioning, family dysfunction, and psychological symptoms in a risk factor model for adolescent inpatients' suicidal ideation severity. *Journal of Clinical Child Psychology, 29*(3), 392–405.

QPR Institute. (2011). What is QPR? Retrieved November 13, 2013, from http://www.qprinstitute.com/about.html.

Ryan, C., Huebner, D., Diaz, R. M., & Sanchez, J. (2009). Family rejection as a predictor of negative health outcomes in white and Latino lesbian, gay, and bisexual young adults. *Pediatrics, 123*(1), 346–352.

Santos R. G., Chartier M. J., Whalen, J. C., Chateau D., & Boyd, L. (2011). Effectiveness of school-based violence prevention for children and youth: cluster randomized controlled field trial of the Roots of Empathy program with replication and three-year follow-up. *Healthcare Quarterly, 14,* 80–91.

Shneidman, E. S. (1998). Perspectives on suicidology: Further reflections on suicide and psychache. *Suicide and Life-Threatening Behavior, 28*(3), 245–250.

Srabstein, J., Joshi, P., Due, P., Wright, J., Leventhal, B., Merrick, J., . . . Riibner, K. (2008). Prevention of public health risks linked to bullying: a need for a whole community approach. *International Journal of Adolescent Medicine and Health, 20*(2), 185–199.

Smith, P. K., & Ananiadou, K. (2003). The nature of school bullying and the effectiveness of school-based interventions. *Journal of Applied Psychoanalytic Studies, 5*(2), 189–209.

Stice, B. D., & Canetto, S. S. (2008). Older adult suicide: perceptions of precipitants and protective factors. *Clinical Gerontologist, 31*(4), 4–30. doi: 10.1080/07317110801947144

Summerville, M. B., Kaslow, N. J., Abbate, M. F., & Cronan, S. (1994). Psychopathology, family functioning, and cognitive style in urban adolescents with suicide attempts. *Journal of Abnormal Child Psychology, 33*(2), 221–235.

Swearer, S. M., & Espelage, D. L. (2004). Introduction: A social-ecological framework of bullying among youth. In D. L. Espelage & S. M. Swearer (Eds.), *Bullying in American Schools: A Social-Ecological Perspective on Prevention and Intervention* (pp. 1–12). Mahwah, NJ: Lawrence Erlbaum.

Trevor Project, The (2013). Retrieved November 12, 2013, from http://www.thetrevorproject.org/.

Twemlow, S. W. (2004). Preventing violence in schools. *Psychiatric Times, 21*(4), 61–67.

Wagner, B. M. (1997). Family risk factors for child and adolescent suicidal behavior. *Psychological Bulletin, 121*, 246–298.

Wenzel, A., & Beck, A. T. (2008). A cognitive model of suicidal behaviour: Theory and treatment. *Applied and Preventive Psychology, 12*, 189–201.

World Health Organization (2002). World report on violence and health. Retrieved February 14, 2010, from http://www.who.int/violence_injury_prevention/violence/world_report/en/full_en.pdf.

15

Minority Stress and Suicide in Lesbians, Gay Men, and Bisexuals

ILAN H. MEYER, DAVID M. FROST, AND SHEILA NEZHAD ■

The minority stress model has been used in many studies to explain the health of sexual minorities but has not been comprehensively used to understand suicide. Meyer (1995, 2003) described minority stress as stress that stems from the social position of lesbian, gay, and bisexual (LGB) people as a stigmatized and disadvantaged minority group in society. According to the minority stress model, the disadvantaged social position of LGB persons exposes them to more stress and fewer coping resources than their heterosexual peers (Meyer, Schwartz, & Frost, 2008). For example, all people who are employed are at risk of losing a job—a major life event that can have adverse health outcomes. Losing a job can happen for a host of reasons, including economic-downturn periods, failed businesses, poor performance at the job, or illness and other conditions that interfere with job performance. The minority stress model suggests that, in addition to these general risks shared by all people, LGB people are at risk of being fired *because* they are LGB. That is, discrimination related to stigma and prejudice against LGB people will put them at higher risk for losing a job than are their non-LGB peers (the same is true of people in other disadvantaged social positions). It is important to note that not only major events, but also everyday experiences of discrimination and microaggressions are sources of stress. These are the gnawing chronic experience of stigma; seemingly minor occurrences that nonetheless can accumulate over time and have serious consequences (Meyer, Ouellette, Haile, & McFarlane, 2011). As a result of exposure to stress, the model predicts, LGB people will experience more adverse health outcomes than heterosexuals proportional to their greater exposure to stress.

Research has generally supported the minority stress hypotheses, showing that LGB people are exposed to more stress than are their heterosexual peers (Meyer et al., 2008), and, in turn, LGBs suffer adverse health consequences across a variety of outcomes, including mental and physical health (Herek & Garnets, 2007; Lick, Durso, & Johnson, 2013). The intersection of sexual and racial/ethnic minority status further exacerbates exposure to minority stress. Racial/ethnic minorities may feel invisible and marginalized, and are often subject to racism within the white LGBT community (Binnie & Skeggs, 2004; Han, 2007). Racial/ethnic minorities are also at risk for homophobia in their communities of color. Some, but certainly not all, communities of color have been shown to be more disapproving of homosexuality than white communities (e.g., Lewis, 2003; Ward, 2005). The church, which is often not approving of homosexuality, has a particularly important place in some communities, especially black and Latino communities (Barnes & Meyer, 2012), making it harder for black and Latino as compared with white LGBs to remove themselves from their communities of origin. Alternatively, racial/ethnic LGBs can receive a lot of support in their communities of origin, and many cherish these affiliations (Meyer & Ouellette, 2009). When they confront homophobia, many LGB persons of color act to combat it in their communities and cope with it in various ways that enhance their ability to embrace their sexual and race/ethnic minority communities (Bowleg, Huang, & Brooks, 2003; Meyer & Ouellette, 2009; Moore, 2010). But because of the added source of stress due to racism, LGB persons of color experience more minority stress and have fewer coping resources than white LGB people (Meyer et al., 2008).

ETIOLOGY OF SUICIDE BEHAVIOR IN SEXUAL MINORITIES

Despite the decades of research demonstrating disparities in suicide behavior between LGBs and heterosexuals, factors contributing to higher rates of suicide attempts among LGBs are not well understood (Haas et al., 2010; Goldsmith, Pellmar, Kleinman, & Bunney, 2002). Garofalo and colleagues (1999) proposed that, in addition to known suicidal risk factors, such as a history of depression and substance use, identification as a sexual-minority identity (gay, lesbian, bisexual, or "not sure") is independently associated with suicidal behavior. But the authors did not specify mediators that may explain this association—What are some experiences that are unique to sexual minorities that place them at risk for suicide behavior? The minority stress model helps articulate the relationship between sexual orientation and suicide behavior.

LGB individuals may be at high risk for suicide behavior both because of the higher likelihood that they have a diagnosed mental disorder, including mood, anxiety, and substance use disorders, and because of their excess exposure to stress and adversities related to homophobia and heterosexism. This is especially true at younger ages when LGB youth approach developmental tasks related to their sexual orientation (McDaniel, Purcell, & D'Augelli, 2001; Spirito & Esposito-Smythers, 2006). In addition to minority stress, sexual minorities are at risk for suicide behavior for all the reasons that heterosexual individuals are at risk for suicide behavior. Our purpose here is to suggest an integrated model of suicide etiology that takes into account both minority stress and other established causes of suicide. We here briefly chronicle these risks.

History of Mental Disorder

As already noted, the main risk factor for suicide attempts is a history of mental disorders, in particular, mood (especially depression) and substance use (especially alcohol use) disorders (Evans, Hawton, & Rodham, 2004; Galaif, Sussman, Newcomb, & Locke, 2007; Spirito & Esposito-Smythers, 2006).

Family Discord, Childhood Trauma, and Abuse

Youth living apart from both parents was associated with increased prevalence of suicidal behavior, even though the death of a parent was not associated with suicide (Evans et al., 2004). Good communication with parents and feeling understood by family members was associated with lower prevalence of suicide behavior. Conversely, family discord seems to be associated with suicide behavior, but mainly for females. Perhaps related to family discord, studies found a relationship between runaway and homeless youth and attempted suicide (Spirito & Esposito-Smythers, 2006). Despite some mixed patterns of results, Evans, Hawton, and Rodham (2004) concluded that, "overall, the results from multivariate analysis indicated that having unsupportive parents is directly associated with suicidal phenomena" (p. 966).

Childhood adversity and life events include sexual and physical abuse; witnessing domestic violence; receiving poor parenting, and parental discord, including parental separation or divorce; and living with substance abusing, mentally ill, or criminal family members (Flouri, 2005; Maniglio, 2011). For example, researchers found that a single adverse childhood experience increased an individual's risk of suicide attempt two- to five-fold, while the presence of more than one adverse experience raised this risk dramatically (Dube et al., 2001). These relationships require further study; for example, it is not clear how the relationship between sexual abuse and suicide behavior is related to other factors, such as mood and substance use disorders and impulsive behaviors, which may act as mediators. Addressing this, Evans, Hawton and Rodham's (2004) review found that in three studies that tested a multivariate model, sexual abuse was independently related to suicide attempts.

Peer Relationships

Peer relationships in adolescence also may be important predictors of suicide. Twelve studies reviewed by Evans, Hawton, and Rodham (2004) found a strong association between poor relationships and suicide behavior. Recent studies suggest that bullying, including physical violence, verbal abuse, and cyber bullying, is independently associated with suicide among youth (Borowsky, Taliaferro, & McMorris, 2013; Espelage & Holt, 2013; Kowalski & Limber, 2013). Interestingly, participation in bullying may be associated with suicide risk factors regardless of whether the youth is the perpetrator, the victim, a bully-victim, or an observer. For example, Espelage and Holt (2013) found that any involvement in bullying increased risk for suicidality among middle school students because of its relationship with delinquency (e.g., lying or cheating, cutting classes, using alcohol, running away, stealing), substance abuse, and depression.

Genetic and Neurobiological Factors

Other studies provide important insights into genetic and biological aspects of suicide. As Mann (2003) described it, suicidal behavior depends in part on a *diathesis*, or predisposition, that includes genetic and neurobiological factors that interact with stress and adversity such as described above (e.g., sexual abuse in childhood). Suicide diathesis increases hopelessness and impulsivity, which are partly related to impaired neurobiological mechanisms. Neurobiological studies account for the interaction of stressful experiences with neurobiological processes such as (among many mechanisms detected) lower serotonergic activity. For example, post-mortem examinations of suicide victims show fewer presynaptic serotonin-transporter sites in the prefrontal cortex (Mann, 2003). Genetic factors are also suggested by studies that show a higher rate of familial suicidal acts, with the concordance rate for suicide and suicide attempts higher in monozygotic than in dizygotic twins. Recent epigenetic studies suggest that early-life adversity may lead to a series of neurobiological changes that persist and put the person at increased risk for suicide. For example, experience of early-life stress and adversity is related to later persistent changes in regulation of the stress-response system, such as the hypothalamic-pituitary-adrenal (HPA) axis. Such changes will lead to pathogenic response to stress and, potentially, suicide in response to adverse stressful experiences later in life (Turecki, Ernst, Jollant, Labonté, & Mechawar, 2012).

Structural and Environmental Risks

Suicide is a "multidimensional malaise" with an interplay of individual, relationship, social, cultural, and environmental factors (Leenaars, 2008). Mościcki (2001) described distal and proximal risk factors, both of which can occur on individual or environmental levels. These risk factors are necessary, but not sufficient, to cause suicidal behavior, as they are very prevalent and most people exposed to them do not attempt suicide. Environmental distal risk factors include a dysfunctional family setting, easy availability of firearms, stigma associated with mental illness, and a lack of environmental protective factors such as community safety. Environmental proximal risk factors include firearms in the home and contagion (the death, including suicide, of an acquaintance). Individual distal risk factors include mental or substance use disorders, a previous suicide attempt, and a family history of mood disorders, suicidality, or physical or sexual abuse. Individual proximal risk factors include stressful life events such as divorce or job loss, and a perceived loss of independence, including incarceration, intoxication, and hopelessness. Protective factors include coping skills, social support, and treatment for mental and substance use disorders (Mościcki, 2001).

Looking specifically at cultural factors in suicide, Chu, Goldblum, Floyd, and Bongar (2010) posited their "Cultural Model of Suicide," which offers three theoretical principles related to the impact of culture on (a) the types of stressors that people are exposed to; (b) meanings associated with stressors and suicide; and (c) how suicidal thoughts, intentions, plans, and attempts are expressed. For example, Zayas and colleagues (2005) explained suicide behavior in Latina youth, arguing that Latina youth are moved toward suicide because of a deep conflict between the norms of adolescent development enforced by their families in the microsystem, and the norms of adolescent development promoted by the host culture in the mesosystem, especially norms related to adolescent autonomy and sexuality.

Extending the Minority Stress Framework to the Study of Suicide Behavior

In Figure 15.1, we present an integrated minority stress model for suicide that reflects the multidimensional etiology of suicide. The model depicts environmental and social vulnerabilities and supports, individual stress and coping experiences, and neurobiological suicide-diathesis factors. The model shows that suicide behavior (attempted and completed suicides) is a function of mental health problems, including depression and substance use, the leading proximal causes of suicide. Suicide is also predicted by the suicide diathesis, which includes genetic, epigenetics, and neurobiological vulnerabilities (including tendency to impulsivity and pessimism). Also, exposure to stress in the immediate and distant past is both directly and indirectly (through its impact on mental health) related to suicide behavior. For example, as shown above, suicide risk can be increased by exposure to adverse life events such as violence, bullying, or a history of childhood sex abuse.

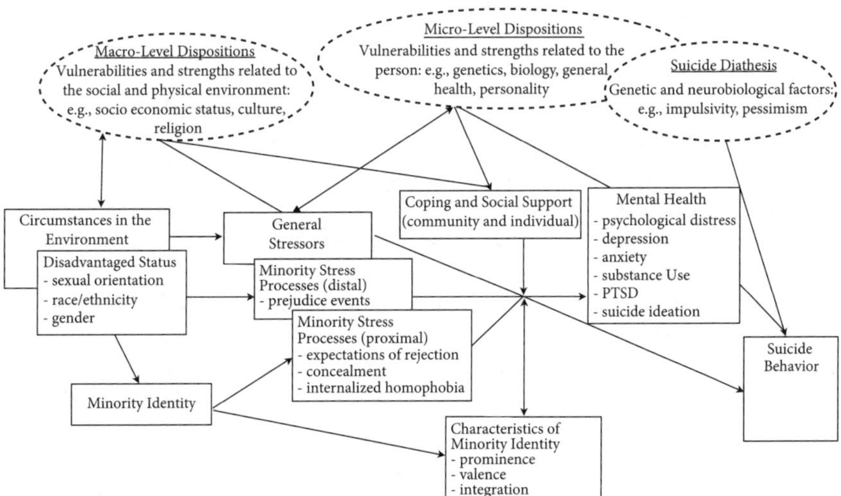

Figure 15.1 Minority stress model in the etiology of suicide ideation and behavior in sexual minorities.

In addition, the model depicts the macro-level influence of environmental (including social and physical) vulnerabilities and strengths and the micro-level influences of personal vulnerabilities and strengths that impact exposure to stress and availability of resources. Suicide diathesis, which directly increases the risk for suicide, is a part of such personal dispositions. Vulnerabilities and strengths can affect multiple elements of the minority stress model. For example, one's culture and religion may be characterized by more intolerance or tolerance toward homosexuality, which, in turn, will affect stress exposure, including life events (e.g., antigay violence) and processes such as internalized homophobia, concealment of LGB identity, and expectations of rejection.

Personal dispositions, such as genetic and biological vulnerabilities and strengths, personality traits, and general health status, can interact with the different elements of the model. As noted above, coping and social support are salutogenic factors in the minority stress model. For example, a person with a greater sense of mastery may be better equipped to cope with stressors than a person with lesser such strengths (Masten, 2001; Ryff & Keyes, 1995). Coping resources also exist at the community level, where they are transferred to the individual through his or her affiliation and through connectedness to a minority community. A greater sense of connection to other similar LGBs may mitigate the impact of stress on health outcome, providing protection through affirmation (Crocker & Major, 1989; Frost & Meyer, 2012; Kertzner, Meyer, Frost, & Stirratt, 2009; Ramirez-Valles, Fegus, Reisen, Poppen, & Zea, 2005).

SUGGESTIONS FOR TREATMENT, PREVENTION, AND POLICY

Medical and Mental Health

- Clinicians and the public need to be educated on the risks of suicide so that interventions can take effect (Mann et al., 2005).
- Specific to youth, school-based prevention measures are needed that aim to increase identification of at-risk youth and connect them with resources, such as peer support, school-wide screening, gatekeeper training, and coping skills training (Gould, Greenberg, Velting & Schaffer, 2003; Mann et al., 2005; Wyman et al., 2008).
- Because depression is present in most suicides, clinical prevention programs must focus on mental health treatment for people at risk and, especially, follow-up care for people who have attempted suicide (Mann et al., 2005).
- Psychotherapy and psychopharmacology are both recommended, with some promising results (Mann et al., 2005; Bridge et al., 2007).
- Additional efforts to prevent suicide among sexual minorities may need to be directed toward identifying non–mentally ill LGB individuals with significant life adversities. Among life events to which LGBs are disproportionally exposed are: discord with parents, parental rejection, homelessness, physical and/or sexual abuse, sexual assault, and antigay violence (Goodenow, Netherland, & Szalacha, 2002; Cochran, Stewart, Ginzler, & Cauce, 2002; Quintana, Rsenthal & Krehely, 2010; Ryan, Huebner, Diaz, & Sanchez, 2009).

- In addition to promoting coping resources that would help all youth, such as enhancing mastery, interventions should enhance youth's understanding of sexuality and of homophobia and promote affiliation with LGBT communities that can enhance the youth's sense of himself or herself as an LGB person.
- Interpersonal clinical interventions may intervene with rejecting families to enhance the youth's family relationships; for example, along the lines of the model provided by the Ryan's Family Acceptance Project (Ryan, Russell, Huebner, Diaz, & Sanchez, 2010; see also http://familyproject.sfsu.edu).

Educators and Parents

- Gay-straight alliances (GSAs) and extracurricular programs that provide a safe space for sexual minority students and educate school communities about lesbian, gay, bisexual, transgender (LGBT) life and history, are an example of a macro-level, school-based, LGBT-affirmative intervention that has been successful at improving school environments, including reduced dating violence, threats, and violence; an increased sense of safety for LGBT youths; and improved health and educational outcomes, such as reducing truancy, injuries at school, and suicide attempts (Burdge, Snapp, Laub, Russell, & Moody, 2013; Goodenow, Szalacha, & Westheimer, 2006).
- Evidence from ecological studies has shown that disparities in suicide attempts between sexual minority and heterosexual students were significantly lower in regions that had a more LGBT-supportive environment than in regions that did not (Hatzenbuehler, 2011; Hatzenbuehler, Birkett, Van Wagenen, & Meyer, 2014). For example, students who attend schools with anti-bullying policies that explicitly mention sexual orientation report lower rates of suicide ideation (Hatzenbuehler & Keyes, 2013).

Researchers and Policy Makers

- Policy interventions, such as establishing protections that would reduce exposure to a stressful environment, are important. For example, laws that protect LGB people from prejudice, discrimination, and violence would help reduce the occurrence of prejudice-related stressors.
- Among such structural interventions are laws that respect gay men's and lesbians' intimate relationships by providing them access to marriage and the benefits afforded to heterosexual married people and their families (Herdt & Kertzner, 2006); and the U.S. Federal Employment Non-Discrimination Act (ENDA), which would protect LGB people from discrimination in the workplace (Malloy & Sears, 2011).

REFERENCES

Barnes, D. M., & Meyer, I. H. (2012). Religious affiliation, internalized homophobia, and mental health in lesbians, gay men, and bisexuals. *American Journal of Orthopsychiatry, 82*(4), 505–515. doi: 10.1111/j.1111/j.1939-0025.01185.x

Binnie, J., & Skeggs, B. (2004). Cosmopolitan knowledge and the production and consumption of sexualized space: Manchester's gay village. *The Sociological Review, 52*(1), 39–61. doi: 10.1111/j.1467-954x.2004.00441.x

Borowsky, I. W., Taliaferro, L. A., & McMorris, B. J. (2013). Suicidal thinking and behavior among youth involved in verbal and social bullying: Risk and protective factors. *Journal of Adolescent Health, 53*(1), S4–S12. doi: 10.1016/j.jadohealth.2012.10.280

Bowleg, L., Huang, J., & Brooks, K. (2003). Triple jeopardy and beyond: Multiple minority stress and resilience among black lesbians. *Journal of Lesbian Studies, 7*(4), 87–108. doi:10.1300/J155v07n04_06

Bridge, J. A., Iyengar, S., Salary, C. B., Barbe, R. P., Birmaher, B., Pincus, H. A., . . . Brent, D. A. (2007). Clinical response and risk for reported suicidal ideation and suicide attempts in pediatric antidepressant treatment. *JAMA: the Journal of the American Medical Association, 297*(15), 1683–1696. doi: 10.1001/jama.297.15.1683

Burdge, H., Snapp, S., Laub, C., Russell, S. T., & Moody, R. (2013). *Implementing Lessons That Matter: The Impact of LGBTQ-Inclusive Curriculum on Student Safety, Well-Being, and Achievement.* San Francisco, CA: Gay-Straight Alliance Network; and Tucson, AZ: Frances McClelland Institute for Children, Youth, and Families at the University of Arizona.

Chu, J. P., Goldblum, P., Floyd, R., & Bongar, B. (2010). The cultural theory and model of suicide. *Applied and Preventive Psychology, 14*, 25–40. doi: 10.1016/j.appsy.2011.11.001

Cochran, B. N., Stewart, A. J., Ginzler, J. A., & Cauce, A. M. (2002). Challenges faced by homeless sexual minorities: Comparison of gay, lesbian, bisexual, and transgender homeless adolescents with their heterosexual counterparts. *American Journal of Public Health, 92*(5), 773–777. doi: 2105/AJPH.92.5.773

Crocker, J., & Major, B. (1989). Social stigma and self-esteem: The self-protective properties of stigma. *Psychological Review, 96*(4), 608–630. doi: 10.1037/0033-295X.96.4.608

Dube, S. R., Anda, R. F., Felitti, V. J., Chapman, D. P., Williamson, D. F., & Giles, W. H. (2001). Childhood abuse, household dysfunction, and the risk of attempted suicide throughout the life span. *JAMA: The Journal of the American Medical Association, 286*(24), 3089–3096. doi: 10.1001/jama.286.24.3089

Espelage, D. L., & Holt, M. K. (2013). Suicidal ideation and school bullying experiences after controlling for depression and delinquency. *Journal of Adolescent Health, 53*(1), S27-S31. doi: 10.1016/j.jadohealth.2012.09.017

Evans, E., Hawton, K., & Rodham, K. (2004). Factors associated with suicidal phenomena in adolescents: A systematic review of population-based studies. *Clinical Psychology Review, 24*(8), 957–979. doi: 10.1016/j.cpr.2004.04.005

Flouri, E. (2005). Psychological and sociological aspects of parenting and their relation to suicidal behavior. *Archives of Suicide Research, 9*, 373–383. doi: 10.1080/13811110500182463

Frost, D. M., & Meyer, I. H. (2012). Measuring community connectedness among diverse sexual minority populations. *Journal of Sex Research, 49*(1), 36–49. doi: 10.1080/00224499.2011.565427

Galaif, E. R., Sussman, S., Newcomb, M. D., & Locke, T. F. (2007). Suicidality, depression, and alcohol use among adolescents: A review of empirical findings. *International Journal of Adolescent Medicine and Health, 19*(1), 27–36. doi: 10.1515/IJAMH.2007.19.1.27

Garofalo, R., Wolf, R. C., Wissow, L. S., Woods, E. R., & Goodman, E. (1999). Sexual orientation and risk of suicide attempts among a representative sample of youth. *Archives of Pediatrics & Adolescent Medicine, 153*(5), 487–493.

Goldsmith, S. K., Pellmar, T. C., Kleinman, A. M., & Bunney, W. E. (Eds.) (2002). *Reducing Suicide: A National Imperative.* National Academies Press.

Goodenow, C., Netherland, J., & Szalacha, L. (2002). AIDS-related risk among adolescent males who have sex with males, females, or both: Evidence from a statewide survey. *American Journal of Public Health, 92*(2), 203–210. doi: 10.2105/AJPH.92.2.203

Goodenow, C., Szalacha, L., & Westheimer, K. (2006). School support groups, other school factors, and the safety of sexual minority adolescents. *Psychology in the Schools, 43*(5), 573–589. doi: 1002/pits.20173

Gould, M. S., Greenberg, T. E. D., Velting, D. M., & Shaffer, D. (2003). Youth suicide risk and preventive interventions: a review of the past 10 years. *Journal of the American Academy of Child & Adolescent Psychiatry, 42*(4), 386–405.

Haas, A. P., Eliason, M., Mays, V. M., Mathy, R. M., Cochran, S. D., D'Augelli, A. R.,... Clayton, P. J. (2010). Suicide and suicide risk in lesbian, gay, bisexual, and transgender populations: Review and recommendations. *Journal of Homosexuality, 58*(1), 10–51. doi: 10.1080/00918369.2011.534038

Han, C. (2007). They don't want to cruise your type: Gay men of color and the racial politics of exclusion. *Social Identities, 13*(1), 51–67. doi: 10.1080/13504630601163379

Hatzenbuehler, M. L. (2011). The social environment and suicide attempts in lesbian, gay, and bisexual youth. *Pediatrics, 127*(5), 896–903. doi: 10.1542/peds.2010-3020

Hatzenbuehler, M. L., Birkett, M., Van Wagenen, A., & Meyer, I. H. (2014). Protective school climates and reduced risk for suicide ideation in sexual minority youths. *American Journal of Public Health, 104*(2), 279–286 doi: 10.2105/AJPH.2013.301508.

Hatzenbuehler, M. L., & Keyes, K. M. (2013). Inclusive anti-bullying policies and reduced risk of suicide attempts in lesbian and gay youth. *Journal of Adolescent Health, 53*(1), S21–S26. doi: 10.1016/j.jadohealth.2010.08.010

Herdt, G., & Kertzner, R. (2006). I do, but I can't: The impact of marriage denial on the mental health and sexual citizenship of lesbians and gay men in the United States. *Sexuality Research and Social Policy Journal of NSRC, 3*(1), 33–49. doi: 10.1525/srsp.2006.3.1.33

Herek, G. M., & Garnets, L. D. (2007). Sexual orientation and mental health. *Annual Review of Clinical Psychology, 3*(1), 353–375. doi: 10.1146/annrev.clinpsy.3.022806.091510

Kertzner, R. M., Meyer, I. H., Frost, D. M., & Stirratt, M. J. (2009). Social and psychological well-being in lesbians, gay men, and bisexuals: The effects of race, gender, age, and sexual identity. *American Journal of Orthopsychiatry, 79*(4), 500–510. doi: 10.1037/a0016848

Kowalski, R. M., & Limber, S. P. (2013). Psychological, physical, and academic correlates of cyberbullying and traditional bullying. *Journal of Adolescent Health, 53*(1), S13–S20. doi: 10.1016/j.jadohealth.2012.09.018

Leenaars, A. A. (2008). Suicide: A cross-cultural theory. In M. M. Leach & F. T. L. Leong (Eds.), *Suicide Among Racial and Ethnic Minority Groups: Theory, Research, and Practice* (pp. 13–37). New York: Routledge/Taylor & Francis.

Lewis, G. B. (2003). Black-white differences in attitudes toward homosexuality and gay rights. *Public Opinion Quarterly, 67*(1), 59–78. doi: 10.186/346009

Lick, D. J., Durso, L. E., & Johnson, K. L. (2013). Minority stress and physical health among sexual minorities. *Perspectives on Psychological Science, 8*(5), 521–548. doi: 10.1177/1745691613497965

Malloy, C., & Sears, B. (2011). *Documented Evidence of Employment Discrimination and Its Effects on LGBT People*. Los Angeles, CA: The Williams Institute.

Maniglio, R. (2011). The role of child sexual abuse in the etiology of suicide and non-suicidal self-injury. *Acta Psychiatrica Scandinavica, 124*(1), 30–41. doi: 10.1111/j.1600-0447.2010.01612.X

Mann, J. J. (2003). Neurobiology of suicidal behaviour. *Nature Reviews Neuroscience, 4*(10), 819–828. doi: 10.1038/nm1220

Mann, J. J., Apter, A., Bertolote, J., Beautrais, A., Currier, D., Haas, A., . . . Hendin, H. (2005). Suicide prevention strategies. *JAMA: The Journal of the American Medical Association, 294*(16), 2064–2074. doi: 10.1001/jama.294.16.2064

Masten, A. S. (2001). Ordinary magic: Resilience processes in development. *American Psychologist, 56*(3), 227–238. doi: 10.1037/0003-066X.56.3.227

McDaniel, J. S., Purcell, D., & D'Augelli, A. R. (2001). The relationship between sexual orientation and risk for suicide: Research findings and future directions for research and prevention. *Suicide and Life-Threatening Behavior, 31*(S1), 84–105. doi: 10.152/suli.31.1.5.84.24224

Meyer, I. H. (1995). Minority stress and mental health in gay men. *Journal of Health and Social Behavior*, 38–56. doi: 10,2307/2137286

Meyer, I. H. (2003). Prejudice, social stress, and mental health in lesbian, gay, and bisexual populations: Conceptual issues and research evidence. *Psychological Bulletin, 129*(5), 674–697. doi: 10.1037/0033-2909.129.5.674

Meyer, I., & Ouellette, S. (2009). Unity and purpose at the intersections of racial/ethnic and sexual identities. In P. L. Hammack & B. J. Cohler (Eds.), *The Story of Sexual Identity: Narrative Perspectives on the Gay and Lesbian Life Course* (pp. 79–106). New York: Oxford University Press.

Meyer, I. H., Ouellette, S. C., Haile, R., & McFarlane, T. A. (2011). "We'd Be Free": Narratives of life without homophobia, racism, or sexism. *Sexuality Research and Social Policy, 8*(3), 204–214. doi: 10.1007/s13178-011-0063-0

Meyer, I. H., Schwartz, S., & Frost, D. M. (2008). Social patterning of stress and coping: Does [*sic*] disadvantaged social statuses confer more stress and fewer coping resources? *Social Science & Medicine, 67*(3), 368–379. Available at http://dx.doi.org/10.1016/j.socscimed.2008.03.012.

Moore, M. R. (2010). Articulating a politics of (multiple) identities. *Du Bois Review, 7*(2), 1–20.

Mościcki, E. K. (2001). Epidemiology of completed and attempted suicide: Toward a framework for prevention. *Clinical Neuroscience Research, 1*(5), 310–323. doi: 10.1016/S1566-2772(01)00032-9

Quintana, N. S., Rosenthal, J., Krehely, J., & Center for American Progress (2010). On the streets: The federal response to gay and transgender homeless youth. Available at http://www.americanprogress.org/issues/lgbt/report/2010/06/21/7983/on-the-streets/.

Ramirez-Valles, J., Fergus, S., Reisen, C. A., Poppen, P. J., & Zea, M. C. (2005). Confronting stigma: Community involvement and psychological well-being among HIV-positive Latino gay men. *Hispanic Journal of Behavioral Sciences, 27*(1), 101–119. doi: 10.1177/0739986304270232

Ryan, C., Huebner, D., Diaz, R. M., & Sanchez, J. (2009). Family rejection as a predictor of negative health outcomes in white and Latino lesbian, gay, and bisexual young adults. *Pediatrics*, *123*(1), 346–352. doi: 10.1542/peds.2007-3524

Ryan, C., Russell, S. T., Huebner, D., Diaz, R., & Sanchez, J. (2010). Family acceptance in adolescence and the health of LGBT young adults. *Journal of Child and Adolescent Psychiatric Nursing*, *23*(4), 205–213. doi:10.1111/j.1744-6171.2010.00246.x

Ryff, C. D., & Keyes, C. L. (1995). The structure of psychological well-being revisited. *Journal of Personality and Social Psychology*, *69*(4), 719–727. doi: 10.1037/0022-3514.69.4.719

Spirito, A., & Esposito-Smythers, C. (2006). Attempted and completed suicide in adolescence. *Annual Review of Clinical Psychology*, *2*, 237–266. doi: 10.1146/annurev.clinpsy,2.022305.095323

Turecki, G., Ernst, C., Jollant, F., Labonté, B., & Mechawar, N. (2012). The neurodevelopmental origins of suicidal behavior. *Trends in Neurosciences*, *35*(1), 14–23. doi: 10.1016/j.tins.2011.11.008

Ward, E. G. (2005). Homophobia, hypermasculinity and the US black church. *Culture, Health & Sexuality*, *7*(5), 493–504.

Wyman, P. A., Brown, C. H., Inman, J., Cross, W., Schmeelk-Cone, K., Guo, J., & Pena, J. B. (2008). Randomized trial of a gatekeeper program for suicide prevention: 1-year impact on secondary school staff. *Journal of Consulting and Clinical Psychology*, *76*(1), 104. doi: 10.1037/0022-006x.76.1.104

Zayas, L. H., Lester, R. J., Cabassa, L. J., & Fortuna, L. R. (2005). Why do so many Latina teens attempt suicide? A conceptual model for research. *American Journal of Orthopsychiatry*, *75*(2), 275–287. doi: 10.1037/0002-9432.75.2.275

PART FIVE

Educational Approaches

16

Bullying, Rejection, and Isolation

Lessons Learned from Classroom Peer Ecology Studies

HANDREA ANITA LOGIS AND PHILIP C. RODKIN ■

Tragic stories of adolescent suicide due to alleged bullying have changed views on bullying from regarding it as a harmless rite of passage to seeing it as a serious public health concern (Hertz, Donato, & Wright, 2013). Most schools have been implementing anti-bullying prevention and intervention programs. Nevertheless, the issue of bullying and suicide persists. A meta-analysis found that school-based anti-bullying programs resulted in a positive and statistically significant effect in reducing bullying, but the overall effect size was small and did not meet the threshold for practical significance (Ferguson, Miguel, Kilburn, & Sanchez, 2007). Another meta-analysis found that school-based anti-bullying programs resulted in changes in students' attitudes, perceptions, and knowledge of bullying, but not in their behaviors (Merrell, Gueldner, Ross, & Isava, 2008). When considering suicide prevention, most studies could not identify a critical ingredient in their school-based programs that leads to successful outcomes (Pelkonen & Marttunen, 2003). One study found that children's reports of suicidal behaviors and depression tended to decrease, but their helping and coping strategies did not improve (King, Strunk, & Sorter, 2011). Although students' levels of suicide attempts went down after participating in a school based psycho-educational program, their reports of suicidal ideation remained stable (Portzky & van Heeringen, 2006).

One of the possible explanations for the ineffectiveness of many anti-bullying programs in North America is the failure to intervene at the environmental level (Swearer, Espelage, Vaillancourt, & Hymel, 2010). Similarly, in terms of suicide prevention programs, there is lack of evidence that purely educational approaches can effectively lead depressed and suicidal youth to seek professional help (Shaffer & Gould, 2000). Drawing from studies focusing on peer social ecologies and youth outcomes, this chapter considers elements of classroom environments that promote healthy peer relationships, which may eventually help reduce bullying and suicidal behaviors. We begin with theories of suicide to uncover specific aspects of bullying that may trigger self-destructive behaviors among youth. We then turn to empirical studies that focus on the association between bullying and suicide, and the effect of classroom structures and teaching practices on bullying and rejection. We provide directions for future research to promote healthier classroom environments for youth. We conclude the chapter with the suggestion that improving youths' feelings of belonging can be among the ways adults can reduce bullying and suicidal behaviors among children and adolescents.

THEORIES OF SUICIDE

The first formally developed theory of suicide comes from the famous French sociologist Emile Durkheim (1951). Durkheim presented three types of suicides that resulted from unbalanced relationships between individuals and their society. Among those three, *egoistic* and *anomic* suicide may be the most suitable with the stories of adolescent suicide due to alleged bullying. Egoistic suicide results from a feeling of disconnection from society. Anomic suicide results from a feeling of pressure from society that creates the idea that death is the only option to escape one's misery. Another theory developed by a clinical psychologist proposed that *psychache*, "the hurt, anguish, or ache that takes hold in the mind," is the basic ingredient of suicide (Shneidman, 1996, p. 13). According to this theory, suicide happens because people want to relieve this unbearable psychache and perceive death as the only solution to end their suffering. From the cognitive perspective, it is the feeling of hopelessness in particular that drives people to commit suicide (Beck, Steer, Kovacs, & Garrison, 1985). Among both psychiatric inpatients and outpatients, those who ultimately committed suicide scored significantly higher on the Beck Hopelessness Scale than those who did not commit suicide (Beck et al., 1985). In summary, these theories postulated that (1) lack of integration with society; (2) severe psychological pain, specifically due to the feeling of hopelessness; and (3) the belief that death is the only way to end the problem are among the main factors that lead to suicide.

Bullying during adolescence has the potential to put youth in any of those states of mind. From a developmental perspective, experiencing interpersonal conflict with peers during adolescence can be especially stressful (Berman, Jobes, & Silverman, 2006). Adolescence is a period of identity formation, when youth actively try to find their niche in the social context and pay more attention to how they are perceived by others (Erikson, 1950/1963, p. 261):

> The growing and developing youth, faced with this physiological revolution within them, and with tangible adult tasks ahead of them are now primarily concerned with what they appear to be in the eyes of others as compared with what they feel they are, and with questions of how to connect the roles and skills cultivated earlier with the occupational prototypes of the day.

Bullying conveys a strong message of rejection and futility, threatening one's sense of belongingness and self-efficacy, which are the two factors that often instigate people's desire to die (Joiner, 2005). However, most people who have been bullied do not commit suicide. Victims of peer harassment who perceive suicide as a heroic or dramatic means of escape are more likely to commit suicide than are youth who perceive it as a stigma (Berman et al., 2006). The ability to enact self-injury (Joiner, 2005), as well as a history of suicide attempts and mental illness (which we will discuss in the next section), can also increase one's likelihood of committing suicide.

BULLYING, SUICIDE, AND PEER ECOLOGIES

The Link Between Bullying and Suicide

Research has shown that the link between bullying and suicide tends to be moderated by depression and delinquency. For example, a cross-sectional study found that middle-school students who identified themselves as a bully, a victim, or a bully-victim, reported higher levels of suicidal behaviors than did students who claimed that they were uninvolved in bullying (Espelage & Holt, 2013). However, when delinquency and depression were taken into account, victims and bully-victims still appeared to have significantly higher levels of suicidal behaviors compared to uninvolved youth, but these differences were reported to be small (Espelage & Holt, 2013). In the longitudinal 1981 Finnish Birth Cohort study, there was no significant association between any bullying involvement in childhood and suicidal ideation ten years later among Finnish adolescent males, after controlling for childhood depression (Klomek et al., 2008). When examining suicide attempts and completed suicide based on Finnish registries, there was again no association between childhood bullying and later suicide attempts or completed suicide among Finnish boys, after childhood psychopathology was accounted for (Klomek et al., 2009). However, the moderating effect of individual psychopathology on the link between bullying and suicide seems to vary by gender. For girls, frequent victimization was still found to be significantly associated with higher levels of suicidal behaviors, even after controlling for depression and delinquency; but for boys, such associations tended to diminish when both psychopathologies were taken into account (Espelage & Holt, 2013; Klomek et al., 2009).

Nevertheless, across gender, the co-occurrence of bullying and mental illnesses increases one's risk of suicidal behaviors. Compared to adolescents who only reported frequent bullying involvement or those who were considered as "at risk" only (reported recent suicidal behavior, moderate to severe depression, and substance abuse impairment), adolescents who both reported bullying involvement and were "at risk" had worse outcomes with regard to depression, suicidal ideation, substance use problems, and functional impairment four years later (Klomek et al., 2011).

Together, studies on the link between bullying and suicide suggest that the co-occurrence of bullying involvement and individual psychiatric disorders, rather than either factor alone, increases one's risk of suicidality. This process seems to fit with a diathesis-stress model, wherein individual psychopathology, such as depression, delinquency, or anxiety, may function as a vulnerability; whereas bullying involvement plays a role as an interpersonal stressor. When individuals with certain vulnerabilities experience bullying, they are more susceptible to developing suicidal ideations or to contemplating suicide than are those who only experience bullying or only have the diathesis.

Other than individual psychopathology, parents, family, and peers are important contextual factors that influence suicidal behaviors among victimized youth. Self-injury, emotional distress, physical and sexual abuse, and parental psychopathology increased the risk of suicidal ideation and attempts among youth who were involved in bullying (Borowsky, Taliaferro, & McMorris, 2013; Herba et al., 2008). In contrast, having authoritative parents, self-reported parental connectedness, perceived care from friends, and a sense of connectedness with school minimized the association between bullying and suicidal ideation, even among those who had a history of suicide attempts (Borowsky et al., 2013; Hay & Meldrum, 2010; Kidd, Henrich, Brookmeyer, Davidson, King, & Sharar, 2006). These protective factors share a common theme: a sense of connection. It seems that children and adolescents who feel connected with their parents, peers, or school are at least partially protected from suicidal behaviors, even though they are bullied or otherwise susceptible to suicide. This premise is consistent with the theory of suicide that having a sense of belonging can sustain one's will to live (Joiner, 2005).

Considering that children and adolescents spend most of their time at school, and most bullying occurs in the school setting (Centers for Disease Control and Prevention [CDC], 2013), perhaps an important intervention effort for both bullying and suicide is to create a social environment that cultivates a sense of connection among students at school. Drawing upon studies of classroom peer ecologies, the next section focuses on classroom structures and teaching practices that are associated with a decrease in peer rejection and social exclusion and an increase in positive relationships.

Classroom Peer Ecologies

The peer social ecology is a proximal setting, a *microsystem*, which Bronfenbrenner (1996, p. xv) describes as "the ultimate mechanism through which development occurs." Interaction within the peer social ecology can take many forms, including frequent affiliation, joint participation in activities, and even negative forms, as is the case with bullying and victimization. As such, the structural aspects of classroom peer ecologies are critical to student learning and effective teaching.

Classroom Hierarchies, Aggression, and Victimization

It has long been thought that more egalitarian or democratic peer ecologies are superior to those in which social capital is held by just a few (e.g., Lewin, Lippitt, & White, 1939; Sherif, 1956). In education settings, a hierarchical social structure can promote hostility, impede cohesion, and lead to the emergence of scapegoats (Cohen & Lotan, 1995). Victimized children are more depressed and have lower self-esteem in classrooms where peer victimization is directed to only a few students than in classrooms where more peers share the plight of peer harassment (Huitsing, Veenstra, Sainio, & Salmivalli, 2010). Our studies have found that aggressive children had the highest social status and victimized children had the lowest social status in classrooms with unequally distributed affiliative connections among students (Ahn, Garandeau, & Rodkin, 2010). Aggressive children also obtained higher status in classrooms where popularity varied greatly from one student to another (Garandeau, Ahn, & Rodkin, 2011). However, in classrooms where friendship networks were more egalitarian, aggressive boys lost social status over the school year (Ahn & Rodkin, 2014). Thus, more egalitarian classrooms where friendship, status, and even peer harassment are more equally shared among students seem to be indicative of healthier, more inclusive classroom environments.

The positive association between aggression and popularity is detrimental to peer social ecologies because, when bullying and aggression are rewarded with power and status, students perceive the aggressors as more accepted (Dijkstra, Lindenberg, & Veenstra, 2008). Moreover, as adolescents tend to conform to the behaviors endorsed by high-status peers and distance themselves from the attitudes of low-status peers (Cohen & Prinstein, 2006), the presence of popular bullies in a classroom may motivate some adolescents to harass their peers in order to gain popularity. Others may choose not to intervene in bullying in order to protect themselves; a bystander role that may only make bullying norms more salient (Juvonen & Galván, 2009; Salmivalli, 2001).

Results from investigating friendship selection and influence among fifth grade students showed that children tended to select their friends based on similarity in popularity—more than on similarity in aggression or prosocial behavior (Logis, Rodkin, Gest, & Ahn, 2013). When children form peer groups based on similarity in popularity, low-status, rejected children may become increasingly marginalized over time, making them an easy target for bullying. When popular peers harass rejected children in order to maintain the status hierarchy in the classroom, others may feel reluctant to intervene. As a result, rejected children may increasingly feel hopeless and lonely, which can eventually lead to suicidal thoughts or behaviors. Hence, being isolated can increase, not only one's risk of bullying, but also one's risk of suicidality.

Teacher Practices Associated with Positive Peer Ecologies

Although teachers are not part of the peer social ecology, they play a unique leadership role in the classroom microsystem. Effective teaching to social dynamics may begin with *attunement* (Gronlund, 1959)—knowing the characteristics and relationships of students as other students view them—and it may culminate with the ability of some teachers to use their knowledge of their classroom's social dynamics towards scaffolding productive, positive relationships between students. Higher levels of attunement are typically associated with better classroom adjustment. For example, greater teacher–student attunement has been associated with anti-aggression norms (Neal, Cappella, Wagner, & Atkins, 2011) and more positive views of school environments, such as a greater sense of school belonging and a greater willingness to defend victims of bullying (Hamm, Farmer, Dadisman, Gravelle, & Murray, 2011). Oftentimes it is difficult for teachers to stay abreast of changing peer dynamics, as many aspects of classroom social dynamics are part of the culture of children and not readily apparent to adults (Rodkin, 2011). For example, our study shows that overall agreement between teachers and students on the measure: "bullies and kids they pick on" in elementary school classrooms is often less than 10% (Ahn, Rodkin, & Gest, 2013).

Other than attunement, teachers' attitudes and interactions with students are also associated with youth outcomes. To test potential teachers' influence on children's peer relationships, Gest and Rodkin (2011) examined teaching practices and peer relationships patterns in elementary school classrooms. They found that students expressed more positive sentiments toward one another in classrooms where teachers placed a strong emphasis on separating students displaying behavior problems and reported higher levels of sympathy and support for shy-withdrawn students. Teachers' observed emotional support was also associated with higher rates of friendship reciprocation among students. Another study found that teachers who showed more warmth, respect, sensitivity to students' needs, and provided many leadership opportunities for children, tended to have classrooms where students perceived their teacher as trustworthy, kind, and warm, and viewed their peers as caring, helpful, and cooperative (Madill, Gest, & Rodkin, 2014).

For phenomena like peer rejection and peer harassment, both the hierarchical nature of classroom peer ecologies and teachers' attentiveness to status hierarchies are associated with the likelihood that rejected children will come to face bullying and peer harassment at school. Our study of elementary school students and their teachers shows that rejected children experience higher levels of peer victimization at the end of the school year in classrooms where harassment was heavily directed towards just a few victims at the beginning of the school year (Serdiouk, Rodkin, Madill, Logis, & Gest, in press). According to attribution theory, children's perceived reasons for their peer relationship problems can determine their subsequent maladjustment. Victimized children who attribute the cause of their peer harassment as internal ("It is something about me"), stable, and beyond their control are more likely to be depressed, anxious, and lonely than victimized children who attribute their peer harassment to an unstable, controllable cause (Graham & Juvonen, 1998). Hence, in classrooms where bullying is only directed towards a few peers, victimized children are more likely to attribute their peer adversity to an internal cause, which can lead to loneliness, low self-esteem, and low self-efficacy—feelings that can increase the risk of suicidal thoughts or behaviors. However, in classrooms where teachers reported making efforts to reduce social status inequality, the rate of peer victimization at the end of the school year was lower (Serdiouk et al., in press).

Overall, these studies suggest that teachers may have the power to reduce bullying and suicidality by using their knowledge of students' relationships to create a classroom characterized by cooperation, friendship, and equality. Such a positive social environment in the classroom creates an opportunity for children who are at risk of bullying and suicide to build positive relationships with their classmates, which can be challenging in an environment that does not promote inclusion and status equality.

Implications

Data from the National Violent Death Reporting System, which includes over 1,000 cases of adolescents who died by suicide, indicate that it is the complex interaction among multiple relationship problems, mental health, and school stressors, rather than a single factor, that triggers suicide (Karch, Logan, McDaniel, Floyd, & Vagi, 2013). Unfortunately, the majority of media reports have typically discounted individual vulnerabilities associated with suicide. Nicole Cardarelli, a manager of State Advocacy and Grassroots Outreach at the American Foundation for Suicide Prevention, stated that this can be a problem: "This death by bullying narrative is really normalizing suicide as a reaction of being bullied. It's emphasizing frequency and similarities among teen suicide deaths, and that's making suicide seem normal, common, or acceptable" (U.S. Department of Education, 2012).

Prevention efforts for bullying and suicide need to be made at different levels in the society. Our studies of classroom peer ecologies suggest that there are conditions in the classroom that can improve social relationships among students, such as an egalitarian peer structure characterized by a more equal distribution of friendship ties and social status. Such a classroom can be beneficial for suicidal youth because it may alleviate their feelings of loneliness and may increase their sense of belongingness. Classrooms that promote cooperation and equality may also be effective in reducing bullying. One possible motivation for children to bully others is to find their niche at school. When bullying becomes the norm, children may be driven to bully others in order to be part of the group. Hence, if children and adolescents can live in an environment where they can find their niche without having to bully others, such as in classrooms with a more egalitarian peer structure and where the teachers are attuned to their students' relationships, then perhaps bullying behaviors can diminish.

A short intervention study among eight- and nine-year-olds shows some promising results that moderately aggressive children can become less aggressive after being paired with a non-aggressive peer (Hektner, August, & Realmuto, 2003). Our study with fifth-grade students suggested that aggressive students would choose prosocial peers as friends—but only if they were previously similar in popularity (Logis et al., 2013). Hence, with knowledge of student popularity and behaviors, teachers might be able to promote supportive friendships through the use of seating arrangements, grouping mechanisms, and class activities that promote cooperation (e.g., Mikami, Boucher, & Humphreys, 2005). Perhaps by pairing an aggressive child with a prosocial peer of similar popularity, a more aggressive child can become more prosocial due to socialization by prosocial friends.

Future Directions

Some studies suggest that not all children who have psychological risk factors (depression, suicidal thoughts, suicidal attempts, functional impairment, and depression) are involved in bullying, and similarly, not all children without psychological risk factors are uninvolved in bullying (e.g., Klomek et al., 2011). Therefore, it would be worthwhile for future studies to examine individual and contextual factors of youth who have psychological risk factors but are uninvolved in bullying to understand the factors that shield them from peer harassment. Previous studies also have been less consistent when it comes to the psychological consequences of being a bully perpetrator. Some studies have found that bullying is related to suicidal ideation (Kaltiala-Heino, Rimpelä, Rantanen, & Rimpleä, 2000; King, Horwitz, Berona, & Jiang, 2013). However, a recent study has found that bully perpetration is not associated with maladjustment in adulthood—including poor physical and mental health, risky behaviors, lack of financial and educational accomplishment, and poor social relationships—after accounting for childhood psychiatric problems and family hardship (Wolke, Copeland, Angold, & Costello, 2013). Future studies may benefit from taking into account the social status of the bully perpetrator to understand such multifinality. Some bullies are popular, but others are rejected; perhaps the rejected bullies are more at risk of future maladjustment than the high-status bullies are.

In addition to identifying individual risk and protective factors for bullying and suicide, knowing specific strategies that some experienced teachers use to successfully build positive relationships with their students and to create egalitarian peer structures can benefit pre-service teachers who may not be well-equipped with effective behavior-management skills. Teacher training in the social dynamics of behavioral management was a fundamental objective of Kurt Lewin and the generation of influential scholars who followed him (Gronlund, 1959; Redl & Wattenberg, 1959). Yet current typical practice in teacher training and development is often inattentive to some fundamental features of classroom peer ecologies, such as the nature of friendships and animosities between children and child peer groups, or the existence of strong status hierarchies that promote aggression and bullying.

Developing a tool to help teachers assess, visualize, and manage classroom social dynamics would be a positive future step towards building more positive classroom climates. Teachers should be able to conduct a quick social-network assessment based on the aggregate perspective of their students. If teachers can identify high-status students early on, they can provide these students with the skills for developing into more effective group leaders (Gronlund, 1959). Identifying rejected and withdrawn students early on also gives teachers the chance to intervene early, perhaps through promoting friendships and providing opportunities for these students to interact with other students in a cooperative manner.

Most of the studies related to classroom peer ecologies discussed in this chapter are drawn from elementary-school settings. However, the issue of bullying and suicide typically emerges when children enter middle school and high school, where peer groups become larger, and aggression predicts social prominence (Cillessen & Mayeux, 2004). Changes in peer structure and peer norms, along with psychological and biological changes that occur during adolescence, may make it more challenging for youth to find their niche. More research is needed to examine whether the same classroom structures and teaching practices associated with positive peer relationships found in elementary classrooms can also be applied in middle- and high-school settings.

IMPLICATIONS FOR PRACTICE, AND SUGGESTIONS

The views on bullying as a serious public health concern imply that intervention and prevention should be conducted with collective efforts to create positive peer social ecologies characterized by acceptance and cooperation. Based on the idea that a healthy environment that promotes inclusion, acceptance, and a sense of belongingness can positively affect children's mental health and development, we propose a few recommendations to help build that climate.

Suggestions for Medical Providers

- Build rapport so that young patients may feel comfortable sharing some issues that they might be experiencing at school or at home, in order to identify early signs of bullying or suicidality and help patients to seek professional help.

Suggestions for Mental Health Providers

- Reduce self-blame among the victims of peer harassment; help them rebuild their self-esteem and self-efficacy; teach coping strategies to deal with interpersonal stress and social skills necessary to build positive relationships with peers.

Suggestions for Parents and Teachers

- Motivate children to try various extracurricular activities to help them identify their abilities and strengths, and to find their niche.
- Help rejected and neglected youth appear favorably among peers by recognizing their positive attitude and talents, or by assigning a leadership role to them.
- Promote friendships among children of different popularity levels, creating opportunities for cooperation in classroom activities, and building positive and respectful relationships with students.

Suggestions for Policy Makers

- Invest in teacher-coaching programs to increase teachers' motivation to take an active role in managing classroom relationships and to increase teachers' sense of efficacy regarding their potential to bring about positive changes in classroom social relationships.

REFERENCES

Ahn, H.-J., & Rodkin, P. C. (2014). Classroom-level predictors of the social status of aggression: Friendship centralization, friendship density, teacher-student attunement, and gender. *Journal of Educational Psychology*

Ahn, H.-J., Rodkin, P. C., & Gest, S. D. (2013). Teacher-student agreement on "bullies and kids they pick on" in elementary school classrooms: Gender and grade differences. *Theory into Practice, 52*, 1–7. doi: 10.1080/00405841.2013.829728

Ahn, H.-J., Garandeau, C. F., & Rodkin, P. C. (2010). Effects of classroom embeddedness and density on the social status of aggressive and victimized children. *Journal of Early Adolescence, 30*, 76–101. doi: 10.1177/0272431609350922

Beck, A. T., Steer, R., Kovacs, M., & Garrison, B. (1985). Hopelessness and eventual suicide: A 10-year prospective study of patients hospitalized with suicidal ideation. *American Journal of Psychiatry, 142*, 559–563.

Berman, A. L., Jobes, D. A., & Silverman, M. M. (2006). *Adolescent Suicide: Assessment and Intervention*. Washington, DC: American Psychological Association.

Borowsky, I. W., Taliaferro, L. A., & McMorris, B. J. (2013). Suicidal thinking and behavior among youth involved in verbal and social bullying: Risk and protective factors. *Journal of Adolescent Health, 53*, 4–12. doi: 10.1016/j.jadohealth.2012.10.280

Bronfenbrenner, U. (1996). Foreword. In R. B. Cairns, G. H. Elder, Jr., & E. J. Costello (Eds.), *Developmental Science* (pp. ix–xvii). New York: Cambridge University Press.

Cillessen, A. H. N, & Mayeux, L. (2004). From censure to reinforcement: Developmental changes in the association between aggression and social status. *Child Development, 75*, 147–163. doi: 10.1111/j.1467-8624.2004.00660.x

Centers for Disease Control and Prevention (2013). 1991–2011 high school youth risk behavior survey data. Retrieved July 2, 2013, from http://apps.nccd.cdc.gov/youthonline.

Cohen, E. G., & Lotan, R. A. (1995). Producing equal-status interaction in the heterogeneous classroom. *American Educational Research Journal, 32*, 99–120. doi: 10.3102/00028312032001099

Cohen, G. L., & Prinstein, M. J. (2006). Peer contagion of aggression and health-risk behavior among adolescent males: An experimental investigation of effects on public conduct and private attitudes. *Child Development, 77*, 967–983. doi: 10.1111/j.1467-8624.2006.00913.x

Department of Education (Sponsor) (2012, August 7). Bullying Prevention Summit, Day 2: Suicide Prevention. Retrieved from http://www.c-spanvideo.org/program/SummitSu.

Dijkstra, J. K., Lindenberg, S. M., & Veenstra, R. (2008). Beyond the classroom norm: The influence of bullying of popular adolescents and its relation to peer acceptance and rejection. *Journal of Abnormal Child Psychology, 36*, 1289–1299. doi: 10.1007/s10802-008-9251-7

Durkheim, E. (1951). *Suicide: A Study in Sociology*. New York: Free Press. (Original work published 1897.)

Erikson, E. H. (1950/1963). *Childhood and Society*. New York: Norton.

Espelage, D. L., & Holt, M. K. (2013). Suicidal ideation and school bullying experiences after controlling for depression and delinquency. *Journal of Adolescent Health, 53*, 27–31. doi:10.1016/j.jadohealth.2012.09.017

Ferguson, C. J., Miguel, C., Kilburn, J. C., & Sanchez, P. (2007). The effectiveness of school-based anti-bullying programs: A meta-analytic review. *Criminal Justice Review, 32*, 401–414. doi: 10.1177/0734016807311712

Garandeau, C. F., Ahn, H.-J., & Rodkin, P. C. (2011). The social status of aggressive students across contexts: The role of classroom status hierarchy, academic achievement, and grade. *Developmental Psychology, 47*, 1699–1710. doi: 10.1037/a0025271

Gest, S. D., & Rodkin, P. C. (2011). Teaching practices and elementary classroom peer ecologies. *Journal of Applied Developmental Psychology, 32*, 288–296. doi: 10.1016/j.appdev.2011.02.004

Graham, S., & Juvonen, J. (1998). Self-blame and peer victimization in middle school: An attributional analysis. *Developmental Psychology, 34*, 587–599. doi: 10.1037/0012-1649.34.3.587

Gronlund, N. E. (1959). *Sociometry in the Classroom*. New York: Harper & Brothers.

Hamm, J. V., Farmer, T W., Dadisman, K., Gravelle, M., & Murray, A. R. (2011). Teachers' attunement to students' peer group affiliations as a source of improved student experiences of the school social-affective context following the middle school transition. *Journal of Applied Developmental Psychology, 32*, 267–277. doi: 10.1016/j.appdev.2010.06.003

Hay, C., & Meldrum, R. (2010). Bullying victimization and adolescent self-harm: Testing hypotheses from General Strain Theory. *Journal of Youth Adolescence, 39*, 446–459. doi: 10.1007/s10964-009-9502-0

Hektner, J. M., August, G. J., & Realmuto, G. M. (2003). Effects of pairing aggressive and nonaggressive children in strategic peer affiliation. *Journal of Abnormal Child Psychology, 31*, 399–412. doi: 10.1023/A:1023891502049

Herba, C. M., Ferdinand, R. F., Stijnen, T., Veenstra, R., Oldehinkel, A. J., Ormel, J., & Verhulst, F. C. (2008). Victimization and suicide ideation in the TRAILS study: Specific vulnerabilities of victims. *Journal of Child Psychology and Psychiatry, 49*, 867–876. doi: 10.1111/j.1469-7610.2008.01900.x

Hertz, M. F., Donato, I., & Wright, J. (Eds.) (2013). Bullying and suicide: A public health approach. *Journal of Adolescent Health, 53*, 1–3. doi:10.1016/j.jadohealth.2013.05.002

Huitsing, G., Veenstra, R., Sainio, M., & Salmivalli, C. (2010). "It must be me" or "It could be them?" The impact of the social network position of bullies and victims on victims' adjustment. *Social Networks, 34*, 379–386. doi: 10.1016/j.socnet.2010.07.002

Joiner, T. (2005). *Why People Die by Suicide*. Cambridge, MA: Harvard University Press.

Juvonen, J., & Galván, A. (2009). Bullying as a means to foster compliance. M. Harris (Ed.), *Bullying, Rejection and Peer Victimization: A Social Cognitive Neuroscience Perspective* (pp. 299–318). New York: Springer Publishing.

Kaltiala-Heino, R. Rimpelä, M., Rantanen, P., & Rimpleä, A. (2000). Bullying at school—an indicator of adolescents at risk for mental disorders. *Journal of Adolescence, 23*, 661–674. doi: 10.1006/jado.2000.0351

Karch, D. L., Logan, J., McDaniel, D. D., Floyd, C. F., & Vagi, K. J. (2013). Precipitating circumstances of suicide among youth aged 10–17 years by sex: Data from the National Violent Death Reporting System, 16 states, 2005–2008. *Journal of Adolescent Health, 53*, 51–53. doi: 10.1016/j.jadohealth.2012.06.028

Kidd, S., Henrich, C. C., Brookmeyer, K. A., Davidson, L., King, R. A., & Shahar, G. (2006). The social context of adolescent suicide attempts: Interactive effects of parent, peer, and school social relations. *Suicide and Life-Threatening Behavior, 36*, 386–395. doi: 10.1521/suli.2006.36.4.386

King, C. A., Horwitz, A., Berona, J., & Jiang, Q. (2013). Acutely suicidal adolescents who engage in bullying behavior: 1-year trajectories. *Journal of Adolescent Health, 53*, 43–50. doi: 10.152/suli.2006.36.4.386

King, K. A., Strunk, C. M., & Sorter, M. T. (2011). Preliminary effectiveness of surviving the Teens® suicide prevention and depression awareness program on adolescents' suicidality and self-efficacy in performing help-seeking behavior. *Journal of School Health, 81*, 581–590. doi 10.1111/j.1746-1561.2011.00630.x

Klomek, A., Sourander, A., Kumpulainen, K., Piha, J., Tamminen, T., Moilanen, I., . . . Gould, M. S (2008). Childhood bullying as a risk for later depression and suicidal ideation among Finnish males. *Journal of Affective Disorders, 109*, 47–55. doi:10.1016/j.jad.2007.12.226

Klomek, A., Sourander, A., Niemela, S., Kumpulainen, K., Piha, J., Tamminen, T., . . . Gould, M. S. (2009). Childhood bullying behaviors as a risk for suicide attempts and completed suicides: A population-based birth cohort study. *Journal of the American Academy of Child and Adolescent Psychiatry, 48*, 254–261. doi:10.1097/CHI.0b013e318196b91f

Klomek, A. B., Kleinman, M., Altschuler, E., Marrocco, F., Amakawa, L., & Gould, M. (2011). High school bullying as a risk for later depression and suicidality. *Suicide and Life-Threatening Behavior, 4*, 501–516. doi: 10.1111/j.1943-278X.2011.00046.x

Logis, H. A., Rodkin, P. C., Gest, S. D., & Ahn, H.-J. (2013). Popularity as an organizing factor of preadolescent friendship networks: Beyond prosocial and aggressive behavior. *Journal of Research on Adolescence, 23*, 413–423. doi: 10.1111/jora.12033

Lewin, K., Lippitt, R., & White, R. K. (1939). Patterns of aggressive behavior in experimentally created "social climates." *Journal of Social Psychology, 10*, 269–299. doi:10.1080/00224545.1939.9713366

Madill, R., Gest, S., & Rodkin, P. (2014). Students' perceptions of social relatedness in the classroom: The roles of emotionally supportive teacher-child interactions, children's aggressive-disruptive behaviors and peer social preference. *School Psychology Review, 43*, 86–105.

Merrell, K. W., Gueldner, B. A., Ross, S. W., & Isava, D. M. (2008). How effective are school bullying intervention programs? A meta-analysis of intervention research. *School Psychology Quarterly, 23*, 26–42. doi: 10.10371045-3830.23.1.26

Mikami, A. Y., Boucher, M. A., & Humphreys, K. (2005). Prevention of peer rejection through classroom-level intervation in middle school. *The Journal of Primary Prevention, 26*, 5–23.doi: 10.1007/s10935-004-0988-7

Neal, J. W., Cappella, E., Wagner, C., & Atkins, M. S. (2011). Seeing eye to eye: Predicting teacher-student agreement on classroom social networks. *Social Development, 20*, 376–393. doi: 10.1111/j.1467-9507.2010.00582.x

Pelkonen, M., & Marttunen, M. (2003). Child and adolescent suicide: Epidemiology, risk factors, and approaches to prevention. *Pediatric Drugs, 5*, 243–265. doi: 10.2165/00128072-200305040-00004

Portzky, G., & van Heeringen, K. (2006). Suicide prevention in adolescents: A controlled study of the effectiveness of a school-based psycho-educational program. *Journal of Child Psychology and Psychiatry, 47*, 910–918. doi: 10.1111/j.1469-7610.2006.01595.x

Redl, F., & Wattenberg, W. W. (1959). *Mental Hygiene in Teaching* (2nd ed.). New York: Harcourt.

Rodkin, P. C. (2011, March). Bullying and children's peer relationships. White paper for the White House Conference on Bullying Prevention. The White House, Washington, D.C. [Reprinted September 2011 in *Educational Leadership, 69*, 10–16.]

Salmivalli, C. (2001). Group view on victimization: Empirical findings and their implications. In J. Juvonen, & S. Graham (Ed.), *Peer Harassment in School: The Plight of the Vulnerable and Victimized* (pp. 398–419). New York: The Guilford Press.

Serdiouk, M., Rodkin, P. C., Madill, R., Logis, H. A., & Gest, S. D. (in press). Rejection and victimization among elementary school children: The buffering role of classroom-level predictors. *Journal of Abnormal Child Psychology.*

Shneidman, E. (1996). *The Suicidal Mind.* New York: Oxford University Press.

Shaffer, D., & Gould, M. (2000). Suicide prevention in schools. In K. Hawton & K. van Heeringen (Eds.), *The International Handbook of Suicide and Attempted Suicide* (pp. 645–660). West Sussex, England: John Wiley & Sons, Ltd.

Sherif, M. (1956). Experiments in group conflict. *Scientific American, 195*, 54–58. doi:10.1038/scientificamerican1156-54

Swearer, S. M., Espelage, D. L., Vaillancourt, T., & Hymel, S. (2010). What can be done about school bullying? Linking research to educational practice. *Educational Researcher, 39*, 38–47. doi: 10.3102/0013189X09357622

Wolke, D., Copeland, W. E., Angold, A., & Costello, E. J. (2013). Impact of bullying in childhood on adult health, wealth, crime, and social outcomes. *Psychological Science, 24*, 1958–1970. doi: 10.1177/0956797613481608

17

The Olweus Bullying Prevention Program

Efforts to Address Risks Associated with Suicide and Suicide-Related Behaviors

SUSAN P. LIMBER, JANE RIESE,
MARLENE J. SNYDER, AND DAN OLWEUS ■

In recent years, attention to bullying has increased markedly among researchers, educators, policy makers, members of the media, and the general public (Kowalski, Limber, & Agatston, 2012). Numerous tragic and high-profile cases of suicide by children and youth have been linked with bullying and have led some members of the public to wrongly assume that bullying frequently leads directly to suicide (Englander & Limber, 2013). Although such conclusions are not supported by existing data, research and experience *do* confirm that there are links between bullying and suicide-related behaviors among youth, such as depression, suicidal ideation, and suicide attempts (Copeland, Wolke, Angold, & Costello, 2013; Espelage & Holt, 2013; Kim, Leventhal, Koh, & Boyce, 2009; Klomek, Marrocco, Kleinman, Schonfield, & Gould, 2007, 2008; Kowalski & Limber, 2013; Olweus, 1993; Pranjić & Bajraktarević, 2010; Reijntjes, Kamphuis, Prinzie, & Telch, 2010; Ttofi Farrington, Lösel, & Loeber, 2011). Moreover, research confirms that such internalizing behaviors are also more likely among students who lack "connectedness" or a sense of belonging to their schools (Jacobson & Rowe, 1999; Resnick et al., 1997; Shochet, Homel, Cockshaw, & Montgomery, 2008) and that positive relationships with peers and close connections with caring adults are important to help youth cope with everyday stressors and with life crises (Shochet, Dadds, Ham, & Montague, 2006). As bullied youth are more likely than other students to feel as if they do not belong in school (Glew, Fan, Katon, Rivara, & Kernic, 2005), efforts to increase their connectedness are critical (Grover, Boberiene, & Limber, in press). In their research to assess precipitating circumstances for suicide among youth (ages 10–17), Karch, Logan, McDaniel, Floyd, and Vagi (2013) found that there was "a complex interaction of multiple relationship, mental health, and school stressors" that were precipitating circumstances for youth suicide, and noted that these stressors "suggest numerous opportunities to intervene and prevent suicidal behavior" (p. S53).

Comprehensive bullying prevention efforts, although no substitute for comprehensive suicide prevention efforts, provide one such important opportunity. They may not only reduce bullying but may also have other positive effects, such as improving peer relationships, enhancing students' sense of school connectedness, and identifying children and youth in need of supportive mental health services. In this context, it is important for individuals who are responsible for bullying prevention efforts in the schools to understand current research on bullying and suicide and its implications for practice within schools. Other chapters [e.g., Holt, Chapter 3; Nickerson & Orrange Torchia, Chapter 4; Orpinas & Horne, Chapter 5] in this volume provide a detailed description of research on bullying and suicide. In this chapter, we will describe the Olweus Bullying Prevention Program (OBPP) and its research base, and will highlight aspects of this comprehensive bullying prevention program that may support suicide prevention efforts in schools.

OVERVIEW OF THE OLWEUS BULLYING PREVENTION PROGRAM

The OBPP was first implemented amidst public concern about possible connections between bullying and suicide. Developed in the early 1980s by bullying researcher Dan Olweus, the OBPP was introduced in elementary and junior high schools in Norway in 1983, at a time when national attention to the issue of bullying had intensified after three adolescent boys died by suicide after having been persistently bullied by their peers.

Goals and Guiding Principles

The OBPP is a framework for positive system change, whose goals are to reduce existing bullying problems among students at school, prevent the development of new bullying problems, and improve peer relations at school (Olweus, 1993; Olweus et al., 2007). In order to meet these goals, school personnel work to restructure the school environment to reduce opportunities and rewards for bullying behavior, shift social norms to create expectations of inclusion and civility, and build a sense of community among students and adults in the school (Olweus, 1993; Olweus et al., 2007).

The OBPP is based on four guiding principles, which have been derived from research on aggression (Baumrind, 1967; Loeber & Stouthamer-Loeber, 1986; Olweus, 1973, 1978, 1979, 1980). Adults in the school community take the lead in building a welcoming school climate by: (1) showing warmth and positive interest in students; (2) applying firm limits to unacceptable behavior, such as bullying; (3) using consistent, non-hostile, non-physical consequences when rules are violated in order to encourage positive behavior change; and (4) model positive behavior for students.

Program Components

These principles have been translated into specific program components at four levels: school-wide, classroom, individual, and community (Olweus et al., 2007). Box 17.1 summarizes all the components of the OBPP. Although it is beyond this scope of this chapter to describe each in detail, several will be highlighted here because: (1) research has suggested that they play key roles in reducing bullying within a school setting; and/or (2) they are particularly relevant to suicide prevention or the coordination of prevention efforts within a school setting.

Establishment of a Bullying Prevention Coordinating Committee

The Bullying Prevention Coordinating Committee (BPCC) is a committee within a school that is responsible for ensuring that all components of the OBPP are

---

Box 17.1

Components of the OBPP

School-Level Components

- Establish a Bullying Prevention Coordinating Committee (BPCC)
- Conduct trainings for the BPCC and all staff
- Administer the Olweus Bullying Questionnaire (grades 3–12)
- Hold staff discussion group meetings
- Introduce the school rules against bullying
- Review and refine the school's supervisory system
- Hold a school-wide kick-off event to launch the program
- Involve parents

Classroom-Level Components

- Post and enforce school-wide rules against bullying
- Hold regular (weekly) class meetings to discuss bullying and related topics
- Hold class-level meetings with students' parents

Individual-Level Components

- Supervise students' activities
- Ensure that all staff intervene on the spot when bullying is observed
- Meet with students involved in bullying (separately for those who are bullied and who bully)
- Meet with parents of involved students
- Develop individual intervention plans for involved students, as needed

Community-Level Components

- Involve community members on the Bullying Prevention Coordinating Committee
- Develop school–community partnerships to support the school's program
- Help to spread anti-bullying messages and principles of best practice in the community

---

implemented with fidelity in the school, and that the OBPP is coordinated with other prevention and intervention efforts at the school, including suicide prevention (Limber, 2011; Olweus et al., 2007; Olweus & Limber, 2010b). The BPCC typically comprises 8–15 members, with representatives from key constituencies at the school, including administrators, teachers, non-teaching staff, counselors and mental health professionals, parents and guardians, and other school personnel who may bring particular expertise (e.g., point-persons for suicide prevention and crisis response, nurses, Title IX representatives, school resource officers). In some cases, the committee may include one or two members from the broader community (e.g., staff from an after-school program or community mental health facility), as well as student representatives where appropriate (e.g., middle, junior, or high schools). The specific responsibilities of BPCC members include attendance at a two-day training by a certified OBPP trainer/consultant; development of a plan to implement the OBPP within the school; communication of this plan to school staff, students, and parents/guardians; careful coordination of the OBPP with other prevention and intervention efforts within the school community; gathering regular feedback from constituents about the implementation of the OBPP; and representation of the program to the broader community (Limber, 2011; Olweus et al., 2007; Olweus & Limber, 2010b).

Training and Consultation for the BPCC and All Administrators, Educators and Non-teaching Staff

Training and ongoing consultation are critical to the successful implementation of the OBPP. In addition to the two-day training for members of the BPCC, a certified Olweus trainer provides at least one year of consultation to the on-site coordinator at each school to assist school personnel in overcoming barriers to program implementation and ensure sustainability. BPCC members (with support from the OBPP trainer) provide a full day of training to the school staff prior to implementing the program. Yearly professional-development trainings for new administrators, teachers, and staff members are encouraged, as are periodic booster trainings for experienced school personnel. During these trainings, all adults are provided information about the prevalence rates of bullying (nationally and in their school building) and the consequences of bullying, and are also alerted to the populations of students who are most likely to be involved in bullying.

As part of their initial training, OBPP trainers are introduced to data on youth suicide and the connections between bullying and suicide, and discuss implications of this research for their training and consultation with schools. They also are provided a document outlining these issues as part of their training and consultation materials (Limber, Snyder, & Riese, 2012) to be shared with BPCC members. This training and supporting document addresses several key issues for trainers for their ongoing consultation with schools interested in implementing the OBPP:

- During their pre-training consultation with school leaders and during their training of BPCCs, OBPP trainers should communicate clearly that children and youth involved in bullying are more likely than others to be depressed, have suicidal ideation, and attempt suicide, but that suicide is a complex issue that typically involves far more than involvement in bullying alone. Trainers are encouraged to spread the message that school personnel who actively work to prevent bullying, who work to build community within classrooms and schools, who are watchful for possible bullying, and who take quick actions to stop bullying are taking logical steps to help prevent suicide. However, these actions do not constitute comprehensive suicide prevention.

- Trainers are encouraged to ask school administrators and members of the BPCC about the specifics of programs and procedures currently in place to prevent and address suicide.
- If a suicide prevention representative and/or crisis response expert for the school is identified, trainers are to encourage administrators to include this person on the BPCC. Alternatively, BPCC members should all be informed whom they should contact if they are concerned about a student, and members of the BPCC, administrators, and other key personnel should be clear as to how to communicate with each other about specific concerns regarding suicide prevention and intervention.
- Trainers are informed, and are encouraged to discuss with school staff, that suicide prevention requires a comprehensive effort to identify mental health resources for students within the school and the larger community, including training for administrators, educators, and parents/guardians about suicide, training about the behavioral indicators that a student may be considering suicide, how to intervene effectively, how to communicate concerns to those who need to know, and how to get immediate help. Evidence-based suicide prevention/intervention strategies should be explored and implemented.
- OBPP trainer/consultants are informed that, although they may be viewed as experts on bullying prevention and intervention, they should not portray themselves as experts or consultants on suicide, unless they have specific professional training or credentials in that regard.
- Finally, trainer/consultants are encouraged to caution educators against using role-play scenarios or videos of bullying behaviors that depict the location or method of an attempted suicide or a death by suicide, as they plan kick-off events, assemblies, or class meetings. The impact of these presentations may be harmful to students who are seriously considering suicide.

Administration of the Olweus Bullying Questionnaire

Another key component of the OBPP is the administration of the Olweus Bullying Questionnaire (OBQ), an anonymous self-report measure, which is administered to students in grades 3–12 prior to implementation of the program and at yearly intervals thereafter (Olweus et al., 2007; Solberg & Olweus, 2003). The OBQ assesses students' experiences with and attitudes about bullying and the climate of the school. A detailed report of building-level findings is produced, which provides school personnel information about students' responses, frequently broken down by gender and grade. Data from the report are used to help raise awareness about bullying and assist in making specific plans to implement the OBPP. Information about bullying prevalence, the length of time bullying has lasted, and students' attitudes about school in general may provide useful information about the number, age, and gender of students who may be at particular risk of bullying. Given the relationship between bullying, school connectedness, and suicide-related behaviors, these data may be useful to school personnel to help them keep abreast of the numbers and characteristics of students who may be at risk for internalizing problems and self-harm. In subsequent years, school personnel will receive a report that highlights changes in key variables over time (presented in terms of relative percentage changes from baseline assessment) to assist them in determining whether, and to what extent, students' experiences with and attitudes about bullying have changed.

Discussion Groups

Recognizing the importance of ongoing learning and support for all school personnel implementing the OBPP, school leaders are encouraged to form discussion groups of teachers and other school staff who meet regularly (e.g., every two weeks) to discuss progress in establishing and maintaining a safe and welcoming school environment, including the implementation of the OBPP, and related issues. These discussion groups provide important structures in which teachers and staff can discuss special topics of concern, such as youth suicide, and share common concerns about students who may exhibit social difficulties or emotional distress, such as aggression toward their peers, being excluded by peers, being depressed or anxious, or experiencing a recent life crisis.

School Rules to Promote Positive Behavior and Address Bullying

So that students, all school employees, and parents/guardians have a clear understanding of the school's expectations for behavior, each school is encouraged to adopt four rules:

1. We will not bully others.
2. We will try to help students who are bullied.
3. We will try to include students who are left out.
4. If we know that somebody is being bullied, we will tell an adult at school and an adult at home (Olweus et al., 2007).

The rules are posted widely and discussed with students and family members. These discussions highlight that, although one of the rules focuses on students who bully (or may consider bullying), three of the four rules focus primarily on the behavior of students who are witnesses to bullying or may be aware of students in distress (Olweus et al., 2007). Collectively, these rules reinforce norms of acceptance and responsibility for one's peers. Stated in somewhat different terms, the rules convey that: "Everyone should have someone to be with" (Rule #3); "We can all help peers who may be in trouble" (Rule #2); and "Adults need to know if kids are in trouble" (Rule #4). Although the rules are specifically focused on bullying, the community-building norms that they promote are broad and apply to all students, including those who are experiencing different types of social and emotional stressors.

Class Meetings

The key classroom-level component of the OBPP involves holding regular group meetings with students about bullying and related issues. These meetings provide a comfortable group structure in which students can talk about bullying and its effects on kids and communities, discuss the roles that they all have to stop and prevent bullying, and increase skills to address bullying (e.g., through role playing). During these meetings, teachers and students also discuss findings from the school's annual survey of students and the positive social norms that already exist at the school on which they can build (e.g., that most students are not directly involved in bullying behavior and most dislike bullying). More broadly, the meetings are intended to build cohesion among the students in the class, provide an opportunity for students to share a wide variety of concerns (including but not limited to bullying), and help teachers keep their fingers on the pulse of students' concerns. Olweus' research found that teachers who systematically held class meetings saw larger reductions in bullying after one year than did those who used them less or not at all (Olweus & Alsaker, 1991; Olweus & Kallestad, 2010).

Because not all teachers are comfortable and skilled in leading such discussions, class meeting resources (videos showing class meetings in action, guides with ideas and strategies for multiple class meetings at different grade levels) were developed (Flerx, Limber, Mullin, Olweus, Riese, & Snyder, 2008; Flerx, Limber, Mullin, Riese, & Snyder, 2009a, 2009b; Snyder, Riese, & Limber; 2013; Snyder, Riese, Limber, & Mullin, 2012). Examples of class meeting topics include: building a positive classroom climate, identifying feelings (e.g., handling anger in healthy ways, building empathy), communication (listening skills, rumors and gossip, electronic bullying), building positive peer relationships (peer pressure, friendship, positive and negative bystander actions), respecting differences and promoting acceptance of differences, and reaching outward (encouraging students to share bullying prevention strategies with others outside of the school context).

Meetings with Students Involved in Bullying

As part of the OBPP, school personnel receive training and support in developing consistent and sensitive procedures to ensure that: (a) all staff intervene immediately if they observe or suspect bullying, and (b) follow-up meetings are held with students who involved in bullying, whenever appropriate. Separate follow-up meetings are held for those who have bullied their peers and for those who have been bullied. Holding such one-on-one meetings with students provides an opportunity for staff to identify difficulties that a student may be experiencing, provide support, and offer referrals to professionals in the community, as appropriate. Depending on the specific situation and requirements of school district policies and state laws, school personnel may involve parents in these meetings with students or communicate with them separately to keep them informed of issues involving their children and seek their support. Given the associations between bullying involvement and suicide-related behaviors, such meetings provide an important opportunity to sensitively "check in" with students about possible depression or suicidal thoughts.

Parental Involvement

Active involvement of parents and guardians is sought to support bullying prevention efforts at the school, as noted in Box 17.1. Parents and other family members attend school-wide events, receive ongoing information about the school's bullying prevention and related efforts, and attend classroom-level parent meetings, which are intended to increase their understanding of bullying and school's efforts to address it (Olweus et al., 2007). One or more parents or guardians also serve on the

BPCC, where they provide guidance to school personnel about program implementation and effective parent engagement. Key messages to parents and guardians, which may be particularly relevant to suicide prevention, include: warning signs that their child may be involved in bullying, what to do if they suspect or know that their child has been involved in bullying, and whom to contact at the school if they have any concerns about their child's behavior.

Connections to the Community

Wide community support is critical to address public health concerns among children and youth, including bullying or suicide (Masiello & Schroeder, 2013). The OBPP encourages community engagement around issues of bullying prevention through the involvement of one or more community members on a school's BPCC, creative engagement of community partners in support of the school's bullying prevention efforts, and collaboration with community members to spread bullying prevention strategies and messages into community settings where children and youth gather (Olweus et al., 2007; Limber, 2011). These community connections are particularly important in order to provide needed resources to children and families in instances where children experience anxiety, depression, psychosomatic illness, suicidal thoughts, or attempt suicide.

Research Basis

Studies conducted in Norway and the United States support the effectiveness of the OBPP. The first evaluation of the OBPP took place in Bergen, Norway, and targeted 2,500 students in grades 5–8 over a period of two and a half years between 1983 and 1985 (Olweus, 1991, 1993, 1997). Findings revealed significant reductions in students' self-reports of being bullied (reductions of 62% after 8 months and 64% after 20 months) and bullying others (reductions of 33% after 8 months and 53% after 20 months). Significant reductions were also reported in teachers' and students' ratings of bullying among students in the classroom. Findings additionally indicated that the program resulted in reductions in self-reports of general antisocial behavior, such as vandalism, theft, and truancy. Reductions in bullying were greater in the classes that had implemented key components of the program (including holding regular class meetings, establishing rules about bullying, and doing role-playing; Olweus & Alsaker, 1991; Olweus & Kallestad, 2010). Finally, Olweus also reported improvements related to aspects of the school climate and students' connectedness with their school. After program implementation, there were significant improvements in in students' perceptions of: satisfaction with school, improved order and discipline, positive social relationships at school, and a positive attitude toward school.

Six follow-up evaluations of the OBPP in Norway involving more than 20,000 students in grades 4–7 from 150 schools revealed consistently positive program effects on students' self-reports of being bullied and bullying others (Olweus & Limber, 2010). Positive outcomes have also been reported with students in grades 8–10, although these results were less consistent and effects have been somewhat weaker (Olweus & Limber, 2010). Of particular note is a five-year follow-up study with 3,000 students across 14 schools, which documented reductions of 40% in self-reports of being bullied and reductions of 51% in self-reports of bullying others (Olweus & Limber, 2010).

The first evaluation of the OBPP in the United States was conducted with elementary and middle school students in South Carolina (Limber, Nation, Tracy, Melton, & Flerx, 2004; Olweus & Limber, 2010a). Participants were predominantly African American, and school districts were located in primarily rural, low socio-economic-status communities. After seven months of program implementation, there were significant Time (pre- vs. post-tests) x Group (intervention vs. comparison group) interactions for students' reports of bullying others. For example, in the intervention schools, there was a 16% decrease in the percentages of students who had bullied others (several times a month or more often during the school term); there was a corresponding 12% increase in bullying others among students in comparison schools, resulting in an overall relative reduction of 28%. There also was an increase over time in self-reported antisocial behavior among students in comparison schools, while there was either no increase or a slower rate of increase in comparison schools with regard to measures of general delinquency, vandalism, school misbehavior, and sanctions for school misbehavior. There were no significant changes in the frequency with which students were bullied, however.

The OBPP was subsequently evaluated in six large public elementary and middle schools in Philadelphia over four years (Black & Jackson, 2007). Two-thirds of the students were from low-income families; 90% were African-American or Latino. Researchers used an observational measure of bullying incident density to assess the frequency of physical, verbal, and emotional bullying during recess (elementary students) and lunch periods (middle-school students). This observational measure consisted of a checklist of bullying behaviors that included physical, verbal, and emotional bullying. Observations of elementary students took place at recess; observations of middle-school students took place during lunch. Evaluators found that bullying decreased 45% over the course of the four years of the project, from 65 incidents per 100 student hours, to 36 incidents.

Bauer and colleagues (2007) used a non-randomized control study to evaluate the OBPP in seven intervention and three control schools in Washington State. Researchers reported positive program effects regarding students' reports that peers actively intervened in bullying incidents (relative risk [RR] = 1.21, 95% confidence interval [CI]: 1.05–1.40). They also observed positive program effects for white students' reports of being physically bullied (RR = .63, 95% CI: .42–.97) and verbally/relationally bullied (.72, 95% CI: .53–.98), although there were no program effects on self-reports of physical or verbal/relational bullying for students of other races/ethnicities.

Most recently, Limber and colleagues (Limber, Olweus, Breivik, & Wang, 2013; Limber & Olweus, 2013) conducted a large-scale evaluation of the OBPP in Pennsylvania with students in grades 3–11. Analyses included more than 72,000 students at baseline assessment who were drawn from 214 schools, who represented several consecutive yearly cohorts, and who were followed over three years (i.e., experienced two years of intervention). Additional analyses included more than 31,000 students at baseline assessment who were drawn from 94 schools, who were followed over four years (i.e., received three years of intervention). Findings revealed significant positive effects of the OBPP on students' reports of being bullied and bullying others over two years and three years for most grades, for boys and girls, and using several different ways to measure students' involvement in bullying. For example, positive findings were observed for global questions about being bullied (i.e., students responding that they had/had not been bullied 2–3 times a month or more often in the past couple of months; odds ratios [ORs] between baseline and Time 2 (T2, two years after baseline) generally ranged from 1.14 to 1.25, depending upon grade level and bullying others (i.e., students responding that they had/had not bullied others 2–3 times a month or more often; ORs between baseline and T2 ranged from 1.41 to 1.62, depending on grade level). Positive findings were also observed for scale scores (i.e., scales that represent the average of nine different forms of being bullied [individual effect sizes ranged from .12 to .18, and school-level effect sizes ranged from .94 to 1.20, depending on grade level] and bullying others (individual effect sizes ranged from .14 to .22, and school-level effect sizes ranged from .75 to 1.30, depending on grade level). Program effects for being bullied and bullying others were somewhat larger for white students, but they were also notable for black and Hispanic students. Program effects for being bullied and bullying others were larger the longer the program was implemented (i.e., two versus three years). There also were positive program effects related to students' attitudes about bullying (e.g., attitudes about how they feel when a student is being bullied) and their reports of others' actions to address bullying (e.g., reports of how much teachers/fellow students had done to address bullying). Analyses suggested that the positive changes over time were not due to "history effects" but rather were due to the effects of the OBPP.

Several research teams have conducted meta-analyses of bullying prevention programs in recent years. That by Ttofi and Farrington (Ttofi et al., 2008; Ttofi & Farrington, 2009) is widely recognized as the most rigorous to date. These authors conclude that comprehensive, school-wide programs can be successful, but that there are significant variations in the effects of different programs. The researchers note that the programs "inspired by the work of Dan Olweus worked best" (Ttofi et al., 2008, p. 69) and that future bullying prevention efforts should be "grounded in the successful Olweus programme" (p. 72).

SUMMARY AND CONCLUSIONS

To be bullied by peers is, for many youth, a very serious, negative life event. Bullied children are more likely than others to experience depression and suicidal thoughts and behavior. Moreover, several longitudinal studies suggest that involvement in bullying is causally related to short-term and long-term depression, suicidal behaviors, and later vulnerability. Research indicates that bullying is one factor among a complex interaction of numerous relationship, mental health, and school stressors that may contribute to suicidal thoughts and behavior, and suggests that there are numerous opportunities to intervene and prevent suicide. One such opportunity is the prevention and reduction of bullying through the implementation of research-based bullying prevention programs, such as the Olweus Bullying Prevention Program, which has been found to reduce bullying and also improve students' perceptions of school life. Systematic bullying prevention efforts should be part of any comprehensive plan for suicide prevention.

REFERENCES

Bauer, N., Lozano, P., & Rivara, F. P. (2007). The effectiveness of the Olweus Bullying Prevention Program in public middle schools: A controlled trial. *Journal of Adolescent Health, 40*, 266–274. doi: 10.1016/j.jadohealth.2006.10.005

Baumrind, D. (1967). Child care practices anteceding three patterns of preschool behavior. *Genetic Psychology Monographs, 75*, 43–88.

Black, S. A., & Jackson, E. (2007). Using bullying incident density to evaluate the Olweus Bullying Prevention Programme. *School Psychology International, 28*, 623–638. doi: 10.1177/0143034307085662

Copeland, W. E., Wolke, D., Angold, A., & Costello, E. J. (2013). Adult psychiatric outcomes of bullying and being bullied by peers in childhood and adolescence. *JAMA Psychiatry, 70*, 419–426. doi: 10.1001/jamapsychiatry.2013.504

Englander, E., & Limber, S. (2013, February 27). Research brief: Bullying and suicide. Retrieved January 23, 2014 from: http://www.stopbullying.gov/blog/2013/02/27/research-brief-suicide-and-bullying

Espelage, D. L., & Holt, M. K. (2013). Suicidal ideation and school bullying experiences after controlling for depression and delinquency. *Journal of Adolescent Health, 53*, S27–S31. doi: 10.1016/j.jadohealth.2012.09.017

Flerx, V. C., Limber, S. P., Mullin, N., Olweus, D., Riese, J., & Snyder, M. (2008). *Class Meetings and Individual Interventions: A How-to Guide and DVDs*. Center City, MN: Hazelden.

Flerx, V., Limber, S. P., Mullin, N., Riese, J., & Snyder, M. (2009a). *Class Meetings That Matter: A Year's Worth of Resources for Grades K–5*. Center City, MN: Hazelden.

Flerx, V., Limber, S. P., Mullin, N., Riese, J., & Snyder, M. (2009b). *Class Meetings That Matter: A Year's Worth of Resources for Grades 6–8*. Center City, MN: Hazelden.

Glew, G. M., Fan, M. Y., Katon, W., Rivara, F. P., & Kernic, M. A. (2005). Bullying, psychosocial adjustment, and academic performance in elementary school. *Archives of Pediatrics & Adolescent Medicine, 159*, 1026. doi: 10.1001/archpedi.159.11.1026.

Grover, H. M., Boberiene, L. V., & Limber, S. P. (in press). Are U.S. schools places of community? Does it matter? In G. B. Melton, (Ed.), *Good Neighbors: Safe and Humane Communities for Children and Families*. Dordrecht, Netherlands: Springer.

Jacobson, K. C., & Rowe, D. C. (1999). Genetic and environmental influences on the relationships between family connectedness, school connectedness, and adolescent depressed mood: Sex differences. *Developmental Psychology, 35*, 926. doi: 10.1037/0012-1649.35.4.926

Karch, D. L., Logan, J., McDaniel, D. D., Floyd, C. F., & Vagi, K. J. (2013). Precipitating circumstances of suicide among youth aged 10–17 years by sex: Data from the National Violent Death Reporting System, 16 states, 2005–2008. *Journal of Adolescent Health, 53*, S51–S53.

Kim, Y. S., Leventhal, B. L., Koh, Y. J., & Boyce, W. T. (2009). Bullying increased suicide risk: Prospective study of Korean adolescents. *Archives of Suicide Research, 13*, 15–30. doi: 10.1080/13811110802572098

Klomek, A. B., Marrocco, F., Kleinman, M., Schonfeld, I. S., & Gould, M. S. (2007). Bullying, depression, and suicidality in adolescents. *Journal of the American Academy of Child & Adolescent Psychiatry, 46*, 40–49. doi: 10.1097/01.chi.0000242237.84925.18

Klomek, A. B., Marrocco, F., Kleinman, M., Schonfeld, I. S., & Gould, M. S. (2008). Peer victimization, depression, and suicidality in adolescents. *Suicide and Life-Threatening Behavior, 38*, 166–180. doi: 10.152/suli.2008.38.2.166

Kowalski, R. M., & Limber, S. P. (2013). Psychological, physical, and academic correlates of cyberbullying and traditional bullying. *Journal of Adolescent Health, 53*, S13–S20. doi: 10.1016/j.jadohealth.2012.09.018

Kowalski, R. M., Limber, S. P., & Agatston, P. W. (2012). *Cyberbullying: Bullying in the Digital Age* (2nd ed.). Malden, MA: Wiley-Blackwell.

Limber, S. P. (2011). Development, evaluation, and future directions of the Olweus Bullying Prevention Program. *Journal of School Violence, 10*, 71–87. doi: 10.1080/15388220.2010.519375

Limber, S. P., Nation, M., Tracy, A. J., Melton, G. B., & Flerx, V. (2004). Implementation of the Olweus Bullying Prevention Program in the Southeastern United States. In P. K. Smith, D. Pepler, & K. Rigby (Eds.), *Bullying in Schools: How Successful Can Interventions Be?* (pp. 55–79). Cambridge, UK: Cambridge University Press.

Limber, S. P., & Olweus, D. (2013). Large scale implementation and evaluation of the Olweus Bullying Prevention Program. Paper presented at the November meeting of the International Bullying Prevention Association, Nashville, TN.

Limber, S. P., Olweus, D., Breivik, K., & Wang, W. (2013). Evaluation of the Olweus Bullying Prevention Program in a large-scale study in Pennsylvania. Manuscript in preparation.

Limber, S. P., Snyder, M., & Riese, J. (2012). Students' involvement in bullying and risk of suicide: Implications for Olweus Bullying Prevention Program trainers and coordinating committees. Unpublished manuscript.

Loeber, R., & Stouthamer-Loeber, M. (1986). Family factors as correlates and predictors of conduct problems and juvenile delinquency. In M. Tonry & N. Morris (Eds.), *Crime and Justice* (Vol. 7). Chicago: University of Chicago Press.

Masiello, M. G., & Schroeder, D. (2013). *A Public Health Approach to Bullying Prevention.* Washington, DC: American Public Health Association.

Olweus, D. (1973). *Hackkycklingar och Översittare: Forskning om Skolmobbning [Bullies and whipping boys: Research on school bullying.]* Stockholm, Sweden: Almqvist & Wiksell.

Olweus, D. (1978). *Aggression in the Schools: Bullies and Whipping Boys.* Washington, DC: Hemisphere (Wiley).

Olweus, D. (1979). Stability of aggressive reaction patterns in males: A review. *Psychological Bulletin, 86*, 852–875. doi: 10.1037/0033-2909.86.4.852

Olweus, D. (1980). Familial and temperamental determinants of aggressive behavior in adolescent boys: A causal analysis. *Developmental Psychology, 16*, 644–660. doi: 10.1037/0012-1649.16.6.644

Olweus, D. (1991). Bully/victim problems among schoolchildren: Basic facts and effects of a school based intervention program. In D. J. Pepler & K. H. Rubin (Eds.), *The Development and Treatment of Childhood Aggression* (pp. 411–448). Hillsdale, NJ: Erlbaum.

Olweus, D. (1993). *Bullying at School: What We Know and What We Can Do.* Oxford, England: Blackwell.

Olweus, D. (1997). Bully/victim problems in school: Facts and intervention. *European Journal of Psychology of Education, 12*, 495–510.

Olweus, D., & Alsaker, F. D. (1991). Assessing change in a cohort longitudinal study with hierarchical data. In D. Magnusson, L. R. Bergman, G. Rudinger, & B. Torestad (Eds.), *Problems and Methods in Longitudinal Research* (pp. 107–132). New York: Cambridge University Press.

Olweus, D., & Kallestad, J. H. (2010). The Olweus Bullying Prevention Program: Effects of classroom components at different grade levels. In K. Osterman (Ed.), *Indirect and Direct Aggression*. New York: Peter Lang.

Olweus, D., & Limber, S. P. (2010a). Bullying in school: Evaluation and dissemination of the Olweus Bullying Prevention Program. *American Journal of Orthopsychiatry, 80*, 124–134. doi: 10.1111/j.1939-0025.2010.01015.x

Olweus, D., & Limber, S. P. (2010b). The Olweus Bullying Prevention Program: Implementation and evaluation over two decades. In S. R. Jimerson, S. M. Swearer, & D. L. Espelage (Eds.), *The International Handbook of School Bullying*. New York: Routledge.

Olweus, D., Limber, S. P., Flerx, V., Mullin, N., Riese, J., & Snyder, M. (2007). *Olweus Bullying Prevention Program Schoolwide Guide*. Center City, MN: Hazelden.

Pranjić, N., & Bajraktarević, A. (2010). Depression and suicide ideation among secondary school adolescents involved in school bullying. *Primary Health Care Research & Development, 11*, 349–362. doi: 10.1017/S1463423610000307

Reijntjes, A., Kamphuis, J. H., Prinzie, P., & Telch, M. (2010). Peer victimization and internalizing problems in children: A meta-analysis of longitudinal studies. *Child Abuse & Neglect, 34*, 244–252. doi: 10.1016/j.chiabu.2009.07.09

Resnick, M. D., Bearman, P. S., Blum, R. W., Bauman, K. E., Harris, K. M., Jones, J., ... Udry, J. R. (1997). Protecting adolescents from harm. *Journal of the American Medical Association, 278*, 823–832. doi: 10.1001/jama.1997.03550100049038

Shochet, I. M., Dadds, M. R., Ham, D., & Montague, R. (2006). School connectedness is an underemphasized parameter in adolescent mental health: Results of a community prediction study. *Journal of Clinical Child and Adolescent Psychology, 35*, 170–179. doi: 10.1207/s15374424jccp3502_1

Shochet, I. M., Homel, R., Cockshaw, W. D., & Montgomery, D. T. (2008). How do school connectedness and attachment to parents interrelate in predicting adolescent depressive symptoms? *Journal of Clinical Child & Adolescent Psychology, 37*, 676–681. doi: 10.1080/15374410802148053

Snyder, M. S., Riese, J., & Limber, S. P. (2013). *High School Class Meetings and Individual Interventions: A Video Training Program for School Staff.* Center City, MN: Hazelden.

Snyder, M., Riese, J., Limber, S. P., & Mullin, N. (2012). *Class Meetings That Matter: A Year's Worth of Resources for Grades 9–12*. Center City, MN: Hazelden.

Solberg, M., & Olweus, D. (2003). Prevalence estimation of school bullying with the Olweus Bully/Victim Questionnaire. *Aggressive Behavior, 29*, 239–268. doi: 10.1002/ab.10047

Ttofi, M. M., & Farrington, D. P. (2009). What works in preventing bullying: Effective elements of anti-bullying programmes. *Journal of Aggression, Conflict and Peace Research, 1*, 13–24. doi: 10.1108/17596599200900003

Ttofi, M. M., Farrington, D. P., & Baldry, A. C. (2008). *Effectiveness of Programmes to Reduce Bullying.* Stockholm, Sweden: Swedish National Council for Crime Prevention.

Ttofi, M. M., Farrington, D. P., Lösel, F., & Loeber, R. (2011). Do the victims of school bullies tend to become depressed later in life? A systematic review and meta-analysis of longitudinal studies. *Journal of Aggression, Conflict and Peace Research, 3*, 63–73.

18

School-wide Bully Prevention Programs and Social-Emotional Learning Approaches to Preventing Bullying and Peer Victimization

DOROTHY L. ESPELAGE, LISA DE LA RUE, AND SABINA K. LOW ■

Research indicates that involvement in bullying in any capacity is associated with higher rates of suicidal ideation and behaviors, with cross-sectional studies finding increased odds ratios of 1.4–10.0 (Kim & Leventhal, 2008). One recent study examined the association between peer victimization and suicidal ideation and attempts across three nationally representative samples of adolescents (Kaminski & Fang, 2009) and found that youth victimized by their peers were 2.4 times more likely to report suicidal ideation and 3.3 times more likely to report a suicide attempt than youth who reported not being bullied. The link between bullying involvement and suicidal behaviors weakens when mediators such as depression and/or anxiety are controlled for, suggesting that bullying may be a catalyst for suicidal behaviors among youth with compromised coping skills or existing mental health problems. Nonetheless, the association continues to be significant (Espelage & Holt, 2013; Nickerson & Torchia, Chapter 4, this volume), and it remains a public health priority to understand the relationship between bullying and suicidal behavior. It stands to reason that prevention efforts to reduce victimization among school-age children could also play a role in preventing the likelihood of repeated victimization and suicidal behaviors. Indeed, a wide range of prevention strategies is employed in schools to reduce bullying, peer victimization, and youth aggression, ranging from individual counseling, peer mentoring, and classroom curriculum, to school-wide approaches (Limber, Riese, Snyder, & Olweus, Chapter 17, this volume; Westheimer, Chapter 19, this volume).

The diathesis-stress framework may be useful in understanding the association between peer victimization and suicidal behaviors. Within this framework, scholars conceptualize bullying and peer victimization as a form of psychological stress that may be traumatic for some youth (Espelage, in press; Keenan et al., 2010; Miller & Beane, 2010). Take, for example, a definition of psychological trauma by McCann and Pearlman (1990). These authors define psychological trauma as an experience that: (a) is sudden, unexpected, or non-normative; (b) exceeds the individual's perceived ability to meet its demands; and (c) disrupts the individual's frame of reference and other central psychological needs. Under this definition, it is conceivable that being frequently verbally and physically victimized by peers and having concomitant fear could be traumatic for some youth. When youth do not have the skills to manage overwhelming emotions, feel powerless to stop the victimization, perceive their school environment as unsupportive, and do not think others can help them stop the bullying, they are at risk for suicidal behaviors (Ybarra, Espelage, & Mitchell, 2014). Research of prevention programs that utilize social-emotional learning approaches to teach skills related to emotion-regulation and utilization of social support and address victimization, are likely to impact the rates of suicidal behavior, given that they can possibly lower victimization experiences and also provide youth with the skills to better cope with these experiences. However, it is also clear that social-emotional programs must be situated within a comprehensive school-wide approach that addresses policies, trains teachers to respond effectively to bullying, and promotes a supportive and safe environment (Espelage, 2012).

In this chapter, we first review the research on bully prevention programs with a focus on the specific elements that drive the greatest reductions in bullying and victimization. Then we describe several school-based bully-prevention programs that have demonstrated reductions of bullying and victimization in a large meta-analytic study (Ttofi & Farrington, 2011). Next, we describe several evidence-based social-emotional learning prevention programs whose content reaches beyond bully prevention and targets multiple risk and protective factors associated with bullying, peer victimization, and violence.

SCHOOL-BASED BULLYING-PREVENTION APPROACHES

Recognizing that the majority of the bully prevention programs have not been rigorously evaluated, what data are available indicate that the efficacy of school violence and bullying prevention programs has varied across countries and contexts (Espelage, 2012; Ttofi & Farrington, 2011). The most comprehensive meta-analysis that applied the Campbell Systematic Review procedures included a review of 44 rigorous program evaluations and randomized clinical trials (RCTs; Ttofi & Farrington, 2011). Almost two-thirds of the studies were conducted outside of the United States or Canada, and one-third of the programs were based on the Olweus Bully Prevention Program (Limber et al., Chapter 17, this volume). Ttofi and Farrington (2011) found that the programs, on average, were associated with a 20%–23% decrease in bullying perpetration, and a 17%–20% decrease in victimization (Ttofi & Farrington, 2011); however, smaller effect sizes were found for RCT designs than in non-RCT designs (an *effect size* provides a measure of the strength of the effect under consideration).

Decreases in rates of *victimization* were associated with the following special program elements: disciplinary methods, parent training/meetings, use of videos, and cooperative group work. In addition, the duration and intensity of the program for children and teachers were significantly associated with a decrease in victimization. However, work with peers (e.g., peer mediation) was associated with an increase in victimization (e.g., Ttofi & Farrington, 2011). This iatrogenic finding is not new. Scholars have argued for a decade that peer mediation is contraindicated for bully prevention (Espelage & Swearer, 2003).

Specific program elements that were associated with decreases in rates of *bully perpetration* (Ttofi & Farrington, 2011) included: parent training/meetings, improved playground supervision, disciplinary methods, classroom management, teacher training, classroom rules, whole-school anti-bullying policy, school conferences, information for parents, and cooperative group work. Furthermore, the number of elements and the duration and intensity of the program for teachers and children were significantly associated with a decrease in bullying in studies in Norway and Europe. Programs tended to be less effective in the United States and in Canada. Of note, programs inspired by the work of Dan Olweus (1993) had the highest effect sizes.

One successful element of the programs that is relevant for this chapter is the use of cooperative group work. In the meta-analysis, this element was defined as teachers working together to learn how to implement cooperative learning and role-playing activities with their students around bullying issues. In many ways, this is similar to the goals of classroom-based social-emotional learning curricula that are being used to combat bullying in schools and our communities. We turn our attention to a definition and brief history of "social-emotional learning" and then describe several promising programs that are used frequently in schools.

SOCIAL-EMOTIONAL LEARNING PROGRAMS

Social-emotional learning (SEL) emerged as a useful framework from different movements that focused on resiliency and the importance of teaching social and emotional competencies to children and adolescents (Elias et al., 1997). The School Development Program (SDP) of the Yale Child Study Center was one of the initial efforts to include psychological, emotional, and moral development as components of academic success (Haynes & Comer, 1993). Within the SDP, the psychological and emotional component was concerned with enhancing students' positive self-evaluation and acceptance, while the moral component focused on helping students make informed decisions and develop skills to resist negative peer pressure (Haynes & Comer, 1993). Consistent with the SDP, social-emotional learning approaches have emerged as a way to prevent many school-based problems and are often conceived as a systematic effort that involves school-wide changes.

Following the emergence of the SDP, New Haven continued to be the early hub of the SEL movement, and included the Yale–New Haven Social Problem Solving Project, developed in collaboration with the schools in which it was to be implemented (Elias & Weissberg, 1990). The framework of this program emphasized the need for students to have cognitive, affective, and behavioral skills; to have opportunities to engage in meaningful interactions to use these skills; and to be consistently reinforced for positive performance (Elias & Weissberg, 1990). These programs and others propelled social-emotional learning to become a large part of the conversation among educators (Elias et al., 1997).

In 1994, a group of researchers, educators, and child advocates who were concerned that health promotion efforts were not producing significant positive results convened to discuss possible new directions (Elias et al., 1997). These individuals explored efforts to enhance positive youth development, to promote social competence and emotional intelligence, and to develop effective drug education, violence prevention, health promotion, character education, service learning, civic education, school reform, and school family–community partnerships. They believed that, unlike the many prevention programs that targeted one specific problem, SEL programming addresses underlying causes of problem health behavior while supporting academic achievement. Thus, SEL approaches and programs, which many of those gathered were implementing, provided a promising direction. These interventions were based on many well-established theories, including theories of emotional intelligence, social and emotional competence promotion, social developmental models, social information processing, and self-management. In addition, behavior change and learning theories also informed the SEL framework, such as the health belief model, the theory of reasoned action, problem behavior theory, and social-cognitive theory (e.g., Greenberg et al., 2003; Hawkins et al., 2004).

The Collaborative for Academic, Social, and Emotional Learning (CASEL) emerged from this meeting with the goal of establishing high-quality, evidence-based SEL as an essential part of preschool through high school education (Collaborative for Academic, Social, & Emotional Learning, 2003; www.casel.org). School-based SEL programs developed to prevent school violence, including bullying, are predicated on the belief that academic skills are intrinsically linked to children's ability to manage their emotions, regulate emotions, and to communicate and problem-solve challenges and interpersonal conflicts (Durlak et al., 2011). Within the SEL framework, there are five interrelated skill areas: self-awareness, social awareness, self-management and organization, responsible problem-solving, and relationship management. Self-regulated learning is both directly and indirectly targeted in these programs, with the use of social-skill instruction to address behavior, discipline, safety, and academics, and to help youth become self-aware, manage their emotions, build social skills (empathy, perspective-taking, respect for diversity), build friendship skills, and make positive decisions (Zins et al., 2004). As students are better able to control their feelings, thoughts, and actions, especially under emotional demands, academic learning is optimized. Furthermore, exercises and opportunities to practice these skills and competences differ in their level of cognitive-emotional complexity to ensure developmentally appropriate interventions that are sustainable.

SEL programs offer schools, after-school programs, and youth community centers a research-based approach to building skills and promoting positive individual and peer attitudes that can contribute to the prevention of bullying. Indeed, school-based violence prevention programs that facilitate social and emotional learning skills, address interpersonal conflict, and teach emotion management have shown promise in reducing youth violence and disruptive behaviors in classrooms (Wilson & Lipsey, 2007). This is especially the case for programs that target peer violence in a coordinated fashion across different micro-contexts of the school ecology (e.g., individual, classroom, school, community). Many of these social-emotional and social-cognitive intervention programs target risk and protective factors that have consistently been associated with aggression, bullying, and victimization in cross-sectional and longitudinal studies (Basile, Espelage, Rivers, McMahon, & Simon, 2009; Espelage, Basile, & Hamburger, 2012; Espelage, Holt, & Henkel, 2003). The reduction of victimization in schools is then expected to have a positive impact on suicidal ideation and behaviors.

Research support for SEL programs is growing. A recent meta-analysis including more than 213 SEL-based programs found that if a school implements a quality SEL curriculum, they can expect better student behavior and an 11-percentile increase in academic test scores in comparison to schools with no SEL programming (Durlak et al., 2011). Schools elect to implement these programs because of the gains that schools see in achievement and prosocial behavior. Studies demonstrate that students exposed to SEL activities feel safer and more connected to their school and academics, build work habits in addition to social skills, and build strong relationships with teachers (Zins et al., 2004).

In summary, social-emotional learning approaches to health promotion are showing promise in reducing aggression and promoting prosocial behavior (Brown et al., 2011; Espelage, Low, Polanin, & Brown, 2013; Frey et al., 2005). It is reasonable to conclude that this success is largely due to the fact that SEL school-based programs parallel the hallmarks of the prevention science framework. First, these programs draw from the scientific literature on the etiological underpinnings of aggression, bullying, school violence, and other problematic behaviors among children and adolescents (Merrell, 2010). Second, risk (e.g., anger, poor impulse control) and protective (e.g., empathy, communication skills) factors are identified from the etiological literature and targeted through direct instruction of skills and opportunities to use skills in different contexts. Third, in relation to bystander intervention, these programs include discussions and content about the barriers or challenges (e.g., fear of being targeted, losing friends) that youth face when they attempt to intervene on behalf of a victim of aggression.

Several RCTs of bullying prevention programs (based on the SEL framework) have attended to the rigorous evaluation of the intervention effects (Brown et al., 2011; Espelage et al., 2013), which is an additional hallmark of prevention science. RCTs of SEL programs have identified implementation as a critical component of producing reductions in aggression and increases in prosocial behavior. As such, in order to have a public health impact, we must move beyond efficacy and focus on adoption, implementation, and sustainability. As schools are increasingly pressed to find time in the day to address psychosocial issues, SEL programs that prevent victimization and its correlates (e.g., social rejection) and also simultaneously improve academic engagement should be rigorously evaluated to make convincing arguments to teachers and school administrators that the use of these resources will produce noticeable benefits.

Next, several school-based SEL programs with strong efficacy data are highlighted. These represent only a small sample of the programs or approaches that are available to schools and communities (see the website www.casel.org for reviews of SEL programming).

EVIDENCE-BASED, SCHOOL-BASED SEL PROGRAMS

Steps to Respect: A Bullying Prevention Program

Steps to Respect: A Bullying Prevention Program© (STR) is designed to help third- through sixth-grade students build supportive relationships with one another (STR; Committee for Children, 2001). The STR program utilizes a whole-school approach to bullying prevention by addressing factors at the staff, peer group, and individual levels. The STR program includes three levels of curriculum (grades 3–4, 4–5, 5–6) that contain content and activities that are developmentally consistent with the cognitive and emotional level of each age group. The program is based on the social-ecological view that intervening at multiple levels is the most effective way to reduce school bullying, given the complex origins, forms, and maintenance factors associated with bullying. Empirical support has shown reductions in playground bullying, acceptance of bullying behavior, and argumentative behavior. At the same time, it has demonstrated increases in agreeable interactions and perceived adult responsiveness in comparison with control schools (Frey et al., 2005). More recently, it has demonstrated reductions in physical perpetration and destructive bystander behavior, and increases in bystander behavior and positive social school climate (Brown et al., 2011), especially among schools with high student engagement in the program (Low, Van Ryzin, Brown, Smith, & Haggerty, 2013). STR relies heavily on adults to deliver scripted training from a curriculum and to continually emphasize those lessons throughout the school year.

Primary bullying prevention strategies address risk factors from a systemic perspective that will influence the maximum number of students. Knowing that primary-level interventions can reach approximately 80% of students in a school encourages school officials and stakeholders to invest time and effort into these systemic efforts (Walker & Shinn, 2002). For example, the first component of the STR program is staff training for "all adults" in the school building, emphasizing that the "staff" includes janitors, bus drivers, mentors, receptionists, school nurses, volunteers, licensed staff, administrators, teachers, assistants, and other adults at school who are involved in the daily lives of students. Training meetings include a scripted training session that provides basic information on the STR program, information on bullying, and training on how to receive bullying reports from students. Administrators, teachers, or counselors who will work directly with students who have been bullied or who are bullying others receive additional training.

The STR curriculum includes lessons to increase students' social-emotional competence and positive social values. Specifically, the program addresses three general skills: First, students learn skills of perspective-taking and empathy, as well as how to manage their emotions. Second, academic skills are also encouraged, by incorporating themes of friendship and bullying into literature-unit activities such as oral expression, writing composition, and analytical reasoning. Third, the curriculum addresses students' social values by encouraging their sense of fairness, and attempts to instill a desire for rewarding friendships. Additionally, there are two literature lessons at each grade level. Students read books that allow opportunities for teachers to address multicultural issues and racism. Frey and colleagues demonstrated (2005) a 25% reduction in playground bullying incidents, compared with a control group, and a decrease in bystanders who encouraged bullying episodes. Furthermore, the effects of the STR program were most pronounced among students who were observed to do the most bullying before program implementation. Other study results included less observed victimization of all children who had previously been victimized, and less destructive bystander behavior among all children who had previously been observed contributing to bullying as bystanders (Hirschstein et al., 2007). A more recent RCT evaluation of STR in 33 California schools indicated that participation in a SEL bully prevention program was associated with higher social skills, reductions in aggression, and reductions in bystanders' assisting the bully among elementary school children (third–sixth graders; Brown et al., 2011).

Second Step: Student Success Through Prevention (Second Step: SSTP)

Second Step: Student Success Through Prevention (Second Step: SSTP; Committee for Children, 2008) is the middle-school curriculum sequence of the kindergarten through eighth-grade Second Step program. Second Step is a social-emotional learning program that also focuses on bullying prevention, sexual harassment, bullying in dating relationships, and substance abuse prevention. The program is composed of 15 lessons at grade 6, and 13 lessons each at grades 7 and 8. Lessons are delivered in one 50-minute or two 25-minute classroom sessions, taught weekly or semi-weekly throughout the school year. Curriculum developers also incorporated classic developmental research on risk and protective factors that address simultaneously multiple problems, reducing the need for a separate program for each concern (Hawkins, Catalano, Kosterman, Abbott, & Hill, 1999). The program targets the following risk factors: inappropriate classroom behavior, such as aggression and impulsivity; favorable attitudes toward problem behavior (e.g. violence, substance abuse); friends who engage in the problem behavior; early initiation of the problem behavior; peer rewards for antisocial behavior; peer rejection; and the following protective factors: social skills, empathy, school connectedness, and adoption of conventional norms about drug use. In addition, the program emphasizes perspective-taking, and in the eighth-grade curriculum, there is a specific focus on discussing stereotypes and prejudice. This program has been used extensively in diverse schools and communities, including Chicago public schools (see mini-documentary; https://www.youtube.com/watch?v=4w06gVinBhc).

Lessons are scripted and highly interactive, incorporating small group discussions and activities, class discussions, dyadic exercises, whole-class instruction, and individual work. Delivery of the lessons is supported through an accompanying DVD, which contains rich media content such as topic-focused interviews with students and video demonstrations of skills. Manualized training covers, not only the curriculum and its delivery, but also an introduction to child developmental stages as related to targeted skills. Lessons are skills-based, and students receive cueing, coaching, and suggestions for improvement on their performance. Lessons are supplemented by "transfer of training" events in which the teacher connects the lessons to events of the day, reinforces students for displaying the skills acquired, identifies natural reinforcement when it occurs, and asks students if they used specific skills during the day's events.

The program is designed to address directly a range of bullying and violent behaviors, including physical, relational, and verbal aggression in peer and dating relationships, as well as sexual harassment. The curriculum targets the peer context for bullying through expanding students' awareness of the full range of bullying behaviors, increasing perspective-taking skills and empathy for students who are bullied, educating students on their influence and responsibility as bystanders, and education and practice on the appropriate, positive responses students can use as bystanders to remove peer support for bullying. Students are taught and practice a range of positive bystander behaviors, from refusing to provide an audience, to directly intervening to stop bullying. By decreasing both active and tacit peer support for bullying, the program is designed to change the peer context, removing the social support that is such a critical driver of bullying and other violent behavior.

Recent research suggests that this program is reducing aggression, homophobic teasing, and sexual harassment, which appear to be the most egregious and overt forms of aggression. More specifically, an RCT in 36 middle schools found that participants who received SEL instruction via Second Step (Committee for Children, 2008) were 42% less likely to report engaging in physical fights after one year in comparison to students in control schools (Espelage et al., 2013) after the sixth-grade curriculum (15 weeks). Furthermore, after two years of SEL curriculum, students in the Second Step schools were 56% less likely to report homophobic victimization and 39% less likely to report sexual violence perpetration than students in the control condition. These findings are particularly important given the elevated risk of suicidal ideation and behaviors among youth who are targets of homophobic language, including gender-nonconforming and lesbian, gay, and bisexual youth (Espelage, Aragon, Birkett, & Koenig, 2008; Robinson & Espelage, 2012, 2013). In order to evaluate whether these effects are maintained as these youth transition to high school, the National Institute of Justice has funded a follow-up study to track these youth for three years of high school (Espelage, Holt, & VanRyzin, 2013). This will be the first study to examine the extent to which SEL programming prevents adverse mental health outcomes and suicidal behaviors.

Informal focus groups with teachers and students were conducted by Committee for Children staff (the developer of Second Step) after this RCT in order to inform the revision of the program. Overall, teachers and students liked the program, but they felt that the lessons were too long, that engagement decreased from sixth to eighth grade because of redundancies, and some felt that the scenarios and the characters in the materials did not reflect their community. This information is being used by Committee for Children as they embark on a revision of the curriculum. This information was also the impetus for the Centers for Disease Control Injury and Prevention funding for another RCT to evaluate a Second Step program against a gendered-enhanced Second Step + program (Espelage, Friedman, & Miller, 2013). Second Step + will include training for teachers and staff around bias-based bullying, sexual harassment, and homophobic name-calling. In turn, these teachers will then implement lessons that discuss gender, gender-based bullying, and bias-based name-calling.

Promoting Alternative Thinking Strategies

Promoting Alternative Thinking Strategies (PATHS; Kusche & Greenberg, 1994): The PATHS program, designed for children in kindergarten through sixth grade, was designated a Blueprints Model Program by the Office of Juvenile Justice and Delinquency Prevention. The PATHS program is based on the affective, behavioral, cognitive, dynamic (ABCD) model of development, and places primary importance on the developmental integration of affect and the development of emotional and cognitive understanding as they relate to social and emotional competence (Kelly, Longbottom, Potts, & Williamson, 2004). The PATHS curriculum builds from a model of development in which children's behavior and internal regulation are functions of their emotional awareness and control, their cognitive abilities, and their social skills (Curtis & Norgate, 2007). Specifically, the PATHS model posits that, during the maturational process, emotional development precedes most forms of cognitive development (Kelly et al., 2004). Following the universal prevention model, which delivers curricula to all students regardless of risk, PATHS was designed to be integrated into existing curricula. Goals of the program include enhancing social and emotional competence and reducing aggression. Classroom teachers deliver most of the curriculum, and take-home activities involve parents. The PATHS framework posits that interventions are most effective when the environment promotes opportunities to use the skills learned (Curtis & Norgate, 2007), and as such promotes full school implementation.

The PATHS curriculum consists of 101 lessons divided into three major units, each containing developmentally sequenced lessons to integrate and build on previous lessons (Curtis & Norgate, 2007). The units include readiness and self-control, feelings and relationships, and problem-solving (Kelly et al., 2004). There is also an additional supplementary unit that contains 30 lessons. Each unit contains aspects of five themes: self-control, emotional understanding, interpersonal problem-solving skills, positive self-esteem, and improved peer communication/relationships.

Several randomized trials of PATHS have indicated positive outcomes, including a reduction in aggressive solutions to problems and increases in prosocial behaviors (e.g., Greenberg et al., 2003).

Recognizing, Understanding, Labeling, Expressing, and Regulating (RULER) Approach

Recognizing, Understanding, Labeling, Expressing, and Regulating (RULER) is a multiyear program available for kindergarten through eighth-grade youth, with units that extend across the academic year (Hagelskamp, Brackett, Rivers, & Salovey, 2013). The design of RULER is based on the achievement model of emotional literacy (Rivers & Brackett, 2011), which includes the development of skills to recognize emotions in oneself and others, understand the causes and consequences of emotions, accurately label emotions, and express and regulate emotions in an appropriate way (Hagelskamp et al., 2013). Emotional literacy is acquired through the acquisition of emotion-related knowledge and skills; learning skills in a safe and supportive environment where the adults model RULER skills; and consistent opportunities to practice using the RULER skills with feedback on their application so that their use becomes refined and automatic. RULER builds social and emotional skills by focusing on the teaching and learning of emotion-related concepts or "feeling words" and by introducing tools for using emotions in the learning environment (Hagelskamp et al., 2013).

An important component of the RULER approach is the inclusion of comprehensive professional development for school leaders and teachers (Hagelskamp et al., 2013). Together, teachers and students analyze the emotional aspects of personal experiences, academic materials, and current events; evaluate how various people, characters, and historical figures felt and managed their feelings; and discuss techniques and use tools for identifying, problem-solving about, and regulating their own and others' emotions (Hagelskamp et al., 2013; Rivers & Brackett, 2011).

Evaluation research shows support for distal outcomes of RULER. After seven months of implementation, students in classrooms that integrated RULER had greater academic and social achievements compared to students in comparison classrooms (Brackett, Rivers, Reyes, & Salovey, 2010). Additionally, longitudinal research has shown that RULER does have sustained impacts on socio-emotional processes in the classroom, and that after two years of implementation, the impact of RULER on classroom quality broadened to include positive effects on the classroom's instructional quality and organization (Hagelskamp et al., 2013).

The Peaceful School Project

The Peaceful Schools Project, developed in 2000, is a philosophy rather than a program (Twemlow, Fonagy, & Sacco, 2004). The goals are consistent with the social-emotional learning framework, with the inclusion of developing healthy relationships between all stakeholders in the educational setting and altering the school climate in permanent and meaningful ways. The Project includes five main components. First, schools embark on a positive-climate campaign that includes counselor-led discussions and the creation of posters that help alter the language and the thinking of everyone in the school (e.g., "Back off, bullies!" or "Stop bullying now"). All stakeholders in the school are flooded with an awareness of the bullying dynamic, and bullying is described as a social relationship problem. Second, teachers are fully supported in classroom-management techniques and are taught specific techniques to diffuse disruptive behavior from a relational perspective rather than from a punishment perspective. Third, peer and adult mentors are used to help everyone in the school resolve problems without blame. These adult mentors are particularly important during times when adult supervision is minimal (e.g., in hallways and on the playground). The fourth component is called the "gentle warrior physical education program." It uses a combination of role-playing, relaxation, and defensive martial arts techniques to help students develop strategies to protect themselves and others. These are essentially confidence-building skills that support positive coping. Fifth, reflection time is included in the school schedule each day. Teachers and students talk for at least ten minutes at the end of the day about bully, victim, and bystander behaviors. By engaging in this dialogue, language and thinking about bullying behaviors can be subtly altered (Twemlow & Fonagy, 2005). In an RCT, elementary students whose schools participated in the Peaceful Schools

Project had higher achievement scores than students from schools without the program; there were also significant reductions in suspensions for acting-out behavior in the treatment schools, whereas the comparison schools had a slight increase in suspensions for problem behavior (Fonagy et al., 2009).

SUMMARY AND SUGGESTIONS

Comprehensive school-wide bully prevention programs have been shown to reduce bullying perpetration and victimization when they have specific program elements (e.g., focus on policy, parental involvement, teacher training, cooperative work, implementation with fidelity, etc.; Ttofi & Farrington, 2011). In conjunction, social-emotional learning approaches in schools are growing in numbers as viable means of preventing school violence, aggression, and peer victimization, and promoting school connectedness as well as academic engagement. At a basic level, social-emotional learning programs and frameworks are similar and inclusive of social-skills training, conflict management, emotion-regulation strategies, interpersonal problem-solving, communication skills, and utilization of social support systems. However, these skills have to be modeled and reinforced by adults in schools in order to bring about school climates that are positive and supportive of youth, especially those at greatest risk for victimization and suicidality (e.g., students with disabilities, gender-nonconforming youth). Additionally, more-specialized programs may be needed for youth who are at a greater risk of suicidal behaviors. The SEL programs described are universal programs, which are provided to all students regardless of risk level, and fall within primary prevention. For youth with elevated symptoms of depression, or for those who otherwise might be at a higher risk for suicide (e.g., trauma history), these programs are important but may not be sufficient. As such, SEL programs should be placed within a more comprehensive system of assessment and supports that enable the identification of students who may need additional assistance.

SUGGESTIONS

For Mental Health and Medical Providers

- Individuals who work with youth need to create opportunities to develop a wide range of skills, including communication, interpersonal problem-solving, emotional regulation, anger management, and impulse control.

For Parents and Teachers

- It is important that youth learn life and social skills to navigate developmental challenges that they will encounter at school, at home, and in the various communities that they interact with. This will allow them to better cope with difficult experiences and have an increased awareness of possible sources of support.
- In order to prevent suicidal behaviors among youth, we have to prevent antecedents such as depression and anxiety that might arise from peer rejection or peer victimization.

- Social-emotional learning strategies described here come in packaged programs, but these skills can be developed and practiced at the dinner table, on the playground, in community centers, and in after-school programs, to name a few places.

For Policy Makers

- Social-emotional learning approaches to prevention that focus on minimizing risk factors and bolstering protective factors must be a priority in the development of policy at all levels (school, community, state, and national).

For Researchers

- While social-emotional learning has not been evaluated as a means of suicide prevention, it has shown some efficacy in reducing physical aggression and reducing language that marginalizes gender non-conforming and lesbian, gay, and bisexual youth. Longitudinal research needs to examine specifically how social-emotional learning programs may help marginalized youth reduce their risk for negative mental health outcomes.

REFERENCES

Basile, K. C., Espelage, D. L., Rivers, I., McMahon, P. M., & Simon, T. R. (2009). The theoretical and empirical links between bullying behavior and male sexual violence perpetration. *Aggression and Violent Behavior, 14*(5), 336–347. doi: 10.1016/j.avb.2009.06.001

Brackett, M. A., Rivers, S. E., Reyes, M. R., & Salovey, P. (2010). Enhancing academic performance and social and emotional competence with the RULER Feeling Words *Curriculum, Learning and Individual Differences, 22*, 218–224.

Brown, E. C., Low, S., Smith, B. H., & Haggerty, K. P. (2011). Outcomes from a school-randomized controlled trial of Steps to Respect: A Bullying Prevention Program. *School Psychology Review, 40*, 423–443. doi: 10.1177/0143034311406813

Collaborative for Academic, Social, and Emotional Learning (CASEL) (2003). *Safe and Sound: An Educational Leader's Guide to Evidence Based Social and Emotional Learning (SEL) Programs*. Chicago, IL: CASEL.

Committee for Children. (2001). *Steps to Respect: A Bullying Prevention Program*. Seattle, WA: Committee for Children.

Committee for Children. (2008). *Second Step: Student Success Through Prevention Program*. Seattle, WA: Committee for Children.

Curtis, C., & Norgate, R. (2007). An evaluation of the Promoting Alternative Thinking Strategies curriculum at Key Stage 1. *Educational Psychology in Practice, 23*, 33–44. doi: 10.1080/02667360601154717

Durlak, J. A., Weissberg, R. P., Dymnicki, A. B., Taylor, R. D., & Schellinger, K. B. (2011). The impact of enhancing students' social and emotional learning: A meta-analysis of school-based universal interventions. *Child Development, 82*(1), 405–432. doi: 10.1111/j.1467-8624.2010.01564.x

Elias, M. J., & Weissberg, R. (1990). School-based social competence promotion as a primary prevention strategy: A tale of two projects. In R. P. Lorion (Ed.), *Protecting the Children: Strategies for Optimizing Emotional and Behavioral Development* (pp. 177–200). New York: Haworth Press.

Elias, M. J., Zins, J. E., Weissberg, R. P., Frey, K. S., Greenberg, M. T., Haynes, N. M., . . . Shriver, T. P. (1997). *Promoting Social and Emotional Learning: Guidelines for Educators.* Alexandria, VA: Association for Supervision and Curriculum Development.

Espelage, D. L. (in press). Ecological theory: Preventing youth bullying, aggression, & victimization. *Theory into Practice.*

Espelage, D. L. (2012). Bullying prevention: a research dialogue with Dorothy Espelage. *Prevention Researcher, 19*, 17–19.

Espelage, D. L., Aragon, S. R., Birkett, M., & Koenig, B. (2008). Homophobic teasing, psychological outcomes, and sexual orientation among high school students: What influence do parents and schools have? *School Psychology Review, 37*, 202–216.

Espelage, D. L., Basile, K. C., & Hamburger, M. E. (2012). Bullying experiences and co-occurring sexual violence perpetration among middle school students: Shared and unique risk factors. *Journal of Adolescent Health, 50*, 60–65. doi: 10.1016/j.jadohealth.2011.07.015

Espelage, D. L. & Holt, M. (2013). Suicidal ideation & school bullying experiences after controlling for depression & delinquency. *Journal of Adolescent Health, 53*, S27–S31. doi: 10.1016/j.jadohealth.2012.09.017

Espelage, D. L., Holt, M. K., & Henkel, R. R. (2003). Examination of peer-group contextual effects on aggression during early adolescence. *Child Development, 74*(1), 205–220. doi: 10.1111/1467-8624.00531

Espelage, D. L., Holt, M., & Van Ryzin, M. (2013). Effects of a middle school social-emotional learning program on teen dating violence, sexual violence, and substance use in high school. Project funded by National Institute of Justice (2013-VA-CX-0008).

Espelage, D. L., Friedman, M., & Miller, E. (2013). Randomized trial of a gender enhanced middle school violence prevention program. Grant funded by National Center for Injury Prevention and Control, Centers for Disease Control and Prevention (1R01CE002340-01).

Espelage, D. L., Low, S., Polanin, J., & Brown, E. (2013). The impact of a middle school program to reduce aggression, victimization, and sexual violence. *Journal of Adolescent Health, 53*(2), 180–186. doi: 10.1016/j.jadohealth.2013.02.021

Espelage, D. L., & Swearer, S. M. (2003). Research on bullying and victimization: What have we learned and where do we go from here? *School Psychology Review, 32*(3), 365–383.

Fonagy, P., Twemlow, S., Vernberg, E., Mize, J., Dill, E., Little, T., & Sargent, A. J. (2009). A cluster randomized controlled trial of a child-focused psychiatric condition and a school systems-focused intervention to reduce aggression. *Journal of Child Psychology and Psychiatry, 50*(5), 607–616. doi: 10.1111/j.1469-7610.2008.02025.x

Frey, K. S., Hirschstein, M. K., Snell, J. L., Edstrom, L. V., MacKenzie, E. P., & Broderick, C. J. (2005). Reducing playground bullying and supporting beliefs: An experimental trial of the Steps to Respect program. *Developmental Psychology, 41*, 479–491. doi: 10.1037/0012-1649.41.3.479

Greenberg, M. T., Weissberg, R. P., O'Brien, M. U., et al. (2003). Enhancing school-based prevention and youth development through coordinated social, emotional, and academic learning. *American Psychologist, 58*, 466–474. doi: 10.1037/0003-066X.58.6-7.466

Hagelskamp, C., Brackett, M. A., Rivers, S. E., & Salovey, P. (2013). Improving classroom quality with the RULER approach to social and emotional learning: Proximal and distal outcomes. *American Journal of Community Psychology, 51*, 530–543. doi: 10.1007/s10464-013-9570-x

Hawkins, J., Catalano, R. F., Kosterman, R., Abbott, R., & Hill, K. (1999). Preventing adolescent health-risk behaviors by strengthening protection during childhood. *Archives of Pediatrics and Adolescent Medicine, 15*(3), 226–234. doi: 10.1001/archpedi.153.3.226.

Haynes, N. M., & Comer, J. P. (1993). The Yale School Development Program process, outcomes, and policy implications. *Urban Education, 28*(2), 166–199. doi: 10.1177/0042085993028002004

Hawkins, J. D., Smith, B. H., and Catalano, R. F. (2004). Social development and social and emotional learning. In: J. E. Zins, R. P. Weissberg, M. C. Wang, and H. J. Walberg (Eds.), *Building Academic Success on Social and Emotional Learning: What Does the Research Say?* (pp. 135–150). New York: Teachers College Press.

Hirschstein, M. K., Edstrom, L. V. S., Frey, K. S., Snell, J. L., and MacKenzie, E. P. (2007). Walking the talk in bullying prevention: teacher implementation variables related to initial impact of the Steps to Respect programme. *School Psychology Review, 36*, 3–21.

Kaminski, J. W., & Fang, X. (2009). Victimization by peers and adolescent suicide in three US samples. *Journal of Pediatrics, 155*, 683–688. doi: 10.1016/j.jpeds.2009.04.061

Keenan, K., Hipwell, A., Feng, X., Rischall, M., Henneberger, B. A., & Klosterman, S. (2010). Lack of assertion, peer victimization and risk for depression in girls: Testing a diathesis-stress model. *Journal of Adolescent Health, 47*, 526–528. doi: 10.1016/j.jadohealth.2010.03.016

Kelly, B., Longbottom, J., Potts, F., & Williamson, J. (2004). Applying emotional intelligence: Exploring the promoting alterative thinking strategies. *Educational Psychology in Practice, 20*, 221–240. doi: 10.1080/0266736042000251808

Kim, Y. S., & Leventhal, B. (2008). Bullying and suicide. A review. *International Journal of Adolescent Medicine and Health, 20*(2), 133–154. doi: 10.1515/IJAMH.2008.20.2.133

Kusche, C. A., & Greenberg, M. T. (1994). *The PATHS Curriculum*. South Deerfield, MA: Channing-Bete Co.

Limber, S. P., Riese, J., Snyder, M. J., & Olweus, D. (2014). The Olweus Bullying Prevention Program: Efforts to address risks associated with suicide and suicide-related behaviors. In P. Goldblum, D. L. Espelage, B. Bongar, & J. Chu (Eds.), *The Challenge of Youth Suicide and Bullying*. New York: Oxford University Press.

Low, S., Ryzin, M. J., Brown, E. C., Smith, B. H., & Haggerty, K. P. (2013). Engagement matters: Lessons from assessing classroom implementation of steps to respect: A bullying prevention program over a one-year period. *Prevention Science, 15*(2), 165–176. doi: 10.1007/s11121-012-0359-1

McCann, I. L., & Pearlman, L. A. (1990). *Psychological Trauma and the Adult Survivor: Theory, Therapy, and Transformation*. New York: Brunner/Mazel.

Merrell, K. W. (2010). Linking prevention science and social and emotional learning: The Oregon Resiliency project. *Psychology in the Schools, 47*(1), 55–70.

Miller, T. W., & Beane, A. (2010). Loss of the safety signal in childhood and adolescent trauma. In T. W. Miller (Ed.), *Handbook of Stressful Transitions Across the Lifespan* (pp. 367–376). New York: Springer Science + Business Media.

Nickerson, A. B., & Torchia, T. O. (2014). Bullying and mental health. In P. Goldblum, D. L. Espelage, B. Bongar, & J. Chu (Eds.), *The Challenge of Youth Suicide and Bullying*. New York: Oxford University Press.

Olweus, D. (1993). *Bullying at School: What We Know and What We Can Do*. Cambridge, MA: Blackwell.

Rivers, S. E., & Brackett, M. A. (2011). Achieving standards in the English language arts (and more) using The RULER Approach to social and emotional learning. *Reading & Writing Quarterly, 27*(1/2), 75–100. doi: 10.1080/10573569.2011.532715

Robinson, J. P., & Espelage, D. L. (2012). Bullying explains only part of LGBTQ-heterosexual risk disparities: Implications for policy and practice. *Educational Researcher, 41*(8), 309–319. doi: 10.3102/0013189X12457023

Robinson, J., & Espelage, D. L. (2013). Peer victimization and sexual risk differences between LGBTQ and heterosexual youth in grades 7–12. *American Journal of Public Health,* 103(10), 1810–1819. doi: 10.2105/AJPH.2013.301387

Ttofi, M. M., & Farrington, D. P. (2011). Effectiveness of school based programmes to reduce bullying: a systematic and meta-analytic review. *Journal of Experimental Criminology, 7*, 27–56. doi: 10.1007/s11292-010-9109-1

Twemlow, S., Fonagy, P., & Sacco, F. (2004). The role of the bystander in the social architecture of bullying and violence in schools and communities. *Annals of New York Academy of Sciences, 1036*, 215–232. doi: 10.1196/annals.1330.014

Twemlow, S. W., & Fonagy, P. (2005). A note on teachers who bully students in schools with differing levels of behavioral problems. *American Journal of Psychiatry, 163*(12), 2387–2389. doi: 10.1176/appi.ajp.162.12.2387

Walker, H. M., & Shinn, M. R. (2002). Structuring school-based interventions to achieve integrated primary, secondary, and tertiary prevention goals for safe and effective schools. In M. R. Shinn, G. Stoner, and H. M. Walker (Eds.), *Interventions for Academic and Behavior Problems: Preventive and Remedial Approaches* (pp. 1–21). Silver Spring, MD: National Association of School Psychologists.

Westheimer, K., & Szalacha, L. A. (2014). Welcoming schools: LGBT and gender inclusive bullying prevention in elementary schools. In P. Goldblum, D. L. Espelage, B. Bongar, & J. Chu (Eds.), *The Challenge of Youth Suicide and Bullying.* New York: Oxford University Press.

Wilson, S. J., & Lipsey, M. W. (2007). School-based interventions for aggressive and disruptive behavior: Update of a meta-analysis. *American Journal of Preventive Medicine, 33*, S130–S143. doi: 10.1016/j.amepre.2007.04.011

Ybarra, M., Espelage, D. L., & Mitchell, K. J. (2014). Differentiating youth who are bullied from other victims of peer-aggression: the importance of differential power and repetition. *Journal of Adolescent Health.* [Published online 10 April 2014].

Zins, J. E., Weissberg, R. P., Wang, M. C., & Walberg, H. J. (Eds.) (2004). *Building School Success Through Social and Emotional Learning.* New York: Teachers College Press.

19

Welcoming Schools

Lesbian, Gay, Bisexual, Transgender, and Gender-Inclusive Bullying Prevention in Elementary Schools

KIM WESTHEIMER AND LAURA A. SZALACHA ■

What does it take for elementary schools or school districts to commit to and implement a bullying prevention approach that is inclusive of students with lesbian, gay, bisexual, transgender (LGBT) families and transgender and gender expansive students[1]? Using the Welcoming Schools program as a case study, this chapter addresses this question by examining the research-based underpinnings of Welcoming Schools, the results of a Welcoming Schools pilot and evaluation, and other lessons learned from schools and communities that have used Welcoming Schools.

Welcoming Schools, a program of the Human Rights Campaign Foundation, addresses identity-based bullying and harassment by helping educators and parents proactively create welcoming climates for diverse students and families. The program content focuses on family diversity, gender inclusiveness, and bias-based bullying. Consistent with the social-ecological model (Bronfenbrenner, 1977), Welcoming Schools engages schools in four levels of intervention among the entire school community:

- Leadership development leading to buy-in from key members of the school community,
- Professional development,
- Family engagement, and
- Inclusive classroom practices, including Welcoming Schools lesson plans.

The program can be tailored to the stated needs of a school or district. Some schools engage with Welcoming Schools because they want to create safe spaces for transgender or gender creative students; some seek out Welcoming Schools because they want to proactively create more culturally responsive schools; and others seek help responding to a crisis involving a student or family who have been excluded or bullied.

THE WELCOMING SCHOOLS FRAMEWORK

The first edition of the Welcoming Schools guide was completed in 2006 by a group of educators, parents, and administrators who recognized a need for elementary-school resources inclusive of diverse families, including those with LGBT parents. The group researched promising and proven practices related to school change and school climate and wrote the guide with these key elements in mind:

1. The most effective way to create school change is to use a systemic ecological approach that engages educators, administrators, parents, and students over time (Frey, Hirschstein, Edstrom, & Snell, 2009; Snell, MacKenzie, & Frey, 2002; Stein, 1995).
2. School curricula should function as both a window and a mirror for students—reflecting the reality of individual students' lives as well as a broader and diverse world (Style, 1996). Most elementary schools do not provide students with LGBT parent mirrors that reflect their family structures, and only a small percentage of students are presented with positive representations of LGBT people, history, or events (Kosciw, Greytak, Bartkiewicz, Boesen, & Palmer, 2012).
3. Bullying and bias are linked (Carter & Spencer, 2006; Kimmel & Mahler, 2003). The majority of school climate and bullying prevention programs ignore this connection and allow negative attitudes and behaviors about targeted groups to proliferate (Espelage & Swearer, 2008).
4. An LGBT-inclusive approach is most likely to be successful if LGBT topics are understood within the broader areas of concerns for elementary schools, such as family diversity, gender stereotyping, and bullying (Kosciw et al., 2012).
5. Schools have a hidden curriculum (Giroux & Penna, 1993) that has as much influence on the school climate as any officially adopted curriculum. This curriculum includes the extent to which educators use inclusive language and representation of diverse communities and cultures; educators' ability to respond to teachable moments; and educators' confidence in the need and their ability to create inclusive environments (Dessel, 2010).
6. Because schools have so much on their plates, they need resources that can be used both as intensive stand-alone resources and in conjunction with existing initiatives and priorities—ranging from social and emotional learning programs to academic learning standards.

Upon completion of the guide, the authors of Welcoming Schools sought out a national organization that could provide resources to make the guide widely available. In 2006, the group signed an agreement that gave the Human Rights Campaign Foundation (HRCF) ownership of Welcoming Schools. Welcoming Schools is currently a project of the HRCF, and the elements outlined above have continued to guide Welcoming Schools at HRCF.

THE WELCOMING SCHOOLS PILOT PROGRAM AND EVALUATION

Welcoming Schools was piloted in 11 public elementary schools in districts in California, Minnesota, and Massachusetts. All were in urban areas, ranging from schools in a small city (population greater than 95,000) to schools in a large metropolitan area (population greater than 800,000). Priority was given to schools with racially/ethnically diverse student bodies.

Program Design: An Ecological Approach

To be included in the pilot, schools needed evidence of central administration approval and were required to demonstrate that some form of LGBT inclusion had already been implemented in the district. Districts pointed to prior inclusive initiatives such as high school gay-straight alliances (GSAs), professional development, or the existence of LGBT-inclusive policies. Schools also had to agree to take part in a multi-pronged approach that included educators, parents/guardians, and students. Pilot components included:

1. Creation of a Welcoming Schools task force that included educators, administrators, and parents/guardians;
2. Two-hour mandatory professional development session for all staff;
3. Eight to twelve hours of professional development for select educators and administrators who would become Welcoming Schools leaders;
4. A well-publicized evening event introducing parents/guardians to the goals of Welcoming Schools; and
5. Selection and teaching of lesson plans to students.

While some schools completed all of these steps in the first year of the pilot, the majority of schools did not complete all of the components of implementation until the second year.

This program design furthered the ecological approach adopted by the authors of Welcoming Schools. It took into consideration the influence of overlapping systems (schools, families, civic organizations) on each member of the school community. It was designed to support individual change agents—to give them a foundation to assess what was needed in what Bronfenbrenner called the "microsystemic level," including settings like individual classrooms, libraries, or administrative offices (Bronfenbrenner, 1994). At the same time, the design recognized the importance of building a foundation among overlapping systems and stakeholders, including families, community organizations, and school boards.

The design encouraged stakeholders to use the program material in a manner consistent with community needs and resources. For example, while Welcoming Schools provided templates for family-engagement events and lesson plans for the classroom, individual schools were led through a process to choose their own materials and to enhance them through connections with existing school initiatives and structures. In this way a school that already was committed to a social and emotional learning or bullying prevention program could align Welcoming Schools to existing structures. This strategy also created a foundation in schools so that if some families opposed the content of Welcoming Schools, a committed and representative group of stakeholders could speak accurately about the program content and take ownership of how the content was being used.

Evaluation Design

A tripartite evaluation of the Welcoming Schools Program was designed to include: (1) an in-depth process-evaluation (including focus group meetings and individual interviews with faculty, staff, parents, and administrators); (2) a preliminary outcome evaluation (surveys pre-implementation, nine months post-implementation and at one-year follow-up); and (3) a community response. The central question was: how do the faculty and administration perceive the impact of Welcoming Schools on the school community?

Inclusivity Climate

The key educational-policy question that this research addresses is whether Welcoming Schools had a measureable, statistically significant impact on school inclusivity in the elementary schools. Freiberg and Stein (1999) define school climate as "that quality of a school that helps each individual feel personal worth, dignity and importance, while simultaneously helping create a sense of belonging to something beyond ourselves" (p. 11). We defined the school inclusivity climate as a quality of the internal environment that is rated by the professional staff regarding the level of safety, tolerance, and respect for all students and families, including those with racially/ethnically diverse members, adopted members, and LGBT individuals. We adapted Szalacha's (2003) measures of school inclusivity developed for high school students, faculty and staff. There were five interrelated measures of school inclusivity: gender expression, child readiness; personal comfort, teaching practices, and overall school inclusivity climate.

Data were collected before and after initial implementation of Welcoming Schools in the 2008–2009 academic year.. On average, survey completion required between 20 and 25 minutes.

Survey

In addition to demographic items, the survey contained 43 questions in six areas of inquiry:

1. The level of knowledge regarding official school policy and procedures regarding harassment and discrimination;
2. Faculty and staff training on diversity and inclusion;
3. The prevalence of taunting and slurs among students regarding difference;
4. Obstacles to addressing family diversity and gender expression in the school;
5. Support needed to address diversity in terms of family diversity and gender expression; and
6. Internal and external inclusivity.

Inclusivity was evaluated by five different measures:

1. Acceptance and support of a broad range of gender expression among students;
2. Student readiness to benefit from discussions of family diversity;
3. Personal comfort level addressing the topics of Welcoming Schools;
4. Intent to incorporate Welcoming Schools into their teaching practices; and
5. Overall school inclusivity climate.

Measures of Internal and External Dimensions of Inclusivity

The Gender Roles Scale measured openness to a variety of gender roles and expressions among children. There were five items measured on a five-point Likert-type scale, from (1) *never* to (4) *very often* (e.g., "It is appropriate for boys who want to take part in activities usually associated with girls—such as playing with dolls or dressing up—to be able to do so").

The Child Readiness Scale measured professional staff's beliefs about their students' cognitive and emotional readiness to discuss different aspects of family diversity. There were six items, measured on a four-point Likert-type scale, from (1) *not at all* to (4) *a great deal* (e.g., "Children in 2nd–3rd grades can benefit from talking about gender roles and expression").

The Personal Comfort Scale measured the professional staff's own personal comfort in dealing with diversity issues in their school. There were 12 items measured on a four-point Likert-type scale, from (1) *very uncomfortable* to (4) *very comfortable* (e.g., "If I had to interrupt students in the hallway using racial/ethnic slurs I would feel. . .").

The Teaching Practices Scale measured the classroom teachers' intent to incorporate more diversity content in their own classrooms. There were four items measured on a five-point Likert-type scale, from (1) *never* to (5) *always* (e.g., "I intend to teach in a way that includes representation of diverse groups—including LGBT people").

The School Inclusivity Climate Scale was designed as an overall measure of acceptance of diversity in the school. The 10-item scale was measured on a five-point Likert-type scale, from (1) *not at all* to (5) *completely.* It contained both attitudinal items (such as, "Children with biracial or multiracial families feel welcome at our school") and behavioral items (such as "How often do you hear other students using gay/lesbian terms as slurs [such as faggot, dyke, that's so gay] in student areas [such as the cafeteria or in the gym]?").

Data Analysis and Reliability and Validity of Measures

After constructing the scales and indices and establishing their psychometric properties, we examined bivariate differences with independent t-tests, correlations, and contingency table analyses. All of the measures of internal and external dimensions of inclusivity were reliable, with Cronbach's alphas ranging from .74–.93, pre- and post-implementation. School members were asked additional items in order to determine the internal validity of the scales and indices using a construct-validity approach. We tested the direction and the magnitude of the predicted correlations between scores on all of the measures of internal and external dimensions of inclusivity. First, all of the five measures were appropriately moderately correlated with each other (from $r = .19$, $p < .001$ to $r = .55$, $p < .001$), indicating that the dimension that each scale measured, while related to the other measures, remained distinct from one another and supported the validity of our measures.

Second, we anticipated that the professional staff's own behavioral comfort would be positively, but moderately, correlated with their perception of the school's overall inclusivity. At both the pre-and post-implementations the correlations were positive, moderate, and statistically significant ($r = .31$, $p < .01$ and $r = .39$, $p < .001$, respectively). Thus, we concluded that the professional staff was able to separate their own comfort levels from their assessment of the school climate as a whole.

Professional Staff Sample

The survey was administered in 11 schools. Overall, 217 professional staff members completed the survey pre-implementation, and 97 completed a post-implementation survey. For both samples, the majority were female, white, heterosexual classroom teachers. Their average age was in the early forties. Overall, they had been educators for 16 years and had been at their present schools an average of eight years.

While Welcoming Schools addresses a broad range of diversities, the results that follow refer specifically to the question posed at the beginning of this chapter, "What does it take for elementary schools or school districts to commit to and implement a bullying prevention approach that is inclusive of students with LGBT families and transgender and gender creative students?" The analysis follows highlights some key findings from the data.

NEEDS EXPRESSED BY EDUCATORS

Educators reported specific needs that were necessary for them to implement an LGBT-inclusive program, including professional development, resources and lesson plans, and administrative and parental support.

Prior to implementation, half of the faculty and staff thought that they needed more professional development time to address issues related to sexual orientation, and 56% said more time was needed to talk about gender roles and expression.

Only 3% believed that too much time was spent addressing sexual orientation, and 1% believed that too much time was spent addressing gender roles and expression.

After the implementation of Welcoming Schools, 40% of educators still wanted more time to discuss sexual orientation issues, and 59% wanted more time to discuss gender roles and expression. One percent of educators said too much time was being spent on sexual orientation and gender.

Prior to implementation, 61% indicated a need for inclusive lesson plans and materials; after the first year of implementation this dropped to 42% ($\chi^2_{(df = 1)} = 17.5$, $p < .001$). Pre-implementation, 57% of educators noted a need for strong administrative leadership, which dropped to 37% post-implementation ($\chi^2_{(df = 1)} = 16.3$, $p < .001$); 54% indicated the need for professional development, which dropped to 38% following implementation ($\chi^2_{(df = 1)} = 14.7$, $p < .001$).

In interviews, educators like this teacher were often appreciative of the resources provided by Welcoming schools and candid about the limitations of their current knowledge:

> We have a number of [same-sex parents] in this school and I think it isn't talked about. I can recall another school where I had a little boy in kindergarten who talked about having two fathers. I could tell he was really uncomfortable. He started to say he had two dads, and then he stopped [after a peer's reaction] and he didn't know how to deal with it and honestly, I didn't know how to deal with it either.

Obstacles to Addressing Family Diversity and Gender Expression

The educators reported a statistically significant lessening of obstacles in addressing sensitive issues in elementary schools after implementing the Welcoming Schools Guide. Prior to program implementation, 54.1% of participants indicated that a major obstacle was their lack of training or resources, and 52.3% indicated a fear of parental dissatisfaction. Post-intervention, the endorsement for "lack of training or resources" dropped significantly, to only 28.3% ($\chi^2_{(df = 1)} = 67.4$, $p < .001$), and only 30.4% still indicated a fear of parental dissatisfaction ($\chi^2_{(df = 1)} = 68.8$, $p < .001$). Educators told researchers that the parents' involvement in Welcoming Schools made them recognize that when parents understood the content of the program, they recognized how many parents wanted a program like Welcoming Schools. As one teacher said, "Schools may hesitate for fear of creating opposition, but parents found the conversation [about Welcoming Schools] with friends at school helpful to implementation."

Internal and External Dimensions of Inclusivity

There were significant positive differences in four of the five measures of inclusivity in all schools: teachers accepting a variety of gender roles and expressions of children; perceptions of their students' readiness to discuss many different aspects of family diversity; their own personal comfort with variations in sexual orientation, and their intent to incorporate more of the Welcoming Schools' lessons in their own classrooms. The measure of school climate inclusivity showed positive differences only in the schools that had fully implemented Welcoming Schools in the first year of the project.

Child Readiness

Every school reported a positive difference in believing that children of every age could benefit from talking about gender roles and expression and families with LGBT parents. Pre-implementation the average was 2.30 (standard deviation [SD] = .61) on a five-point range; and post-implementation the average was 4.49 (SD = .55, t = 29.8, $p < .001$). One administrator commented that, "I am very pleased with even the informal lessons I have seen in the classrooms. I've seen teachers discussing the three main parts of the program and can honestly say that I do believe that the kids here understand these components."

Gender Roles and Expression

Prior to implementation, the educators rated their openness to diverse expressions of gender and gender roles as 3.70 (SD = .73) on a five-point range. Ratings of openness were significantly higher post-implementation, at 4.47 (SD = .55, t = 9.14, $p < .001$), indicating a positive difference in the belief that girls and boys should have greater freedom in gender expression.

Teachers observed firsthand that having open conversations about gender and diversity was positive for their students. One educator described a fifth-grader who:

> ...had been having horrible tantrums at school and getting suspended frequently. He would fly off in a rage and pull down bulletin boards, kick over garbage cans, and so on. After doing the lessons on family diversity and gender, he came out [as transgender] to his teacher and to the principal. His behavior calmed down and he had very few behavioral referrals for the rest of the year. When the principal asked him why he was no longer having behavior problems he said, "I'm not angry anymore. My secret is out."

Personal Comfort

The same positive growth was reported in the educator's personal comfort in dealing with diversity issues in their school, as evidenced by the significant difference from a pre-implementation score of 3.34 (SD = .45) on a four-point range to an average of 3.57 (SD = .42, t = 4.2, $p < .05$).

Some educators who thought they were comfortable including LGBT parents and people in their classroom recognized that they were not comfortable taking proactive steps to be inclusive. One educator recognized the limits of her approach prior to Welcoming Schools:

> I, myself, have a student in my class who has parents of the same gender and it has never come up as a discussion. It's never been talked about.... It's not that I don't feel comfortable talking about it, I just feel it has never come up as an issue. But now that all the discussion about the Welcoming Schools curriculum has come up, I have often thought about how that particular child might feel left out at times because it has never been discussed.

Intent to Incorporate Welcoming Schools

Similarly, there was a significant positive difference among educators in intent to address issues of LGBT and gender role/expression diversity in their classrooms/school, from a pre-implementation average of 1.92 (SD = 1.01) to a post-implementation average of 4.21 (SD = 1.72, t = 14.5, $p < .001$) on a five-point scale. One teacher observed, "This school has always been accepting of diverse backgrounds... now there is a bit more accountability and awareness of expectations on the part of faculty." There was a significant positive difference in educators reporting of their willingness to teach lessons involving adoption and single-parent issues, with a pre-implementation average of 1.73 (SD = 1.34) and a post-implementation average of 3.22 (SD = 1.29) on a five-point scale.

School Inclusivity Climate

A statistically significant difference was also found in the school inclusivity climate in the schools that had completed all of the pilot elements, including: formation of a Welcoming Schools task force, professional development for the full faculty, training of a team of Welcoming Schools Leaders, a community event for parents and guardians, and teaching of lesson plans. In the district that successfully completed all elements, school inclusivity climate increased significantly. As one educator noted, "The staff taught more diversity lessons than in past years. The lessons have had a positive effect on students' attitudes." Schools that had not completed the full implementation showed some positive growth post-implementation, but these rates did not differ significantly across all schools.

The Use of Welcoming Schools Lessons

Among classroom teachers, there were significant positive differences in all five measures of dimensions of inclusivity based on whether they had taught one or more lessons from the Welcoming Schools Guide. Those who had used the lessons in their classrooms noted higher levels of openness to diverse expressions of gender and gender roles compared to teachers who had not used the lessons (M = 4.76, SD = .42 vs. 4.07, SD = .97; t = 3.27, $p < .01$). The same significantly positive growth was reported in the classroom teachers' ratings of child readiness to benefit from discussions of diversity, personal comfort in dealing with diversity issues, and overall assessment of their school's inclusivity climate. The greatest difference was in teachers' willingness to incorporate more of the Welcoming School content in their teaching in the future. On a five-point scale, those who had already taught lessons rated their likelihood as 4.10 (SD = .85) in contrast to those who had not yet taught lessons ($M = 2.72$, $SD = 1.15$, $t = 4.76$, $p < .001$).

DISCUSSION

After the first year of implementation of the Welcoming Schools guide, despite variability in use, there is credible evidence that such a program can have a measureable, statistically significant, positive impact on the attitudes and assessments of the adult members of the school community and the school climate. Quantitative and qualitative data gathered in the pilot program identify key factors that can help or hinder the implementation of LGBT-inclusive initiatives in the early grades, including administrative support and leadership, involvement of parents and guardians, and training and resources.

Administrative Support and Leadership

In their pre-tests, educators identified administrative support as the second most important element required to implement LGBT- and gender-inclusive initiatives. In interviews and surveys, educators said they needed to know that administrators would "have their back" if controversy arose as a result of using Welcoming Schools. This support became a reality in one school district when administrators responded to concerns from a small group of parents that deemed Welcoming Schools inappropriate because of its LGBT-inclusive content. The superintendent of this district wrote a district-wide letter in support of Welcoming Schools, concluding: "Our schools can, and should be, places where students are free to learn unencumbered by fear. It's their right and our responsibility."

Administrators may also need help responding to controversy. In one district, media training to equip administrators to respond to questions about Welcoming Schools helped allay fears about how to respond to controversy. In another district, a staff person in the central office kept upper-level administrators well informed about the progress of Welcoming Schools, and helped frame any complaints in the context of how Welcoming Schools was helping the district meet its educational goals.

One of the largest challenges of maintaining the momentum of Welcoming Schools came with administrative leadership changes. One district had a strong program for two years, despite a supportive superintendent being replaced by an administrator who was vocal in her discomfort with Welcoming Schools. However, other changes at the administrative level and the hiring of a third superintendent in three years made continuing formal implementation of Welcoming Schools challenging.

Involvement of Parents and Guardians

Educators identified fear of opposition from parents and guardians as one of the biggest obstacles to implementing an LGBT- and gender-inclusive program in their schools. This fear diminished significantly after participating in Welcoming Schools for one year. Interviews with educators and administrators indicated that this fear diminished because parents were invited into the process of launching the program from the beginning, as members of the leadership team and in planning family events. The transparency of the program was key, as was the recognition that the majority of parents, when they learned what Welcoming Schools was, were in favor of the program.

The parents helped create events that were designed to be inclusive of all families and children, such as this event:

> At a family forum at one of pilot school, 45 parents attended a pasta dinner. To prepare kids for the family forum, the school made a Family Diversity Tree. Each child made a leaf of his/her family, and the leaf was placed on the tree in the auditorium where the family forum was held. For the main event of the evening, the principal pre-selected several families to talk about their family and how it is unique.
>
> A multiracial family discussed the role culture plays in their family, and how they made sure their children were connected to the cultures of both parents. They discussed their different religions and ways that they expose children to both religions. The next family was parented by two mothers. Their daughter spoke about her feelings on having two moms. She discussed how we are no different than other families. The daughter in the last pre-selected family was in a wheelchair. Her mother, who is single, shared how important her daughter is to her. The daughter talked about how her mother takes care of her and is the best mom.
>
> Afterward, other children briefly discussed their families. These students came from African-American families, Indian families, Caucasian families, religiously diverse families, and grandparent-headed households. The overarching themes from all the children were: My parents care for me, we have lots of fun together, and they love me.

The willingness to engage with parents who might not agree with Welcoming Schools was another factor in diminishing fear about use of the program. A family forum in one school included a showing of the film *That's a Family*, which features children from diverse families—including multiracial, same-sex, single-parent, and adoptive families—talking about their families. A Latino father who attended the forum expressed his concern about the program to a Latino upper-level administrator who presented at the forum. The administrator listened to the father's concerns and encouraged him to become more engaged in the school community. The father, who had previously been unengaged in the district, subsequently became part of a task force for Latino families in the school.

Educators and administrators heard from parents thanking them for Welcoming Schools. The day after the forum described above, a member of a Welcoming Schools task force was approached on the street by a parent who thanked her for the forum. The parent said that on the way home she had the best conversation about diversity that she had ever had with her son! Like educators, parents were also thankful to have an opportunity to examine their own comfort levels addressing LGBT topics with their children:

> My own 10-year-old sits at the dinner table and says, "Oh, you're being so gay"... Well, as a parent I'm also trying to come to terms with how comfortable I feel discussing these things.

Training and Resources

In the pre-survey, 54.1% of participants indicated that a major obstacle was their lack in training or resources. Over half also stated that they needed more professional development time addressing topics related to sexual orientation and gender. Post-intervention, the lack in training or resources dropped significantly, to 28.3%.

The rollout of resources and lesson plans for pilot schools was based on a process designed to create a foundation for the content of Welcoming Schools before educators introduced lesson plans. Lesson plans were introduced after time had been spent on leadership development, professional development, and family engagement. These foundational activities provided resources to help adults create inclusive classrooms, with a strong emphasis on responding to teachable moments with students (e.g., responding to comments such as, "That's so gay," "How can she have two dads?" and "Why does he like to play with dolls?"). Professional development also focused on ways to have a more gender-expansive classroom, where activities were not labeled for boys or girls, and educators provided examples of people doing non–gender stereotypical activities.

Summary

The pre- and post-surveys of the first academic year of implementation clearly documented educators' and communities' perceived continuing need for such a program in their schools. Most importantly, there was demonstrable, significant change in school climate that occurred over the course of only nine months, particularly for schools that implemented all components of the program in the first year. This is notable because it would be expected that school climate change would not occur within a single academic year (George, White, & Schlaffer, 2007).

The educators reported a statistically significant lessening of obstacles in addressing sensitive issues. Concerns about lack of training and materials were halved, and fear of parental dissatisfaction dropped by 23%. Nonetheless, almost a third still indicated a fear of parental dissatisfaction. This suggests that while the trainings and community meetings helped prepare teachers and foster mutual trust between parents and the schools, there is still more to be addressed in this domain.

There are limitations to the findings of our first-year survey. Because the number of people who filled out the post-survey was smaller than the number who filled out the pre-survey, there could be a systematic bias in those that were returned, and they may not be representative of the school as a whole. The 11 schools each had different levels of implementation, and it is crucial to bear in mind that the preexisting climate of each school differed from the others. This preexisting climate can affect the implementation of Welcoming Schools at every level of its process.

RECOMMENDATIONS

A host of lessons for educators, administrators, parents and school partners can be gleaned from the experiences of schools using Welcoming Schools. Lessons specifically related to introducing LGBT- and gender-inclusive content in bullying prevention and school climate into schools include the following.

For Mental Health Professionals

- Research the policies of your professional organizations in relation to LGBT and gender inclusion.
- Meet with colleagues to discuss ways to make your work more reflective of the professional policies and statements related to LGBT and gender inclusion.
- Work in collaboration with educators, administrators, and parents to create more inclusive schools.
- Have visible signs of diversity in your offices, including posters or books with diverse families and that portray diverse examples of gender expression.

For Parents and Guardians

- Talk with your child and his or her friends about the climate at their school. Ask about hurtful teasing, name-calling, or bullying.
- Learn the connections among LGBT inclusion, school climate, and academic achievement.
- Educators and administrators need to know that there are parents who are eager to see more LGBT-inclusive content in schools. Make your support visible to in writing, in person and in public forums.
- Reach out to administrators and educators who you think are committed to creating more LGBT-inclusive schools. Discuss strategies that have been successful for implementing new programs and initiatives in the past and also what current initiatives might be a foundation to build an LGBT-inclusive approach. Review school policies to find opportunities for further inclusion.
- Reach out to the Parents Teachers Organization/ Parents Teachers Association or (PTO/PTA) and other parents/guardians in your school community. Be an ally. Develop allies. Work with a diverse range of concerned families to create a safe and caring school for all children.
- Have a plan in place if there is a leadership change to educate and gain buy in from new leaders.

For Teachers and School Administrators

- Engage a broad cross-section of the school community to spearhead implementation, keeping parents aware of the reasons for the initiative.

- Connect the initiative with existing school priorities and programs. These can include academic goals, school improvement plans, school missions, and other bullying prevention or school climate initiatives.
- Pay attention to the formal curriculum as well as the informal curriculum.
- Have a plan in place if there is a leadership change to educate and gain buy-in from new leaders.
- Provide educators with professional development that builds on their skills and knowledge and gives them with concrete tools to create better learning environments.

For Administrators (District and Building)

- Be prepared to respond to controversy in a matter-of-fact way that allows dissent to be expressed and keeps a focus on the big picture of students' academic, social, and emotional growth.
- Review school policies and look for opportunities for further inclusion.
- Make sure educators know that you support LGBT-inclusive initiatives. Let them know in meetings and in written materials. It is valuable for educators to hear from multiple administrators multiple times that LGBT-inclusive work is supported.

NOTE

1. Students who are gender expansive express their gender based on their internal sense of what feels "right and comfortable," not what is societally expected.

REFERENCES

Bronfenbrenner, U. (1977). Toward an experimental ecology of human development. *American Psychologist, 32*, 513–531.

Bronfenbrenner, U. (1994). Ecological models of human development. In *International Encyclopedia of Education* (Vol. 3, 2nd ed.). Oxford, England: Elsevier. Reprinted in: M. Gyavain & M. Cole, (Eds.), *Readings on the Development of Children* (2nd ed., pp. 37–43). New York: Freeman.

Carter, B. B., & Spencer, V. G. (2006). The fear factor: Bullying and students with disabilities. *International Journal of Special Education, 21*(1), 11–23.

Dessel, A. (2010). Prejudice in schools: Promotion of an inclusive culture and climate. *Education and Urban Society, 42*(4), 407–429. doi: 10.1177/0013124510361852.

Espelage, D. L., & Swearer, S. M. (2008). Addressing research gaps in the intersection between homophobia and bullying. *School Psychology Review, 37*(2), 155–159.

Freiberg, H. J., & Stein, T. A. (1999). Measuring, improving, and sustaining healthy learning environments. In H. J. Freiberg (Ed.), *School Climate: Measuring, Improving, and Sustaining Healthy Learning Environments* (pp. 11–29). Philadelphia, PA: Taylor and Francis.

Frey, K. S., Hirschstein, M. K., Edstrom, L. V., & Snell, J. L. (2009). Observed reductions in school bullying, nonbullying aggression and destructive bystander behavior: A longitudinal evaluation. *Journal of Educational Psychology, 101*(2), 466–481. doi: 10.1037/a0013839

George, M. P., White, G. P., & Schlaffer, J. J. (2007). Implementing school-wide behavior change: Lessons from the field. *Psychology in the Schools, 44*(1), 41–51. doi: 10.1002/pits.20204.

Giroux, H., & Penna, A. (1993). Social education in the classroom: The dynamics of the hidden curriculum. In H. Giroux & D. Purpel (Eds.), *The Hidden Curriculum and Moral Education* (pp. 100–121). Berkeley, CA: McCutchan Publishing.

Kimmel, M., & Mahler, M. (2003). Adolescent masculinity, homophobia, and violence: Random school shootings, 1982–2001. *American Behavioral Scientist, 46*(10), 1439–1458. doi: 10.1177/0002764203046010010.

Kosciw, J. G., Greytak, E. A., Bartkiewicz, M. J., Boesen, M. J., & Palmer, N. A. (2012). *The 2011 National School Climate Survey: The Experiences of Lesbian, Gay, Bisexual and Transgender Youth in Our Nation's Schools*. New York: GLSEN.

Snell, J., MacKenzie, E., & Frey, K. (2002). Bullying prevention in elementary schools: The importance of adult leadership, peer group support, and student social-emotional skills. In M. Shinn, H. Walker, & G. Stoner (Eds.), *Interventions for Academic and Behavior Problems II: Preventive and Remedial Approaches* (pp. 351–372). Bethesda, MD: National Association of School Psychologists.

Stein, N. (1995). Sexual harassment in school: The public performance of gendered violence. *Harvard Educational Review, 65*(2), 145–163.

Style, E. (1996). Curriculum as window and mirror. *Social Science Record*, 35–42.

Szalacha, L. A. (2003). Safer sexual diversity climates: Lessons learned from an evaluation of Massachusetts' Safe Schools Program for Gay and Lesbian Students. *American Journal of Education, 110*(1): 58–88. doi: 10.1086/377673

20

The LET's CONNECT Intervention

Targeting Social Connectedness, Bullying, and Youth Suicide Risk

CHERYL A. KING, POLLY Y. GIPSON, AND KIEL OPPERMAN ■

Suicide is the second leading cause of death among youth, ages 10–18 years, in the United States (Centers for Disease Control and Prevention, 2013). Moreover, approximately 6% of adolescent girls and 2% of adolescent boys report a lifetime history of suicide attempt (Nock et al., 2013). Responding to this substantial public health problem, the National Strategy for Suicide Prevention strongly recommends the development of effective prevention and intervention strategies to prevent suicide attempts and suicides (U.S. Department of Health and Human Services [DHHS], 2012).

Many existing school- and community-based suicide prevention strategies for adolescents are based on a mental health model that emphasizes the importance of recognizing suicide risk and mental health or substance use disorders in adolescents—or the symptoms of these disorders—and referring the adolescents for treatment. Examples include school-wide screening approaches such as the TeenScreen Program (Husky, McGuire, Flynn, Chrostowski, & Olfson, 2009; Scott et al., 2008; Shaffer et al., 2004) and the Signs of Suicide (SOS) program (Aseltine, 2003). Although these approaches are promising, they are also subject to a number of the barriers associated with poor utilization of the mental health system. It is estimated that about 80% of the children and adolescents who are identified as needing mental health services do not receive such care, and that the uninsured have an especially high rate of poor mental health care utilization (Kataoka, Zhang, & Wells, 2002). Furthermore, referral for treatment does not ensure treatment linkage, treatment adherence, or treatment effectiveness (Asarnow et al., 2011).

THE LET'S CONNECT STRATEGY—TARGETING SOCIAL CONNECTEDNESS

Rather than focusing on the recognition and treatment of mental disorders, Links to Enhancing Teens' Connectedness (LET's CONNECT) focuses on the problems of bullying victimization, perpetration, and impaired social connectedness. It is a community-based mentorship intervention for youth at elevated risk for suicidal behavior because of one or more of these problems. As such, the intervention model is based on previous research and theory pertaining to social connectedness, peer victimization and bullying, and suicide risk. We are examining the effectiveness of LET's CONNECT in a randomized controlled trial, funded by the Centers for Disease Control (CDC) and Prevention, to determine if it is effective in (a) preventing the initial occurrence of suicidal behavior, and (b) improving adolescents' perceived peer and community connectedness.

INTEGRATING RESEARCH, THEORY, AND PREVENTION PERTAINING TO SOCIAL CONNECTEDNESS, PEER VICTIMIZATION/BULLYING, AND SUICIDE RISK

Social connectedness can be defined as closeness to an individual or group, perceived caring from others, sense of belonging, and relationship satisfaction (for a review, see Barber & Schluterman, 2008). It has been conceptualized in terms of the perceived quality of or satisfaction with relationships, and the subjective experience of belonging and feeling supported (Barber & Schluterman, 2008). Given that connectedness is a key component of several psychological theories focusing on depression and suicide risk, it is perhaps not surprising that the National Strategy for Suicide Prevention identified strengthening connectedness among individuals, families, and communities as one possible strategy for preventing suicidal behavior.

The concept of social integration is rooted in Durkheim's (1897) work, which proposed that stable social structures are protective against suicide. Similarly, a major interpersonal theory of depression, Coyne's interactional theory of depression, argues that negative social interactions are key components in explaining the development and maintenance of depression (Coyne, 1976). More recent theoretical models emphasize the possible beneficial effects of social connectedness on adolescent outcomes via direct and indirect positive effects on problem-solving, the availability of helpful information (Heaney & Israel, 2002), and the reframing of negative events or problems in a more adaptive and less distorted manner (Thoits, 1995). Finally, Joiner's interpersonal theory of suicidal behavior (Joiner, 2005) emphasizes thwarted belongingness as a principal component of the desire for death.

Converging evidence suggests that problems in social connectedness, including being the victim or perpetrator of peer bullying, are associated with suicidal ideation and behavior (Borowsky, Taliaferro, & McMorris, 2013; Espelage & Holt, 2013; King & Merchant, 2008; Klomek et al., 2013). Lack of social support is associated with social avoidance (La Greca & Lopez, 1998), loneliness (Mahon, Yarcheski,

Yarcheski, Cannella, & Hanks, 2006), delinquency, bullying, and both internalizing and externalizing behaviors (Scolte, van Lieshout, & van Aken, 2001). Additionally, perceived peer rejection and low levels of friendship support have been directly associated with higher levels of suicidal ideation among adolescents (Prinstein, Boergers, Spirito, Little, & Grapentine, 2000).

Peer victimization has been strongly associated with an increased likelihood of suicidal ideation and suicide attempts in multiple studies (Baldry & Winkel, 2003; Borowsky et al., 2013; Espelage & Holt, 2013; Liang, Flisher, & Lombard, 2007; Park, Schepp, Jang, & Koo, 2006). Russell and Joyner (2001) examined data from the National Longitudinal Study of Adolescent Health (ADD Health) study and reported that, even after taking into account the effects of sexual orientation, hopelessness, depression, alcohol abuse, and family/friend history of suicidal ideation and behavior, adolescents who reported histories of victimization were more likely to report suicidal thoughts and attempts. Furthermore, Friedman and colleagues (2006) found that for gay male adolescents, bullying mediated suicidal ideation and attempts. More recently, Borowsky and colleagues (2013) analyzed data on 130,908 students in the sixth, ninth, and twelfth grades and reported that suicidal thinking or a suicide attempt was reported by 22% of bully perpetrators, 29% of bully victims, and 38% of bully perpetrators–victims. This is one of several studies indicating that the perpetrators of peer bullying are also at increased risk for suicide. In fact, Klomek and colleagues (2013) found that high school students who, at baseline, endorsed bully perpetration and were at risk for suicide, reported greater amounts of suicidal ideation at a two-year follow-up than those who were only at risk for suicide. These studies suggest the need to target bully perpetrators and victims in a prevention-based approach to address the interpersonal precursors of suicidal ideation and behavior.

CULTURAL CONSIDERATIONS FOR BULLYING VICTIMIZATION AND SUICIDE PREVENTION

Although cultural considerations are important to our understanding of youth bullying and suicide, it is challenging to pinpoint which factors may matter most, due to the under-representation of ethnic minority youth in empirical investigations and the broad array of potential culturally based risk and protective factors.

As a starting place, however, the prevalence rates for youth suicide and suicide attempts differ significantly across groups defined by race and ethnicity. American Indian/Alaskan Native adolescent females and males are at the highest risk for a death by suicide (CDC, 2013). Regarding suicidal behaviors, Latina adolescents report more attempts within a one-year period (13.5%) than their African American and Caucasian counterparts (8.8% and 7.9%, respectively; CDC, 2012). Similarly, some studies suggest no differences in bullying prevalence across racial and ethnic groups (Nansel et al., 2001; Seals & Young, 2003), while others suggest differences in bullying victimization across these groups, with African American youth at lower risk than their Latino and Caucasian peers (Spriggs, Iannotti, Nansel, & Haynie, 2007).

Perhaps of greater importance to preventive efforts, there are cultural factors that may elevate risk within groups, such as isolated living environments for

American Indian/Alaskan Native youth (Freedenthal & Stiffman, 2007); acculturation stress for Latinos (Duarté-Vélez & Bernal, 2007); and racial/discriminatory stress and access to firearms for African American adolescents (Joe & Kaplan, 2002). Similarly, there are cultural factors that may protect youth from suicidal outcomes. For example, religiosity/spirituality and perceived family/community connectedness (a target of the LET's CONNECT intervention) have been found to serve as protective factors from suicidal behaviors across ethnic groups (Goldston et al., 2008). Future research is warranted to better understand the interplay of risk and protective factors, and which strategies to recommend within and across adolescent ethnic groups to prevent suicidal behavior.

PREVIOUS STUDIES OF YOUTH-MENTORING PROGRAMS AND MENTAL HEALTH OUTCOMES

Promising findings have been reported in several previous studies of youth-mentoring programs. De Wit and colleagues (2007) conducted a relatively small randomized controlled trial of the Big Brothers Big Sisters youth-mentoring program in a sample of youths aged 7 to 14 years who were either matched ($n = 39$) or waitlisted ($n = 32$) and assessed 12 months later. At follow-up, youths in the intent-to-treat group demonstrated marginally better scores than the control group on self-report measures of emotional problems, social anxiety, teacher social support, and self-control skills (at trend levels). The effectiveness of the Communities in Schools of San Antonio youth-mentoring program was examined in a randomized study of 525 youth (elementary through high school; Karcher, 2008). Youth in the intervention group ($n = 252$) received "standard services" plus one hour per week of mentoring for eight months. Youth in the control group ($n = 264$) received "standard services," including educational enhancement activities, guidance, and tutoring. Results indicated small but positive intervention effects on measures of self-esteem, connectedness to peers, and perceived social support. Similarly promising findings were reported by King, Vidourek, Davis, and McClellan (2002), who evaluated the effectiveness of the Healthy Kids Mentoring Program, a multidimensional mentoring program for fourth-graders targeting self-esteem and connectedness. Participation selection was based on low self-esteem, engagement in risky health behaviors, depression, alcohol or other drug abuse, and failing classes. The program was associated with significant improvements in students' self-esteem and positive connections to school, peers, and family. Students who were mentored were also less likely to be depressed or be involved in bullying and fighting. To our knowledge, this is the only previous study of a mentorship program that examined peer victimization or peer bullying.

LET'S CONNECT EFFECTIVENESS TRIAL

In LET's CONNECT, participants are recruited from a general pediatric emergency department in an urban area where approximately 56.6% of residents self-identify as African American, 37.4% as Caucasian, 3.9% as Hispanic, 0.5% as American Indian/Alaska Native, 0.5% as Asian, and 3.9% identifying with two or more races

(U.S. Census Bureau, 2013). Eighty-one percent of residents are high school graduates or higher, and 11.5% have obtained a bachelor's degree or higher. Approximately 38% of residents live below the poverty line, and the median household income is $26,621 (U.S. Census Bureau, 2013). Although we do not have baseline data on all youth screened regarding those who self-identify as LGBT, it may be helpful to note that, in a nationally representative sample of high school students, an estimated 1.0% to 2.6% identify as gay or lesbian, 2.9% to 5.2% as bisexual, and 1.3% to 4.7% are unsure of their sexual identity (Kann et al., 2011).

Though these poverty and unemployment rates create an environment in which residents face increased hardships, a socio-ecological framework posits that proximal processes (e.g., interactions with others) play an important part in development above and beyond the role of environment (Bronfenbrenner, 1994). Social support and connectedness are protective factors for at-risk adolescents (e.g., King & Merchant, 2008; Scales et al., 2008), and have been shown to add incremental validity to environmental factors when predicting mental health outcomes such as suicide attempts, depression, and externalizing behaviors (Kaslow et al., 2005; Taylor, Budescu, Gebre, & Hodzic, 2012).

The emergency department (ED) is an ideal location for screening and comprehensive assessment efforts aimed at identifying at-risk adolescents due to long waiting times and the fact that approximately one-third of adolescents utilize ED services each year (Britto et al., 2001). In our LET's CONNECT project, youth in the ED are approached for participation if they meet the following criteria: (1) 12 to 15 years of age; (2) parent/legal guardian present; and (3) resident of study-catchment area. Exclusion criteria include: (1) lifetime history of a suicide attempt; (2) a life-threatening condition; (3) previous participation or participation in another ongoing research study; and (4) severe cognitive impairment.

Screening Phase

We screen eligible youth for whom parent/guardian informed consent and adolescent assent is obtained. The self-report screen includes the Peer Experiences Questionnaire (Prinstein, Boergers, & Vernberg, 2001) to assess bully perpetration and victimization, and the UCLA Loneliness Scale–Revised (Russell, Peplau, & Curtrona, 1980) to assess interpersonal connectedness. It requires approximately five minutes for completion. If adolescents score above our established cut-point on the screening measure, we assess recent suicidal ideation and lifetime history of a suicide attempt. We exclude youth with a positive suicide attempt history because the primary objective of this project is to prevent the initial onset of suicidal behavior in at-risk youth.

Baseline Evaluation

In the baseline evaluation, youth are asked to complete measures about their perceived levels of connectedness across contexts (i.e., parent-family, community, school, peer); suicidal ideation/behavior, including non-suicidal self-injury; and other areas of functioning, such as alcohol/drug use, self-esteem, sexual orientation, religiousness/spirituality, and major life events. Parent/guardian measures include the youth's mental healthcare utilization, strengths and difficulties, and social adjustment.

Following the baseline assessment, youth are randomized to either the LET's CONNECT intervention or enhanced treatment-as-usual condition (E-TAU), which includes community mental health resource information. Youth randomized to the intervention are then scheduled for a home-based meeting at which we recapitulate the LET's CONNECT intervention, addressing questions and concerns; facilitate the youth's natural mentor nomination; and learn more about the youth's engagement in activities, social strengths, and areas for growth. We also inform the youth and family of the community mentor assignment and facilitate the scheduling of an initial meeting with the youth, natural, and community mentors.

LET's CONNECT Mentorship

The primary role of the community mentors (adults at least 25 years of age who meet screening and background-check criteria) is to facilitate the youth's connection to them as supportive individuals and to community-based organizations and activities. They participate in a six-hour training program that provides psycho-education about mentoring, adolescent development, and effective communication with youth. Additionally, the topic of bullying is covered extensively, including information about types of bullying (e.g., physical, relational, cyber), warning signs (e.g., internalizing/externalizing symptoms), and strategies mentors can employ to assist victims and perpetrators. Mentors engage in various exercises, such as vignettes to practice action-plan development and the importance of attending to diversity considerations, broadly defined (e.g., socioeconomic status, sexual orientation, family constellation). Finally, a thorough discussion of project logistics is reviewed, allowing ample time to answer questions.

Community mentors are matched to youth based on gender (for girls only), interests, neighborhood proximity, and other relevant considerations. They receive a mentor guidebook that includes a regularly updated description of community organizations and activities, and are expected to collaborate with the youth in developing an action plan for engaging in activities that enhance connectedness. These community mentors are expected to have regular face-to-face contact, approximately six hours per month for the first 12 months and four hours per month during the final four months. They are compensated with hourly wages for their face-to-face time with the youth and have access to limited community activity funds.

The role of the natural mentor—a family member or someone who is "like family" to the youth—is also to serve as a supportive person. This mentor also works collaboratively with the youth to develop and implement an action plan that facilitates the youth's connectedness with other individuals and the community. Like community mentors, natural mentors must be at least 25 years of age and, if not the parent/guardian, participate in a screening progress.

The LET's CONNECT prevention specialists are mental health professionals with a minimum of a master's degree in a mental health or related field of study, in addition to previous experience working with adolescents and their families.

These individuals undergo an internal certification process that includes substantial project-specific training. Their activities are key to the successful implementation of all aspects of the intervention. These include providing psycho-education to mentors; facilitating meetings to discuss progress toward the youth's action plan goals as well as mentor–youth or mentor–mentor relationships; disseminating resource information for community activities; serving as creative problem-solvers when challenges arise; and maintaining flexible availability to accommodate participants' schedules, provide support, and address concerns. Natural and community mentors are also expected to engage in telephone check-ins with the prevention specialist to assess progress with the mentor–youth relationship, action plan implementation, and to address barriers that may arise.

Operation 72

Operation 72 was devised to assist in the alleviation of attrition for those assigned to the LET's CONNECT intervention condition. This procedure was implemented following our four-month pilot trial. More specifically, for those families randomized to the intervention group, we examined their dates of consent and initial home-based meeting. It was evident that a more rapid launch for this meeting contributed to youths' successful launch within the mentorship program, decreasing attrition rates. Thus, we set 72 hours from the date of consent as our goal to schedule and, if possible, conduct the home-based meeting. Prior to scheduling the home-based meeting, the community mentor is contacted for a collaborative discussion regarding the potential match with a youth. The consent/assent form signed by the youth and parent/guardian indicates that information about the youth will be shared with the mentor (e.g., reason for positive screen, personal/school adjustment, and mental health treatment history). Should the mentor agree the match is a good fit, a meeting involving the mentor, youth, and parent will be scheduled to occur shortly after the first home-based meeting with the youth and parent/guardian. This is based on our experience that quickly engaging youth and their families in the first intervention meeting increases their buy-in and rapport, which in turn decreases attrition. Families of lower socioeconomic status often lack access to important resources (e.g., childcare or transportation), leading to an increased number of barriers when becoming involved in a new extracurricular activity. For a family who is experiencing these types of difficulties, moving quickly and efficiently to launch a program is important; otherwise, it may become perceived as less feasible for the family or become a low priority, given their other concerns.

Communications to Maintain Investment and Participation

The urban area in which LET's CONNECT is conducted has experienced significant urban decay over recent decades, resulting in increased poverty rates associated with income and employment volatility, and residential instability (Western, Bloome, Sosnaud, & Tach, 2012). The presence of such adversity may lead to frequent changes in telephone numbers or other means of communication. Because of this, we have found it is important to use a wide variety of communication tools, such as obtaining contact information of relatives/trusted friends; obtaining social media user-names and email addresses; and obtaining a release of information to the youth's school. We are finding that for some youth and their families, electronic communication provides the most stable form of contact, changing less frequently than residences and telephone numbers.

Communications between our research staff and participating youth, families, and community mentors are essential. For the intervention condition, a monthly newsletter is sent to community mentors communicating pertinent information (e.g., upcoming connectedness events/activities, changes in study procedures). For adolescents in intervention and E-TAU conditions, postcards are sent several times each year. One postcard is sent to each youth participant for his or her birthday, and additional postcards are sent near seasonal holidays (e.g., Thanksgiving) to thank youth for their participation and remind them of upcoming follow-up assessments. Additionally, at the baseline evaluation, youth and their parent or guardian are informed of the 6- and 16-month follow-up evaluations and provided with an appointment card indicating their approximate date of follow-up.

Youth Positive Screens

To date, we have screened 692 youth in the LET's CONNECT project. These youth are between the ages of 12 and 15 years ($M = 13.5$ years), and just over half of them are female (56.2%). Approximately two-thirds of them are African American; approximately one-third are Caucasian. A majority of their families receive public assistance.

Our screening measures provide preliminary prevalence rates of bully victimization and perpetration in the study sample. Using the Peer Experiences Questionnaire and its established cut score of ≥ 17 for females and ≥ 19 for males (Vernberg, Jacobs, & Hershberger, 1999), 148 of our participants thus far (21.4%) have screened positive for peer victimization over the past four months, while 41 participants (5.9%) have screened positive for bully perpetration during the same time period. On the UCLA Loneliness Scale (Russell et al., 1980), 113 youth (16.3%) have screened positive for low levels of social connectedness. No significant differences between victimization type (i.e., bully victim/perpetrator) and ethnicity or race have emerged. Correlations between the screening measures (i.e., bully victimization and perpetration, low interpersonal connectedness) and the baseline Suicidal Ideation Questionnaire–Junior (SIQ-JR; Reynolds, 1988) scores are each positive and significant, except for bully perpetration and SIQ-JR (see Table 20.1).

CONCLUSIONS, AND DIRECTIONS FOR FURTHER RESEARCH

Youth suicide risk, bullying victimization, and bullying perpetration are major public health concerns, and low levels of social connectedness have been associated with each of these. LET's CONNECT has been developed in an effort to prevent the

Table 20.1. Correlations Among LET'S CONNECT Screening Variables and Suicidal Ideation

Variable	Bully Victimization	Bully Perpetration	UCLA Loneliness
Bully Perpetration	.526***		
UCLA Loneliness Scale	.430***	.268***	
SIQ-JR (n = 129)	.241**	.091	.233**

NOTE: SIQ-JR = Suicidal Ideation Questionnaire–Junior; SIQ-JR is administered at baseline, resulting in a sample size of 129.
**$p < .01$
***$p < .001$

initial onset of suicidal behavior in youth at elevated risk by improving their social connectedness with others and their community. The study is currently underway, and results are pending. Whether or not this particular intervention is found to be effective, because youth in our society are embedded within multiple ecological contexts, a perceived sense of connectedness to families, school, peers, and the community at large may serve as a protective factor against adverse outcomes and enhance overall well-being.

Suggestions for Medical Providers

- When determining whether or not to conduct a suicide risk screen, consider social/interpersonal risk factors such as peer victimization, bully perpetration, and more generally, lack of social connectedness as "red flags" for the importance of such screening.
- When there is evidence of peer aggression or bully perpetration, always conduct a suicide risk screen, as a bully perpetrator may be at risk for suicidal behavior and suicide, and may also be a victim of bullying.
- A brief suicide risk screen can be conducted in a few minutes. One can begin with a statement of understanding, such as, "Given these difficulties with peers and how painful these can be sometimes, I wonder if you have had thoughts of killing yourself, of suicide?" It is appropriate to ask in a few different ways and to allow time for slower responding. If the screen suggests possible suicidal thoughts, a referral for a more comprehensive risk assessment is indicated.
- Work with your team to prepare a list of mental health professionals to whom you can refer youth who screen positive for elevated risk for suicide. When in doubt, refer for a psychiatric evaluation.
- If you have any concerns about a youth you are treating, give the youth and the parent/guardian each a crisis card with emergency numbers, such as for the National Lifeline (1-800-273-8255).

Suggestions for Parents and Teachers

- Talk with your child or students regularly, leaving the door open to talking about difficulties with peers. It is fine to ask your child or student

direct questions about peer relationships, about emotional distress, and about the possibility that they are having suicidal thoughts.
- If your child or student is unwilling to discuss peer relationships, emotional distress, or personal struggles with you at this time, encourage your child to talk with another trusted adult.
- Trust your understanding of your child or student and your own observations and anxieties. If you observe a change in behavior in the direction of more aggression, more social withdrawal, or more depression or irritability, share that you are concerned about him or her. Ask your child or student if they are feeling down, struggling with peers, or having thoughts of suicide. When in doubt, parents are encouraged to seek a mental health evaluation for their children; teachers are encouraged to share their concern with the identified school personnel for such concerns, and with the child and the child's parent.
- Keep in mind that social connectedness and positive peer relationships are important to youth's sense of well-being and positive growth. Facilitate social skill development, positive involvement in healthy peer activities, and engagement in structured peer activities with adult support and supervision (school clubs, sport teams, etc.).

Suggestions for Mental Health Providers

- An evaluation of peer victimization, peer bullying and, more generally, social connectedness, is an important component of a comprehensive mental health or psychiatric evaluation and, more specifically, a suicide risk assessment.
- Understand that the bully perpetrator may also be a victim of bullying, and may be at as high or higher risk for suicidal behavior and suicide. When there is evidence of peer aggression or bully perpetration, conduct a suicide risk assessment and consider other appropriate interventions.
- Consider interventions to enhance social and community connectedness, and assist youth and families in coping with and responding to peer bullying.

Suggestions for Policy Makers

- Develop guidelines for the core elements within effective anti-bullying programs and address ways in which communities can incorporate cultural and community-level tailoring.
- Seek legislative action at the community, state, and/or national level to implement comprehensive anti-bullying programs for bully perpetrators, victims, and bystanders within schools and other contexts (e.g., juvenile justice, activity-based organizations, physical/mental health centers).
- When drafting anti-bullying laws/policies, include broad, behaviorally based items of various types bullying (e.g., cyber, relational, physical) to capture groups that may be at even higher risk for peer victimization, such as lesbian, gay, bisexual, transgender, and questioning youth; religious minorities within the identified region; and youth identified by other minority status within a particular setting (e.g., race/ethnicity, socioeconomic status).

- Prioritize funding for surveillance studies of the incidence/prevalence of bullying behaviors; develop, implement, and systematically assess the efficacy and effectiveness of anti-bullying youth programs; and facilitate the broad dissemination of findings to stakeholders, practitioners, and fellow researchers.

AUTHOR NOTE

The LET's CONNECT community mentorship intervention and effectiveness trial described in this chapter was supported by a CDC grant (U01-CE-001940-01) and National Institute of Mental Health (NIMH) K24 (MH077705) award to Dr. Cheryl King.

REFERENCES

Asarnow, J. R., Baraff, L. J., Berk, M., Grob, C. S., Devich-Navarro, M., Suddath, R.,...Tang, L. (2011). An emergency department intervention for linking pediatric suicidal patients to follow-up mental health treatment. *Psychiatric Services, 62*(11), 1303–1309.

Aseltine, R. H., Jr. (2003). An evaluation of a school based suicide prevention program. *Adolescent & Family Health, 3*(2), 81–88.

Baldry, A. C., & Winkel, F. W. (2003). Direct and vicarious victimization at school and at home as risk factors for suicidal cognition among Italian adolescents. *Journal of Adolescence, 26*(6), 703–716.

Barber, B. K., & Schluterman, J. M. (2008). Connectedness in the lives of children and adolescents: A call for greater conceptual clarity. *Journal of Adolescent Health, 43*(3), 209–216. doi: 10.1016/j.jadohealth.2008.01.012

Britto, M. T., Klostermann, B. K., Bonny, A. E., Altum, S. A., & Hornung, R. W. (2001). Impact of a school-based intervention on access to healthcare for underserved youth. *Journal of Adolescent Health, 29*(2), 116–124.

Borowsky, I. W., Taliaferro, L. A., & McMorris, B. J. (2013). Suicidal thinking and behavior among youth involved in verbal and social bullying: Risk and protective factors. *Journal of Adolescent Health, 53*(1 Suppl), S4–S12.

Bronfenbrenner, U. (1994). Ecological models of human development. In M. Gauvain & M. Cole (Eds.), *Readings on the Development of Children* (2nd ed., Vol. 3, pp. 37–43). New York: Freeman.

Centers for Disease Control and Prevention (2012). Suicide: Facts at a glance. Retrieved September 11, 2013, from http://www.cdc.gov/violenceprevention/pdf/suicide-datasheet-a.PDF.

Centers for Disease Control and Prevention (2013). Web-based Injury Statistics Query and Reporting System (WISQARS). Retrieved July 8, 2013, from http://www.cdc.gov/injury/wisqars/index.html.

Coyne, J. C. (1976). Toward an interactional description of depression. *Psychiatry: Journal for the Study of Interpersonal Processes, 39*(1), 28–40.

De Wit, D. J., Lipman, E., Manzano-Munguia, M., Bisanz, J., Graham, K., Offord, D. R.,...Shaver, K. (2007). Feasibility of a randomized controlled trial for evaluating the effectiveness of the Big Brother Big Sisters community match program at the national level. *Children and Youth Services Review, 29*, 383–404.

Duarté-Vélez, Y. M., & Bernal, G. (2007). Suicide behavior among Latino and Latino adolescents: Conceptual and methodological issues. *Death Studies, 31*(5), 425–455. doi: 10.1080/07481180701244579

Durkheim, E. (1897). *Suicide*. New York: Free Press.

Espelage, D. L., & Holt, M. K. (2013). Suicidal ideation and school bullying experiences after controlling for depression and delinquency. *Journal of Adolescent Health, 53*(1 Suppl), S27–S31. doi: 10.1016/j.jadohealth.2012.09.017

Freedenthal, S., & Stiffman, A. R. (2007). "They might think I was crazy": Young American Indians' reasons for not seeking help when suicidal. *Journal of Adolescent Research, 22*(1), 58–77. doi: 10.1177/0743558406295969

Friedman, M. S., Koeske, G. F., Silvestre, A. J., Korr, W. S., & Sites, E. W. (2006). The impact of gender-role nonconforming behavior, bullying, and social support on suicidality among gay male youth. *Journal of Adolescent Health, 38*(5), 621–623. doi: http://dx.doi.org/10.1016/j.jadohealth.2005.04.014

Goldston, D. B., Molock, S. D., Whitbeck, L. B., Murakami, J. L., Zayas, L. H., & Hall, G. C. N. (2008). Cultural considerations in adolescent suicide prevention and psychosocial treatment. *American Psychologist, 63*(1), 14–31.

Heaney, C. A., & Israel, B. A. (2002). Social networks and social support. In K. Glanz, B. K. Rimer & F. M. Lewis (Eds.), *Health Behavior and Health Education: Theory, Research, and Practice, 3rd Edition* (pp. 185–209). San Francisco, CA: John Wiley & Sons.

Husky, M. M., McGuire, L., Flynn, L., Chrostowski, C., & Olfson, M. (2009). Correlates of help-seeking behavior among at-risk adolescents. *Child Psychiatry and Human Development, 40*(1), 15–24.

Joe, S., & Kaplan, M. S. (2002). Firearm-related suicide among young African-American males. *Psychiatric Services, 53*(3), 332–334. doi: 10.1176/appi.ps.53.3.332

Joiner, T. E. (2005). *Why People Die by Suicide*. Cambridge, MA: Harvard University Press.

Kann, L., Olsen, E. O., McManus, T., Kinchen, S., Chyen, D., Harris, W. A., & Wechsler, H. (2011). Sexual identity, sex of sexual contacts, and health-risk behaviors among students in grades 9–12—youth risk behavior surveillance, selected sites, United States, 2001–2009. *Morbidity & Mortality Weekly Report Surveillance Summary, 60*(7), 1–133.

Karcher, M. J. (2008). The Study of Mentoring in the Learning Environment (SMILE): A randomized evaluation of the effectiveness of school-based mentoring. *Prevention Science, 9*, 99–113.

Kaslow, N. J., Sherry, A., Bethea, K., Wyckoff, S., Compton, M. T., Grall, M. B., . . . Parker, R. (2005). Social risk and protective factors for suicide attempts in low income African American men and women. *Suicide and Life-Threatening Behavior, 35*(4), 400–412. doi: 10.1521/suli.2005.35.4.400

Kataoka, S. H., Zhang, L., & Wells, K. B. (2002). Unmet need for mental health care among U.S. children: Variation by ethnicity and insurance status. *The American Journal of Psychiatry, 159*(9), 1548–1555. doi: 10.1176/appi.ajp.159.9.1548

King, C. A., & Merchant, C. R. (2008). Social and interpersonal factors relating to adolescent suicidality: A review of the literature. *Archives of Suicide Research, 12*(3), 181–196.

King, K. A., Vidourek, R. A., Davis, B., & McClellan, W. (2002). Increasing self-esteem and school connectedness through a multidimensional mentoring program. *Journal of School Health, 72*, 294–299.

Klomek, A. B., Kleinman, M., Altschuler, E., Marrocco, F., Amakawa, L., & Gould, M. S. (2013). Suicidal adolescents' experiences with bullying perpetration and victimization during high school as risk factors for later depression and suicidality. *Journal of Adolescent Health, 53*(1 Suppl), S37–S42. doi: 10.1016/j.jadohealth.2012.12.008

La Greca, A. M., & Lopez, N. (1998). Social anxiety among adolescents: Linkages with peer relations and friendships. *Journal of Abnormal Child Psychology, 26*(2), 83–94.

Liang, H., Flisher, A. J., & Lombard, C. J. (2007). Bullying, violence, and risk behavior in South African school students. *Child Abuse & Neglect, 31*(2), 161–171.

Mahon, N. E., Yarcheski, A., Yarcheski, T. J., Cannella, B. L., & Hanks, M. M. (2006). A meta-analytic study of predictors for loneliness during adolescence. *Nursing Research, 55*(5), 308–315.

Nansel, T. R., Overpeck, M., Pilla, R. S., Ruan, W. J., Simons-Morton, B., & Scheidt, P. (2001). Bullying behaviors among US youth: Prevalence and association with psychosocial adjustment. *JAMA: Journal of the American Medical Association, 285*(16), 2094–2100.

Nock, M. K., Green, J. G., Hwang, I., McLaughlin, K. A., Sampson, N. A., Zaslavsky, A. M., & Kessler, R. C. (2013). Prevalence, correlates, and treatment of lifetime suicidal behavior among adolescents: Results from the National Comorbidity Survey Replication Adolescent Supplement. *JAMA Psychiatry, 70*(3), 300–310. doi: 10.1001/2013.jamapsychiatry.55

Park, H. S., Schepp, K. G., Jang, E. H., & Koo, H. Y. (2006). Predictors of suicidal ideation among high school students by gender in South Korea. *Journal of School Health, 76*(5), 181–188.

Prinstein, M. J., Boergers, J., Spirito, A., Little, T. D., & Grapentine, W. L. (2000). Peer functioning, family dysfunction, and psychological symptoms in a risk factor model for adolescent inpatients' suicidal ideation severity. *Journal of Clinical Child Psychology, 29*(3), 392–405.

Prinstein, M. J., Boergers, J., & Vernberg, E. M. (2001). Overt and relational aggression in adolescents: Social-psychological adjustment of aggressors and victims. *Journal of Clinical Child Psychology, 30*(4), 479–491.

Reynolds, W. M. (1988). *Suicidal Ideation Questionnaire: Professional Manual*. Odessa, FL: Psychological Assessment Resources.

Russell, D., Peplau, L. A., & Curtrona, C. E. (1980). The revised UCLA Loneliness Scale: Concurrent and discriminant validity evidence. *Journal of Personality & Social Psychology, 39*, 472–480.

Russell, S. T., & Joyner, K. (2001). Adolescent sexual orientation and suicide risk: Evidence from a national study. *American Journal of Public Health, 91*(8), 1276–1281.

Scales, P. C., Benson, P. L., Moore, K. A., Lippman, L., Brown, B., & Zaff, J. F. (2008). Promoting equal developmental opportunity and outcomes among America's children and youth: Results from the National Promises Study. *The Journal of Primary Prevention, 29*(2), 121–144.

Scolte, R. H. J., van Lieshout, C. F. M., & van Aken, M. A. G. (2001). Perceived relational support in adolescence: Dimension, configurations, and adolescent adjustment. *Journal of Research on Adolescence, 11*(1), 71–94.

Scott, M. A., Wilcox, H. C., Schonfeld, S., Davies, M., Hicks, R. C., Tuner, J. B., & Shaffer, D. (2008). School-based screening to identify students not already known to school professionals: The Columbia Suicide Screen. *American Journal of Public Health, 99*, 1–6.

Seals, D., & Young, J. (2003). Bullying and victimization: prevalence and relationship to gender, grade level, ethnicity, self-esteem, and depression. *Adolescence, 38*(152), 735–747.

Shaffer, D., Scott, M., Wilcox, H., Maslow, C., Hicks, R., Lucas, C. P., . . . Greenwald, S. (2004). The Columbia Suicide Screen: Validity and reliability of a screen for youth suicide and depression. *Journal of the American Academy of Child & Adolescent Psychiatry, 43*(1), 71–79.

Spriggs, A. L., Iannotti, R. J., Nansel, T. R., & Haynie, D. L. (2007). Adolescent bullying involvement and perceived family, peer and school relations: commonalities and differences across race/ethnicity. *Journal of Adolescent Health, 41*(3), 283–293. doi: 10.1016/j.jadohealth.2007.04.009

Taylor, R. D., Budescu, M., Gebre, A., & Hodzic, I. (2012). Family financial pressure and maternal and adolescent socioemotional adjustment: Moderating effects of kin social support in low income African American families. *Journal of Child and Family Studies, 23*(2), 242–254. doi: 10.1007/s10826-012-9688-8

Thoits, P. A. (1995). Stress, coping, and social support processes: Where are we? what next? *Journal of Health and Social Behavior, 35*, 53–79.

U.S. Census Bureau (2013). State & County Quickfacts: Flint, Michigan. Retrieved September 11, 2013, from http://quickfacts.census.gov/qfd/index.html.

U.S. Department of Health and Human Services (HHS) Office of the Surgeon General and National Action Alliance for Suicide Prevention (2012). *2012 National Strategy for Suicide Prevention: Goals and Objectives for Action*. Washington D.C.

Vernberg, E. M., Jacobs, A. K., & Hershberger, S. L. (1999). Peer victimization and attitudes about violence during early adolescence. *Journal of Clinical Child Psychology, 28*(3), 386–395.

Western, B., Bloome, D., Sosnaud, B., & Tach, L. (2012). Economic insecurity and social stratification. *Annual Review of Sociology, 38*, 341–359. doi: 10.1146/annurev-soc-071811-145434

PART SIX

Public Health Approaches

21

National and State-Level Approaches to Youth Suicide and Bullying Prevention

DEWEY CORNELL AND ROXANA MARACHI

There are national and state-level approaches to suicide prevention as well as national and state-level approaches to bullying prevention; the challenge for the field is to identify areas of overlap and potential synergy. As noted by the American Foundation for Suicide Prevention (2013), "The relationship between bullying and suicide is complex. While it alone does not cause suicide, bullying can be a contributing factor, putting youth who are already vulnerable at increased risk for self-harm" (p. 1). For this reason, bullying interventions could contribute to suicide prevention efforts, and similarly, suicide screening might identify students who are being bullied, and thus strengthen intervention and support efforts.

NATIONAL APPROACHES TO SUICIDE AND BULLYING PREVENTION

Since the 1999 landmark Surgeon General's report on suicide prevention (U.S. Public Health Service, 1999), there have been extensive efforts among multiple federal agencies to develop and update a national suicide prevention strategy (U.S. Department of Health and Human Services [HHS], Office of the Surgeon General, and the National Action Alliance for Suicide Prevention, 2012; hereafter USDHHS, 2012).

Although the majority of national-level approaches for suicide and bullying prevention have operated independently of one another and charted separate courses in the past decade, more recent efforts are integrating the work of multiple agencies to promote strategic plans for reducing risk in both areas (U.S. Department of Education [USDOE], 2013; USDHHS, 2012). The National Strategy for Suicide Prevention (NSSP) reflects important developments in the understanding of suicide and suicide prevention. One key development is the recognition that suicide prevention is not solely a mental health issue to be addressed by mental health agencies. Grounded in a socio-ecological framework for prevention, the NSSP report emphasizes a public health approach and coordinated efforts to promote action at multiple levels, including federal, state, tribal, and local governments, as well as schools and community-based organizations (USDHHS, 2012). The NSSP report establishes four strategic directions for action, each with goals that align with bullying prevention efforts.

STRATEGIC DIRECTION 1: HEALTHY AND EMPOWERED INDIVIDUALS, FAMILIES, AND COMMUNITIES

The first strategic direction is to create supportive environments that promote the health and well-being of the general population and reduce barriers to seeking help for problems such as mental illness, substance abuse, and other risk factors for suicide (USDHHS, 2012). The NSSP report notes shared risk and protective factors for suicide and bullying, emphasizes the need to eliminate biases associated with seeking mental health services, and suggests efforts to promote awareness that effective treatment is possible. Like those who are at risk for suicide, victims of bullying may be too ashamed or embarrassed to seek help, and they may not recognize that bullying can be stopped. Similarly, individuals who know someone who is being victimized need to recognize the importance of encouraging that person to seek help.

The Office of Civil Rights (OCR) in the U.S. Department of Education has initiated an important national anti-bullying effort that fits well with the emphasis of Strategic Direction 1 on maintaining a supportive environment for individuals who may need assistance. In a series of "Dear Colleague" letters on harassment and bullying, the OCR highlighted the legal obligation of school authorities to protect students from sexual and gender-based harassment, as well as other forms of harassment based on race, national origin, or disability status that may constitute a violation of the students' civil rights (USDOE/OCR, 2010). The letters advise schools that they have an obligation under Title IX to take proactive measures such as educational programs and staff training to prevent discriminatory behavior and to make comprehensive victim services available when harassment occurs.

Another important national strategy is to improve the quality of media representations of suicide. This includes recommendations for responsible reporting of suicides by news agencies and accurate portrayals of suicide and mental illness by the entertainment industry (USDHHS, 2012). In the field of bullying prevention, there is concern that media reports could perpetuate a stereotypical link between bullying and suicide (Feldman Hertz, Donato, & Wright, 2013). It is important that suicide not be portrayed as a direct consequence of bullying, so that victims of bullying are not encouraged to see suicide as a response to their victimization.

STRATEGIC DIRECTION 2: CLINICAL AND COMMUNITY PREVENTIVE SERVICES

The second national strategic direction for suicide prevention is to promote more effective clinical and community-based prevention services (USDHHS, 2012). This includes objectives such as training healthcare providers to screen patients for suicide risk and helping community service providers implement more effective, evidence-based prevention programs. Because suicide and bullying share many risk and protective factors, prevention efforts that promote healthy development contribute to both suicide and bullying prevention efforts.

In an effort to communicate best practices with the general public, the Federal Partners in Bullying Prevention have hosted a series of webinars addressing key issues related to bullying prevention, including harassment laws related to bullying and best practices in intervention and prevention of bullying (USDOE, 2013). The federally supported Safe and Supportive Schools Technical Assistance website has archived webinars on bullying prevention strategies for school and classroom environments (http://safesupportiveschools.ed.gov/index.php?id=65).

A key preventive approach for both bullying and suicide is the integration of social and emotional learning programs in schools to support students' self-awareness, self-management, social awareness, relationship skills, and responsible decision-making (Greenberg, Weissberg, O'Brien, Zins, Fredericks, Resnik, & Elias, 2003). A 2011 meta-analysis of 213 studies found that social and emotional learning (SEL) programming improved social and emotional skills and classroom behavior, lowered emotional distress such as stress and depression, and improved student attitudes about themselves, others, and school (Durlak, Weissberg, Dymnicki, Taylor, & Schellinger, 2011). The quality of program implementation is a critical factor, since programs that were not well implemented (missing program elements, staff without adequate training, etc.) were less effective.

STRATEGIC DIRECTION 3: TREATMENT AND SUPPORT SERVICES

To offer the most immediate and effective access to intervention, suicide prevention should be promoted as a core component for all health-related services (USDHHS, 2012). Organizations should have systems in place to implement effective clinical and professional practices for assessing and treating those identified as at risk for suicidal behaviors. For students who have been severely victimized by bullying, this support strategy is an immediate form of intervention. Students who have endured extreme forms of bullying or peer abuse should be referred for mental health support. Furthermore, care and support should be provided for those who have been affected by suicide deaths and attempts.

Both suicide and bullying prevention efforts often follow the public health model that operates on three levels: *universal* strategies that target the entire population (in schools, the entire student body), *selective* strategies for subgroups at heightened risk for the problem, and *indicated* (or targeted) strategies for the individuals who are at high risk or are already experiencing the problem (Waldvogel, Reuter, & Oberg, 2008). Within a social-ecological framework that outlines the often-overlapping roots of suicide and violence, national-level prevention efforts emphasize the involvement of comprehensive systems at national, state, territorial, local, and organizational levels to address prevention (USDHHS, 2012). To be effective, prevention efforts should be culturally attuned, developmentally appropriate, and locally relevant. Given their similar approaches to prevention, it may be useful for bullying prevention specialists to have gatekeeper training on risk factors for suicidal behavior, and for suicide prevention specialists to include information on bullying in their training.

STRATEGIC DIRECTION 4: SURVEILLANCE, RESEARCH, AND EVALUATION

Sustainable prevention and intervention efforts will depend on ongoing, accurate, efficient, and effective use of national surveillance systems to determine best practices. Communication systems that allow for collection, analysis, and use of relevant information can be instrumental in moving prevention and intervention efforts forward. Research on both suicide and bullying prevention should continue to evaluate the development, impact, and implementation of prevention and interventions systems.

There have been several efforts to promote valid and reliable measures for research and evaluation purposes. One example is the *Compendium of Assessment Tools for Measuring Violence-Related Attitudes, Behaviors, and Influences Among Youth,* published by the Centers for Disease Control (CDC; Dahlberg, Toal, Swahn, & Behrens, 2005). Another example is the competitive grants offered through the Safe and Supportive Schools Program to support eleven states in their efforts to measure school climate and improve school safety. The grants program included support for school administrators to obtain survey information on bullying and harassment, along with funding for interventions in high-need schools.

There are serious challenges in conducting accurate and effective research on bullying and suicide prevention. In contrast to the comparatively straightforward definitions and measurements of suicide, suicidal behaviors, and attempts, there is great variability and complexity in definitions and measurement of "bullying" (American Educational Research Association, 2013).

Current national datasets may also be lacking important demographic information that could improve our basic understanding of prevalence rates. Rates of suicide by LGBT populations are currently unknown, because death certificates do not identify sexual orientation (USDHHS, 2012). The National Violent Death Reporting System (NVDRS) attempts to address this issue; however, it is limited in scope and is only available in 16 states (CDC, 2013a). The most current dataset available on the national prevalence of suicide is the Web-based Inquiry Statistics Query and Reporting System, or WISQARS (CDC, 2013b).

There are several national efforts to improve the quality of data available on bullying and harassment, especially for groups that have experienced high rates of victimization. The U.S. Department of Education plans for the Civil Rights Biennial Data Collection to require schools to report instances of harassment or bullying based on race, sex, national origin, disability, and religion (USDOE/OCR, 2013). In addition, the National Center for Education Statistics is developing questions about sexual orientation, gender identity, and schools' experiences for use in the High School Longitudinal Study and the National Crime Victimization Survey's School Crime Supplement (Kim, 2013). The availability of more reliable data on the incidence of bullying and harassment based on sexual orientation, race, and disability will have a major impact on policy and practice. Schools will become more cognizant of bullying and harassment directed at particular populations and be able to focus their efforts accordingly.

One area for further research on strategic prevention is the role of social media communication in outreach and intervention efforts. Current research has not yet included large-scale analyses of social media strategies or their effectiveness. It may be worthwhile to examine patterns and trends of social media communications to determine which kinds of content are most valuable, most commonly shared, yield the highest traffic to resource sites, and provide the greatest access and connection to help lines and resources for assistance.

CIVIL RIGHTS LAWS

The terms "bullying" and "harassment" are often used interchangeably, but there are some important conceptual and legal differences. Bullying is usually defined as repeated intentional actions by someone that harm or humiliate a weaker or less powerful victim (Cornell & Cole, 2011), whereas harassment refers to any repeated conduct that is offensive or harmful to the victim (The Law Dictionary, http://thelawdictionary.org/harassment/). Bullying differs from harassment because it involves a power imbalance between the aggressor and victim, whereas there is no requirement for a power imbalance in harassment. From this perspective, bullying is a kind of harassment, and laws about harassment have direct relevance for bullying. Certain forms of harassment are prohibited by a wide variety of federal and state laws designed to prevent discrimination. For example, discrimination based on race, color, sex, or national origin is prohibited by the Title VII of the Civil Rights Act of 1964 (with important amendments in the Civil Rights Act of 1991 and the Lily Ledbetter Fair Pay Act of 2009; Title VII of the Civil Rights Act of 1964, http://www.eeoc.gov/laws/statutes/titlevii.cfm). Discrimination based on disability is prohibited by Section 504 of the Rehabilitation Act of 1973 and Title II of the Americans with Disabilities Act of 2004. Anti-discrimination laws are powerful tools for reducing the societal and interpersonal stress that can contribute to suicide.

In 1999, the Supreme Court ruled that school authorities had a responsibility to prevent sexual harassment that takes place between students (*Davis* v. *Monroe County Board of Education,* 1999). In this case, a fifth-grade girl was sexually harassed repeatedly by a classmate, and even though school authorities were aware of the harassment, they made little effort to stop it. The family sued on the basis of the Title IX provision that "no person shall, on the basis of sex, be excluded from participation in, be denied the benefits of, or be subjected to discrimination under any education program or activity receiving federal financial assistance" (20 U.S.C. §1681a). This is a landmark case with broad implications for bullying and opens the door for more cases arguing that schools should take action to stop harassment that constitutes a civil rights violation.

In 2013, the U.S. Office of Special Education and Rehabilitative Services (OSER) issued guidance to school authorities emphasizing their obligation to prevent the bullying of students with disabilities. Allowing a student with a disability to be bullied could constitute a denial of educational services guaranteed under the Individuals with Disabilities Education Act. Although the federal law protects the rights of students with disabilities, OSER authorities also observed, "Bullying of any student simply cannot be tolerated in our schools. A school where children don't feel safe is a school where children struggle to learn. Every student deserves to thrive in a safe school and classroom free from bullying" (Yudin, 2013, p. 1).

Civil rights legislation has important implications for school authorities because they may be held responsible for the protection of youth in case of any misconduct (on or off school grounds) that creates a "hostile and offensive environment" and is based on race, color, national origin, sex, or disability (Office for Civil Rights [OCR], 2010). In such cases, districts must respond in accordance with federal civil rights statutes and regulations (Goodemann, Zammitt, & Hagedorn, 2012; OCR, 2010).

STATE APPROACHES TO SUICIDE PREVENTION

States play a key role in suicide prevention by providing localities with training and resources to implement comprehensive and effective programs. As recommended by the National Governors Association (Goldrick, 2005), state campaigns can increase public awareness about suicide prevention, and they can guide authorities to adopt high-quality programs. A critical element of a statewide effort is to fund a dedicated suicide prevention office that can provide training and coordination of services as well as foster multi-agency collaboration. However, only a few states have a freestanding state government office for suicide prevention, and most rely on public–private coalitions with a state staff member who coordinates training and other initiatives.

State policies on suicide prevention are diverse. As the American Foundation for Suicide Prevention (2013b) concluded, "While all U.S. States have some form of suicide prevention plan in place, no two states currently address the issue in the same way." For example, there is wide variation in state legislation to promote training and education in suicide prevention through the public schools. Only three states have statutes that require both training for school personnel and student education concerning suicide prevention. However, eight states have requirements for school personnel training but not student education, and four states require student education but are silent on training school personnel. Still other states merely encourage rather than require training or education. Altogether, 29 states either require or encourage training for school personnel, and 20 states either require or encourage student education, but 12 states have no school-focused suicide prevention statute.

New Jersey has for many years had one of the lowest adolescent suicide rates in the nation and has been singled out as a model for statewide prevention practices (Guild, Freeman, & Shanahan, 2004; New Jersey Department of Children and Families (DCF)-Division of Child Behavioral Health Services, n.d.). Although it is not possible to distinguish the most critical causal factors among the wide variety of prevention efforts in New Jersey, an independent evaluation highlighted components such as the high degree of collaboration among state and local agencies, the presence of psychiatric screening centers and crisis hotlines in every county, and the prevalence of school-based awareness curricula and programs to teach social skills and reduce stress. The evaluation also noted New Jersey's legislative efforts to limit adolescent access to firearms. Several studies have concluded that reducing adolescent access to firearms can reduce suicide rates (Lubin, Werbeloff, Halperin, Shmushkevitch, Weiser, & Knobler, 2010).

One of the most valuable state suicide prevention efforts is gatekeeper training, which is the systematic education of individuals to recognize when someone might be suicidal, to express concern and make appropriate inquiries, and when appropriate, take action to obtain assistance. The Suicide Prevention Resource Center (2013) describes 37 different gatekeeper training programs variously designed for educators, health professionals, law enforcement officers, parents, friends, and other groups. Question, Persuade, and Refer (QPR; QPR Institute, 2013) is one of the most widely used gatekeeper training programs and has been listed with the National Registry of Evidence-based Programs and Practices (NREPP).

Many states have established gatekeeper training programs. For example, the Maine Suicide Prevention Program (2013) has an impressive array of training programs crafted for different stakeholders. A Tennessee study found that gatekeeper training increased knowledge of suicide prevention and self-efficacy (Keller et al., 2009). And a Virginia study found that school counselors and teachers who participated in QPR training not only demonstrated increased knowledge of suicide risk factors, they also applied their training by questioning more students and making "no-harm contracts" and outside referrals (Reis & Cornell, 2008). These studies suggest that training can have an impact on gatekeepers, but there is a pressing need for more direct evidence that gatekeeper training reduces suicide rates (Isaac et al., 2009).

LESBIAN, GAY, BISEXUAL, AND TRANSGENDER CONCERNS

No group better represents the nexus of suicide risk and bullying than lesbian, gay, bisexual, and transgender (LGBT) youth (see Chapter 8 in this volume). There is indirect, correlational evidence that state and school policies can have a protective effect on the stresses experienced by LGBT youth. One study found that adults reporting lesbian, gay, or bisexual status reported higher levels of dysthymia, generalized anxiety disorder, and post-traumatic stress disorder if they were living in a state with policies that did not protect them from hate crimes and employment discrimination (Hatzenbuehler, Keyes, & Hasin, 2009). Furthermore, a study of Oregon eleventh-graders found that lesbian, gay, and bisexual students reported lower rates of suicide attempts when they attended schools with anti-bullying policies that specifically included sexual orientation as a protected status (Hatzenbuehler & Keyes, 2013). In 2011, the Department of Education reminded schools of their obligation under the Equal Access Act to allow gay-straight alliances and similar clubs for LGBT youth (USDOE, 2011).

STATE APPROACHES TO BULLYING

State laws and policies regarding bullying are rapidly evolving. Before 1999, no states had laws concerning bullying, but by 2012, all but one state (Montana) had enacted legislation (Sacco et al., 2012). There is considerable variation across states, but 49 states have required local school authorities to develop policies on bullying (Sacco et al., 2012). Policies typically offer a definition of bullying, prohibit bullying behavior, and require school authorities to investigate bullying incidents. Only 13 states direct schools to provide mental health services to victims, although many policies mention mental health needs (Nickerson, Cornell, Smith, & Furlong, 2013).

There is concern that enforcement of state-required anti-bullying policies could lead school authorities to overlook cases that also constitute harassment that represents a civil rights violation (USDOE/OCR, 2010). As described above, the Office for Civil Rights has determined that school authorities are obligated under civil rights laws to investigate and end discriminatory harassment, and furthermore, to take steps to eliminate a hostile environment and prevent such acts from recurring. One limitation of the civil rights approach to harassment, however, is that many forms of bullying may not be based on traits of race, color, national origin, sex, religion, or disability. Children and adolescents may be bullied for virtually any reason (e.g., being perceived as overweight or underweight, too tall or too short). School policies that address all forms of bullying are necessary. And although federal protections are limited to specific categories of harassment, many states have legislation that recognizes the rights of all students to a public education free from discrimination (General Accounting Office, 2012).

Another concern is that states might encourage zero-tolerance policies toward students who engage in bullying ("Education Dept.," 2012). The American Psychological Association's Zero Tolerance Task Force (2008) criticized zero-tolerance policies for mandating a severe punishment that is applied to all violations regardless of the circumstances, and concluded that there is no scientific evidence to support claims that zero tolerance improves student behavior or renders schools safer. Zero-tolerance practices such as automatic school suspension fail to address the reasons why students engage in bullying and may have a chilling effect on reporting by both students and adults (Limber, 2010; Stopbullying.gov, 2012). Furthermore, harshly exclusionary disciplinary policies have been found to contribute to the school-to-prison pipeline and to have a disproportionate impact on students of color, of low socioeconomic status, and with disabilities (Gonsoulin, Zablocki, & Leone, 2012; Osher, et al., 2012).

State policy makers can turn to a large body of research on effective bullying prevention and intervention practices (Nickerson et al., 2013). As outlined by Nickerson and colleagues (2013), schools need strong leadership committed to carrying out a comprehensive anti-bullying program. Anti-bullying programs begin with a clear and comprehensive anti-bullying policy that defines bullying; provides guidelines for staff, students, and parents in how to respond to bullying; and establishes consequences and interventions for those involved in bullying. Staff training is another essential ingredient, since studies have found that teachers often fail to identify bullying or do not intervene when they observe it. Schools also need to use evidence-based programs, guided by regular assessments of the prevalence of bullying and related aspects of school climate. Overall, bullying prevention relies fundamentally on establishing a school culture of mutual respect and acceptance, a structured and supportive climate that engenders positive peer relationships and healthy student development.

SYNTHESIS

General Conclusions

- There are many areas of overlap in prevention policies regarding suicide and bullying.
- Mental health services must be readily available in both school and community settings, and barriers to seeking services must be overcome.
- There is a need for routine collection of reliable information on the nature and prevalence of both bullying and suicide-related behavior in order to inform public policy and guide prevention and intervention efforts.

Suggestions

For Mental Health Providers

- Mental health providers should look for a history of peer victimization among suicidal youth and should be sensitive to possible suicidality among youth who are victims of bullying.

For Parents and Teachers

- Parents and teachers need education to increase their awareness of mental health problems and concerns associated with both bullying and suicide.
- Gatekeeper training can help parents and teachers improve their ability to identify mental health concerns that can lead to suicide.
- Schools must become more actively engaged in creating positive learning environments that prevent bullying and harassment.

For Policy Makers

- More public education is needed concerning the value of mental health services and school-based programs to address bullying as well as suicide risk.
- There is a need for greater emphasis on evidence-based practices, along with research to identify and improve those practices.
- Civil rights laws against discrimination protect some students from harassment in school, but broader policies are needed to protect all students.

REFERENCES

American Education Research Association (2013). *Prevention of Bullying in Schools, Colleges, and Universities: Research Report and Recommendations.* Washington, DC: American Educational Research Association.

American Foundation for Suicide Prevention (2013a). Anti-bullying and anti-cyberbullying policies. Retrieved from https://www.afsp.org/advocacy-public-policy/state-policy/anti-bullying-and-anti-cyberbullying-policies.

American Foundation for Suicide Prevention (2013b). State suicide prevention initiatives and plans. Retrieved from https://www.afsp.org/advocacy-public-policy/state-policy/state-suicide-prevention-initiatives-and-plans.

American Psychological Association Zero Tolerance Task Force (2008). Are zero tolerance policies effective in the schools? An evidentiary review and recommendations. *American Psychologist, 63*, 82–862.

Centers for Disease Control and Prevention (2013a). NDVRS: National Violent Death Reporting System. Retrieved from http://www.cdc.gov/violenceprevention/nvdrs/index.hmtl.

Centers for Disease Control and Prevention (2013b). WISQARS: Web-based Injury Statistics Query and Reporting System. Available at www.cdc.gov/injury/wisqars. Accessed June 30th, 2013.

Cornell, D., & Cole, J. (2011). Assessment of bullying. In S. R. Jimerson, A. B. Nickerson, M. J. Mayer, & M. J. Furlong (Eds.), *The Handbook of School Violence and School Safety: International Research and Practice* (2nd ed., pp. 289–303). Mahwah, NJ: Routledge.

Dahlberg, L. L., Toal, S. B., Swahn, M., & Behrens, C. B. (2005). *Measuring Violence Related Attitudes, Behaviors, and Influences Among Youths: A Compendium of Assessment Tools (2nd ed.).* Atlanta, GA: Centers for Disease Control and Prevention, National Center for Injury Prevention and Control.

Davis v. Monroe County Board of Education, 526 U.S. 629 (1999).

Durlak, J. A., Weissberg, R. P., Dymnicki, A. B., Taylor, R. D., & Schellinger, K. B. (2011). The impact of enhancing students' social and emotional learning: A meta-analysis of school-based universal interventions. *Child Development, 82*(1), 405–432. doi: 10.21111/j.1467-8624.2010.01564.x

"Education Department hosts third annual bullying prevention summit" (2012). C-Span. Retrieved from http://www.c-span.org/Events/Education-Dept-Hosts-Third-Annual-Bullying-Prevention-Summit/10737432871/.

Feldman Hertz, M., Donato, I., & Wright, J. (2013). Bullying and suicide: A public health approach (editorial). *Journal of Adolescent Health, 53*, S1–S3. doi: 10.1016/j.jadohealth.2013.05.002

General Accounting Office (2012). School bullying: Extent of legal protections for vulnerable groups needs to be more fully assessed. Retrieved from http://www.gao.gov/products/GAO-12-785T.

Goldrick, L. (2005). Youth suicide prevention: Strengthening state policies and school-based strategies. Retrieved from National Governors Association Center for Best Practices: http://www.nga.org/files/live/sites/NGA/files/pdf/0504SUICIDEPREVENTION.pdf.

Gonsoulin, S., Zabkocki, M., & Leone, P. (2012). Safe schools, staff development, and the school-to-prison pipeline. *Teacher Education and Special Education: The Journal of the Teacher Education Division of the Council for Exceptional Children, 35*(4), 309–319. doi: 10.1177/0888406412453470

Goodemann, C., Zammitt, K. A., & Hagedorn, M. (2012). The wolf in sheep's clothing: Student harassment veiled as bullying. *Children & Schools, 34*(2), 124–127.

Greenberg, M. T., Weissberg, R. P., O'Brien, M. U., Zins, J. E., Fredericks, L., Resnik, H., & Elias, M. J. (2003). Enhancing school-based prevention and youth development through coordinated social, emotional, and academic learning. *American Psychologist, 58*(6/7), 466–474. doi: 10.1037/0003-066X.58.6-7.466

Guild, P. A., Freeman, V. A., & Shanahan, E. (2004). *Promising Practices to Prevent Adolescent Suicide: What We Can Learn from New Jersey.* University of North Carolina at Chapel Hill, Cecil G. Sheps Center for Health Services Research.

Hatzenbuehler, M. L., & Keyes, K. M. (2013). Inclusive anti-bullying policies and reduced risk of suicide attempts in lesbian and gay youth. *Journal of Adolescent Health, 53,* S21–S26. doi: 10.1016/j.jadohealth.2012.08.010

Hatzenbuehler, M. L., Keyes, K. M., & Hasin, D. S. (2009). State-level policies and psychiatric morbidity in lesbian, gay, and bisexual populations. *American Journal of Public Health, 99,* 2275–2281. doi: 10.2105/AJPH.2008.153510

Isaac, M., Elias, B., Katz, L. Y., Belik, S., Deane, F. P. (2009). Gatekeeper training as a preventative intervention for suicide: A systematic review. *Canadian Journal of Psychiatry—Revue Canadienne de Psychiatrie, 54,* 260–268.

Keller, D. P., Schut, L. J., Puddy, R. W., Williams, L., Stephens, R. L., McKeon, R., & Lubell, K. (2009). Tennessee Lives Count: Statewide gatekeeper training for youth suicide prevention. *Professional Psychology: Research and Practice, 40,* 126–133. doi: 10.1037/10014889.

Kim, A. (2013, June 28). Departments of Education and Justice to collect data about LGBT student experiences. Robert F. Kennedy Center for Justice and Human Rights. Retrieved from http://bullying.rfkcenter.org/2013/06/28/depts-of-education-and-justice-to-collect-data-about-lgbt-student-experiences/.

Limber, S. P. (2010). Implementation of the Olweus Bullying Prevention Program: Lessons learned from the field. In D. Espelage & S. Swearer (Eds.), *Bullying in North American Schools: A Social-Ecological Perspective on Prevention and Intervention* (2nd ed., pp. 291–306). New York: Routledge.

Lubin, G., Werbeloff, N., Halperin, D., Shmushkevitch, M., Weiser, M., & Knobler, H. Y. (2010). Decrease in suicide rates after a change in policy reducing access to firearms in adolescents: A naturalistic epidemiological study. *Suicide and Life-Threatening Behavior, 40,* 421–424. doi: 10.1521/suli.2010.40.5.421

Maine Department of Health and Human Services (2013). Maine Suicide Prevention Program. Retrieved from http://www.maine.gov/suicide/index.htm.

New Jersey Department of Children and Families (DCF)- Division of Child Behavioral Health Services (n.d.). New Jersey Youth Suicide Prevention Plan, 2011–2014. Retrieved from: http://www.state.nj.us/dcf/documents/behavioral/prevention/preventionplan.pdf

Nickerson, A., Cornell, D., Smith, D., & Furlong, M. (2013). School anti-bullying efforts: Advice for education policymakers. *Journal of School Violence, 12,* 268–282. doi: 10.1080/15388220.2013.787366

Osher, D., Coggshall, J., Colombi, G., Woodruff, D., Francois, S., & Osher, T. (2012). Building school and teacher capacity to eliminate the school-to-prison pipeline. *Teacher Education and Special Education: The Journal of the Teacher Education Division of the Council for Exceptional Children, 35,* 284–295.

Reis, C., & Cornell, D. (2008). An evaluation of suicide gatekeeper training for school counselors and teachers. *Professional School Counseling, 11,* 386–394. doi: 10.5330/PSC.n.2010-11.386

QPR Institute (2013). QPR gatekeeper training for suicide prevention listed in the National Registry of Evidence-Based Practices and Policies. Retrieved from http://www.qprinstitute.com/.

Sacco, D. T., Silbaugh, K., Corredor, F., Casey, J., & Dohert, D. (2012). An overview of state anti-bullying legislation and other related laws. Retrieved August 19, 2012, from http://cyber.law.harvard.edu/sites/cyber.law.harvard.edu/files/State_Anti_bullying_Legislation_Overview_0.pdf.

Stopbullying.gov (2012). Misdirections in bullying prevention and intervention. Retrieved from http://www.stopbullying.gov/prevention/at-school/educate/misdirections-in-prevention.pdf.

Suicide Prevention Resource Center (2013). Comparison table of suicide prevention gatekeeper training programs. Retrieved from http://www.sprc.org/library_resources/items/comparison-table-suicide-prevention-gatekeeper-training-programs.

U.S. Department of Education (2011, June 14). Open letter releasing the legal guidelines regarding the Equal Access Act and recognition of student-led non-curricular groups. Retrieved from: http://www2.ed.gov/policy/gen/guid/secletter/index.html?src=rt.

U.S. Department of Education, Office for Civil Rights, (2010, October 26). Dear Colleague letter: Harassment and bullying. Retrieved from http://www2.ed.gov/about/offices/list/ocr/letters/colleague-201010.html.

U.S. Department of Education (2013, June). *Federal Partners in Bullying Prevention Efforts Summary.* Washington, DC: Office of Safe and Healthy Students.

U.S. Department of Education, Office for Civil Rights (2011, April 4). Dear Colleague letter: Sexual violence. Retrieved from http://www2.ed.gov/about/offices/list/ocr/letters/colleague-201104.pdf.

U.S. Department of Education, Office for Civil Rights (2013, August 29). Civil rights data collection. Retrieved from http://www2.ed.gov/about/offices/list/ocr/data.html.

U.S. Department of Health and Human Services (HHS), Office of the Surgeon General, and National Action Alliance for Suicide Prevention. *2012 National Strategy for Suicide Prevention: Goals and Objectives for Action.* Washington, DC: HHS, September 2012.

U.S. Public Health Service (1999). The Surgeon General's call to action to prevent suicide. Washington, DC. Online at http://profiles.nlm.nih.gov/ps/access/NNBBBH.pdf.

Waldvogel, J. L., Reuter, M., & Oberg, C. N. (2008). Adolescent suicide: Risk factors and prevention strategies. *Current Problems in Pediatric and Adolescent Health Care, 38*(4), 110–125. doi: 10.1016/j.cppeds.2008.01.003

Yudin, M. (2013). Keeping students with disabilities safe from bullying. Official Blog of the U.S. Department of Education. Retrieved from http://www.ed.gov/blog/2013/08/keeping-students-with-disabilities-safe-from-bullying/.

22

Bullying, Suicide, and the Media

WHITNEY BLISS, SAMANTHA PFLUM, LAURA SCIACCA, AND PETER GOLDBLUM ■

When exploring the role of mass media in bullying and suicide, it is important to make the distinction between the ways in which the term "mass media" is used. It is often a term used to describe journalistic media, which convey news through television, radio, print, and digital media forms. It can also be used to describe the various modes for delivering messages to wide audiences (Potter, 2013). Given these dual definitions, this chapter addresses the role of both in the prevention of bullying and suicide. The first section explores the way that the mass media—particularly journalistic media—influence perceptions and behaviors related to bullying and suicide. The second section examines how bullying and suicide prevention programs and campaigns have used various forms of media to reach audiences at different levels of the ecological systems model. The chapter concludes with recommendations for how to maximize mass media's role in the prevention of bullying and suicide.

MASS MEDIA'S PLACE IN THE ECOLOGICAL SYSTEMS MODEL

In Bronfenbrenner's (1977) conception of the ecological systems model of development, mass media were placed in the "exosystem." By his definition, the exosystem influences contexts and key players in the individual's life but does not interact with the individual directly. Mass media fit well in this layer of the model, as they may exert influence on an individual's parents, school system, or the regulations that govern these elements in a child's life. As a component of the exosystem, mass media also permeate the macrosystem to influence national culture and policy.

One element of mass media that muddles its place in the ecological systems model is the fact that they are directly "consumed" by the individual. While the relationship between mass media and individual is not yet sufficiently complex and interactive to warrant media's placement in the "microsystem," the emergence of Internet-based media has eroded the previously unidirectional influence of print and television-based mass media. The Internet has created an environment hospitable to participatory media, which is marked by decreased reliance on corporate news outlets, greater opportunities for citizen journalism, and an overall increase in opportunities for individual interactivity with media (Bowman & Willis, 2003). The line between mass media and consumer has also been blurred by corporate news media's foray into social media networks such as Twitter and Facebook. This increase in the complexity and ease of interaction between the individual and the media suggests that media's current place in the exosystem may not be as well defined as originally conceived by Bronfenbrenner in 1977.

NEWS MEDIA AND SUICIDE

Journalists' handling of suicide events is a subject that has received significant attention from researchers, and for good reason. Pirkis and Blood (2001) conducted an analysis of 42 studies examining the influence of nonfiction accounts of suicide in newspapers, on television, and in books on subsequent completed suicides. From this analysis, they made a compelling argument for a causal effect of suicide reporting on increases in suicide deaths. This argument was based on factors such as consistency of such patterns, the temporal logic tying such reports to proximate increases in suicide rates, and a "dose–response" effect between the frequency of reporting on a suicide and notable increases in numbers of deaths (Pirkis & Blood, 2001). Other researchers have also noted significant links between reporting of suicide and subsequent increases in suicidal acts (see Stack, 2005, for a review). Of particular relevance are the connections between suicide reporting and activation of suicidality in youth, a population that is especially susceptible to such media influence (Gould, Jamieson, & Romer, 2003).

These well-documented associations have necessitated the formulation of journalistic guidelines for reporting on suicide. One of the most comprehensive guidelines, *Recommendations for Reporting on Suicide* (2012), comes from collaboration between the American Association of Suicidology, the Centers for Disease Control, and other public health, suicide prevention, and media organizations and institutions. The stated objective of these guidelines, which were based on a review of over 20 studies of media effects on suicide, is the avoidance of suicide "contagion" (or "copycat suicides"). The guidelines define suicide contagion as "when one or more suicides are reported in a way that contributes to another suicide" (American Association of Suicidology et al., p. 1). The authors do not specify if this guidance is meant to address adult or youth suicide in particular; rather, they refer to the need to protect "vulnerable populations" (p. 1).

The primary goal of these guidelines is to avoid the sensationalizing of reports regarding suicide. Sensationalizing a story may include headlines featuring the means of death or descriptions of the suicide rate using charged language such as "skyrocketing." The guidelines also recommend against overemphasis on the mourning process (e.g., publication of photos of memorial services). They also suggest treating suicide as a public health problem rather than a crime. This can be accomplished by highlighting the complexity of suicide and its relationship to mental illness rather than attributing it to a single cause such as a personal failure. In addition, the guidelines promote the incorporation of stories of individuals who had suicidal crises but successfully received help. Finally, the guidance calls for the inclusion of information on suicide resources (such as crisis numbers and treatment options) as well as a list of common indicators of suicidality (e.g., talk about hopelessness, burdensomeness, or wanting to die).

Though these recommendations were based on research and written in collaboration with media and journalistic organizations, preliminary evidence suggests these guidelines have not consistently been followed. One study, by Tatum, Canetto, and Slater (2010), investigated U.S. newspapers' adherence to an earlier iteration of these guidelines in the two years following their release. While only 19% of stories included an image deemed "inappropriate," over half detailed the method and location, and fewer than 7% reported on warning signs of suicide, risk factors, depression, or resources for prevention and treatment (Tatum, Canetto, & Slater, 2010). In a more comprehensive review of studies investigating suicide reporting and subsequent changes in suicide rates, Bohanna and Wang (2012) found several instances of responsible reporting corresponding with reductions in suicide rates. However, they also found significant variance in the degree to which different countries adhered to these guidelines, as well as a widespread lack of knowledge of national and international suicide-reporting guidelines among journalists.

There has also been concern about the effectiveness of these recommendations in the Internet age. Gunn and Lester (2012) expressed concern that the great number of hits available for Internet searches on suicide makes it nearly impossible to avoid the effects of repetitive reporting. They also suggested that the ease of online communication could create an environment that is well suited to near-instant glorification of suicide. For example, a high-profile teen suicide could compel a flurry of celebrity condolence tweets, which may be strongly activating to other suicidal teens already feeling alone and unloved. The authors also noted the potential for online news media to provide equally swift access to helping resources, though they commented that many online news sources do not currently provide these resources. These concerns and recommendations were also echoed by *Recommendations for Reporting on Suicide* (2012), with additional suggestions for managing social media issues such as negative commenting on Facebook memorial pages.

NEWS MEDIA AND BULLYING

Compared to the robust literature investigating mass media reporting on suicide, there has been a relative dearth of literature exploring mass media's coverage of bullying incidents. Despite an absence of analyses of bullying-related news stories in the general youth population, increased reporting has been observed regarding youth bullying and suicide in the lesbian, gay, bisexual, transgender, and queer (LGBTQ) community. Sciacca and colleagues (2011) conducted an analysis of 403 news reports from 2003 to 2011 and found a surge in reporting on this subject in 2010, which coincided with the suicide death of several gay-identified adolescents and young adults, including college student Tyler Clementi. This upward reporting trend was mostly focused on Clementi and a handful of other high-profile suicide deaths, suggesting that the increase in articles was due to an increase of media attention on several individuals rather than an increase LGBTQ bullying-related suicides. Actual rates of completed suicides in the LGBTQ community have been difficult to ascertain, due in part to the infrequency of inquiry into sexual orientation in psychological autopsies following suicide (van Heeringen & Vincke, 2000).

Given the interest in media coverage of bullying and suicide and the potential for negative outcomes similar to those found in irresponsible reporting on suicide, the United States Department of Health and Human Services (DHHS) convened a task force to address the topic of bullying coverage in the news media (DHHS, 2013a). This group compiled a list of best practices for reporting on bullying. Some of these best practices include guidance like that in the suicide-reporting recommendations discussed previously, such as relying on knowledgeable sources, balancing tragic stories with stories of hope, providing information on helping resources such as crisis lines, and conceptualizing bullying as a complex public health problem. Other guidance is more specific to bullying, such as ensuring that this descriptor is being used in accordance with the government's definition, which inherently excludes adults. This is intended to eliminate overuse of the term "bullying" to refer to adult behaviors such as workplace abuse.

DHHS (2013a) also provided a list of practices to avoid, including not overstating the problem of bullying and avoidance of terms such as "epidemic." DHHS cautions against this overstatement because of its potential to normalize bullying, which may reduce attempts to stop the behavior. Another possible overstatement the guidelines warn against is the link between bullying and suicide. Many media reports do not take the time to describe the complex relationship between bullying and suicide and instead portray bullying as the sole cause of suicide. This may normalize suicide as a response to bullying, which could lead to suicide contagion in the wake of such reporting. Another potential reporting pitfall is either the invisibility or mischaracterization of the individual who perpetrated the bullying. There is concern about bullies being portrayed as "murderers" in the event that a bullying victim dies by suicide. Such an outcome might lead to criminal investigations, civil lawsuits, and other impediments to dialogue and healing for the community, the family of the victim, and the bully and their loved ones.

The Robert F. Kennedy Center for Justice and Human Rights' Project SEATBELT (2013), an evidence-based, multisystem bullying prevention and intervention program, also set forth specific guidelines for responsible reporting of bullying. Using the argument that media set a tone of normalcy and can influence youth, parent, and community behavior, many of their recommendations echo the guidelines by the DHHS (2013a). However, Project SEATBELT guidelines also caution against overly associating bullying and school violence (e.g., school shootings). Project SEATBELT warns that oversimplified connections between being a victim and perpetrating violence against others may give the impression that such violence is a normal response to being bullied. This oversimplified connection between bullying and youth violence may also be connected to the expectation of memorialization or notoriety. The organization also suggests that the media take steps to report on positive outcomes, such as former bullies who have stopped violent behavior and peers who have successfully intervened.

USE OF MASS MEDIA IN PREVENTION PROGRAMS

Despite aforementioned concerns regarding traditional coverage of suicide and bullying events, mass media can also serve as a vehicle for widespread sharing of valuable information through prevention and intervention programs. Considering the technology utilization of many youth today, the Internet could be an especially effective medium for delivering suicide and bullying prevention messages and helping services. Before we examine select programs that have incorporated mass media in various ways, a discussion of prevention and intervention communications classification can assist in understanding the different ways in which media efforts work to reduce bullying and suicide.

Health Promotion Using an Ecological Systems Model

In 2010, a Centers for Disease Control (CDC) panel of experts on bullying and suicide determined that bullying and suicide are both public health problems and would probably be responsive to public health prevention and intervention approaches (Hertz, Donato, & Wright, 2013). One method of exploring ways that mass media can help prevent bullying and suicide is to view health promotion in an ecological fashion. McLeroy and colleagues (1988) proposed a health promotion model that describes communications delivered at five different levels: intrapersonal, interpersonal, institutional, community, and policy. Intrapersonal health promotion involves efforts that directly target the individual, with the purpose of inciting changes in the individual's knowledge, skills, and attitudes. Interpersonal-level health promotion focuses on central figures in an individual's life, with the goal of influencing the individual through their interactions with these figures. Institutional-level health promotion aims to influence the individual by addressing the organizations in which they are embedded. Community-level health promotion works through the multiple community agencies and organizations that collectively interact with the individual and with each other. Finally, policy-level health promotion is intended to influence regulations, procedures, and laws, which create effects that trickle down to the individual through all other layers of the ecological system (see Table 22.1).

Table 22.1. Individual Impacts of Ecological Levels

Ecological Level	**Impacts Individual Through...**
Intrapersonal	Direct contact
Interpersonal	Social influence from friends, family, peers, teachers, etc.
Institutional	Institutional influence (work and school policies, promotions, environments)
Community	Community (houses of worship, neighborhoods, and other organized groups)
Policy	Laws and regulations that govern the nation, states, communities, and institutions

Using the health promotion avenues described above (McLeroy et al., 1988), it is possible to investigate and categorize current suicide and bullying prevention program media usage. The process of categorization is not only helpful for clarifying what audiences are being accessed and what mode of prevention the messaging is serving; the process also assists in identifying areas where further media efforts could be directed. Although it is outside of the scope of this chapter to analyze all major bullying and suicide prevention programs, several different types of programs and campaigns will be examined in order to highlight the variety of media that can be used to influence behavior related to bullying and suicide.

Bullying Prevention Programs

In addition to providing the media guidelines described above, the DHHS has also developed a comprehensive suicide prevention campaign, hosted at Stopbullying.gov. DHHS uses its website to provide bullying prevention information at several different levels of the ecological model (DHHS, 2013b). The website's "How to Talk About Bullying" section targets parents, school personnel, and other adults at the interpersonal health promotion level. Specific suggestions include guidelines for talking to kids about bullying, methods for teaching them what bullying is, and strategies for fostering resiliency by connecting youth with hobbies and other sources of social support outside of school. The website also provides tools for school administrators to assess bullying in their school, shape anti-bullying policies, educate staff, and enhance overall school safety. These tools can assist both bullied and peer bystander children at the organizational level. In addition, Stopbullying.gov provides guidance for mobilizing partnerships among related organizations, promoting health at the community level.

Another branch of StopBullying.gov's campaign is its partnership with the Ad Council to produce and distribute several television and print public service announcements (PSAs) related to bullying (Ad Council, 2013). The 30-second televised PSAs target parents and encourage them to visit Stopbullying.gov to learn more about helping their children be "more than a bystander." The print PSA also targets parents and encourages them to teach their children about peer intervention. In terms of the ecological systems model of health promotion, this type of advertising targets individual change—in this case, the potential peer intervener—through interpersonal interactions with parents.

Interestingly, the Ad Council's website for their bullying prevention campaign not only links parents to Stopbullying.gov, but also directs them to The Bully Project (www.thebullyproject.com), an anti-bullying education campaign affiliated with the 2011 film *Bully.* In addition to catapulting the creation of The Bully Project, however, the film also garnered criticism for its oversimplification of links between bullying and suicide. Specifically, one of the film's focal bullying victims, Tyler Long, had a mental health history that included diagnoses of bipolar disorder, Asperger's disorder, and attention-deficit hyperactivity disorder (Bazelon, 2012). None of these diagnoses was mentioned in the film as a possible contributor to his suicide (Lowen, Hirsch, Waitt, Warren, & Hirsch, 2011). The Ad Council's decision to direct consumers to the homepage of a film that, by DHHS's guidelines, does not conform to responsible representation of bullying, is an example of some of the difficulties that are inherent in balancing responsible representations of bullying and suicide with a desire to tell a story that is appealing to an audience.

A disproportionate focus on consumer appeal over evidence-based prevention has also manifested in other bullying prevention campaigns. One example of this is the website STOMP Out Bullying (http://www.stompoutbullying.org). The website features a variety of celebrity PSAs encouraging kids to "stomp out bullying." The celebrities repeat messages of how important it is to "stomp out bullying," along with advice about treating others with kindness and honoring differences. Fewer than half of the internal links on the website are related to the actual prevention of bullying, however, such as education about bullying or ways to reduce bullying, while the other internal links are devoted to the foundation, promotion, and funding of the STOMP Out Bullying campaign itself. In addition, the information that is provided on bullying does not include references or clear indications that the campaign is based on evidence-based prevention models. One especially questionable segment of the website is entitled "Are you a bully?" (STOMP Out Bullying, 2013). The page offers a quiz to tell the user if they are a bully and baits these users with the prospect of being "cool" if they cease being a bully. The page implores these accused bullies to think about the cruel things they have done and then "tell a trusted adult." Both beneficial and harmful effects of this campaign and others like it are difficult to determine because of ill-defined program implementation protocols and no clear plan for outcome evaluation.

A primary problem with media campaigns, especially those that target multiple ecological systems, is their inability to evaluate their precise impact. However, preliminary evidence indicates that the utilization of certain kinds of media can influence both student perceptions of bullying as well as bullying behaviors themselves. One example of this is the BeatBullying model, which has been used in the United Kingdom (The BeatBullying Group, no date). The primary feature of the model is a peer mentor system that includes face-to-face meetings at school and online chats through the BeatBullying website. The website also includes adult counselors who mentor, supervise, and provide assistance for more serious problems. An evaluation of this program found that both bullying behaviors and perceptions of bullying went down significantly after BeatBullying's implementation, and the online mentoring in particular was praised for providing a confidential space for students to share their struggles (Banerjee, Robinson, & Smalley, no date).

Although BeatBullying's successful implementation of online mentoring suggests an advantage to utilizing Internet-based services in youth bullying prevention efforts, more traditional forms of media have also proven effective in positively modifying bullying attitudes and behaviors. One study, by Perkins, Craig, and Perkins (2011), investigated the ability of a poster-based social norms campaign to change students' perceptions of bullying, as well as acts of bullying. The messaging on posters was based on a survey of the students on bullying attitudes and behaviors and made statements such as "4 out of 5 students do not spread rumors about other students." In this pre-post design, researchers discovered that the social norms messaging was associated with decreased reports of bullying perpetration and victimization as well as reductions in perceived prevalence of bullying. It is difficult to determine if these findings are largely due to the specific intervention or the power of media to influence behavior. However, these results do suggest that individual-level health messaging using poster-based media can be effective in reducing bullying. Importantly, this study also surveyed students on how often they saw the posters. Perkins and colleagues (2011) found that greater reported exposure to the posters was associated with reduced perceptions of bullying and decreases in bullying behaviors.

Suicide Prevention Programs

Internet-based digital media, such as social networks, have received much attention for their role in the advent and evolution of cyber-bullying (see Chapter 7 of this volume). However, many organizations are taking advantage of youth's connectedness to such media forms in order to reach out to individuals who are vulnerable to suicide. One prime example is the National Suicide Prevention Lifeline (NSPL), a federal suicide prevention effort run by the U.S. Substance Abuse and Mental Health Services Administration (SAMHSA, n.d.a). The NSPL may be best known for its suicide prevention hotline, 1-800-273-TALK, but it has made a significant foray into online digital media as well. The NSPL primarily targets intrapersonal and interpersonal levels of influence and also has special prevention efforts aimed at youth.

The NSPL website features a variety of methods to encourage help-seeking. In addition to the telephone hotline, users in crisis can chat online via text with a volunteer. For those who may be reluctant to utilize crisis-intervention services, there is also a gallery of YouTube videos where individuals talk about their reasons for contacting the crisis line. This is particularly important because it can reassure potential users that the services are not only for those who are acutely suicidal. The website also provides information for individuals who are concerned about a friend or loved one, including how to report suicidal messages on Facebook, Twitter, and other social media networks. The site even gives users the opportunity to send an e-card to someone who may be struggling with life difficulties, suicidality, and/or grief. NSPL also has made efforts to specifically target youth in crisis, creating a young adult–oriented sister page called "You Matter" (SAMHSA, n.d.b). In addition to providing access to the crisis line, this page features a blog written by young adults for young adults that features information about resiliency, coping, help-seeking, and supporting struggling friends. It also provides individuals with links to the "You Matter" campaign via social media like Facebook and Twitter. Although not all aspects of NSPL's multifaceted suicide prevention efforts have been studied, there is evidence that suicide crisis hotlines are effective in reducing hopelessness, intent to die, and psychological anguish in suicidal callers (Gould, Kalafat, HarrisMunfakh, & Kleinman, 2007). Preliminary research has also indicated that text-based suicide intervention is effective in increasing youth help-seeking behavior (Evans, Davidson, & Sicafuse, 2013). One strength of the NSPL's website is that its pages consistently refer the user to the crisis line and to its synchronous text-based crisis services, creating a relatively closed system free of distracting external links that could derail help-seeking intentions.

The NSPL is geared toward a wide range of individuals in crisis, from youth to older adults. However, there are other suicide prevention programs and campaigns that focus primarily on youth and, in particular, on sexual and gender minorities. Research indicates these populations are at increased risk for suicidal ideation and behavior compared to non-gender and sexual minorities (Fitzpatrick, Euton, Jones, & Schmidt, 2005; Silenzio, Pena, Duberstein, Cerel, & Knox, 2007). In response to this disproportionate risk, the Trevor Project serves as the nation's only suicide prevention crisis service intended solely for sexual and gender minorities from ages 13–24 (The Trevor Project, 2013). As a youth-oriented program, the Trevor Project has capitalized on the use of both traditional and digital forms of media, including the crisis phone line, online crisis chat, crisis intervention via text message, as well as a social networking service for gender and sexual minorities and their allies. In addition to these individually directed services, the Trevor Project also offers education and resource kits for adults, which helps them access the individual youth at the interpersonal level through their interactions with teachers, parents, and other adult mentors. Although program evaluation for the Trevor Project is not readily available online or in the scientific literature, it uses many of the same demonstrated-effective crisis intervention media forms as the NSPL.

Though much attention has been given to Internet-based prevention campaigns using digital media, there is also evidence to suggest that youth suicide prevention campaigns using more traditional media can have positive effects on community health. One example of such an effort was the Louisiana Partnership for Youth Suicide Prevention (LPYSP) media campaign that ran from 2007 to 2008. Jenner, Woodward Jenner, Matthews-Sterling, Butts, and Williams (2010) investigated whether the media campaign translated into increased usage of the NSPL. The campaign was composed of billboards, bus boards, newspaper ads, radio PSAs, and movie theater PSAs, which contained the message "If you or someone you know is suicidal, call 1-800-273-TALK." This type of message was aimed at suicidal youth, both directly and through interpersonal interactions with concerned peers, parents, teachers, or caring adults. With the exception of the radio PSA, Jenner and colleagues (2010) found that all modalities contributed separately and significantly to the amount of calls received by the hotline. However, it was unclear whether increases in service usage were a result of individuals' responding to the messaging or because another concerned individual persuaded them to call after witnessing the messaging. Additionally, there is uncertainty as to whether increased calling was from at-risk youth or from adults, though the researchers did find that the youth-targeted movie theater PSA had the strongest unique effect on help-seeking behaviors (Jenner et al., 2010).

Summary and Limitations

The bullying and suicide prevention campaigns highlighted in this chapter represent only a small sample of the many programs attempting to reach vulnerable individuals within different ecological systems. Most intervention efforts appeared to use an intrapersonal approach to public health awareness by directly targeting the affected individual. Also common were efforts aimed at individuals in the youth's microsystem, such as peers, friends, parents, and teachers. Other layers of the ecosystem, such as the meso-, exo-, and macrosystems, were often not the direct targets of prevention and intervention campaigns, though several major prevention organizations such as the American Foundation for Suicide Prevention (www.afsp.org/advocacy-public-policy) and the Trevor Project (www.thetrevorproject.

org/section/advocacy-landing-page) provide avenues for individuals to learn about ways they can influence local, state, and federal levels of policy. In this sense, the media tools in these prevention campaigns may indirectly affect meso-, exo-, and macrosystems through bottom-up activation of at-risk individuals and their friends, families, teachers, and other loved ones.

Although there is a strong theoretical and empirical basis for the importance of targeting different levels of an individual's social-ecological system (see Chapter 25 of this volume), the current literature has not afforded empirical examinations of exactly how these multilevel media efforts affect the individual. For example, in a campaign that targets both inter- and intrapersonal levels, how can an agency know whether the desired outcome was obtained by their message impacting the individual or impacting someone else in that person's microsystem? Given the complexity of the nested ecological system, particularly ones that expand beyond the microsystem, it would seem that such research might be dauntingly complex. Therefore, in lieu of an in-depth, empirical understanding of how media campaigns and prevention efforts filter through the layers of the ecological system, it will continue to be important for prevention programs to rely on theoretical knowledge to inform future utilization of media.

Despite the relative scarcity of media campaign program evaluations, particularly ones that assess how messaging translates into program utilization, this should not discourage organizations from attempting to understand the ways that health promotion communications affect outcomes. Campaign effects should focus, not only on changes in behavior and attitudes (e.g., Banerjee et al., n.d.; Jenner et al., 2010) but also on the mechanisms that facilitated these changes (e.g., seeing a poster, participating in a training, using a particular crisis service mode such as telephone, text, or chat). Attention paid to these processes would not only benefit future program efforts but would also benefit public health communications as a field.

SUGGESTIONS

Parents and Educators

- When selecting bullying and/or suicide prevention programs for school use, ensure that the program is evidence-based. If this information cannot be found on the program's website or other materials, contact the organization directly.
- Choose programs that operate on multiple levels of an individual's socio-ecological system, such as those that direct prevention and intervention efforts at students, peers, parents, and educators.
- Teach youth about media literacy, including media's impact on attitudes and behaviors and the ways that social media, journalism, and advertising deliberately work to shape consumers.
- Introduce youth to safe helping websites that screen their social networking components to prevent vulnerable individuals from being exposed to activating content from other users.
- Introduce youth to helping services that have multiple, secure, confidential avenues of access. If an adolescent is reluctant to call a crisis phone line, they may be more willing to access crisis services through online chat or text.

Journalists and Editors

- Utilize evidence-based media guidelines for reporting of bullying and suicide.
- Create internal policies on the reporting of these events based on the published guidelines.
- Editors should facilitate discussion of responsible reporting among staff, including the challenges of balancing consumer safety with the need to deliver engaging content.

Media Consumers

- Support news outlets that adhere to responsible reporting of suicide and bullying.
- Be aware that not every bullying and suicide program/campaign is backed by research. Some campaigns rely heavily on celebrity endorsements and merchandising but provide little evidence-based content.

REFERENCES

Ad Council (2013). Bullying prevention. Retrieved November 2, 2013, from http://www.adcouncil.org/Our-Work/Current-Work/Safety/Bullying-Prevention.

American Association of Suicidology, American Foundation for Suicide Prevention, Annenberg Public Policy Center, Canterbury Suicide Project—University of Otago, Columbia University Department of Psychiatry, ConnectSafely.org, . . . UCLA School of Public Health (2012). *Recommendations for Reporting on Suicide*. Retrieved October 10, 2013, from http://reportingonsuicide.org/Recommendations2012.pdf.

Banerjee, R., Robinson, C., & Smalley, D. (n.d.). Evaluation of the Beatbullying [*sic*] Peer Mentoring Programme. Retrieved October 10, 2013, from http://www.sussex.ac.uk/Users/robinb/bbreportsummary.pdf.

Bazelon, E. (2012, March 29). The problem with "Bully." *Slate*. Retrieved October 15, 2013, from http://www.slate.com/articles/news_and_politics/bulle/2012/03/bully_documentary_lee_hirsch_s_film_dangerously_oversimplifies_the_connection_between_bullying_and_suicide_.html.

Bowman, S., & Willis, C. (2003). We media: How audiences are shaping the future of news and information. The Media Center at the American Press Institute. Retrieved September 25, 2013, from http://www.hypergene.net/wemedia/download/we_media.pdf.

Bronfenbrenner, U. (1977). Toward an experimental ecology of human development. *American Psychologist, 32*(7), 513–531. doi: 10.1037/0003-066X.32.7.513

Evans, W. P., Davidson, L., & Sicafuse, L. (2013). Someone to listen: Increasing youth help-seeking behavior through a text-based crisis line for youth. *Journal of Community Psychology, 41*(4), 471–487. doi: 10.1002/jcop.21551

Fitzpatrick, K. K., Euton, S. J., Jones, J. N., & Schmidt, N. B. (2005). Gender role, sexual orientation and suicide risk. *Journal of Affective Disorders, 87*(1), 35–42. doi: 10.1016/j.jad.2005.02.020

Gould, M., Jamieson, P., & Romer, D. (2003). Media contagion and suicide among the young. *American Behavioral Scientist, 46*, 1269–1284. doi: 10.1177/0002764202250670

Gould, M. S., Kalafat, J., HarrisMunfakh, J. L., & Kleinman, M. (2007). An evaluation of crisis hotline outcomes part 2: Suicidal callers. *Suicide and Life-Threatening Behavior, 37*(3), 338–352. doi: 10.1521/suli.2007.37.3.338

Gunn, J. F. III, & Lester, D. (2012). Media guidelines in the Internet age. *Crisis: The Journal of Crisis Intervention and Suicide Prevention, 33*(4), 187–189. doi: 10.1027/0227-5910/a000171

Hertz, M. F., Donato, I., & Wright, J. (2013). Bullying and suicide: A public health approach. *Journal of Adolescent Health, 53*(1 Supp), S1–S3. doi: 10.1016/j.jadohealth.2013.05.002

Jenner, E., Woodward Jenner, L., Matthews-Sterling, M., Butts, J. K., & Williams, T. E. (2010). Awareness effects of a youth suicide prevention media campaign in Louisiana. *Suicide and Life-Threatening Behavior, 40*(4), 394–406. doi: 10.1521/suli.2010.40.4.394

Lowen, C., Hirsch, L., Waitt, C., & Warren, N. (producers); & Hirsch, L. (director) (2011). *Bully* [motion picture]. New York: The Weinstein Company.

McLeroy, K. R., Bibeau, D., Steckler, A., & Glanz, K. (1988). An ecological perspective on health promotion programs. *Health Education & Behavior, 15*(4), 351–377. doi: 10.1177/109019818801500401

Perkins, H., W., Craig, D. W., & Perkins, J. M. (2011). Using social norms to reduce bullying: A research intervention among adolescents in five middle schools. *Group Processes & Intergroup Relations, 14*(5), 703–722. doi: 10.1177/1368430210398004.

Pirkis, J., & Blood, R. W. (2001). Suicide and the media: Part I. Reportage in nonfictional media. *Crisis: The Journal of Crisis Intervention and Suicide Prevention, 22*(4), 146–154. doi: 10.1027//0227-5910.22.4.146

Potter, W. J. (2013). Synthesizing a working definition of “mass” media. *Review of Communications Research, 1*(1), 1–30. Retrieved September 29, 2013, from http://www.rcommunicationr.org/

Robert F. Kennedy Center for Justice and Human Rights (2013). Why media matters. Retrieved October 3, 2013, from http://bullying.rfkcenter.org/wp content/uploads/2013/07/ RFK_Seatbelt_WhyMediaMatters.pdf.

Sciacca, L. M., Jimenez, C., Wang, F., Pflum, S., Joseph, K., & Testa, R. (2011, August). Recent media accounts of LGBT suicides due to bullying: New trend or old news. Paper presented as part of a symposium entitled “Exploring the Link Between Bullying and Suicide,” 119th Annual American Psychological Association Convention, August 4–11, 2011, Washington, DC.

Silenzio, V. M. B., Pena, J. B., Duberstein, P. R., Cerel, J., & Knox, K. L. (2007). Sexual orientation and risk factors for suicidal ideation and suicide attempts among adolescents and young adults. *American Journal of Public Health, 97*(11), 2017–2019. doi: 10.2105/AJPH.2006.095943

Stack, S. (2005). Suicide in the media: A quantitative review of studies based on nonfictional stories. *Suicide and Life-Threatening Behavior, 35*(2), 121–133. doi: 10.1521/suli.35.2.121.62877

STOMP Out Bullying. (2013). Retrieved on October 25, 2013 from http://www.stompoutbullying.org on

Tatum, P. T., Canetto, S. S., & Slater, M. D. (2010). Suicide coverage in U.S. newspapers following the publication of the media guidelines. *Suicide and Life-Threatening Behavior, 40*(5), 524–534. doi: 10.1521/suli.2010.40.5.524

The BeatBullying Group (n.d.). BeatBullying: The model. Retrieved November 10, 2013, from http:// www.beatbullying.org/the-model/.

The Trevor Project (2013). Programs and services. Retrieved October 2, 2013, from http://www.thetrevorproject. org/pages/programs-services.

U.S. Department of Health and Human Services (2013a). Media guidelines for bullying prevention. Retrieved October 16, 2013, from http://www.stopbullying.gov/news/media/index.html.

U.S. Department of Health and Human Services (2013b). Prevent bullying. Retrieved October 16, 2013, from http://www.stopbullying.gov/prevention/index.html.

U.S. Substance Abuse and Mental Health Services Administration (n.d.a). National Suicide Prevention Lifeline. Retrieved October 6, 2013, from http://www.suicidepreventionlifeline.org/.

U.S. Substance Abuse and Mental Health Services Administration (n.d.b). You Matter. Retrieved October 14, 2013, from http://www.youmatter.suicidepreventionlifeline.org/.

van Heeringen, C., & Vincke, J. (2000). Suicidal acts and ideation in homosexual and bisexual young people: A study of prevalence and risk factors. *Social Psychiatry and Psychiatric Epidemiology, 35*(11), 494–499. doi: 10.1007/s001270050270

23

The Mental Health Consequences of Antibullying Policies

MARK L. HATZENBUEHLER, JENNIFER HIRSCH, RICHARD PARKER, CONSTANCE NATHANSON, AND AMY FAIRCHILD ■

Bullying has recently emerged in the public discourse as a problem that warrants a legal response. Within the last decade, there has been a proliferation of antibullying laws at both the school district and state levels (Limber & Small, 2003; Srabstein, Berkman, & Pyntikova, 2008; U.S. General Accounting Office, 2012). Already in 2007, 75% of public school students in the United States grew up in states that had antibullying policies (Srabstein et al., 2008). In addition, individuals have begun to initiate court cases against school districts whose policies are believed to harm students (e.g., *Doe* v. *Anoka-Hennepin School District No. 11* et al., 2011), such as schools' failure to adopt inclusive antibullying policies that protect lesbian, gay, bisexual, and transgender (LGBT) youths (e.g., *Pratt* v. *Indian River School District* et al., 2009). The topic of bullying has also received increased attention in the media (Bazelon, 2012; Scott, 2012), and several prominent organizations have begun to address the issue. Both the United Nations and the White House have convened conferences on bullying, and the Centers for Disease Control and Prevention held an expert panel in 2011 on bullying and suicide.

Despite the proliferation of antibullying policies, and the recognition that they may be effective in addressing bullying behaviors (Srabstein et al., 2008), there has been limited investigation of whether such policies do, in fact, reduce bullying and associated health problems, including suicide. In our chapter, we discuss this topic, with a particular focus on LGBT youth, where the empirical work on antibullying policies and mental health has largely been conducted.[1] As our review indicates, the available data raise more questions than they currently answer. Consequently, after discussing methodological challenges and reviewing the literature, we discuss multiple research gaps in an effort to motivate additional work in this area. We also advance the importance of an interdisciplinary, multi-method approach to the study of antibullying policies and mental health.

METHODOLOGICAL APPROACHES IN STUDYING THE MENTAL HEALTH CONSEQUENCES OF ANTIBULLYING POLICIES

We discuss four methodological approaches that can be used to evaluate the impact of antibullying policies on mental health. This is not meant to be an exhaustive list, but rather an introduction to common strategies used in quasi-experimental designs (for a more in-depth coverage, see Shadish, Cook, & Campbell, 2002).

Cross-Sectional Designs

In the first approach, researchers use cross-sectional designs to examine whether the presence of antibullying policies in schools is associated with a reduction in bullying and adverse mental health outcomes (e.g., suicide attempts). In these cross-sectional studies, there are two potential types of comparison studies. One type compares schools with and without antibullying policies within the same school district. One advantage of such a design is that it reduces confounding because schools within the same district are often (though certainly not always) comparable on observable and unobservable factors that may affect mental health outcomes (e.g., poverty rates). Another practical advantage is that these studies are easier to conduct than other designs because they typically cover a relatively small geographical area. However, such within-district comparison groups are rare; because antibullying policies are often implemented at the district level, there is no variation in the policy within districts. A second type of study is a between-jurisdiction comparison. In these studies, researchers compare jurisdictions (typically another school district or another state) with and without antibullying policies. One limitation of this comparison approach is that school districts (or states) with and without antibullying policies may differ in ways other than the policy (e.g., level of gun ownership), which may in turn be associated with the mental health outcome of interest (e.g., suicide attempts).

Although cross-sectional studies can provide important information on mental health correlates of antibullying policies, they have a number of limitations. In particular, with these designs, it is unclear whether an observed effect is due to antibullying policies' being causally related to mental health outcomes, or whether the relationship is due to a third, unmeasured variable (i.e., to confounding). Although one can control for many potential confounders of the relationship between antibullying policies and suicide attempts, there is still the possibility of unmeasured confounding, which may produce spurious relationships between the independent and dependent variables.

Pre-Post Design

A second methodological approach that improves on cross-sectional designs is the pre-post study. In this design, measures of the outcome (e.g., suicide attempts) are available before an antibullying policy is implemented. Researchers then examine the same group of respondents after they are exposed to an antibullying policy (e.g., their school district or state implements an antibullying policy) and observe whether there is a change in their mental health status (e.g., percentage who report attempting suicide). The pre-post design provides data on short-term changes in mental health (e.g., suicide attempts) resulting from antibullying policies; however, any reduction in suicide attempts might reflect natural variation in this outcome over time (e.g., seasonal effects on mental health). Moreover, another event could occur during the implementation of the antibullying policy that also affects suicidality (e.g., media coverage of suicide attempts, the introduction of a suicide hotline in the school district or state). This event would introduce a threat to the internal validity of the study (known as a "history threat"; see Shadish et al., 2002).

Time-Series Analysis

Time-series analysis, which represents a third methodological approach, addresses some of these limitations and therefore offers an important complement to a pre-post design. Time-series analyses require multiple time points both before and after the policy is implemented (rather than just two time points as in a pre-post test). Such designs make it easier to determine whether changes in the outcomes around the time of the policy implementation are larger than typical variation over time (Wagenaar & Komro, 2011), strengthening one's ability to make causal inferences about the mental health impact of antibullying policies.

Dose–Response Relationships

A fourth type of analysis, which can be combined with other approaches, is to test for a "dose–response" relationship between antibullying laws and mental health outcomes. As indicated in a comprehensive report on bullying laws compiled by the U.S. Department of Education (2011), there is substantial variation in the "dose" of these laws; that is, states and districts differ in the extent of coverage of 16 key components of antibullying laws (e.g., training and prevention, consequences of prohibited conduct). Thus, one can classify states or districts according to "low," "medium," and "high" categories with respect to the strength of their antibullying laws. If one finds that the magnitude of the change in the mental health outcomes "tracks" the dose (e.g., small or no change in suicide attempts in low-dose cities and large changes in the high-dose cities), these results strengthen causal inferences about the effect of antibullying policies on mental health outcomes (Wagenaar & Komro, 2011).

METHODOLOGICAL CHALLENGES IN STUDYING THE MENTAL HEALTH CONSEQUENCES OF ANTIBULLYING POLICIES

As these approaches illustrate, there are significant methodological challenges to studying the impact of antibullying policies on bullying behaviors and associated health outcomes. One is that, as with other social exposures of interest to public health researchers (e.g., discrimination, poverty, childhood adversity), it is rarely feasible (or ethical) to randomly assign individuals to attend schools with and without antibullying policies. Indeed, the passage and implementation of antibullying laws is rarely under the control of researchers. Consequently, the field must rely on observational or quasi-experimental designs, in which random assignment is not possible. It is important to note, however, that quasi-experimental studies, when carefully designed, can provide essential information about the impact of social factors and conditions on health and well-being (Shadish et al., 2002).

There are also practical considerations that pose additional methodological challenges to the study of antibullying policies and mental health. Given the nature of drafting and implementing policies, it can often take considerable time for policy-level changes to occur, which can impede researchers' ability to study their effect on health. On the other hand, some policies are hastily put together, often in response to a perceived or actual crisis (e.g., a suicide attempt following a bullying incident). In this case, it can be extremely difficult to obtain measures of the outcome (e.g., mental health or suicide attempts) before the policy was implemented, which is necessary in order to examine within-individual change. Finally, studying the health impact of antibullying policies can be resource-intensive and costly, even in cross-sectional designs, because one ideally needs multiple schools and, if conducting a time-series analysis, multiple assessment points. Obtaining consent from school districts to collect such data is difficult. Furthermore, most existing population-based datasets of youth that contain measures of bullying and mental health (e.g., Youth Risk Behavior Surveillance studies) typically do not release data below the state level, which prevents looking at within-state variation in the impact of antibullying policies on mental health.

RESEARCH EVIDENCE ON SOCIAL POLICIES AND MENTAL HEALTH IN LESBIAN, GAY, AND BISEXUAL POPULATIONS

Despite the methodological challenges to studying policies and mental health, there is a small but emerging literature suggesting that social policies that differentially target sexual minorities for social exclusion (e.g., constitutional amendments banning same-sex marriage) can affect the health of LGB populations. For instance, research demonstrates that the prevalence of psychiatric disorders is significantly higher among LGB adults living in states with policies that do not extend protections to gays and lesbians (i.e., sexual orientation is not accorded protected-class status in hate crime or employment non-discrimination acts), compared to LGB respondents living in states with more protective policies (Hatzenbuehler, Keyes, & Hasin, 2009). Similarly, LGB adults who lived in states that passed constitutional amendments banning same-sex marriage in 2004 experienced a significant increase in psychiatric and substance disorders in the 12 months following the amendments; LGB adults who lived in states that did not ban same-sex marriage did not experience an increase in mental health problems (Hatzenbuehler, McLaughlin, Keyes, & Hasin, 2010).

These studies indicated that some social policies have detrimental mental health consequences for LGB populations. The converse may also be true; recent research indicates that enacting social policies that protect sexual minorities may improve their health. In the 12 months after the legalization of same-sex marriage in Massachusetts, Hatzenbuehler and colleagues (2012) found a substantial reduction in several mental and physical health problems among gay and bisexual men, including a 14% decrease in depression and an 18% decrease in hypertension. Researchers also observed nearly a 15% reduction in medical and mental healthcare utilization and costs among gay and bisexual men, suggesting that their improvements in health translated into a reduced need for health care. In contrast, during this same time period, healthcare costs increased for the general population in Massachusetts. These results are broadly consistent with studies showing that social policies, even those not specifically concerned with health, produce health effects downstream (Williams et al., 2008).

RESEARCH EVIDENCE ON ANTIBULLYING POLICIES AND SUICIDE ATTEMPTS: A CASE STUDY IN LESBIAN, GAY, AND BISEXUAL YOUTH

The aforementioned research did not examine antibullying policies per se; nevertheless, the evidence indicates that policies that increase discrimination may exacerbate sexual orientation disparities in mental health, which suggests that policies with the opposite goal might also have the opposite effect (i.e., be effective in preventing disparities). In fact, a recent study specifically evaluating associations between antibullying policies and suicide risk in LGB youth provides initial evidence for a protective effect of such policies (Hatzenbuehler & Keyes, 2013). In this study, researchers coded school district websites and student handbooks across 197 school districts to determine whether the districts had any antibullying policies (harassment and antidiscrimination policies were not included in this category) and, if so, whether these policies gave sexual orientation a protected-class status. Thus, these data made it possible to differentiate between: (1) the absence of antibullying policies; (2) the presence of antibullying policies including specific categories (e.g., gender, race, religion), but not sexual orientation ("restrictive" policies); and (3) antibullying policies that were inclusive of sexual orientation ("inclusive" policies). These data on antibullying policies were then linked to the Oregon Healthy Teens (OHT) survey, a population-based dataset of eleventh-grade public school students (n = 1,413 LGB students, or 4.4%). Because information on location of residence for the study participants was only available at the county level, the measures of antibullying policies were aggregated from the district to the county level by dividing the number of school districts with antibullying policies by the total number of school districts in the county. Variables of the proportion of school districts that had restrictive and inclusive antibullying policies within each of 34 Oregon counties were created.

The study revealed four noteworthy findings. First, as the proportion of school districts that adopted antibullying policies inclusive of sexual orientation increased, rates of past-year suicide attempts among lesbian and gay youths decreased. Specifically, lesbian and gay youths living in counties with fewer school districts with inclusive antibullying policies were 2.25 times more likely (95% confidence interval [CI]: 1.13, 4.49) to have attempted suicide in the past year compared to those living in counties where more districts had these policies (see Figure 23.1). Moreover, inclusive antibullying policies were significantly associated with a reduced risk for suicide attempts among lesbian and gay youths, even after

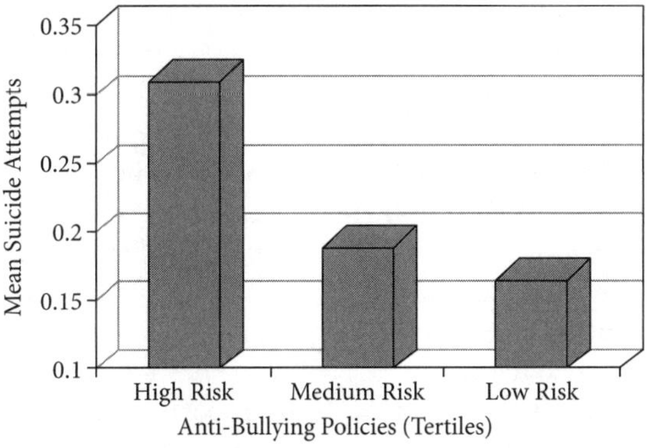

Figure 23.1 Associations between antibullying policies and suicide attempts in LGB youth.

controlling for sociodemographic characteristics (sex, race/ethnicity) and exposure to peer victimization (odds ratio [OR] = 0.18, 95% CI: 0.03–0.92).

Second, antibullying policies that did not include sexual orientation (i.e., "restrictive" policies) were not associated with lower suicide attempts among lesbian and gay youths (OR = 0.38, 95% CI: 0.02–7.33). Thus, policies had to include sexual orientation in the list of protected-class statuses in order to be effective in protecting lesbian and gay youths from attempting suicide. These results suggest the importance of specifically including sexual orientation in antibullying policies that enumerate protected groups, in order to signal supportive and inclusive school environments for lesbian and gay students.

Third, inclusive antibullying policies were not associated with a decreased risk for suicide attempts in the total heterosexual sample, documenting specificity of the results to lesbian and gay youths. However, it is important to note that enumerated policies are most relevant to specific subgroups of heterosexual youth who are most likely to be targets of bullying (e.g., racial/ethnic minorities, overweight/obese youth). Thus, it is possible that enumerated policies would protect these subgroups against suicide risk; however, because the study did not code for other groups that were protected in the inclusive policies, it was not possible to test this hypothesis.

Fourth, in addition to being associated with a reduction in suicide attempts, peer victimization of all youth was also less likely to occur in counties with a greater proportion of school districts with inclusive antibullying policies. These results suggest one potential mechanism linking inclusive antibullying policies to reduced risk of suicide attempts in lesbian/gay youth. In addition, these results demonstrate that policies protecting sexual-minority adolescents may confer benefits for heterosexual youths as well, in the form of reduced bullying behaviors.

Although this study suggested that antibullying policies have beneficial mental health consequences for gay and lesbian youth, these data were cross-sectional. Thus, it is not possible to determine whether antibullying policies are causally related to suicide attempts, or whether such policies reflect more supportive environments for sexual-minority youth. Additional studies, including those that utilize quasi-experimental designs, are needed to strengthen causal inferences regarding the effect of antibullying policies on LGBT mental health.

GAPS IN THE LITERATURE TO BE EXPLORED IN FUTURE RESEARCH

The study of the mental health impact of antibullying policies is in its infancy. Below, we highlight several critical directions for future inquiry in order to advance this inchoate literature. Although there is a fairly large literature on antibullying programs in schools (for a review of antibullying evaluation programs, see Ryan & Smith, 2009), we were only able to locate one study specifically evaluating the mental health impact of antibullying *policies* (Hatzenbuehler & Keyes, 2013). Thus, more studies are needed to address this research question.

LGBT youth represent one group that is disproportionately targeted by bullying, but other populations of adolescents, including overweight/obese adolescents (Puhl & Latner, 2007) and students with disabilities (Rose, Monda-Amaya, & Espelage, 2011), are also especially vulnerable to peer victimization and bullying. However, there are currently no empirical data on whether antibullying policies are effective in protecting these and other vulnerable youth against the negative mental health sequelae of bullying. These questions are important to answer because the policies enacted may be intentionally framed to provide protections to many enumerated classes, so it is vital to know whether this broad inclusiveness in framing is effective in protecting these other groups, who may also be targets of bullying. It may, conversely, be true that a focus on more general practices of discrimination attenuates the impact on LGBT youth by shifting the focus of intervention away from preventing specific homophobic and gender-normative bullying practices. Furthermore, youth facing intersectional inequalities (i.e., those with multiple stigmatized identities, such as Black gay youth) could potentially benefit from policies that address multiple forms of stigma and discrimination simultaneously; the conceptual literature on intersectionality (McCall, 2005) underlines the urgency of learning about the impact of anti-bullying policies on other marginalized groups and people living with multiple marginalized statuses.

In addition to studies that examine main effect relationships between antibullying policies and mental health, research on mediators and moderators of these relationships is also warranted. The study by Hatzenbuehler and colleagues (2013) found that victimization of all youth was less likely to occur in counties with a greater proportion of school districts with inclusive antibullying policies. This research suggests that antibullying policies may be effective in reducing bullying and victimization, which are established risk factors for suicidality in youth (Russell & Joyner, 2001). There are many ways antibullying policies could reduce bullying behaviors, ranging from changing social norms in the school, to enforcement practices (e.g., increased punishment for bullying). It is currently unknown which of these mechanisms is the "active ingredient" in effective antibullying policies. Thus, an important direction for future studies is to identify the processes linking antibullying policies to improved mental health, which will inform the development of more effective antibullying policies that can target these specific mechanisms.

With respect to potential moderators, there is currently substantial heterogeneity in the kinds of antibullying policies that have been passed in states and school districts, as well as in the groups that are covered as protected classes (U.S. General Accounting Office, 2012). In a comprehensive review of antibullying policies, for example, Srabstein and colleagues (2008) found that only 16 out of 35 state policies incorporated comprehensive public health antibullying principles, which include "a clear definition of bullying, an explicit articulation of a bullying prohibition, implementation of prevention and treatment programs, and acknowledgment of the association between bullying and public health risks" (p. 15). Although it seems plausible that these more comprehensive policies would be more likely to protect the mental health and well-being of vulnerable youth, this hypothesis has yet to be empirically tested. Thus, an important avenue for future inquiry is to examine whether the strength and comprehensiveness of antibullying policies serves as a moderator of mental health outcomes among youth (see discussion of dose–response relationships above).

ADOPTING AN INTERDISCIPLINARY APPROACH TO THE STUDY OF ANTIBULLYING POLICIES AND MENTAL HEALTH

The study of antibullying policies and mental health requires an interdisciplinary response, drawing on and integrating theories and methods from such diverse fields as law, psychology, anthropology, sociology, and history. Antibullying research, however, has drawn only superficially on the full range of methods and theories from the social sciences. Noticeably absent from this literature, for example, are historical studies, despite the fact that historical studies across the field of public health policy research have made it clear that the range of possible policy solutions is shaped by the ways in which problems emerge and are framed. Children bullying other children is hardly a new phenomenon, and a great deal of scholarship has described bullying in schools (Nansel et al., 2001) and has discussed the health and social psychological consequences of bullying (e.g., Arseneault et al., 2010); however, remarkably, there is no social history of the emergence of bullying as a focus of public health concern, despite the recent outpouring of popular and scholarly interest in the topic (Bazelon, 2012; Scott, 2012). Particularly powerful would be historical studies that incorporate ideas from the sociology of public problems (Gusfield, 1981): understanding the circumstances under which any issue gains traction and draws attention as needing remediation is critical in crafting effective policy responses (e.g., Lerner, 2011). Little is known, however, about how emerging evidence, sustained advocacy, and political opportunity converged to create a proliferation of legislation to address these issues across the nation (U.S. Department of Education, 2011; U.S. General Accounting Office, 2012), or about how these legal initiatives have been implemented at the institutional level. Historical analyses can begin to fill these gaps in the literature.

Social movement theory (Tarrow, 1998) would be another powerful conceptual tool to use in analyzing the history of the policy response to bullying. In the course of not even a decade, school bullying has moved from being a topic that was primarily discussed in the specialized confines of research on education or adolescent health, to become the focus of documentaries, social media campaigns, legislation across the country, and a great deal of other collective activity. This organized social response can only be properly understood and analyzed when considered in relation to broader knowledge about the circumstances under which social movements have effectively mobilized to create social change. Situating the social movement that has arisen under the banner of "bullying prevention" in relation to the social science of collective action can provide insight into why the movement has been effective, where it has been, and how it could be more effective in those cases, and contexts where it has not been. Very little work has been done that incorporates this sort of interdisciplinary, multi-method approach to address the broad question of how, to what extent, and under what circumstances antibullying policies can emerge to enhance the mental health of youth.

In terms of methodology, ethnography could be a crucial complement to the policy history that we have described above. Fine-grained ethnographic case studies of the actual institutional responses to antibullying policies can illuminate the circumstances that shape both institutional commitment to implementation as well as the characteristics of that implementation. For instance, what actually happens in schools that implement antibullying policies? How does the institutional climate change? If it does not change, what institutional and cultural barriers prevent the uptake and maintenance of antibullying policies? Careful ethnographic research in schools, informed by the concepts from the sociological study of institutional change outlined above, could be a powerful tool for uncovering barriers and facilitators of policy change so that effective dissemination of policies across diverse social contexts becomes possible. Resistance to such policies and programs is common, and neither the sources of resistance nor how resistance may be overcome are well understood. Ethnographic research could answer two specific questions in this regard. First, *how do various stakeholders describe and experience the institutional climate* in terms of discrimination and bullying, both in general and regarding LGBT youth in particular, both currently and in the past? Second, *what are the internal social processes and interactions that have produced each specific institutional response* to the common policy context? This includes exploring:

1. ownership of new initiatives,
2. how framing reflects and shapes the actions taken by school leadership,
3. the cultural legitimacy of laws establishing sexual orientation and gender identity as protected classes,
4. local championship and its effects on forms of implementation, and
5. institutional structures that support or challenge the implementation process.

Our point is not to argue for an ethnographic study focused principally on school climate, as a good deal of work has already been done to describe schools as institutions where heteronormativity and rigid gender roles are reproduced (e.g., Pascoe, 2007). Rather, what is needed is an understanding the process of policy formation and implementation and the complex social processes involved in the transformation of institutional climate around antibullying.

We see several potential benefits of an interdisciplinary approach to the study of antibullying policies. The simultaneous use of multiple approaches deepens our understanding of the impact of antibullying policies by making possible the triangulation of multiple sources of data. In addition, different approaches enable researchers to address certain issues related to this topic that are not possible with the other approaches. For instance, the implementation of a policy will vary depending on local and institutional conditions. While policy translation is receiving ever more focus in health sciences research, very little of that work has explored the institution-level factors that determine the variability in how a particular policy is implemented (Burris et al., 2010).

CONCLUSIONS AND SUGGESTIONS

We end by discussing several conclusions based on the topics covered in this chapter as they relate to different constituencies interested in antibullying policies and mental health.

General Conclusions

- Social policies are health policies; that is, social policies affect multiple factors (e.g., resources, social relationships, behaviors) that in turn contribute to health outcomes (Williams et al., 2008). This chapter explored whether and how social policies related to bullying affect the mental health of adolescents.
- The nature and extent of protections available to adolescents who are bullied depend on the policies where they attend school (U.S. General Accounting Office, 2012). Thus, antibullying policies represent one particularly important protective factor that may buffer vulnerable youth against the negative mental health consequences of bullying.
- The literature on antibullying policies and mental health is relatively new, with only one published study examining associations between antibullying policies and suicide attempts among LGB youth (Hatzenbuehler & Keyes, 2013).
- This study found that LGB youth were 2.25 times more likely to attempt suicide if they lived in counties with fewer school districts with inclusive antibullying policies (i.e., policies in which sexual orientation was listed as a protected-class status). Moreover, the antibullying policies had to include sexual orientation in the list of protected-class statuses in order to be effective in protecting lesbian and gay youths from attempting suicide. Victimization of all youth was also less likely to occur in counties with a greater proportion of school districts with inclusive antibullying policies. This research is consistent with studies demonstrating that rates of psychiatric disorders among LGB adults are lower in states that enact policies that protect sexual minorities (Hatzenbuehler et al., 2009, 2010, 2012).

Suggestions for Mental Health Providers

- Mental health providers typically focus on intrapersonal (e.g., cognitions, emotions) and interpersonal (e.g., peer and family relationships) factors that contribute to mental health problems in youth. While these factors are important, youth are also embedded in other systems—including schools, neighborhoods, communities, and states—that affect their health and well-being (Bronfenbrenner, 1979). Thus, mental health practitioners should be aware that supra-individual factors, including antibullying

policies that affect school climates, may be determinants of adolescent mental health.
- Practitioners should also help educate clients and their parents about the role that such factors may play in contributing to mental health problems.
- Mental health practitioners are important, but underutilized, advocates for their clients. When appropriate, practitioners should therefore help clients and their parents change school climates through altering district and state policies related to bullying.

Suggestions for Parents and Teachers

- Parents and teachers are encouraged to become aware of the antibullying policies in their states and school districts.
- When these policies are not in line with best practices, parents and teachers are encouraged to work with appropriate individuals (e.g., legislators, superintendents) to draft new policies that adequately protect youth.
- Parents and teachers should be aware that available research suggests that policies that explicitly include categories of students (e.g., LGBT) may be more effective in reducing suicides and other mental health consequences of bullying than policies without such explicit protections.

Suggestions for Policy Makers

- Policy maker interest in addressing bullying can have a clear impact on law and policy; therefore, those who have taken a clear interest should sustain and broaden their efforts, encouraging colleagues in other districts/states to promote simpler policies that explicitly protect a wide range of youth.
- There is currently substantial heterogeneity in the nature and extent of these laws; only a minority of antibullying policies includes funds available for the implementation of prevention and treatment programs for bullying (Srabstein et al., 2008; U.S. Department of Education, 2011), which is critical if law and policy are to achieve their full potential.
- It is important that antibullying policies provide comprehensive solutions to addressing bullying (Srabstein et al., 2008), and that such policies be based upon the best available evidence.
- Policy makers can meaningfully contribute to creating this evidence base by setting aside funding for testing the impact of antibullying policies on bullying behaviors and related health outcomes.

Suggestions for Researchers

- There are several gaps in the literature on antibullying policies and health that deserve greater empirical attention in future research, including: utilizing designs that afford greater ability to establish causal inference (e.g., quasi-experimental studies, time-series analyses); examining whether antibullying policies protect youth who, like LGBT students, are disproportionately targeted by bullying; and identifying mediators and moderators of the relationship between antibullying policies and mental health.

- Future studies should also leverage the strengths of interdisciplinary, multi-method approaches to studying these research questions. In particular, research would benefit from greater attention to disciplinary fields (e.g., history, sociology of social movements) and methods (e.g., ethnography) that have heretofore been underemployed in the study of antibullying policies.
- As social science data on the mental health impact of antibullying policies become increasingly available, researchers should make this information available to policy makers. Continued partnerships between researchers and policy makers will ensure that effective policies are crafted to protect all youth against the negative consequences of bullying.

NOTE

1. Although this chapter focuses on LGBT youth, several studies in this review did not include measures of gender identity. In those cases, we use "LGB" to indicate that the study only assessed measures of sexual orientation (i.e., self-identification as lesbian, gay, or bisexual).

REFERENCES

Arseneault, L., Bowes, L., & Shakoor, S. (2010). Bullying victimization in youths and mental health problems: "Much ado about nothing"? *Psychological Medicine, 40*, 717–729. doi: 10.1017/S0033291709991383

Bazelon, E. (2012). Lady Gaga, anti-bullying crusader. *Slate*. Retrieved from http://www.slate.com/articles/news_and_politics/bulle/2012/03/lady_gaga_launches_her_born_this_way_foundation_at_harvard_.html

Bronfenbrenner, U. (1979). *The Ecology of Human Development: Experiments by Nature and Design*. Cambridge, MA: Harvard University Press.

Burris, S., Wagenaar, A. C., Swanson, J., Ibrahim, J. K., Wood, J., & Mello, M. M. (2010). Making the case for laws that improve health: A framework for public health law research. *Milbank Quarterly, 88*, 169–210. doi: 10.1111/j.1468-0009.2010.00595.x

Doe vs. Anoka-Hennepin School District No.11 et al. (2011). United States District Court, District of Minnesota. Filed on July 21, 2011.

Gusfield, J. R. (1981). *The Culture of Public Problems: Drinking-Driving and the Symbolic Order*. Chicago: University of Chicago Press.

Hatzenbuehler, M. L., & Keyes, K. M. (2013). Inclusive anti-bullying policies reduce suicide attempts in lesbian and gay youth. *Journal of Adolescent Health, 53*(1 Suppl), S21–S26. doi: 10.1016/j.jadohealth.2012.08.010

Hatzenbuehler, M. L., Keyes, K. M., & Hasin, D. S. (2009). State-level policies and psychiatric morbidity in lesbian, gay, and bisexual populations. *American Journal of Public Health, 99*, 2275–2281. doi: 10.2105/AJPH.2008.153510

Hatzenbuehler, M. L., McLaughlin, K. A., Keyes, K. M., & Hasin, D. S. (2010). The impact of institutional discrimination on psychiatric disorders in lesbian, gay, and bisexual populations: A prospective study. *American Journal of Public Health, 100*, 452–459. doi: 10.2105/AJPH.2009.168815

Hatzenbuehler, M. L., O'Cleirigh, C., Grasso, C., Mayer, K., Safren, S., & Bradford, J. (2012). Effect of same-sex marriage laws on health care use and expenditures in sexual minority men: A quasi-natural experiment. *American Journal of Public Health, 102*, 285–291. doi: 10.2105/2011.300382

Lerner, B. H. (2011). *One for the Road: Drunk Driving Since 1900*. Baltimore, MD: Johns Hopkins University Press.

Limber, S. P., & Small, M. A. (2003). State laws and policies to address bullying in schools. *School Psychology Review, 32*, 445–455.

McCall, L. (2005). The complexity of intersectionality. *Signs, 30*, 1771–1800. doi: 10.1086/426800

Nansel, T. R., Overpeck, M., Pilla, R. S., Ruan, W. J., Simons-Morton, B., & Scheidt, P. (2001). Bullying behaviors among US youth: Prevalence and association with psychosocial adjustment. *Journal of the American Medical Association, 285*, 2094–2100. doi: 10.1001/jama.285.16.2094

Pascoe, C. J. (2007). *Dude, You're a Fag: Masculinity and Sexuality in High School*. Berkeley: University of California Press.

Pratt v. *Indian River School District* et al. (2009). United States District Court, Northern District of New York. Filed on April 8, 2009.

Puhl, R. M., & Latner J. D. (2007). Stigma, obesity, and the health of the nation's children. *Psychological Bulletin, 133*, 557–580. doi: 10.1037/0033-2909.133.4.557

Rose, C. A., Monda-Amaya, L. E., & Espelage, D. L. (2011). Bullying perpetration and victimization in special education: A review of the literature. *Remedial and Special Education, 32*, 114–130. doi: 10.1177/0741932510361247

Russell, S. T., & Joyner, K. (2001). Adolescent sexual orientation and suicide risk: Evidence from a national study. *American Journal of Public Health, 91*, 1276–1281. doi: 10.2105/AJPH.91.8.1276

Ryan, W., & Smith, J. D. (2009). Antibullying programs in schools: How effective are evaluation practices? *Prevention Science, 10*, 248–259. doi: 10.1007/s11121-009-0128-y

Scott, A. O. (2012). Behind every harassed child? A whole lot of clueless adults. *New York Times* movie review. Retreived from http://www.nytimes.com/2012/03/30/movies/bully-a-documentary-by-lee-hirsch.html?_r=0

Shadish, W., Cook, T., & Campbell, D. (2002). *Experimental and Quasi-Experimental Designs for Generalized Causal Inference*. Boston: Houghton Mifflin.

Srabstein, J. C., Berkman, B. E., & Pyntikova, E. (2008). Antibullying legislation: A public health perspective. *Journal of Adolescent Health, 42*, 11–20. doi: 10.1016/j.jadohealth.2007.10.007

Tarrow, S. (1998). *Power in Movement: Social Movements and Contentious Politics*. Cambridge, MA: Cambridge University Press.

U.S. Department of Education. (2011). Analysis of state bullying laws and policies. Washington, DC: USDOE. Available at: http://www2.ed.gov/rschstat/eval/bullying/state-bullying-laws/state-bullying-laws.pdf.

U.S. General Accounting Office. (June 8, 2012). School bullying: Legal protections for vulnerable youth need to be more fully assessed. Testimony before the Committee on Health, Education, Labor and Pensions, U.S. Senate.

Wagenaar, A. C., & Komro, K. A. (2011). Natural experiments: Design elements for optimal causal inference. *Public Health Law Research (PHLR) Methods Monograph Series*. Retrieved from http://publichealthlawresearch.org/sites/default/files/downloads/resource/WagenaarKomroPHLR-MethodsModule.pdf

Williams, D. R., Costa, M. V., Odunlami, A. O., & Mohammed, S. A. (2008). Moving upstream: How interventions that address the social determinants of health can improve health and reduce disparities. *Journal of Public Health Management & Practice, 14,* S8–S17. doi: m10.1177/0741932510361247

PART SEVEN

Conclusions and Future Directions

24

Comment Chapter

Adapting Interpersonal Psychotherapy for Depressed Adolescents (IPT-A) for Adolescents Who Engage in Bullying Behaviors and Are at Risk for Suicide

ANAT BRUNSTEIN KLOMEK AND LAURA MUFSON ■

There are only a few indicated individual psychotherapeutic interventions for bullies, victims, and bully-victims who are depressed or suicidal (e.g., Berry & Hunt, 2009; Tang & Huang, 2013). Tang and Huiang (2013) found interpersonal psychotherapy for adolescents (IPT-A) to be effective in improving anxiety and depression in adolescents experiencing bullying. Mufson and colleagues are currently conducting a study examining an adaptation of the school-based Interpersonal Psychotherapy Adolescent Skills Training (IPT-AST) prevention model (Young, Mufson, & Davies, 2006) for victims of bullying who also report subsyndromal depression and social anxiety symptoms.

There are several reasons to adapt IPT-A for adolescents involved in bullying behavior and at risk for suicide. Both bullying and suicide among adolescents are forms of aggression: one toward the self, and one toward others, and both can be dangerous. In addition, many psychosocial factors known to be associated with the increased risk of suicidal behavior among adolescents are similar for those involved in bullying or cyber-bullying behavior. These include: poor mental health (e.g., major depression, anxiety, conduct), maladaptive coping strategies (e.g., difficulty in efficient problem-solving, deficits in emotion-regulation skills), aggression/impulsivity, hopelessness, low self-esteem, difficult family characteristics (e.g., abuse, family dysfunction/conflict, parenting style), and peer and social difficulties (e.g., affiliation with students involved in bullying, lack of social support systems) (Borowsky et al., 2013; Espelage & Holt, 2013; Gould et al., 2003; Sourander et al., 2010). Psychotherapies that are based on skill building may teach and practice emotional, behavioral, social, and interpersonal skills, which are relevant to bullying, cyber-bullying, and suicide prevention. IPT-A is a psychotherapy for depressed adolescents that is considered evidence-based (Mufson et al., 1999, 2004; Rossello & Bernal, 1999). (For a full description of the treatment, please see the treatment manual: Mufson et al., 2004.) In the current commentary, we will describe how IPT-A can be clinically used with adolescents who are involved in bullying/

cyber-bullying behavior and are at risk for suicide; however, this application has not yet been empirically tested.

INTERPERSONAL PSYCHOTHERAPY FOR ADOLESCENT SUICIDE PREVENTION (IPT-ASP)

Mufson and colleagues have adapted IPT-A for depressed adolescents who engage in non-suicidal self injury (NSSI) (Jacobson & Mufson, 2012) and for depressed adolescents with suicidal ideation or behavior (IPT-ASP) (Mufson et al., 2013). The suicide prevention adaptation focuses on the links among depression, suicidal behavior, and interpersonal problems. The IPT-ASP adaptation was developed in a unique setting that allowed for participation in a day-treatment program, a brief stay when necessary in an inpatient unit, and the use of adjunctive medication treatment. IPT-ASP comprises twice-weekly treatment sessions for eight weeks, followed by weekly treatment for 12 weeks. Sessions are held with the adolescent, caregivers, or both. IPT-ASP involves several additional elements: increased parental involvement, use of an interpersonal safety plan, earlier introduction of communication skills to aid in emotion regulation, and an expanded focus on suicide prevention. Psycho-education was expanded to include psycho-education for adolescents and parents or caregivers on suicide prevention, and "teen tips" were expanded to include methods for preventing suicidal behavior (e.g., emphasis that suicide is "a permanent solution to a temporary problem," knowledge that suicidal urges come in waves, trying to avoid impulsivity, etc.). In addition, parent tips for parenting a suicidal child were created (e.g., setting suicide prevention as the most important priority, monitoring the child's suicidality, setting limits, etc.). The Depression Circle technique was also expanded to incorporate suicidal ideation and behavior in order to understand the link between emotions, relationship difficulties (including bullying involvement), and suicidal behavior (Mufson et al., 2013).

The Depression/Suicide Circle used in IPT-ASP is a technique designed to help understand the interpersonal function of depression and suicidal behavior. The therapist and adolescent try to uncover all the interpersonal, behavioral, and emotional factors that led up to the suicidal ideation or behavior, as well as those that existed both during and after the suicidal ideation or behavior. The goal is to identify the interpersonal, behavioral, and emotional links in the chain that ultimately resulted in the suicidal behavior (Mufson et al., 2013). The Interpersonal Safety Plan was adapted from the Safety Plan developed by Stanley and Brown (2012) by adding an explicitly interpersonal focus. It is a written and comprehensive plan that includes a set of steps the adolescent can take if he or she is thinking about suicide. The steps start with identifying the emotional, behavioral, and interpersonal triggers to their suicidal ideation, identifying things the adolescent can do by themselves to soothe and decrease these thoughts, progresses to things they can do with others, or significant others they can contact when they are at risk (starting with family members and continuing with professionals). Lastly, the Safety Plan includes discussion about where the adolescent can go for help (e.g., the emergency room) if none of the previous strategies is effective. The plan is written during the first session with the adolescent, is shared with the parents, and then continues to be used as part of the ongoing therapeutic process.

ADAPTING IPT-A FOR ADOLESCENTS WHO ENGAGE IN BULLYING AND ARE AT RISK FOR SUICIDE

The suggested model should include the original IPT-A manual with the suicide-prevention adaptations. The goals of treatment should be: reduction of the bullying behavior (bullying, victimization, or both), improvement in interpersonal functioning, and reduction of the depression symptoms and suicidal risk. The suggested protocol should be one to two weekly sessions in the first eight weeks and weekly sessions for additional 12 weeks. Sessions should be with the adolescent, parents, or both. The work with parents is central in all three phases of the treatment (see below for details about working with parents in each phase).

Initial Phase

The initial phase (weeks 1–4) will include four major components. Safety measures are the first component. A Safety Plan should be completed first, because these adolescents are at risk for suicide (see above). In addition, a Bullying Prevention Plan should be conducted in a collaborative effort. The aim of the bullying prevention plan is to reduce or prevent future bullying and cyber-bullying behavior. It is a written plan of action created by the therapist and the youth involved in bullying others that essentially charts the course of what the youth should do if they begin to experience bullying urges or start to bully or cyber-bully others. The plan has hierarchical steps, including the identification of warning signs for bullying behavior, use of internal coping strategies, use of external-interpersonal coping strategies, and involvement of an adult or professional provider. The Safety Plan and the Bullying Prevention Plan should be periodically reviewed, discussed, and expanded as skills are added. Second, there should be a focus on both the bullying behavior and any depression, mood symptoms, or suicidality, providing psycho-education about all of these issues, evaluating the need for psychiatric consultation, and instilling hope for recovery. In addition, the therapist gives the adolescent the Limited Sick Role, which is a temporary status recognizing that depressive illness keeps the adolescent from functioning at full capacity, while encouraging him to participate in as many of his normal activities as possible. By assigning the Limited Sick Role, the blame for poor performance is removed from the adolescent and is placed on the illness. In this phase, it is important to work toward increasing youths' self-awareness, as some bullies and victims may be reluctant to acknowledge their bullying behavior and emotions openly. The therapist should aim to link the interpersonal issues and bullying involvement to the depression, mood symptoms, and suicidality.

During the initial sessions, the therapist teaches the adolescent to rate his mood and the bullying behavior on a scale of 1 to 10, separately for each. The therapist and adolescent use these scales on a weekly basis to monitor the impact of interpersonal and bullying events and mood on each other. One way to focus on all of the links between bullying, mood, and suicidal behavior is to create a depression and suicide circle (Mufson et al., 2013). In addition to conducting the standard circle described above, it is important to identify the vulnerability factors, and activating events, feelings, and behaviors linked to bullying or cyber-bullying. Third, the exploration of the adolescent's significant relationships with peers, parents, and other adults should be achieved through the use of the Closeness Circle and Interpersonal Inventory (Mufson et al., 2004). The Closeness Circle, like the Standard Circle in IPT-A, includes the significant people in the adolescent's life (both positive and negative), and additionally should incorporate victims and perpetrators of bullying, as well as others involved in the bullying behavior (bystanders, school personnel, etc.). In the interpersonal inventory, the therapist and adolescent explore the different interpersonal relationships that are relevant to their mood. It is important to include parents and others (who may be not involved in the bullying), as well as those who are involved in the bullying behavior (in any role). While doing this, the therapist is forming hypotheses about which interpersonal issues may be most related to the current bullying behavior and depression symptoms or suicide risk. Lastly, based on the inventory, the therapist identifies the primary problem area that will be the focus of the remainder of treatment (Mufson et al., 2004).

Three of the four original problem areas may be most relevant for adolescents who are involved in bullying behavior and at risk for suicide. *Interpersonal role dispute* is the problem area identified when an adolescent is involved in bullying and also reports having frequent conflicts with other significant people. The goal is to help the adolescent interact with others in ways that reduce conflict and/or bullying involvement. *Interpersonal role transition* is the identified problem area when an adolescent or family is having a difficult time adjusting to a life change that entails playing a new social role. Role transitions can occur because of developmental changes or other life changes, including the beginning of involvement in bullying or victimization. The goal in this problem area would be to better understand how this role impacts the bully's or victim's life, as well as to teach coping skills for moving forward. *Interpersonal deficits* may be the identified problem area when an adolescent is bullying others or is victimized by others and lacks the social and communication skills to establish and maintain appropriate peer relationships (Mufson et al., 2004).

Middle Phase

In the middle phase (weeks 5–15), therapist and adolescent work within the identified problem area. The therapist and adolescent address changes in mood, present risk for suicide, interpersonal relationships, and bullying behavior with IPT-A techniques. At the start of each session, her mood, suicidality, and interpersonal functioning domains (including bullying involvement) are reviewed. If the adolescent is still reporting suicidal behavior, she can be seen twice weekly until week 8.

There are several techniques that can be adapted for use with adolescents who bully or are victimized, or both, and are at risk for suicide (Mufson et al., 2004). Emotion-identification strategies can be very useful for both bullies and victims, who frequently need help with increasing their awareness, understanding, and adaptive expression of emotions. Emotion cards (Mufson et al., 2004) can be used to learn about the range of emotions, monitor their levels of intensity, and learn ways to regulate emotions in order to control one's behavior. The therapist and adolescent write different emotions on cards in order to learn about all types of possible emotions (i.e., positive, negative, mixed), learn to identify them, label them correctly, legitimize the negative and mixed ones, and monitor their current intensity level (i.e., on a scale from 0–10). Emotion-regulation skills are relevant for both bullying and suicide prevention. Teaching adolescents to cope with their emotions by expressing them verbally (to themselves and to others) may decrease both suicidal and bullying risk. The regulation of emotions can start with things the adolescent can do by himself (e.g., sports, journaling) to things he can do with the help of others (either as distracting or as calming skills). An important emphasis should be that communication is more effective when one is emotionally regulated ("Strike when the iron is cold"). This may be crucial in some of the victims' responses to their own bullies.

Another useful IPT-A technique is communication analysis (Mufson et al., 2004). The goal is to help the adolescent recognize the impact of verbal and nonverbal communications on others, and to help her perceive how modifying this communication (what she actually says and how she says it) may affect the outcome of the interaction and associated feelings of both parties. In bullying interactions, it is very important that this technique be conducted with no criticism or blaming of the perpetrator or victim. The assumption with bullies is that they can control their negative behavior but they are not stopping it because it serves a social and emotional function. By conducting a communication analysis, the therapist and adolescent can try to understand the underlying function of the bullying behavior and can modify the interaction in a way that the underlying function is fulfilled without bullying others. With victims, the assumption is that they have no control over the bully's behavior, but they can learn to modify their communication patterns and reactions, and, as a result, deal more effectively with the bullying. The communication analysis includes dissecting a bullying interaction into the behavior exhibited and words said by each person, and then discussing the message sent by the behavior and words and their impact on the feelings of both people involved. The therapist and adolescent discuss how changing the perpetration and victimization communication and behavior (even in small ways) at various points in the interaction, may result in a different outcome (e.g., victim ignoring provocation, with different and more assertive body language). The adolescent is asked about what he might have said or done differently, how the outcome could have been different as a result (e.g., bully gaining power by prosocial behavior) and then how he might have felt differently at the conclusion of the interaction.

In the next step, the therapist presents various interpersonal and social skills and communication strategies that could be helpful, including: assertiveness (using "I statements"), initiating and maintaining positive social relationships; acknowledging the other person's perspective ("Give to get"), and other teen-friendly tips (Mufson et al., 2013). With both bullies and aggressive victims (Fung, 2012), an important component should be empathy skills and perspective-taking ("putting yourself in the other's shoes").

Decision analysis is another technique that may be used as part of IPT-A. For youth who bully others, the objective is to help the adolescent to identify a goal or motivation for the bullying interaction, to understand that there are alternative solutions to the problem associated with this interaction, and to evaluate a more effective behavior or strategy (Mufson et al., 2004). The reasons why adolescents bully one another (e.g., gaining power, feeling in control) are often complex and multiply determined. Once the adolescent has identified a possible alternative (e.g., feeling strong in a positive way; affiliating with students who do not bully others), the therapist and adolescent map out how to communicate or behave differently to achieve that goal and role-play the associated interaction in the session until the adolescent is ready to implement it. With victims, a decision analysis can be conducted as to how to respond to peer bullying behavior. The therapist and adolescent should consider alternative courses of action in order to resolve a problem or reach a goal (e.g., "make sure you are accompanied by one supportive peer during recess") and then to evaluate the likely consequences of different possible courses of action. Based on this process, one solution is chosen and practiced.

During sessions, the therapist and adolescent role-play interactions using these techniques while refining, reinforcing, and reevaluating how to use them successfully. Interpersonal experiments to do outside of the session related to the bullying behavior are developed by the therapist and adolescent arising out of situations and skills that are practiced and role-played in the session. These may include practicing social skills and assertiveness for victims and practicing alternative behaviors for bullies.

Termination Phase

The termination phase (weeks 16–20) focuses on relapse-prevention for the adolescent's depression and suicidality, as well as the bullying involvement. In this phase, the therapist and adolescent clarify warning symptoms of future depressive symptoms, suicidal behavior, and bullying behaviors. In addition, the teen and therapist work together to identify adaptive strategies used in the middle phase that can be generalized to future interpersonal and social situations, and the need for further treatment is discussed.

Parent involvement is integral to IPT-A. In the initial phase, parents provide diagnostic information and, with the therapist and adolescent, discuss confidentiality and set appropriate expectations for the intervention. It is important for the parents to help the adolescent struggle with the bullying behavior instead of blaming or criticizing her. One helpful way is to join the adolescent in a supportive manner in trying to understand the involvement in the bullying behavior as an external problem that she can collaboratively try to reduce. In the middle phase, parents are involved to help youth with new and adaptive emotional skills, communication styles, problem-solving, and to be supportive of efforts to change their interpersonal behavior. In the termination phase, parents review the adolescent's progress and help her make decisions about the need for continuing treatment.

In summary, IPT-A may be beneficial for use with adolescents who are involved in bullying or cyber-bullying behavior and are at risk for suicide. The adaptation presented here has not yet been empirically tested; therefore, studies of this suggested intervention are needed for confirmation of its effectiveness with this population.

REFERENCES

Berry, K., & Hunt, C. J. (2009). Evaluation of an intervention program for anxious adolescent boys who are bullied at school. *Journal of Adolescent Health, 45*(4), 376–382. doi: 10.1016/j.jadohealth.2009.04.023

Borowsky, I. W., Taliaferro, L. A., & McMorris, B. J. (2013). Suicidal thinking and behavior among youth involved in verbal and social bullying: Risk and protective factors. *Journal of Adolescent Health, 53(1)*, 4–12. doi: 10.1016/j.jadohealth.2012.10.280

Espelage, D. L., & Holt, M. K. (2013). Suicidal ideation and school bullying experiences after controlling for depression and delinquency. *Journal of Adolescent Health, 53*(1), 27–31. doi: 10.1016/j.jadohealth.2012.09.017

Fung, A. L. (2012). Intervention for aggressive victims of school bullying in Hong Kong: A longitudinal mixed-methods study. *Scandinavian Journal of Psychology, 53*(4), 360–367. doi: 10.1111/j.1467-9450.2012.00953.x

Gould, M. S., Greenberg, T., Velting, D. M., & Shaffer, D. (2003). Youth suicide risk and preventive interventions: A review of the past 10 years. *Journal of the American Academy of Child & Adolescent Psychiatry, 53*, 1155–1162. doi: 10.1097/01.CHI.0000046821.95464.CF

Jacobson, C. M., & Mufson, L. (2012). Interpersonal psychotherapy for depressed adolescents adapted for self-injury (IPT-ASI): Rationale, overview, and case summary. *American Journal of Psychotherapy, 66*(4), 349–374.

Mufson, L., Weissman, M. M., Moreau, D., & Garfinkel, R. (1999). Efficacy of interpersonal psychotherapy for depressed adolescents. *Archives of General Psychiatry, 56*, 573–579. doi: 10.1001/archpsyc.56.6.573

Mufson, L., Dorta, K. P., Wickramaratne, P., Nomura, Y., Olfson, M., & Weissman, M. M. (2004). A randomized effectiveness trial of interpersonal psychotherapy for depressed adolescents. *Archives of General Psychiatry, 61*(6), 577–584. doi: 10.1001/archpsyc.61.6.577

Mufson, L. Dorta, K. P., Moreau, D., & Weissman, M. M. (2004). *Interpersonal Psychotherapy for Depressed Adolescents* (2nd ed.). New York: Guilford Publications.

Mufson, L., Rynn, M., Goldberg, P., Brunstein-Klomek, A., Rapp, A., Puliafico, A., ...Seracini, A. (2013). IPT-A adapted for depressed youth engaging in suicidal behavior: Preliminary outcomes and experiences. Presented at the International Society for Interpersonal Psychotherapy (ISIPT) Conference, June 13, 2013, Iowa City, IA.

Rossello, J., & Bernal, G. (1999). The efficacy of cognitive-behavioral and interpersonal treatments for depression in Puerto Rican adolescents. *Journal of Consulting Clinical Psychology, 67*(5), 734–745. doi: 10.1037/0022-006x.67.5.734

Sourander, A., Brunstein-Klomek, A., Ikonen, M., Lindroos, J., Luntamo, T., Koskelainen, M.,...Helenius, H. (2010). Psychosocial risk factors associated with cyberbullying among adolescents: A population-based study. *Archives of General Psychiatry, 67*(7), 720–728. doi: 10.1001/archgenpsychiatry.2010.79.

Stanley, B., & Brown, K. G. (2012). Safety planning intervention: A brief intervention to mitigate suicide risk. *Cognition and Behavior Practice, 19*, 256–264. doi: 10.1016/j.cbpra.2011.01.001

Tang, T. C., & Huang, S. Y. (2013). Interpersonal psychotherapy for treating psychological disturbances in adolescents who experienced bullied experiences: Randomized case control study. *European Psychiatry, 28*(1), 1.

Young, J., Mufson, L., & Davies, M. (2006). Preliminary efficacy of interpersonal psychotherapy-adolescent skills training: An indicated preventative intervention for adolescent depression. *Journal of Child Psychology and Psychiatry, 47,* 1254–1262. doi: 10.1111/j.1469-7610.2006.01667.x

25

Developing an Ecological Approach to Address Challenges of Youth Bullying and Suicide

Recommendations for Research, Practice, Policy, and Training

DOROTHY L. ESPELAGE, PETER GOLDBLUM, JOYCE CHU, BRUCE BONGAR, SAMANTHA PFLUM, AND LISA DE LA RUE ■

Addressing the challenges associated with both bullying and youth suicide requires a comprehensive approach that targets all levels of the social ecology and engages all members of society. A social-ecological approach demands that we pay attention to the individual mental health issues of youth and their families, while also considering the larger sociocultural and institutional predictors that create unsafe spaces for youth. These unsafe spaces may exacerbate risk factors for suicide behaviors, including bullying and other forms of victimization, and as such require targeted interventions. Consistent with the original writings of Bronfenbrenner (1979) and the more recent conceptualization of bullying (Espelage, in press) and suicide prevention (King & Merchant, 2008), the authors in this book have argued that both the antecedents of bullying and suicide behaviors are situated within multiple systems. In order to successfully reduce youth bullying and suicide, prevention efforts should target these multiple systems through research findings from educational and prevention science, public health approaches to community mental health, and cross-cultural psychology.

As discussed in several chapters in this book (Chapter 3, Chapter 6, Chapter 7, Chapter 8, Chapter 10, Chapter 16, and Chapter 19), social-ecological approaches to understanding and preventing bullying and suicide should involve the microsystems that surround youth, such as peers, family members, community members, school staff, and other adults (Bronfenbrenner, 1979). These microsystems influence one another in both positive and negative ways, and are also situated within several overlapping systems that interlink within the mesosystem (Bronfenbrenner, 1994). Bullying involvement and risk for suicidal behavior can be significantly reduced if prevention and intervention efforts address the complex direct and indirect (interaction) effects of a youth's environment. For example, a school's climate influences the likelihood of teachers' intervening when they witness incidents of bullying (Espelage, Polanin, & Low, in press). The school climate also predicts whether teachers will be supported in their antibullying efforts by the entire school community, including administrators and families. Authors of this book have offered a wealth of recommendations that address both bullying and suicide prevention efforts within the various microsystems and mesosystems, which will be summarized here.

RECOMMENDATIONS FOR PARENTS AND TEACHERS

A consistent message from national and international experts in this volume is for parents and educators to be aware and ready to respond to signs of bullying involvement and suicidal ideation and behavior. Nickerson and Torchia (Chapter 4; this volume) prompt parents and educators to note things like bruises, torn clothing, missing property, and changes in mood and behavior. However, simply looking for signs is not enough to counteract bullying involvement. Orpinas and Horne (Chapter 5; this volume) articulate the importance of building meaningful and caring relationships in families, classrooms, and schools. Families need to prioritize time to learn from and listen to each other, to discuss psychological distress (e.g., depression, anxiety, depression, isolation, substance use) and suicide openly, and to encourage each other to talk through stressful situations.

By developing strong, communicative, and flexible relationships with their students, teachers can convey that they are comfortable talking about concerns such as bullying and suicide. These are key practices for suicide prevention and can help ameliorate psychiatric symptoms that co-occur with bullying and suicide (Chapter 6; this volume). When considering the increase in cultural diversity within families (e.g., different levels of acculturation, immigrant status, language use, and different cultural styles in dealing with stress), many youth and their parents experience cultural conflict that can heighten psychological distress. In these cases, educators must work with families to negotiate these conflicts and to minimize adverse academic, relational, and psychological outcomes (Chapter 8; this volume). Regardless of the cultural challenges, all families need to pay particular attention to youths' peer relationships and the potential for quarrels, rejection, and humiliation.

In the same vein, teachers need to create classrooms where bullying is not tolerated, and must engage in practices that promote inclusion, respect, and active problem-solving. Logis and Rodkin (Chapter 16; this volume) suggest that teachers create collaborative opportunities for youth of varying levels of popularity to learn from one another. In addition, educators and parents need to advocate school-wide comprehensive approaches that promote respectful behaviors, teach social-emotional strategies to enhance students' interactions with others, and create safe spaces for youth to support each other through struggles with bullying and suicidality (Chapter 2; this volume; Chapter 18; this volume).

With the advent of increased technology utilization among youth, cyber-bullying has become a serious, prevalent concern (Chapter 7; this volume). Ongoing conversations need to happen naturally in homes and in classrooms about the responsible use of technology; youth should also be educated on methods to protect themselves from victimization or to decrease hostile behavior towards others. Technology is here to stay, and youth, families, and schools are all influenced by the time they spend interacting with social media and visiting social networking sites. Parents need to be intentional in their monitoring of their children's use of computers, social media, and electronics (Chapter 7; this volume), especially given the research that finds that face-to-face bullying and victimization is causally linked to online bullying and victimization (Espelage, Rao, & Craven, 2013).

Many of the authors challenge the common cultural tendency to ignore mental health concerns among children, adolescents, and young adults, and they encourage all adults who interact with youth to become familiar with mental health symptoms (Chapter 21; this volume). It is imperative that teachers and students understand how youth with mental health diagnoses are especially vulnerable to the effects of bullying (Chapter 6; this volume). Parents and educators should work to foster greater understanding of mental illness among youth, and should avoid behaving in ways that stigmatize youth who demonstrate psychiatric symptoms, particularly suicidality (Berman et al., 2006; Chapter 13; this volume). Both the American Foundation for Suicide Prevention and the Stop Bullying website (www.stopbullying.gov) provide comprehensive information about bullying and suicidal behaviors, and can serve as valuable resources for parents, teachers, and communities. While it is important for teachers and school staff to implement strategies to help their students, parents also play a critical role in ensuring that schools have antibullying policies in place that are consistent with best practices. Individually and through parent organizations such as the Parent Teacher Association (PTA), parents need to advocate generally for safe and welcoming schools, and when needed, specific bullying and suicide prevention programs (Chapter 23; this volume).

Sexual and gender minority youth (i.e., lesbian, gay, bisexual, transgender [LGBT]) are a specific group of students who are especially vulnerable to peer victimization and bullying. LGBT youth are also particularly susceptible to the negative outcomes of victimization and bullying, including increased suicide risk (Espelage, Birkett, Aragon, & Koenig, 2008; Hershberger & D'Augelli, 1995; Goldblum et al., 2012; Pilkington & D'Augelli, 1995; Robinson & Espelage, 2011; Savin-Williams & Ream, 2003). LGBT youth often face stigma and discrimination in multiple contexts, and many are faced with hostile, rejecting, or unsupportive home environments (Chapter 15; this volume; Pilkington & D'Augelli, 1995). Poteat and Rivers (Chapter 10; this volume) encourage parents to work towards acceptance of their child's sexual orientation or gender identity and to serve as advocates for their child's physical and psychological well-being before and after "coming out." Parents should also be active in communicating with youth about dating, meeting partners, and making healthy sexual decisions (Robinson & Espelage, 2013). Parents of sexual minority youth can also assist their child in establishing LGBT-sensitive clubs (e.g., a gay-straight alliance [GSA] at his/her school). The presence of GSAs in schools has been shown to be associated with an increased sense of safety among LGBT youth, as well as improved health and educational outcomes such as reduced truancy, fewer injuries at school, and fewer suicide attempts

(Burdge, Snapp, Laub, Russell, & Moody, 2013; Chapter 13; this volume; Goodenow, Szalacha, & Westheimer, 2006; Chapter 23; this volume). Teachers of all educational levels (K–12) should be educated about sexual identity and gender diversity in youth, and should work to communicate this knowledge and consideration to all students in a developmentally appropriate manner (Chapter 11; this volume; Chapter 19; this volume).

Recommendations for Mental Health and Medical Providers

Corona and colleagues (Chapter 13; this volume) set out a mandate for medical and mental health providers. All youth-serving providers should familiarize themselves with emerging research and best practices in the field of suicidology and youth violence, particularly bullying. Several national organizations, including the Substance Abuse and Mental Health Services Administration (SAMHSA: http://www.nrepp.samhsa.gov), provide evidence-based registries for easy access to comprehensive information. Providers are urged to consult the SAMHSA registry to familiarize themselves with options for treating suicidal clients and preventing bullying. Corona and colleagues strongly encourage practitioners to be mindful of their own biases toward chronically victimized and suicidal youth. They encourage providers to be patient and to avoid labeling or promoting a pathological view of youth who engage in suicidal behaviors (Berman et al., 2006).

When working with ethnic minority populations, Tormala and colleagues (Chapter 8; this volume) offer culturally competent practices that will promote disclosure and trust between clients and providers. Providers must be aware of their implicit biases and stereotypes, evaluate a family's experiences with bias and discrimination, understand that ethnic minority families may initially consult primary or emergency medical care rather than mental health providers, and assess for family and community connections that have been disrupted due to mental health symptoms or suicidality. Hudley (Chapter 9; this volume) challenges professionals who work in youth prevention programs to "engage in ongoing processes of program- and self-evaluation to assure the relevance of particular program leaders and content to the culture(s) they are intended to serve" (p. XX).

Given the high prevalence of both bullying and suicidality among LGBT students (Chapter 10; this volume), Testa and Hendricks (Chapter 11; this volume) propose that all providers must educate themselves on the provision of culturally competent services for transgender and gender nonconforming youth by accessing resources such as the World Professional Association of Transgender Health Standards of Care, Version 7 (Coleman et al., 2011), and the American Counseling Association's (ALGBTIC, 2009) Competencies for Counseling with Transgender Clients. For both sexual and gender minorities, school officials and mental health practitioners must understand that LGBT youth may present with specific life events that present unique challenges, such as parental rejection, homelessness, hate-related victimization, prejudice, and discrimination. Meyer and colleagues (Chapter 15; this volume) call attention to the utility of interpersonal clinical interventions with rejecting families to minimize family discord and promote acceptance (e.g., the Family Acceptance Project, http://familyproject.sfsu.edu).

Mental health services need to be readily available in schools (Chapter 21; this volume) and school-based prevention measures are indispensable for connecting youth at risk for suicide with community resources (Chapter 15; this volume), including referrals for mental health services and psychopharmacological interventions as needed. Mental health practitioners must query about peer victimization experiences when youth present with suicidal ideation or attempts. Practitioners can also work closely with parents to impact school-level policies and advocate for their clients' safety from victimization at school (Chapter 23; this volume).

Pediatricians and other health care professionals are often the first individuals to have contact with youth at risk for suicide and those who are involved in bullying (bullies, victims, or bully-victims). To identify children who are involved in bullying, the American Academy of Pediatrics advises pediatricians to ask screening questions during wellness exams and patient visits (Committee on Injury, Poison, and Violence Prevention, 2009; StopBullying.gov, n.d.). Pediatricians need to screen for bullying experiences in and out of the home (including experiences online), suicidal ideation, and suicidal behaviors during each visit (Chapter 3; this volume) (see http://www.stopbullying.gov/resources-files/roles-for-pediatricians-tipsheet.pdf for more screening information). Stress-related physical symptoms could be related to peer conflict or bullying at school and/or difficulties at home (e.g., parental arguments and divorce, relocation, parental substance abuse, conflict with siblings, etc.). Bauman (Chapter 7; this volume) notes that 90% of young people who committed suicide had seen a primary care physician within the past year (Tingley, 2013). She cautions physicians not only to ask if a youth is suicidal, but also to ask "What would make you think about suicide?" School nurses are also likely to have frequent interactions with youth who are experiencing bullying or isolation at school. As such, school nurses must understand the signs of victimization and suicidal behaviors, and should communicate their concerns to the school staff, initiate a referral for a screening, and follow up on the progress of the referral. Finally, given the risk of at-home gun storage for suicidal youth, pediatricians should talk to parents about guns and gun safety for families who do have guns in their home (Chapter 5; this volume).

As we review the changes required of mental and medical health professionals brought about by problems that cross multidisciplinary lines of practice and training, the need for new paradigms of professional training becomes apparent. While some disciplines such as social work and public health have long held the systemic models for understanding community and physical and mental health problems, others such as clinical psychology and psychiatry have been slow to adapt their training and practice models (Chu et al., 2012). Nowhere is the need for an integrated community-based approach more apparent than in the development of youth bullying and suicide prevention programs. In their groundbreaking article on the Public Psychology Doctoral Training Model, Chu and colleagues (2012) responded to the President's Commission on Mental Health (2003). The authors lamented the lack of public access to consistent, evidence-based mental health care, centering their concern on the disjointed care that clients received. This fragmentation is exacerbated within the multiple systems that have been charged with preventing suicide and bullying. For instance, schools and their personnel are frequently unfamiliar with mental health and medical resources. Too often, health professionals see their mandates ending at the school door, and subsequently avoid consulting with those who have more direct contact with the child. At times, such professionals even avoid working closely with parents. According to Chu and colleagues (2012), psychology graduate students need to develop competencies consistent with public psychology, understanding the multiple systems that impact their clients and being willing to advocate for the clients within institutions. This advocacy may take the form of educational advising on symptoms of bullying and suicide, the provision of referral strategies, and consultation with parents and teachers on how to protect their children.

RECOMMENDATIONS FOR POLICY MAKERS AND POLICY ADVOCATES

School and governmental policies have an impact on citizens' perception of community safety and openness, particularly for stigmatized minority populations (Chapter 23; this volume; Chapter 19; this volume). As with all issues that have a widespread impact on various groups within our society, great interest—and, at times, conflicts—arise as to how our institutions should officially react to the prevalence of bullying and suicide among American youth. Without advocacy, difficult and politically charged problems may go unaddressed for expedient or political reasons. An infamous example of this was the federal government's slow action to address the AIDS epidemic, which only changed as citizens demanded government action. As youth bullying and suicide becomes understood within the realm of public health, greater resources to develop evidence-based interventions are available. At the same time, as the problem moves to the national stage, active interest groups are becoming increasingly divided at all levels of care: national, state, local, and community. Hatzenbuehler and colleagues (Chapter 23; this volume) describe innovative policy-level research to help inform suicide and bullying interventions that consider the unique geographic characteristics that might predict the prevalence and antecedents to mistreatment of LGBT youth.

Clearly, research funding of this sort is sorely needed to understand the risk and protective factors that moderate or mediate the association between youth bullying and suicidal behaviors. Even more, funding is needed to extend this basic micro- and meso-level research to include examination of gender, culture, sexual orientation, race and ethnicity, and other factors that may strengthen the connection between bullying and suicidality. Research is also needed to assess the efficacy and sustainability of community and school-based interventions that show promise in reducing aggression toward vulnerable populations, such as students with disabilities and sexual or gender minority youth (Chapter 18; this volume).

RECOMMENDATIONS FOR RESEARCHERS

Increasingly, states are passing comprehensive policies about bullying and discrimination that explicitly require protection based on enumerated personal characteristics, including sexual orientation, gender identity or expression, and race. It is imperative that longitudinal studies of victimization associated with sexual orientation and gender identity be conducted in relation to these policy changes (Chapter 23; this volume) so that the impact of these policies can be understood. In addition, there needs to be greater investment in research that examines the unique bullying dynamics surrounding vulnerable populations, and such research should increasingly consider the experiences of groups such as Native American youth, immigrant populations, and students with disabilities.

To date, the usefulness of research in directing policy and interventions has been hampered by the lack of methodological rigor. As articulated in the introductory chapter of this volume (Chapter 1; this volume), researchers often do not agree on consistent definitions of "bullying" and frequently use different assessments when examining bullying involvement. These methodological inconsistencies make it difficult for researchers to draw conclusions across studies. An even more complex problem is the inconsistent use of newer research designs that are capable of understanding the interactions between several possible antecedent conditions and multiple outcomes. As national research funding sources become more involved in violence and suicide research and research universities continue to train researchers interested in the area, more consensus on definitions and appropriate research methodologies should be articulated. That said, given the challenges of multilevel research, authorities should continue to encourage research that has community support and participation, and that continues to use both qualitative and quantitative (mixed methods) approaches.

Another challenge within the bullying and school violence research literature is the fact that scholars have tended to study individual types of aggression or violence in isolation, and have only recently recognized the need to examine multiple forms of violence simultaneously. The change in these research efforts has been catalyzed by the high incidence of poly-victimization and overlap of victimization experiences during a person's lifespan (Hamby & Grych, 2013). For example, in-school bullying victimization, verbal aggression, and physical aggression during early adolescence have been shown to be strong predictors of involvement in homophobic name-calling and sexual harassment among middle-school students (Birkett & Espelage, in press; Espelage, Basile, & Hamburger, 2012; Espelage, Low, & De La Rue, 2012; Poteat & Espelage, 2007). Furthermore, many of these forms of aggression and victimization share common risk and protective factors (e.g., lack of empathy, attitudes supportive of aggression; Espelage, Green, & Polanin, 2012), and are often maintained and reinforced in similar peer contexts (Dishion & Owen, 2002; Espelage, Holt, & Henkel, 2003; Low, Espelage, & Polanin, 2013). As such, future research should examine the relationships among bullying, homophobic name-calling, sexual harassment, and suicidal behaviors in order to identify shared and unique influences, as well as to maximize the efficacy of interventions (Hamby & Grych, 2013).

To illustrate this concept in terms of extant research on bullying perpetration, a longitudinal study of middle- and high-school youth demonstrated that bully perpetration shows relatively little change during middle school and declines further in high school (Espelage, Holt, et al., 2014; Nansel et al., 2001). Moreover, a recent meta-analysis of bullying intervention programs indicated significant reductions in bully perpetration prior to the seventh grade, but in eighth grade there is a sharp drop to an average efficacy of zero (Yeager, Fong, Lee, & Espelage, in press), with an actually negative effect being found in high-school samples. Given the saliency of bias-based bullying in high school, evaluations of school-based programs that focus on addressing homophobia, gender diversity, disability status, and immigration concerns are needed.

As identified throughout this book, there is a need for more research on the efficacy of bully prevention programs and social-emotional learning programs for suicide prevention. Indelible causal links between bullying and suicide frequently have been assumed and publicized; however, this connection needs to be further examined within the research literature to fully understand whether prevention programs implemented in schools are able to impact suicide behaviors. More research on the overlap between bullying and suicidal behaviors, focusing on protective factors across the social-ecological framework, is needed to illustrate a more comprehensive picture of the relationship between bullying and suicide.

As young people become more immersed in technology, researchers will need to continue exploring the incidence of bullying and discrimination in online spaces and gaming environments. It is likely that future bullying intervention efforts will need to be tailored to address specific experiences in social media and other online venues.

RECOMMENDATIONS FOR MEDIA: JOURNALISTS, EDITORS, AND CONSUMERS

The mass media plays an important role in the public discourse on bullying and suicide. Moreover, the advent of the Internet and social media has allowed positive and negative media effects to permeate multiple layers of a child's socio-ecological system. Public officials (Sebelius, 2013) have credited spontaneous media discussion and campaigns with the effect of forcing attention to the problem of youth violence, bullying, and suicide. One example of a spontaneous, viral media campaign is the "It Gets Better Project" a web-based campaign where individuals upload short videos assuring victimized sexual and gender minority that "life gets better." According to their website (http://www.itgetsbetter.org), as of this writing, 50,000 individuals had uploaded personal videos and there were 50 million page-views of at least one of them. In terms of sheer volume, it is hard to believe that intentional public health messaging could possibly compete with such a widespread project.

Public health theory uses the terms *diffusion* and *dissemination* to describe how new health attitudes and knowledge are spread. Diffusion is "the overall spread of an innovation, the process by which an innovation is communicated through certain channels over time among the members of a social system," while dissemination "is the planned, systematic effort designed to make a program or innovation more widely available" (Oldenburg & Glanz, 2008). As public health specialists and concerned citizens, we hope to benefit from the positive messaging from mass and social media, at the same time being aware of the potential for damaging and false information.

More recently, there has been great concern that social media itself can be a vehicle for relational bullying. In Chapter 22 in this volume, Bliss, Pflum, Sciacca, and Goldblum reviewed the existing literature on best practices for media professionals to utilize the positive aspects of media while decreasing its potential harm. Beginning with editors, their recommendations advise the creation of internal policies on the reporting of bullying and suicide based on published guidelines, the *Recommendations for Reporting on Suicide* (American Association of Suicidology et al., 2012). Editors should facilitate discussions of responsible reporting among staff, including the challenges of balancing consumer safety with the need to deliver engaging content. They should rely on news outlets that adhere to responsible reporting of suicide and bullying (American Association of Suicidology et al., 2012). Finally, consumers must be aware that not all bullying and suicide programs or campaigns are backed by research. Some campaigns rely heavily on celebrity endorsements and merchandising but provide little evidence-based content.

CONCLUSION

This book examined extant research, the majority of which indicates that involvement in bullying in any capacity is associated with higher rates of suicidal ideation and behaviors. The specific mechanisms of this increased suicide risk can be varied, with multiple pathways (e.g., social, cultural, ecological, psychiatric, minority stress model, etc.) by which bullying can beget suicide. In addition, special populations of transgender, sexual minority, disabled, or ethnic minority individuals may be uniquely vulnerable to bullying and suicide.

What becomes clear from our understanding of the complex social-ecological forces at play is that the prevention of suicide, bullying, and in particular, suicide as a result of bullying, is not a simple problem with a simple answer. In this concluding chapter, we have expounded upon guidance for parents, teachers, mental and medical health care providers, policy makers and advocates, researchers, and media in tackling the issue of prevention of bullying and suicide. The overarching public health and social-ecological approaches of this book illuminate the message that efforts must span multiple levels of stakeholders within our societal context in order to enact the awareness, education, and action needed to turn the tides of prevention and change. It is our hope that all stakeholders can utilize this book to guide research, new curricular development, clinical practice, and program development that encourages community members and professionals to undertake new roles within a community perspective. These new and essential community perspectives can create a sociocultural context conducive to early intervention and prevention of bullying to avert negative consequences of suicidal ideation and behaviors amongst affected youth.

REFERENCES

American Association of Suicidology, American Foundation for Suicide Prevention, Annenberg Public Policy Center, Canterbury Suicide Project—University of Otago, Columbia University Department of Psychiatry, ConnectSafely.org,... UCLA School of Public Health. (2012). *Recommendations for Reporting on Suicide*. Retrieved May 28, 2014, from http://reportingonsuicide.org/Recommendations2012.pdf.

Association for Lesbian, Gay, Bisexual, and Transgender Issues in Counseling (ALGBTIC) (2009). *Competences for Counseling with Transgender Clients*. Alexandria, VA: ALGBTIC.

Berman, A. L., Jobes, D. A., & Silverman, M. M. (2006). *Adolescent Suicide: Assessment and Intervention* (2nd ed.). Washington, DC: American Psychological Association.

Birkett, M., & Espelage, D.L. (in press). Homophobic name-calling, peer-groups, and masculinity: The socialization of homophobic behavior in adolescents. *Social Development.*

Bronfenbrenner, U. (1979). *The Ecology of Human Development.* Boston, MA: Harvard University Press.

Bronfenbrenner, U. (1994). Ecological models of human development. In *International Encyclopedia of Education* (Vol. 3, 2nd ed.; 1643–1647). Oxford, England: Elsevier.

Burdge, H., Snapp, S., Laub, C., Russell, S. T., Moody, R. (2013). *Implementing Lessons That Matter: The Impact of LGBTQ-Inclusive Curriculum on Student Safety, Well-Being, and Achievement.* San Francisco, CA: Gay-Straight Alliance Network; and Tucson, AZ: Frances McClelland Institute for Children, Youth, and Families at the University of Arizona.

Chu, J. P., Emmons, L., Wong, J., Goldblum, P., Reiser, R., Barrera, A. Z., & Byrd-Olmstead, J. (2012). Public psychology: A competency model for professional psychologists in community mental health. *Professional Psychology: Research and Practice, 43*(1), 39–49. doi: 10.1037/a0026319.

Coleman, E., Bockting, W., Botzer, M., Cohen-Kettenis, P., DeCuypere, G.,... Zucker, K. (2011). Standards of care for the health of transsexual, transgender, and gender-conforming people, version 7. *International Journal of Transgenderism, 13.4*, 165–232. doi: 10.1080/15532739.2011.700873

Committee on Injury, Violence, and Poison Prevention (2009). The role of the pediatrician in youth violence prevention. *Pediatrics, 124*(1), 393–402.

Dishion, T. J., & Owen, L. D. (2002). A longitudinal analysis of friendships and substance use: Bidirectional influence from adolescence to adulthood. *Developmental Psychology, 38*, 480–491. doi: 10.1037/0012-1649.38.4.480

Espelage, D. L. (in press). Ecological theory: Preventing youth bullying, aggression, and victimization. *Theory into Practice.*

Espelage, D. L., Aragon, S. R, Birkett, M., & Koenig, B. (2008). Homophobic teasing, psychological outcomes, and sexual orientation among high school students: What influence do parents and schools have? *School Psychology Review, 37*, 202–216.

Espelage, D. L., Basile, K. C., & Hamburger, M. E. (2012). Bullying perpetration and subsequent sexual violence perpetration among middle school students. *Journal of Adolescent Health, 50*(1), 60–65. doi: 10.1016/j.jadohealth.2011.07.015

Espelage, D. L., Low, S., & De La Rue, L. (2012). Relations between peer victimization subtypes, family violence, and psychological outcomes during adolescence. *Psychology of Violence, 2*(4), 313–324. doi: 10.1037/a0027386

Espelage, D. L., Holt, M. K., & Henkel, R. R. (2003). Examination of peer-group contextual effects on aggression during early adolescence. *Child Development, 74*(1), 205–220. doi: 10.1111/1467-8624.00531

Espelage, D. L., Low, S., Polanin, J. R., & Brown, E. C. (2013). The impact of a middle school program to reduce aggression, victimization, and sexual violence. *Journal of Adolescent Health, 53*(2), 180–186.

Espelage, D. L., Polanin, J., & Low, S. K. (in press). Teacher and staff perceptions of school environment as predictors of student aggression, victimization, and willingness to intervene in bullying situations. *School Psychology Quarterly.*

Espelage, D. L., Rao, M. A., & Craven, R. (2013). Relevant theories for cyberbullying research. In S. Bauman, J. Walker, & D. Cross (Eds.), *Principles of Cyberbullying Research: Definition, Methods, and Measures* (pp. 49–67). New York: Routledge.

Goldblum, P., Testa, R. J., Pflum, S., Hendricks, M. L., Bradford, J., & Bongar, B. (2012). The relationship between gender-based victimization and suicide attempts in transgender people. *Professional Psychology: Research and Practice, 43*(5), 468–475.

Goodenow, C., Szalacha, L., & Westheimer, K. (2006). School support groups, other school factors, and the safety of sexual minority adolescents. *Psychology in the Schools, 43*(5), 573–589. doi: 10.1002/pits.20173

Hamby, S., & Grych, J. (2013). *The Web of Violence: Exploring Connections Among Different Forms of Interpersonal Violence and Abuse*. New York: Springer.

Hershberger, S. L., & D'Augelli, A. R. (1995). The impact of victimization on the mental health and suicidality of lesbian, gay, and bisexual youths. *Developmental Psychology, 31*(1), 65–74.

King, C. A., & Merchant, C. R. (2008). Social and interpersonal factors relating to adolescent suicidality: A review of the literature. *Archives of Suicide Research, 12*(3), 181–196. doi: 10.1080/13811110802101203

Nansel, T. R., Overpeck, M., Pilla, R. S., Ruan, W., Simons-Morton, B., & Scheidt, P. (2001). Bullying behaviors among US youth: Prevalence and association with psychosocial adjustment. *Journal of the American Medical Association, 285*, 2094–2100.

Oldenburg, B. F., & Glanz, K. (2008). Diffusion of innovations. In Karen Glanz, Barbara K. Rimer and K. Viswanath (eds.), *Health Behavior and Health Education: Theory, Research, and Practice* (pp. 313–333). United States: Jossey-Bass Inc.

Pilkington, N. W., & D'Augelli, A. R. (1995). Victimization of lesbian, gay, and bisexual youth in community settings. *Journal of Community Psychology, 23*(1), 34–56.

Poteat, V. P., & Espelage, D. L. (2007). Predicting psychosocial consequences of homophobic victimization in middle school students. *The Journal of Early Adolescence, 27*, 175–191. doi: 10.1177/0272431606294839

Robinson, J. P., & Espelage, D. L. (2011). Inequities in educational and psychological outcomes between LGBTQ and straight students in middle and high school. *Educational Researcher, 40*, 315–330. doi: 10.3102/0013189X11422112

Robinson, J., & Espelage, D. L. (2013). Peer victimization and sexual risk differences between LGBTQ and nontransgender heterosexual youth in grades 7–12. *American Journal of Public Health, 103*(10), 1810–1819. doi: 10.2105/AJPH.2013.301387.

Savin-Williams, R. C., & Ream, G. L. (2003). Suicide attempts among sexual-minority male youth. *Journal of Clinical Child and Adolescent Psychology, 32*(4), 509–522.

Sebelius, K. (2013). Bullying Prevention Awareness Month. Retrieved May 28, 2014, from http://www.hhs.gov/news/press/2013pres/10/20131021a.html

Stopbullying.gov (n.d.). *Roles for Pediatricians in Bullying Prevention and Intervention*. Retrieved May 28, 2014, from http://www.stopbullying.gov/resources-files/roles-for-pediatricians-tipsheet.pdf.

Tingley, K. (2013). The suicide detective. *New York Times Magazine*, June 28. Retrieved from www.nytimes.com/2013/06/30/magazine/the-suicide-detective.

INDEX